HISTORICAL ESSAYS ON BRITISH COLUMBIA

HISTORICAL ESSAYS ON BRITISH COLUMBIA

Edited by
J. Friesen
H. K. Ralston

The Carleton Library No. 96
Published by McClelland and Stewart Limited
in Association with the Institute of
Canadian Studies, Carleton University

THE CARLETON LIBRARY

A series of reprints, original works and new
collections of source material relating to Canada,
issued under the editorial supervision of the Institute
of Canadian Studies of Carleton University, Ottawa.

Table of Contents

Introduction

The area of the western North American Cordillera that in 1871 joined the Canadian confederation as British Columbia had seen nearly one hundred years of European exploration and settlement. This process had intersected only briefly with the development of the communities making up the eastern portions of the new transcontinental federation. After completion of a railroad link, when a substantial union became possible, the Pacific province already exhibited an outlook that was largely a product of this separate evolution. The first formal histories of British Columbia, which appeared as the railway neared completion, reflected this self-consciousness, and succeeding decades of British Columbia historiography have reinforced the feeling of distinctiveness in the community. It can be argued that this distinctiveness is a myth, a variation in a pervasive North American culture, discernible only to the eye of faith. But, even so, the myth has grown and expanded and has contributed to a conviction among both citizens and outside observers that British Columbia is, as Charles Mair suggested so long ago, *sui generis*, "in, but not of Canada."

* * *

Separated from the rest of Canada by the Rocky Mountains, segmented and divided within itself by awe-inspiring forests, magnificent mountain ranges and formidable river systems, the Pacific region remained virtually unknown to the European world until well into the eighteenth century. Imperial Russia first touched the fringes of the area before 1750, but almost two decades had passed since the fall of New France before Spain and Britain began seriously to explore and map the inlets, islands and fiords of the North Pacific coast. British Columbia was initially approached from the west, but the Montreal fur traders were in the same period reaching towards the Pacific. Alexander Mackenzie, Simon Fraser and David Thompson of the North West Company explored the major river routes and began the inland fur trade of New Caledonia. With the amalgamation of the North West Company and the Hudson's Bay Company in 1821, the link with the St. Lawrence was broken and the Pacific slope became part of the same empire as Red River; a fur trade autocracy, governed by hierarchical authority from London.

In the 1830's and 1840's the Hudson's Bay Company, faced by encroaching settlement from the United States, withdrew gradually from its operations south of the Columbia River and increased its interest in the lucrative fur trade of the northern coast. In 1843 Chief Factor James Douglas chose a spectacular site at the southern tip of Vancouver's Island for the new Fort Victoria, which, after the settlement of the Oregon Boundary dispute and official British withdrawal from the Columbia, became the administrative and supply centre for the Pacific operations of the "Honourable Company."

As American pressure on British Pacific territory increased, Britain, to ensure her territorial integrity north of the forty-ninth parallel, in 1849 granted the Hudson's Bay Company proprietary rights to Vancouver Island. The Royal Navy was thus assured of a north Pacific base, but only a token group of settlers came to the distant colony. Richard Blanshard, the Colonial Office's appointee as Governor, found that he had few colonists, that he was expected to finance personally his living expenses, and, most important, that in the shadow of the Hudson's Bay Company his authority was meaningless. Indeed, the Imperial government was only recognizing the political reality of the situation on Vancouver Island, when, in 1851, it appointed Chief Factor James Douglas to succeed the ineffectual Blanshard.

During the early years of Douglas' governorship, the social atmosphere of the fur trade still dominated the society of Fort Victoria. Built mostly of wood and close to the wilderness, surrounded and often inundated by Indian tribes from all along the northern coast, the small town yet exuded an air of quiet dignity, uncommon on the North American frontier. The school and chapel, the nascent agricultural and lumbering activity, and the presence of the wives and families of traders and townsmen gave the village a settled appearance. Many of the trappings of Victorian England were evident in the gardens, styles of dress and the rigidly-maintained social order. The increasing use by the Pacific squadron of the Royal Navy of nearby Esquimalt gave an added dimension to social and economic life, and the presence of the naval officers provided an uncommon lustre to an otherwise commercial society.

The discovery, in 1858, of gold on the mainland transformed the mountainous interior. Thousands of gold-seekers streamed into the country, mostly by sea from California. The fur trading empire of the Hudson's Bay Company now had to accommodate that sporadic and shifting mining frontier which it had so long excluded. Victoria itself became the centre of supply and entertainment for the miners who worked on the lower Fraser River and later in the Cariboo. And inevitably the quiet English atmosphere within Fort Victoria was rapidly replaced by the more frenzied air of a North American frontier boom town. American saloons and American businesses were established near the harbour, while Chinese, Jewish and Black establishments reflected the growing diversity of population. The mainland was declared a Crown Colony on November 19, 1858, and James Douglas, no longer Chief Factor of the Hudson's Bay Company, served as Governor of both Vancouver Island and British Columbia.

With the Royal Engineers to provide protection and build the vital communication links with the interior gold fields, Douglas was able to maintain a firm British rule in face of the rapid influx of American miners. Yet not only did he seek to uphold British sovereignty, but like Judge Matthew Begbie and the newly arrived Anglican Bishop Rt. Rev. George Hills, he sought to establish "another England on the Pacific." In a speech at the Mansion House in London, the Bishop succinctly expressed such attitudes. "In Columbia let the institutions of England be planted, her freedom, her laws, her religion. . . . Let there be a union of philanthropic and religious minds. Let the British territory be a spot where sympathy will be shown the oppressed." This strong British sentiment was reinforced by the appointment of many colonial officials from Britain, by the Hudson's Bay Company's well-tended family links with "home," by the presence of the Royal Navy, the Royal Engineers, and by the active social work of the Anglican clergy.

Canadians in the colonies, generally looked down upon by this official element, were excluded both from administrative positions and from the social circles of the governing elite. Even in 1867, confederation with the British colonies in Eastern North America seemed a remote possibility, and only the Canadians in the interior at Yale and Barkerville felt the occasion one for celebration. But the economic depression which had begun in 1865 slowly changed the attitudes of the British colonists. In 1866 the island colony and the gold colony had for pragmatic economic reasons joined in the united colony of British Columbia, and some British Columbians were perhaps dimly aware that British government support for maritime union on the Atlantic and Pacific coasts was only a prelude to imperial pressure for a confederation of all British North American colonies.

A bargain with Canada was finally sealed, but with little affection. Many former British colonists saw themselves as in "conquered country" and the leaders of the new province could not yield their emotional ties with the glittering centre of a world empire for the political and social life of a crude lumber town on the Rideau. As historian Margaret Ormsby has emphasized, the union was not based on sentiment "and could not permanently exist unless it served the material advantage of the people." In fact, the call for "better terms" from Ottawa became for British Columbia politicians a popular slogan which was intensified in times of economic distress, and which gained strength from the province's loose ties with national political parties.

Confederation came when British Columbia was at the nadir of its economic fortunes, in the midst of its first faltering steps to re-establish its economy on the exploitation of natural resources other than alluvial gold. Coal mining and salmon canning provided a modest base for the growth of the first twenty years that saw Victoria develop as a nascent metropolis, its businessmen dominating the hinterland and linking it to San Francisco, London and Liverpool. In the next two decades, demand on the Prairies and a speculative boom in the Kootenays established the wood products and lode mining industries in their present leading positions, in that heavy and often reckless exploitation of natural wealth that has characterized the province's growth. These years also saw the business and financial leadership of British Columbia pass from Victoria to the new metropolis of Vancouver.

The first decade of the twentieth century marked the peak years of a population growth that saw the province's population virtually doubling in each decade to reach over half a million in 1921, ten times that of 1871. Prosperous British Columbia attracted many of the immigrants who flooded into Canada in the years between 1901 and 1911. The majority of the immigrants to British Columbia were from the British Isles; some were the familiar "remittance men," the younger sons of English gentry who, complete with cricket bats and croquet mallets, came to the Cariboo and Okanagan; but most were from industrial Britain— those cloth-capped workingmen who were to set their stamp on politics and social life, especially in Vancouver. Canadians also joined the stream, helping to offset the conscious "Britishness" of the province. Another stream of immigrants, Japanese and Sikhs, who in increasing numbers joined Chinese residents, brought violent demands for restrictions on Asian immigration.

In the years following the First World War, more Canadians, particularly from the prairies and Ontario, settled in the province, and Vancouver reinforced its metropolitan status, completely overshadowing Victoria and dominating the economic life of British Columbia. Yet, in the succeeding years of depression, the city was to experience greater hardship than probably any other urban area in Canada. With its temperate climate, Vancouver became a haven for the single drifters or the farm families who were no longer equipped to cope with the severe prairie winters. Welfare budgets and middle-class charity were strained. The militant industrial unions and radical political parties which had always had a firmer foothold in British Columbia than elsewhere in Canada now found many new adherents, and these strong class antagonisms survived the return of prosperity during the Second World War.

The confidence of British Columbians in themselves and the destiny of their province, briefly shaken in the 1930's, returned in full measure in the war and post-war years. As population and economic indicators resumed their seemingly inexorable upward climb, the province turned increasingly in upon itself. The intense "Britishness" of the early years may have passed, succumbing to a more cosmopolitan population and wider trading horizons, but it seems to have been replaced by only a nominal Canadianism. Fiercely proud of the splendour of their surroundings, British Columbians have maintained their somewhat complacent, limited identity, reflected in the narcissistic quality of their public life. The centre of the political arena in British Columbia has remained in Victoria, just as business and culture has centred in Vancouver. The relationship between British Columbia and Canada has all too frequently been one of Canada fulfilling the needs and demands of the Pacific province. In return, British Columbia has never imposed itself on the larger society nor sought to reform or change that society. Not for British Columbians the role in national parties of Nova Scotians—for few, if any, British Columbia representatives in federal cabinets have attained widespread recognition outside their home territory. In marked contrast also is this relationship to that between Canada and the prairie provinces, who with almost religious zeal have sought "to give life to that persistent sectional dream of the west, to merge the section with the nation."

The darker side of provincial exclusiveness has been the treatment of groups who did not easily fit the perceived pattern. The campaign for restriction on Asian immigration, the forced relocation of Japanese-Canadians, the policies and attitudes to the Doukhobours and the continued denial of aboriginal rights to the majority of the Indians of the province, all provide examples of the sometime narrowness of the province's public opinion and is force in maintaining an insular and largely self-satisfied society.

* * *

Articles and books on the history of British Columbia make up the bulk of the entries in the eight volume *Dictionary-Catalogue of the Provincial Archives of British Columbia*, which reproduces the holdings of the most extensive collection of printed works on the subject.

Journalists, bibliophiles, public servants and teachers have all contributed to the writing of the province's history. And like the prairie provinces, the dedicated and talented amateurs have contributed substantial monographs and have brought to the Provincial historical societies and journals both their enthusiasm and sympathy and their personal intimate links with the historical past. Such writers have shared with professional and academic historians a fascination with material progress, a nostalgia for the romantic days of a unique colonial past, and above all a passion for the magnificence of the land itself. Not unexpectedly, but perhaps unfortunately, it has been largely left to the "professional" historians to deal with the vital questions of the role of race and class in their society, to self-consciously attempt to define the elusive identity of the Pacific province and, with a characteristic British Columbian's ambivalence towards the nation, to challenge the metropolitan interpretations of Canadian history.

Any brief survey of developments in British Columbia historiography must of necessity concentrate on only a few of both these professional and non-professional historians. However, consideration of the works and careers of major figures, such as H. H. Bancroft, R. E. Gosnell, E.O.S. Scholefield, Judge F. W. Howay, Professor W. N. Sage, and Professor M. A. Ormsby, can illustrate not only the recurrent themes in the writing of British Columbia history, but also the changing position and role of the historian himself. Such a selection may also indicate some of their fields of concern, for in their work can be seen that pronounced emphasis on the colonial past, particularly on the period of Hudson's Bay Company rule. Fur traders' journals, fur trade society, Company history and the early politics of Vancouver Island have attracted many students from within and outside the province. As in many new fields of historical research, political narrative and political biography have had a large place, though curiously, the various aspects of Dominion-Provincial relations have attracted more attention than colonial-Imperial relations. In the 1930's, however, as elsewhere in Canada, more attention was given to social and economic history, and in later decades the international contexts of British Columbia history have received wider consideration.

The earliest historical accounts of British Columbia are to be found in a genre of popular writings, for instance those of Mathew Macfie and R. C. Lundin Brown, publicizing in the 1860's the newly-discovered gold fields, or those of A. C. Anderson and G. M. Sproat, which were directed at the prospective immigrant. The first formal histories were an outgrowth of these publicist activities and appeared in the decade after the arrival of the Canadian Pacific Railway. Their appearance reflected two facets of British Columbia's situation – her geographical position on North America's Pacific rim, and her political position in the new Dominion of Canada. H. H. Bancroft's *History of British Columbia*, following his *History of the Northwest Coast*, was part of a multi-volume series, produced in San Francisco, on the history of western North America. Alexander Begg collaborated in a biographical dictionary of a commercial type popular in nineteenth century North America, and in 1894 produced a *History of British Columbia* for the Toronto firm of William Briggs —evidence of central Canadian curiosity about the new far western domain. The work of Begg, who has rejoiced in the nickname of "Old Paste and Scissors," will not repay a modern reading (although inexplicably reprinted by a multi-national publisher from his recently-acquired Canadian list). Bancroft, however, produced substantial if erratic works.

Hubert Howe Bancroft did not live in the province and was never a part of the society of which he wrote. A man of unlimited energy and business acumen, Bancroft, a bookseller, printer and publisher, turned to the writing of history as a commercial venture. Believing that historical research, at times a lengthy and tedious task, could be broken down into a series of relatively simple tasks, not necessarily to be carried out by the historian, he developed an organization for this purpose, later somewhat derisively known as "the history factory." Researchers in major libraries brought together an encyclopaedic compendium of available knowledge on the Pacific coast. Where necessary, personal reminiscences were solicited and manuscripts purchased—all brought together in a then new, complex system of card catalogues and files. Other employees then pulled together a dramatic and literary record of the recent past of the west coast of North America. The preparation of Bancroft's history stimulated reflections on the past by British Columbians who had played important roles in the society and politics of the previous decades. Held today in the Bancroft Library at Berkeley, these various reminiscences, some written and some oral, are a miscellany of caustic "neighbourly" comment, remembered lives of valour, family pride and various shades of political invective, whose merits at publication were vigorously and at times bitterly debated by British Columbians.

Of equal interest to a modern observer is the application by Bancroft to British Columbia history of a framework of development, derived from a larger North American experience, and intended to parallel in its processes the growth of the Pacific States he had outlined in other volumes. Yet even this outside interpreter emphasized the distinctiveness of the British Columbia experience in the lengthy dominance of the Hudson's Bay Company and the continued strength of a British presence.

The strength of the British connection was a theme which British Columbia historians of the early twentieth century found profoundly satisfying and in this they were no different from their Imperialist counterparts elsewhere in English Canada. For them the Imperial tie was one which gave to their province that special place in the firmament which it had not achieved, and perhaps did not desire, in Confederation. The arrival of the Canadian Pacific Railway was welcome to these British Columbians not because it joined together a new nation, but because it made British Columbia the final link in an Imperial chain. R. E. Gosnell boasted that "throughout the length and breadth of the Empire there is no part where the people as a whole are so wholly and unreservedly devoted to the idea of Imperial unity and British institutions as is British Columbia."[1]

If these ideas were indeed accepted, it was because Gosnell, author of pamphlets and articles on Imperial federation and a prominent organizer of the British Empire League of British Columbia, played no small part in their promotion and maintenance. Born in Quebec, educated in Ontario, he arrived in British Columbia in 1888 and embraced his new home with all the ferocity of a convert. In a view which was to re-appear with variations in subsequent British Columbia writing, he eulogised this Pacific province which "had a peculiar fascination for the majority of strangers, and few who came to stay for a time ever left, or if they did leave longed to return again. In truth, the atmosphere of a British Columbia city holds him who breathes it with a grip not felt under other skies."[2]

Gosnell began his working life as a journalist but his later career, together with that of his colleague E.O.S. Sholefield, saw significant development for the writing of history, particularly the creation in Victoria of a provincial centre which began to assemble a great breadth of materials relating to British Columbia. As secretary of the Provincial Bureau of Information, the author of a series of yearbooks of British Columbia, first Provincial librarian and first Provincial Archivist, Gosnell began to lay the necessary foundations for the development of British Columbia history. In addition, Gosnell as a journalist, political advisor, and civil servant, was a not insignificant participant in the society and politics of which he wrote.[3]

Although Gosnell produced a *History of British Columbia* in 1906, his most substantial work was *History of British Columbia: Sixty Years of Progress*, co-authored in 1913 with E.O.S. Scholefield, his successor at the Provincial Library and Provincial Archives. In the post-confederation section, Gosnell outlined themes which were to dominate British Columbia history for decades.

His emphasis on plenty and abundance is perhaps to be expected from a successful immigrant, and author of immigration pamphlets. But the leap from the riches of the environment to the inevitability of provincial progress is one which has since been made with almost painful regularity, particularly by popular writers. For Gosnell, the connection was clear. "The huge mineral wealth which had been exposed and exploited; the vast shoals of fish that swarmed in the contiguous sea and the inland waters: the density and extent of the forests; the fertility and adaptability of the soil already brought under the plough, the geographical situation in regard to the Pacific trade; the charms and salubrity of the climate, the rare opportunities for sport afforded by the abundance and wide habitat of game; the magnificent resources of scenery—all these happy causes combined to render certain, under favourable conditions, the great fortune that awaited the country."[4]

The uniqueness of British Columbia was striking not only in its environment but also in its society, its politics, and as Bancroft had suggested, in its past. And here, too, Gosnell's interpretations have enjoyed a longer currency than perhaps they deserve. Politically, he saw British Columbia as unique because its attitude to Confederation differed markedly from that of the prairie west and the St. Lawrence. Accepting, as others have since, the judgment of Dr. J. S. Helmcken, a member of the Confederation delegation to Ottawa, Gosnell stressed that Confederation was not sought as a solution for political deadlock, and that it could only become accepted if it furthered the material development of British Columbia.

Politics within British Columbia too, Gosnell argued, had not followed established Canadian patterns, partly, in his view, because of the strength of sectional interests within the province, and a political milieu which was less a matter of principle and party than of personal inclination and private allegiance—interpretations which have been challenged all too infrequently. For Gosnell British Columbia was also unique in that she alone faced the burden of oriental immigration in what he felt was essentially and by right a white man's country. The Japanese were the most offensive to British Columbia's sensibilities for "their word is not dependable and their motives always ulterior. They have the gloss of politeness and extreme courtesy, a frenchified exterior of conduct; but remove ever so little of cuticle and you reveal the Tartar." The Chinese he regarded as a lesser danger. They were, as a rule, "industrious, honest, faithful to their employers, cleanly in person, and without desire to assimilate or to establish themselves on the land ... they are admirably useful as servants, as economic machines. . . . "[5] For years anti-oriental and anti-Asiastic legislation appeared in the provincial legislatures as regularly as Parliament sat. It was, as Gosnell drily noted, a "robust plant of unfailing bloom," and the historian-journalist and public servant shared the concerns of his province.

In Gosnell's view, British Columbia's "society" was not composed of the logger, the farmer or the miner, but "the pioneers of British Columbia ... were essentially a superior class of men and women" whose ideal was the self-made man of commercial and business success.[6] Like his contemporaries and successors, Gosnell relished the civilised urban and genteel past of these British Columbian commercial heroes, "those halcyon days to which older men of the present generation can now look back, moderate work, frequent holidays, wholesome recreation and sport, gay evenings, congenial free handed social life, beautiful environment, a climate like that of England itself ... no greedy competition. Businessmen went late to their offices and came away early." Not for British Columbians the virtues of hard physical labour that prairie writers have extolled; nor the combination of Protestant religion, thrift and prosperity which has seemed important to Ontario. Neither was her theme the survival of culture and people in a hostile nation and against a harsh landscape that Quebec has nursed, nor the dimly perceived estrangement between man and land which has permeated much of the search for a Canadian identity; but, for the Pacific province there has persisted a vision of harmony between the distant grandeur of the land, and the ease, gentleness and civility of the societies which developed on the coast and in the sheltered valleys of the interior.

Gosnell left a legacy not only in historical collecting, research and writing, but in the training he is said to have given to his more stable and more sober successor at the Provincial Library and Archives. Ethelbert Olaf Scholefield was born in England and came to Victoria with his father, an Anglican minister, when he was twelve. From pageboy in the legislative assembly he became assistant to Gosnell at the Provincial Library, succeeding him as Librarian in 1898, and in 1910 added the responsibility of the Provincial Archives. Although his own enthusiasm was for the coastal history of North West America he made some attempt to expand the materials of the Archives by interviewing and collecting written, oral and visual materials in the interior towns. In the opinion of a later historian, the Archives and the *Archives Memoirs* series he began are the main monuments of his relatively brief career.[7] Yet Scholefield as an historian and collaborator with both Gosnell and Judge Howay was a link in the development of historical writing in British Columbia. He shared their predilection for the biographical and heroic approach; he joined with them in their regard for gentlemen of "refinement and education" and their longing for the world they had lost—Victoria "the sylvan retreat, idyllic in its simplicity." He echoed too their admiration for British ties and business values and indeed in speaking of the Hudson's Bay Company saw the two as divinely entwined. For with its "superb organization . . . and administration as effective as it was far reaching, the Company held the land until, in the fullness of time, it became an integral part of the Empire." For Scholefield, the "commercial spirit of the Anglo-Saxon race [was] . . . one of the greatest propelling forces that the world has ever known," and it was from this force British Columbians drew their identity and their satisfactions.

The monuments to Gosnell and to Scholefield are two provincially-sponsored institutions in the capital—a library, variously called the Provincial or the Legislative Library, and the Provincial Archives of British Columbia. The delayed and painful birth of a university in the province and the penury of its early years, made these two institutions indispensable to the writer of British Columbia history. They remain so; for not until the donation to the University of British Columbia of the extensive libraries of F. W. Howay and Robie Reid was there any other comparable collection inside the province. Even in these days of mechanical reproduction, the great holdings of British Columbia newspapers and government records are unduplicated.

Frederick William Howay was an important transitional figure, linking the journalist-civil servant Gosnell to the university-trained historian Walter Sage, though his work in volume surpassed them both. Judge F. W. Howay is usually remembered for the four-volume history of British Columbia he co-authored with Schole-field, and although this was certainly an important work of collation and interpretation and remained as the standard work on provincial history for forty-five years, it was by no means the limit of his contri-bution. A New Westminster lawyer who devoted his leisure to the writing and collecting of British Columbia history, he built a mag-nificent library of material on the north west coast which later be-came the basis of a special collection at the University of British Co-lumbia. His particular interest was the maritime fur trade, and to this he applied all his training as a lawyer and his enthusiasm for local history. Howay's presidential address to the Royal Society of Canada[8] is an instructive example of his bibliophilia, his regard for precise rules of evidence, his meticulous research techniques and his interest in and grasp of the international factors in the early history of British Columbia.

Like Gosnell, Howay was an important part of the small society of which he wrote. A boyhood friend of Richard McBride, and later a classmate of Premier Bowser, his own political role lay in forming a public consciousness about British Columbia's past, and developing a literary culture in the province. He supported and participated in several literary and historical societies, and served on many public boards, including the senate of the University of British Columbia. His numerous speeches to organizations throughout the province, and his support of so many cultural activities gave him a closer knowledge of the society of which he wrote and brought him a public respect beyond the bor-ders of British Columbia. It was to Judge Howay that publishers turned when they needed a "British Columbia" chapter for a text-book, an encyclopaedia, or for a general interpretation of provincial history for the Cambridge History of the British Empire. Howay's professional honours at the national level, and the wider audience for his works, mark a transition in the writing of British Columbia history. Boosterism had passed; Canadian influence in the province had strengthened in the intervening years and this was evident in Howay's life and work.

Howay himself had been educated at Dalhousie Law School, and his wider view of his nation-community was reflected in his work. For Howay, British Columbia's entry into Confederation was not a burdensome decision imposed by a retreating colonial power, nor was it the closing of the "thin red line." Rather it was to be interpreted as a time of renewed faith, and above all of progress through the eventual introduction of responsible govern-ment, views which are strikingly portrayed in his two major bio-graphical articles on Governor Seymour and Governor Musgrave. grave.

Howay's own eclecticism and his many professional contacts in national and international historical associations are perhaps both reflected in the attention he gave to new areas of provincial history. As perhaps befits an historian of the maritime fur trade, he gave new emphasis to the role of Indians in British Columbia; but his work also included accounts of the Overlanders, Black immigration, an interest in the Spanish at Nootka, in the Royal Engineers, in camp life in the Cariboo, and in the continuing "problem" as he saw it, of oriental immigration into British Columbia, a subject he treated no more extensively, though more soberly, than his predecessors. To a modern reader, much of Howay's periodical literature remains a tedious recitation of detail, with little, if any, broad interpretive sweep. The literary style of his articles reflects the lawyer rather than the historian, and seldom in these tightly written pieces is there room for the reveries of other writers on the *splendor sine occasu*. It is in Howay's standard history of British Columbia, in his immense productivity, in his personal influence on later scholars (although he was never formally a teacher), and in the place he made for British Columbia and its historians at a national level, that one should seek his contributions.

In the period after the First World War Howay and his fellow amateurs continued to hold the field. In 1922 they founded the British Columbia Historical Association, which published four volumes containing historical articles. Also begun at this time was the Okanagan Historical Society *Report*, now the oldest continuously published historical periodical in British Columbia. But with the creation of a history department at the University of British Columbia, professionally-trained historians began to be attracted to the study of British Columbia history. Most prominent among these newcomers was Walter Sage, the first of the province's historians to combine writing and research with a full-time teaching post at the University of British Columbia.

Born in London, Ontario, the son of an Anglican minister, educated at English schools and colleges, Sage was among the first Ph.D.'s in Canadian history from the University of Toronto. He came to the University of British Columbia at the end of the First World War, and by 1932 had become head of the department, a position he held for twenty years. He was, by one account, an ideal department head when the University of British Columbia was a small and closely-knit group of students and faculty. He was also, a competent, though not brilliant historian, never approaching Howay in his range and detail, nor equalling his student Margaret Ormsby in literary accomplishment. Like both Howay and Ormsby however, he was recognized as the British Columbian representative at national and international historical meetings. He also served a long term on the Historic Sites and Monuments Board, was President of the Canadian Historical Association and of the Pacific Coast Branch of the American Historical Association, a Vice-President of the Champlain Society, and a Fellow of the Royal Society.

Sage's early interests followed the well-worn tracks of the romance of the fur trade and the colonial pasts, interests which complemented Howay's work in these years, and which culminated in the publication in 1930 of his major work, *Sir James Douglas and British Columbia*. Based on his thesis, this was, as has been suggested, "a narrative and anecdotal history . . . rather than an incisive biographical study." Yet it "contained the germs for broader interpretations," some of which would be developed by Dr. Sage himself and others by his students. Sage however had already gone beyond these concerns to develop some broader interpretations of provincial history, and to attempt to incorporate a British Columbia perspective into Canadian history.

Like his colleagues elsewhere, Sage was influenced by environmentalist arguments, as his 1928 "*Aspects of the Frontier in Canadian History* suggests. Following somewhat in this vein is his *Geographical and Cultural Aspects of the Five Canadas* (1937), in which Sage demonstrated how far he had moved from his earlier colonial-political interests to this relatively "unworked field, the interrelation of the geographical and cultural interpretations" of Canada. Though a British Columbian, he spoke for all regional historians when he stressed the distinct and characteristic contribution which each cultural region had offered in the building of the Dominion. In the era of the Rowell-Sirois Commission he provided strong counterpoints to those emergent historians of the St. Lawrence who saw the history of the Canadas as merely the extension of the metropolis to its natural and rightful hinterland. This page of Sage's work came to fruition in 1942 with the publication, in collaboration with Howay and Angus, of *British Columbia and the United States*, which attempted to place British Columbia in the regional context of the North Pacific Slope. Although this was one of the first full-scale attempts to bring British Columbia's history out of isolation, Harold Innis was harshly critical of the parochial implications of the book's intent, and of the fact that it did not "link up B.C. in any broad interpretative way with Canada." In his supremely central Canadian manner Innis also lectured Howay and Sage on their strong pro-British, pro-British Columbia, pro-

Hudson's Bay and anti-Methodist sentiments, charges they would for the most part have been delighted to confirm.

Sage had begun to develop new and important ideas about the writing of Canadian history, and he had sought to bring a professional regional perspective to the interpretation of national history. From this, Sage gained not only an increased national recognition, but he also developed a growing identification with British Columbia and a need to interpret the province to itself as well as to the larger community. Yet Sage's search for the distinctiveness of British Columbia moved little beyond that of his predecessors. In 1930 he began a seminar at the University of British Columbia in British Columbia history, and was active in expanding academic interests in provincial history, particularly at the M.A. level. But his own version of British Columbia remained in the main startlingly familiar, with its stress on the importance of the maritime frontier, the forming role of the gold rush and fur trade, the envisioned role of the province as a gateway to the Orient, and the continued strength of British sentiment. Although he did recognize also a role for the "constant pressure of the United States," and the "mining camp" psychology of the Pacific province, unhappily he never developed these themes further.

During the 1930's, opportunities for research and publication expanded. A series of graduate theses on British Columbia, virtually all of which are still unpublished, was produced at the University of British Columbia. In this decade, too, the leadership of the Provincial Archives was taken over by historians who had begun their training at the University of British Columbia; W. Kaye Lamb in 1934 and Willard Ireland in 1940. New professional standards were evident in the *British Columbia Historical Quarterly*, launched in 1937, with Lamb as editor, and co-sponsored by the Provincial Archives and the British Columbia Historical Association. The pages of this journal came to reflect the growing diversity of interest in British Columbia history, especially in social, economic and religious history, although the overwhelming bias was still toward the fur trade and gold rush eras.

The years of the Second World War and the immediate post-war period were not marked by any great expansion of the interest in British Columbia history—this came during the preparations for the celebration in 1958 of the centennial of the founding of the gold colony of British Columbia. This sparked, in addition to the standard history by Margaret Ormsby commissioned by the centennial committee, a rush of popular books and articles. This interest was sustained and even increased in the 1960's and early 1970's by the historical activities associated with the celebrations of the centennials of the union of British Columbia and Vancouver Island in 1966, the Canadian Confederation in 1967, and the entry of British Columbia into that confederation in 1971.

A growing public interest was paralleled by an expansion in the number of professionally-trained historians with interests in British Columbia. The creation of the universities of Victoria and Simon Fraser, followed by a network of communities colleges, created a demand for historians with interests in regional and local history. The graduate program at the University of British Columbia, which after 1964 offered training at the Ph.D. level, expanded to provide candidates for these vacancies. The Provincial museum in Victoria sought to staff a new history division, and the provincial archives offered additional positions. All these developments were mirrored in a new journal, *B.C. Studies*, which commenced publication in 1969 under the auspices of the three universities.

The major figure among British Columbian historians in this period was Margaret Ormsby. Like Walter Sage, she taught in the history department at the University of British Columbia, and like him, she became head of the department, a post she held for ten years. Margaret Ormsby's origins and experience of British Columbia are unique among the province's major historians. Not only was she a woman in a time, place and profession which were not notoriously welcoming, but she came from a small interior town in the Okanagan, the daughter of those "quiet well-read fruit farmers" of the valley. The valleys, the human scale of her experience, and the strength of the landscape itself are themes to which she has continued to turn.

Educated at the University of British Columbia, with an early specialty in medieval history, she completed her Ph. D. for Bryn Mawr on Dominion-Provincial relations in British Columbia, and returned shortly thereafter to teach at the provincial university. In 1964 she became head of a growing and difficult department in uneasy years for university administrators. Like Howay and Sage she served on the Historic Sites and Monuments Board, is a Fellow of the Royal Society, and a past President of the Canadian Historical Association. And, like Sage, through her teaching and supervision of numerous theses, she has left an impact for some time to come on the writing of British Columbia history.

Ormsby's early published works were mainly political history of the immediate post-Confederation period, and were derived from her thesis research. Although politics remained "clearly Miss Ormsby's first love," she is one of the few people to have given much attention to agricultural history, and her article on the "United

Farmers of B.C.: An Abortive Third Party"[10] should be more easily available than it is.

Professor Ormsby's interpretations of British Columbia's past have, not surprisingly, changed over time. In her earlier writings she seemed to be more concerned with the integrating factors drawing British Columbia towards Canada. She stressed the "frontier democracy," the ties of education and religion, which by the time of the completion of the transcontinental railroad had made "British Columbia . . . manifestly Canadian in spirit and custom."[11] Later in her career, particularly in her one volume history of the province and in her presidential address to the Canadian Historical Association, Ormsby became less sure of the rapid Canadianisation of the province, of its innate democracy, and the closeness of its links to other areas of Canada or North America. By 1966 Ormsby spoke "as a Westerner," stressed the deep gulf in social and political values which separated east and west, and reminded her audience of the continuing influence on the Pacific slope of the London metropolis. She saw that popular democracy tempered by "a conservatism drawn from a long tradition of submitting to restriction imposed, like law and order, by outside authorities," in a far west which as late as 1913 was, she suggested, only "nominally Canadian."[12]

British Columbia: A History remains Margaret Ormsby's most important book. In a single volume, it combined the fast pace and wide range necessary for a popular history with a firm grasp of interpretive themes of provincial development. In her discussion of the post-Confederation period, she broke much new ground, particularly in economic and social history, yet retained control of the taut organization of the book. Though accused by some of a whiggish view of British Columbia history, she avoided the boosterism and unrestrained optimism of earlier historians, while sharing their enthusiasm for fur trade and gold colony, their concern for a gentler way of life, and their stress upon the distinctiveness of the "spoilt child of confederation."

The centennial history also impressed on Ormsby and her researchers a clear view of the state of the writing of the province's history. In a brief and little noticed article, she outlined the neglected aspects of British Columbia's past and the consequent "needs and opportunities" for further work.[13] In almost every area—economic history, political biography, company and labour histories, religious and social history—she pointed out the wide gaps that existed in our understanding of B.C. history. Even in the apparently overworked colonial period, she argued, much of the available work existed only in descriptive and outline forms. Since the early

1960's, a steady flow of M.A. and Ph.D. theses under her direction have begun to fill some of these gaps, particularly in the fields of labour, religion, company history and Indian-European relations.

Ormsby herself returned to the colonial period to consummate, in her *Dictionary of Canadian Biography* article on James Douglas, a long-term interest in the fur trader and governor, a man whom, many years before she had characterized as the "most significant individual in B.C. history," who "more than any other man had set his stamp both on the people and the institutions." To Ormsby, Douglas was a man of physical prowess and iron nerve, a largely self-made man who had distinguished himself in more than one career. Highly conscious of the power he wielded and the respect he commanded, Ormsby's regard for "old square toes" rests on his practicality, energy and especially on what she sees as his humanitarian and judicious use of power, views which perhaps reflect her conscious liberalism and her own participation in professional and public life.

In her poetic "Horizontal View," Ormsby like Sage before her, tried to interpret the west and British Columbia to her colleagues and fellow Canadians. "Everyone plots the things he cares for most," she suggested, and set out first to stress the uniqueness of the west, but also to place in the perspective of her wider view "the pervasiveness of the northern wilderness, of the voids that separate settlement from settlement, and of the lonely desolation that in Canada surrounds the work of man." As a British Columbian, she returned to the small valleys, to the intimate society "in which it is possible for individuals to be well known to one another, and where the pleasant custom of seeing and knowing one another produces love for the citizens rather than a love of the soil."

Recent years have seen a great expansion in the teaching of British Columbia history. Provincial history is now offered at the undergraduate and graduate level; not only at the University of British Columbia, Simon Fraser University and the University of Victoria, but also at the many community colleges established throughout the province where British Columbia and local studies are frequently in demand. At colleges and universities outside the province, British Columbia history is also taught from time to time in conjunction with prairie history.

The writing and function of British Columbia history has also changed considerably in this last decade. Like prairie history it has both suffered and benefitted from the splintering into more numerous and perhaps more rigorous disciplines. For some, British Columbia history is no longer the avocation it was; it seems to have become merely another field of historical research—a different set of source materials to test typotheses formed elsewhere.

This late flowering and increasing diversity in B.C. studies, for example in the field of art history, has made the choice of essays a difficult one. Our selection, perhaps unavoidably, reflects our own interests in labour history and ethnohistory, and we too, have felt the need to interpret British Columbia to others as much as to herself.

In making our selection we aimed above all to provide a representative picture of historical writing in British Columbia and to indicate some of the changes which have taken place in the past century. Thus we sought the typical rather than the esoteric articles, and we chose not necessarily the "best" writing of each historian, for that was not always to be found in convenient form, but the article that we thought represented the career or interests of the author. In addition to interpretive articles, we have also included a representative selection from the variety of reminiscences, biographical and descriptive writing which have at times dominated British Columbia history. Thus our selection ranges from the work of the early collectors, such as Bancroft, Kerr, Gosnell and Morice, through the extensive and detailed work of Howay, to the academic writing of students like Isobel Bescoby, archivists Lamb and Ireland and Professors Sage and Ormsby. Newer work and recent interests are indicated in the articles by Roy, Jamieson, Ralston, Macdonald and Fisher, while the approaches of "outside" historians can be seen in the work of Dobie, Caves and Holton and Careless.

We lingered with regret over the articles we left behind; the writings of the gifted amateur Leonard Norris in the Okanagan Historical Society reports, or the delightful article on Sointula, the Finnish utopian settlement, in the *British Columbia Historical Quarterly*. Some essays, such as the conclusion to Paul Phillips *No Power Greater*, were not available to us, and others of excellent quality were still very recent and readily available. Undoubtedly, our selection will not satisfy all the interests of its prospective readers, but we hope it will offer a flavouring of the historical literature of British Columbia.

We have benefitted from the advice and criticism of Dr. M. A. Ormsby, Dr. P. Roy, Dr. A. C. Cairns, Dr. J. Wright, Ms. J. Gresco and Ms. Margaret Andrews, from the patience of Professor Carman Bickerton, and from the generous financial participation of the history division of the National Museum of Man in the early stages of the preparation of this book.

J. Friesen, University of Manitoba

Notes

1. R. E. Gosnell and E. O. S. Scholefield, *A History of British Columbia: Sixty Years of Progress* (n.p., 1913), pt. 1, p. 5. See also on this theme Allan Smith's brief but excellent paper on the early historiography of British Columbia (unpublished).
2. Gosnell, *op. cit.*, pt. II, p. 9.
3. Gosnell was editor of the Victoria Colonist 1904-1906, and private secretary to provincial premiers Dunsmiur and McBride.
4. Gosnell, *op. cit.*, pt. II, p. 16.
5. R. E. Gosnell, "British Columbia and British International Relations," *The Annals of the American Academy of Political and Social Sciences*, vol. XLV (Jan. 1913), p. 11.
6. Allan Smith, unpublished paper, *op. cit.*
7. Walter N. Sage, "Some Early Historians of British Columbia," *British Columbia Historical Quarterly*, vol. 24, no. 1.
8. Given in 1924, and entitled "The Early Literature of the Northwest Coast."
9. M. A. Ormsby, "W. N. Sage," *Canadian Historical Review*, Vol. XLV, no. 2 (June 1964), pp. 180-182.
10. *B.C.H.Q.*, vol. xvii
11. M. A. Ormsby, "Canada and the New British Columbia," Canadian Historical Association *Report*, 1948.
12. M. A. Ormsby, "A Horizontal View," Canadian Historical Association *Report*, 1967.
13. *British Columbia Library Quarterly*, vol. 23, April 1960.

1. Alexander Caulfield Anderson, Fur Trader and Scholar
H. H. Bancroft

HUBERT HOWE BANCROFT *(1832-1918), a San Francisco book-seller and publisher, promoted a history-writing "industry" on Western North American topics. This short extract—actually a lengthy footnote—was chosen to illustrate the extensive use by the Bancroft "team" of interviews with individuals.*

While at Victoria in 1878 I made the acquaintance of Mr Anderson, and spent much of my time with him in studying Northwest Coast affairs. Indeed, without that experience and the information then given me by Anderson, Tolmie, Finlayson, and others, I do not see how I could have written with any degree of completeness or correctness a history either of Oregon or of British Columbia. Anderson was the most scholarly of all the Hudson's Bay Company officers; Tolmie was keen and practical; Finlayson intellectual and courtly. Sir James Douglas, Mr Work, and Mr Ogden unfortunately were dead, but their respective families kindly placed at my disposal all the information within their reach. I speak of all these gentlemen elsewhere. I will give here only a brief biographical and bibliographical sketch of Mr Anderson and his works.

The more immediate result of my many interviews with Mr. Anderson is a manuscript *History of the Northwest Coast*, comprising 285 pages, and covering the entire field of Oregon affairs to 1846, and of matters relating to New Caledonia and British Columbia to date. So far as possible, the needless repetition of facts already in print was avoided. He as well as I knew well enough what was wanted, and as neither of us had time to waste, we confined ourselves pretty closely to inquiries into the domain of unrevealed facts. A thousand important events are thus for the first time placed upon record and a thousand incidents heretofore but vaguely stated are explained. In style, Mr. Anderson is somewhat pompous, pedantic, and diffusive in parading himself before

---

1 *Source*: Bancroft, H.H., *History of British Columbia, 1792-1887* (San Francisco, 1887).

the world, while in bringing into proper prominence the deeds of his associates a false delicacy makes him painfully reticent. This is a habit common to all the officers of the great monopoly, who, after living in deadly fear of speaking of company affairs for a score or two of years, almost tremble in their old age to set their tongues wagging over these old-time and sacred secrets. But for his honesty, courtesy, his sound business sense, and discriminating analysis of character, we may well forgive him a few superfluous words and high-sounding sentences. Throughout the whole work, particularly in the first pages, the facts are sadly jumbled, being thrown together as they arose in our minds, without regard to chronological or other order; but when segregated from the confused mass, by the system of note-taking obtaining in my Library, and being brought into conjunction with parallel facts and contemporaneous incidents, almost every sentence is a jewel which finds its proper fitting. To the personal work of Mr. Anderson are appended certain *Autograph Notes by the late John Stuart*, written at Torres, Scotland, in 1842, and consisting of caustic criticism of a previous narrative by Mr. Anderson. While that work of Anderson's is as a whole highly eulogized by Stuart, parts of it were pronounced apocryphal, and other parts exaggerated. This indeed would be the case with any work which could be written. Place three or even two of these old Hudson's Bay men in a room to discuss general affairs in which they had all participated, and hot words if not blows are sure to follow. In his *Notes*, Stuart takes exceptions to the dark side only of Indian character which Anderson chooses to dwell upon, and to the boundaries Anderson gives to New Caledonia, which Stuart says are too limited, and the like. To all this Anderson replies in such a way as to bring out the real state of affairs in the clearest possible manner.

And now for a brief biography, leaving details to their proper place in the history. Alexander Caulfield Anderson, a native of Calcutta, educated in England, was a youth of eighteen, having served the Hudson's Bay adventurers as clerk but one year when in 1832 he first appeared at Fort Vancouver. After participating in the founding of the posts at Milbank Sound and on the Stikeen, in the summer of 1835 he was appointed to Mr. Ogden's district of New Caledonia, and reached Fort George about the beginning of September. He was then despatched with a party by way of Yellowhead Pass to Jasper House to meet the Columbia brigade, and bring back goods for the New Caledonia district. Two months afterward he was appointed to the charge of the post at the lower end of Fraser Lake, his first independent command. In the autumn of 1839 he was removed to Fort George, and in the spring of 1840 accompanied the outgoing brigade to Fort

Vancouver, and in the autumn of the same year was appointed to the charge of Fort Nisqually. In the Autumn of 1841 Mr. Anderson left Nisqually and passed the winter at Fort Vancouver. Next spring he went with the express to York Factory, returned in October and proceeded to Fort Alexandria, to the charge of which he had been appointed, and remained there till 1848, having meanwhile been promoted. In that year he was appointed to the Colville district, succeeding Chief Factor John Lee Lewes. At Colville he remained, making annual trips with supplies and bringing out the furs to Fort Langley till 1851, when he went to Fort Vancouver as assistant to Mr. Ballenden, and succeeded temporarily to the superintendence till 1854, when he retired from active service. Marrying, he passed a few years near the house of his father-in-law, James Birnie, and then purchased a home at Cathlamet. In 1858 he went to Victoria to inquire into the gold discoveries. Douglas urged him to accept office and bring his family and assist in the affairs of the colony, which he did, since residing at Rosebank, Saanich, near Victoria. In 1876 he was appointed by the Dominion government commissioner to settle the Indian land differences in British Columbia, and continued to act in that capacity until the commission was dissolved in 1878. On his retirement from the Hudson's Bay Company's service in 1853-4, he received two years' retiring furlough in addition to the usual retired interest, which continued for seven years subsequently. It was as chief trader that he left the service of the company, his commission as chief factor being dependent on his returning to take charge of New Caledonia, where he had already passed a year; but the education of his family demanded that he should reside nearer the conveniences of civilization. In 1846 Mr. Anderson made an exploration for a route from Alexandria down the Fraser Valley to Fort Langley, and in 1847 a similar survey from Kamloops down the Thompson to the Mouth of the Nicola; thence by way of Lytton to Yale and Langley. The lines then traced afterward became the main routes of access to the interior. In 1858, in order to obtain means for transport of goods to the newly discovered gold-diggings, he recommended and directed the opening of a road from the head of Harrison Lake by way of Lake Anderson to the crossing of the Fraser, where Lilloet was afterward located. Five hundred miners were employed on the work, and the road thus constructed was used for the transport of all supplies, until the road along the Fraser was made. In personal appearance, at the time I saw him, he being then sixty-three years of age, Mr. Anderson was of slight build, wiry make, active in mind and body, with a keen, penetrating eye, covered by lids which persisted in a perpetual and spasmodic winking, brought on years ago by snow-field exposures, and now become habitual, and doubtless as disagreeable to him as to his friends. In speech he was elegant and precise, and by no means so verbose as in his writings, and in carriage, if not so dignified as Finlayson, his manner would do him credit at St. James.

2. Extract from the *Biographical Dictionary of Well-Known British Columbians*
J. B. Kerr

JOHN BLAINE KERR *(ca. 1863-1927) was an Ontario-born news-paperman who worked on papers in Vancouver and Rossland. The introduction to the* Dictionary *is an early piece of historical criticism. Kerr, reflecting the views of many pioneer British Columbians, charged Bancroft with numerous inaccuracies.*

Carne, Frederick, Jr., son of Frederick and Harriet Carne, was born August 18th, 1856, at Burealstone, Devonshire, Eng. In 1864 he came to British Columbia with his parents, who settled at Victoria. Here Mr. Carne went to school till he reached the age of fifteen. Since that time he has been continuously in business in Victoria. In 1883 he, in conjunction with Mr. Munsie, opened the grocery business the firm now conducts. Mr. Carne is also engaged with Mr. Munsie and Mr. A. J. Bechtel in the sealing business, and with these gentlemen has three schooners on the water. Two of their vessels have been seized by the United States revenue cutter, one, the Caroline, in 1886, which was loaded with all her cargo, and the Pathfinder, in 1889, which they recovered, the captain bringing her to Victoria with the prize crew on board. Mr. Carne is a member of the Order of Foresters. In 1885 he married Miss Agnes Gowan, of Victoria.

Erb, Louis E., (Victoria), was born in Fulda, Prussia, in January, 1830, and lived there till he was sixteen years old, when he went to Bavaria. While in Munich he studied the theory of brewing at Liebig's College, and afterwards obtained a practical knowledge of the business in breweries, in Bavaria, Austria and Hungary. He then went to Warsaw, where he had charge of a large brewing establishment for several years. From Warsaw he went to Constantinople to take charge of a business there, and from Constantinople he removed to Bucharest, Roumania, where he conducted a brewing establishment for two years. In 1863 he came to

---

Source: J. B. Kerr, *Biographical Dictionary of Well-Known British Columbians* (Vancouver, 1890), pp. 120-1 (Carne), p. 161 (Erb), p. 176 (Guichon), pp. 243-44 (Munroe and Munsie), p. 267 (O'Reilly), p. 291 (Sayward).

America, and for a year had charge of one of the largest breweries in New York. He then came west to San Francisco where, after a few year's residence, he removed to British Columbia. He was in Lillooet when the Big Bend excitement broke out, and he started a brewery in Seymour City, at the head of Shuswap lake. When the Big Bend excitement failed, Mr. Erb went to Cariboo, where he took charge of the principal brewery in Barkerville, where he remained till the Mosquito creek excitement broke out when he started a brewery there and conducted it till the mines were worked out. In the spring of 1870, he went to Victoria and purchased an interest in the Victoria Brewing Co., which he worked up to what it now is, the largest brewing business in British Columbia.

Guichon, Laurent, (Ladner's Landing), one of the earliest French settlers of British Columbia, was born in 1836 at Chambery, in the province of Savoie, France, where his father M. Jean Guichon, had an extensive farm. Mr. Guichon spent his early life in Savoie where he received his education. In 1857 he went to California where he was engaged in mining enterprises until 1850, when he left the Golden State and came to British Columbia, making Lytton his headquarters. During nine years Mr. Guichon, in partnership with his brother, Mr. Charles Guichon and a friend, Mr. Vincent Girod, carried on a very extensive and remunerative business in mining supplies and general merchandise from Yale to Quesnelle and Cariboo. In 1869 Mr. Charles Guichon left the firm and in 1873 Mr. Guichon sold out all his interests to his partner, Mr. Girod, and settled in Nicola Valley where he resided ten years. In 1883 Mr. Guichon removed to New Westminster where he speculated to a considerable extent. In the fall of the same year he bought the farm he now cultivates at Ladner's Landing and in 1886 built a store on his property, which he afterwards sold, devoting his whole attention to agricultural pursuits. Mr. Guichon married Perome, ninth daughter of Antoine Rae, a landed proprietor of Chambery, by whom he has six children.

Munro, Alexander, (Victoria), chief factor of the Hudson's Bay Company, was born in the town of Tain, Rosshire, Scotland, in 1824. In early life he was engaged in different pursuits—law, banking, etc.—first in Scotland and afterwards in England. He arrived on Vancouver Island in 1857 in the Hudson's Bay Company's service, and has since remained in and near Victoria. He witnessed the great gold rush of 1858. For many years past he has been factor of the Hudson's Bay Company and accountant of their western department, comprising the whole of British Columbia, and has also had charge of their lands and those of the Puget's Sound Agricultural Company in this Province. After the many changes which have taken place under his observation during the third part of a century he is now, on the eve of his retirement, the senior chief factor in the company's service. His life has been a busy and industrious one, but not eventful in comparison with the lives and stirring experiences of many of his predecessors—those adventurous, manly pioneers and veterans who smoothed the way, to a great extent for their successors by themselves undergoing the privations, the arduous labors and "perils by flood and field" incident to establishing not merely the company's trading posts but British authority also, and therewith happily introducing the dawn of civilization among savage tribes scattered over the wide continent from Canada to Alaska and the Arctic regions.

Munsie, William, (Victoria), was born in Pictou county, Nova Scotia, on January 4th, 1849, and educated at Pictou. After leaving school he served his apprenticeship to the foundry business in Truro, and remained their [sic] for four years. In 1874 he went to San Francisco, where for four years he was employed at this business. In 1878 he came to British Columbia and settled in Victoria, where he established a stove business for Mr. Joseph Spratt, of the Albion Iron Works, and designed and manufactured the first stoves ever made in British Columbia. He remained with Mr. Spratt for over six years. In 1885 he formed a partnership with his present associate, Mr. F. Carne, and established the grocery business the firm now conducts. In the same year in conjunction with Mr. A. J. Bechtel he purchased the schooner Caroline and engaged in the sealing industry. The following year they purchased another vessel, and have since been adding to their fleet.

O'Reilly, Hon. Peter, (Victoria), born in Ireland and educated there. Subsequently entered the civil service and was appointed a lieutenant in the revenue police. Came to British Columbia in 1858 and in April, 1859, was appointed assistant gold commissioner and stipendiary magistrate, and later in the same year was appointed high sheriff. He sat in the Legislative Council of British Columbia from 1863 till confederation. In 1864 he was appointed chief gold commissioner, and in 1881 Indian reserve commissioner, which latter office he still holds.

Sayward, William Parsons, (Victoria), born December 9th, 1818, at Thomastown, Maine, U.S.A., where his father James Sayward, was a shipmaster. Attended Thomastown grammar school till seventeen years of age, when he learned the carpenter trade. In 1838 he went to Florida where he resided for three years and then returned to his native place. He subsequently spent three years in Boston, Mass., and in 1846 again went to Florida and till March, 1849, lived in Key West. In 1849 he removed to California and settled in Sacramento, where he passed two years. In 1851 he removed to San Francisco and engaged in the lumber trade there till June, 1858, when he came to British Columbia and settled at Victoria. He established his lumber business at Victoria shortly after his arrival and has since continued to conduct it. He was married in Victoria to Miss Chambers. He is a member of the Oddfellows' Order and has twice been president of the Pioneer Society.

3. The Massacre at Chinlac
Adrian Gabriel Morice

ADRIAN GABRIEL MORICE, O.M.I. *(1859-1938), a Roman Catholic missionary, wrote extensively on the history and anthropology of the Canadian west. This selection offers an interesting example of what is now called ethno-history.*

About ... [1745] ... a most melancholy event, which was to cause a permanent change in the ethnographical map of the country, had happened at the confluence of the Stuart and Nechaco Rivers. There stood at that time a flourishing village called Chinlac, the population of which was allied by blood and dialect to the Lower Carriers of what is now called Stony Creek. The principal chief was a certain Khadintel, a man who enjoyed the consideration of his subjects, and who must have been well up in years, since he had two wives with a large number of children.

For some time previous to 1745, the report had been current amongst his people and their friends of other localities that the Chilcotins intended to avenge on him the death of one of their notables, and, agreeable to anticipations, a very large band of those Southern Dénés did come in due time, and in one morning practically annihilated the whole population then present at Chinlac. A few only owe their life to their temporary absence or to a speedy flight.

At the time of the catastrophe the head chief, Khadintel, was on a tour of inspection of his snares, some distance down the Nechaco. He had reached the rapid next to the confluence of the two rivers, paddling up in a large canoe with two other men, when he suddenly caught sight of a large number of canoes coming down stream.

"The Chilcotins!" he exclaimed. "Run up the bank and flee for your lives. I am the one they want, and I alone ought to die."

His companions were no sooner out of sight than a volley of arrows was whizzing around him, which he so dexterously dodged that, partly because his life appeared charmed to his aggressors, and partly because they thought it prudent to keep for any

Source: A. G. Morice, *The History of the Northern Interior of British Columbia* (Toronto, 1905), pp. 114-19.

possible emergency the few remaining arrows in their possession after the great expenditure of them they had made in the morning, Khalhpan, the captain of the war party, ordered a suspension of hostilites. Then, addressing his bold adversary, he said:

"Khadintel, you have the reputation of being a man. If you are such, dance for me."

Whereupon the Chinlac chief commenced the dance of a *toeneza* on the beach of the river, just to show that his heart was above fear and emotion. When he had finished he warned his departing enemy that, in the course of a few years, he would return his visit.

The spectacle which met Khadintel's eyes on his return to his village was indeed heart-rending. On the ground, lying bathed in pools of blood, were the bodies of his own two wives and of nearly all his countrymen, while hanging on transversal poles resting on stout forked sticks planted in the ground, were the bodies of the children ripped open and spitted through the out-turned ribs in exactly the same way as salmon drying in the sun. Two such poles were loaded from end to end with that gruesome burden.

Aided by his two companions, Khadintel religiously burnt all the bodies, and placed the bones which had partially escaped destruction in leather satchels adorned with long fringes which, in the course of time, he entrusted to the care of the surviving relatives of Khalhpan's victims. Then he prepared the vengeance due to such an unprovoked crime and, early in the spring of the third year after the massacre, he found himself at the head of a large band of braves he had gathered from among the few survivors of the Chinlac population and the allied villages of Thachek, Nulkreh (Stony Creek) and Natleh (Fraser Lake).

Having reached the Chilcotin valley, at a place which, from the topographical details now furnished by the old men, must be identified with the plain where the modern village of Anarhem stands, the avenging party beheld from the top of the third terrace, or last of the superposed plateaus, in the thickets of which they discreetly passed the night, a long row of lodges, indicating a very large population.

Khalpan, the Chilcotin chieftain, had a younger brother known as 'Kun'qus, a man most powerfully built and of a very amiable disposition. Expecting reprisals for his brother's misdeed, that influential Chilcotin had built a palisade round his house, wherein he lived with a wife taken from among his own tribe and a second partner, a Carrier woman, with her little brother, whom the members of Khalpan's expedition had brought him from Chinlac.

He had just gone to prepare laths for the erection of a salmon trap, when, early in the morning, he was surprised to hear, all of a sudden, the uproarious clamors of the avenging party who, from different points of vantage, were storming his village. Running home in all haste, he gave the alarm to the sleeping population, and as he rushed into his house he passed his Carrier wife and her brother escaping in the direction of their attacking countrymen. He lost some time in trying to pursue them armed with a war-club which, to defeat his purpose, the woman had previously fastened to the wall of the lodge.

By that time, several Chilcotins had already fallen before the rage of the Carriers, when 'Kun'qus, aided by his first wife, hastily donned his double armor, consisting of a device made of dried rods of hardened amelanchier wood, over which he spread the *pesta*, a sleeveless, tunic-like cuirass of moose-skin covered with a coat of glued sand and gravel. Thus attired, he went out and started shooting wildly until his supply of arrows was exhausted, keeping between his legs, till he fell pierced by an arrow, a little son of his, whom he loved above all his other children.

The Carriers, who now recognized him, seeing him practically powerless, assailed him from all parts. But with a large stone dagger, whose blade he had mounted at the end of a stick, he kept them all at bay, so that they could hardly hurt him, inasmuch as their missiles were of no avail against his double armor. In this predicament they remembered the boast of a confederate, a little man of insignificant parentage named Yoentoelh, who had previously offered to catch the big Chilcotin for them. Bidden to make good his boast, Yoentoelh rushed at 'Kun'qus, leading him to use his lance, which he skilfully dodged at the very instant that he seemed doomed to destruction, and grasping its shaft before 'Kun'qus could strike again, gave his countrymen the long-sought-for opportunity. Seizing the warrior from every available quarter, they snatched from him all the native finery in which he was attired, a beautiful ceremonial wig adorned with dentalium shells, a costly breastplate, and a necklace mostly of the same material. Then, under a heavy stroke from a warclub launched on the forepart of his head, 'Kun'qus fell down never to rise again. Then, falling on his helpless body with all kinds of weapons, they made of it an unrecognizable mass of flesh.

The Carriers had now gratified their lust for vengeance.

Indeed, the destruction of Chinlac was more than avenged. There the Chilcotins had set up two poles loaded with children's bodies, while the Carriers did not return to their country before they had put up as a trophy three such poles with similarly innocent victims.

Meanwhile, Khalhpan, the primary cause of the whole trouble, had been vainly sought for by the avenging northerners. He was absent, and did not come back until a short time after their departure. His feelings can be imagined when he came in sight of his village, now transformed into a solitude, peopled only by dogs howling around the mangled remains of their masters. Taking with him a few of the fugitives he found gloomily prowling about the field of carnage, he set out in pursuit of the retreating Carriers.

These had just forded a river at a point where a sandbank in the middle cut it in two, and they were in the act of putting on their foot-gear again, when Khalhpan was sighted on the opposite side of the stream. Khadintel immediately advanced to meet him.

"People say that you are a man, and you would fain pass yourself off as a terrible warrior," he said, in the best Chilcotin he could command. "If you be such, come on, Khalhpan; come on, and retreat not."

Whereupon the Chilcotin chief advanced as far as the sand-bank; but at the sight of his powerlessness against such a host of enemies, he began to cry and to turn back.

"Now, Khalhpan," insisted his triumphant foe, "when, all alone against your people, I was cornered on the river bank and you wanted to kill me, I danced at your bidding. If you are a man, dance now for me, as I did for you."

But his adversary merely returned as far as the sand islet, when the sight of the multitude facing him, and the remembrance of all his relatives gone and of his beloved daughter, now dragged into slavery, were too much for him. He requested his adversary to spare her life, and broke into violent sobbing, which seeing, Khadintel, in tones full of scorn, cried across the river:

"Khalhpan, it is upon men that we came down to avenge a great wrong. I see that you are a woman, therefore I allow you to live. Go in peace, and weep to your heart's content."

The affront to the Carrier tribe was thus washed out in blood, but the destruction wrought by the Chilcotin marauders remained irreparable. In the course of time, the few persons who had escaped the massacre of 1745 settled among their friends of Thachek and Lheitli (Fort George). As to their own village, a bare spot on the right bank of the Stuart River, and the several trails leading out of it, are all that now remain of what was formerly the home of a thriving community.*

*After the destruction of his native village Khadintel remarried, and by his last wife he had a daughter named Samalh'ti, who died in 1842 at the age of about ninety. She was then older than another woman who died recently among the Dénés leaving after her four generations of descendants. Samalh'ti is our authority for the date of the Chinlac massacre.

4. A Greater Britain on the Pacific.
R. E. Gosnell.

R. EDWARD GOSNELL *(1860-1931)*, *newspaperman and civil servant, was, at various times, first British Columbia provincial
librarian, first provincial archivist, secretary to the premier and
founder of the provincial bureau of information. His imperialist
views were shared by many English-Canadians in other parts of
the country.*

It is not a far cry from the time when British Columbia was part
of the great terra incognito, designated as Indian Territory, over
which the Hudson's Bay Company had exclusive trading privileges, and the year 1907, when Sir Wilfrid Laurier, as Premier of
the nine prosperous provinces of Canada, and the unorganized
districts attached thereto—the whole of what was formerly known
as British North America—sat in the councils of the Empire and
represented the views of the government of the first dominion in
that Empire. It is only fifty years since British Columbia disinte-
grated from the Oregon of that day, and became a colony of
Great Britain. Her late Gracious Majesty Queen Victoria had
already reigned twenty years when that occurred and was of
middle age. It seems only yesterday that she laid the sceptre
down. Yet in that short space of time vast changes have taken
place in the West of North America, and not in the least remarkable way in the West of His Majesty's domain. These changes
have been so great and momentous and have so altered the
destinies of the British Empire itself that few persons, even those
who have witnessed them all, realize their extent, character and
import. The object here, however, is not to be retrospective or
historical, except in so far as may be necessary to institute some
parallels conveying a more or less tangible impression of progress
achieved and therefrom draw conclusions as to the future.

In 1857, there was no means of communication overland
between the east and west of the North American continent,
except the prairie ship, the primitive, wearily winding caravan—
the emigrant train of pioneer days. There were still millions of

Source: *Westward Ho! Magazine*, *II*, 1908, pp. 7-13.

buffaloes on the prairie. West of the line of the Mississippi there were not yet half a million of people of European extraction. Apart from the few servants of the Hudson's Bay Co., scattered here and there at long intervals, there was not a white man on the mainland of British Columbia. On Vancouver Island which had been a Crown colony since 1849, there were possibly not more than 300 white persons all told. The news of the discovery of gold in the interior rivers and streams had just begun to percolate into the outside world through laggard channels. A reminiscent article in April Cornhill from the pen of Admiral Moresby ... deals with the oppressive solitude of the dense forests, with their children the Red Men and their primitive savagery with the long winding and deep dark inlets that so numerously indent the northwest coast of the continent; with wild beasts and the winged animals in an unexploited paradise of sport; with Nature in its very pristine forms and solemn majesty and with the few adventurous fur traders who were pioneering for the generation to come. "So little known, in fact was Vancouver (Island) in 1852," he writes "that when the news came to the officers' mess of H.M. Thetis. (a crack 35 gun frigate) of an order to proceed there straightway, I scarcely think even our hope of sport had any more concrete form than a vague notion of forest and stream, fur and fish," and in conclusion he strikes almost a pathetic key.

"As I lay my pen down the vision of the forest primeval and its children fades, and there rises in its place the roar of civilization, the teeming life of the cities that are and will be throned on the North Pacific.

"So the world changes; so our feverish activities fill the space between the silences; but to an old sailor who recalls many men and things in the peace of his last days, it is difficult sometimes to distinguish phantom and reality, and easier to believe that the pines are still waving in their solitude and the rivers running undisturbed to the great ocean."

For the purpose of comparison it is impossible to quote statistics of a time before which there was nothing. To show the progress that has been made we cannot go back as far as 1857, because while there were gold discoveries in that year, and in the following year excitements, inrush of population and government of a kind, as there had been in California ten years before, these were but the bases or germs, of a social and industrial organization that took many years to develop. As in the Middle and Pacific States, there was no real, at least rapid, progress until railways were built. So the history of British Columbia did not commence until about twenty years ago upon the completion of the C.P.R. There were as I have said, government, a small population, incipient commerce, trade and industry, but after the preliminary spurts incident to mining excitements, there was stagnation. Taking into consideration all things, more especially geographical remoteness, isolation, and mountainous exterior, the progress achieved since that time has been as remarkable as—if not more remarkable than—anything witnessed in the world during a very remarkable quarter of a century.

The states of Washington, Oregon and California in their development, and being largely similar in natural conditions what applies to them applies equally well to the country north of them, and in making comparisons I wish to include both. The reason for this rests upon the fact that causes and effects as revealed all along this long line of territory in addition to being largely contemporaneous are also very closely correlated. That is important to bear in mind. Statistics confined to a strictly mathematical basis might seem to prove that the American states referred to had relatively advanced much faster than British Columbia, and that is true; but it must be clearly understood that as these three states represented the western shore line of a great Republic that for many years made phenomenal strides—longer and faster than those made by Canada—it was but natural and inevitable that they should with it. Today in Canada people do not mourn over the fact that the United States for all these years, in material development, outstripped it actually and relatively. The very start that country got over Canada, while the latter was struggling with its hard physical conditions and knotty political problems, made it all the more difficult for Canadians to keep up in the race. Canada was not only handicapped in competition, by almost every possible adverse condition, for a share of the attention and immigration its great rival was receiving, but nearly two millions of her own population were carried away in that apparently never-ceasing floodtide to join their fortunes with those of their Yankee cousins. The steady plodding of the Canadian and the filling up of United States lands finally brought him to his opportunity, when the tide has begun to flow back again to the northward, promising to make the twentieth century Canada's, as the nineteenth was peculiarly that of her neighbour. The discipline of working and waiting and struggling was worth more in making national character than riches and fine linen. So, therefore, if British Columbia has lagged behind Washington, Oregon and California, which present many similar natural conditions and opportunities, in the past, it has not been without good, I might say, national cause; but the very reasons which caused the Pacific

Coast states to stride so fast for a time will cause this province to stride still faster in the future. The latter possesses some advantages which her neighbours do not, and similar advantages in a greater degree, as I shall attempt to show.

Readers do not require to be reminded that prior to 1846, Oregon, Washington and the greater part of British Columbia, as at present constituted, were included in that lone land of shadowy metes and bounds then known as the Oregon territory, and, indifferently, some times as Columbia. There were, as they also know, very conflicting claims as to the right of sovereignty. Those of the British extended as far south as the Columbia river, while the United States wanted the earth as far north as Alaska, a claim, by the way, which gave rise to the political shibboleth in the latter country at one time of "54, 40 or fight," a phrase attributed to that erratic genius of American fame in railways and finance, the late George Francis Train, and incorporated by him into some rather remarkable doggerel. Prior to the settlement of the boundary question the whole of the territory in dispute was appraised as practically valueless by the people of both countries, as reference to literature of the time will show. The missionaries and the first settlers in Oregon may be excepted from this general category, but they were recent arrivals, and like the Israelites of old they got, this new Canaan, for Uncle Sam this land of milk and honey, by simply entering in and taking possession of it. I might quote Robt. Greenhow, the distinguished librarian at Washington, as I have done on other occasions, to show the accepted American view of the country—a land hopeless in the expectancy of important commercial or industrial results, and forbidding all expectation of a transcontinental or transpacific trade developing through it or out of it. Or I might also quote some of the British writers on the same subject to practically the same effect. How dimly the potential present was then perceived by the very wisest and best informed men we may best judge by the accomplishments of the meanwhile.

It is not necessary to discuss the merits of the Oregon dispute. Like some other international disputes we have had with our near neighbours, it settled itself somehow in a haphazard way. There is a story told by the late Roderick Finlayson in his privately published diary. Finlayson was the factor of the Hudson's Bay Co.'s fort at Victoria, when Capt. Gordon, brother of the then premier of Great Britain, paid him a visit in his ship H.M.S. "America," to obtain information in order to assist the Imperial government in settling this bothering dispute. Mr. Finlayson states that Gordon was quite disgusted to find that fish were caught with lines and bait instead of with a rod and flies. He was equally disgusted with his attempts to stalk deer in a country where the thickets were too dense to be penetrated after the quarry had been sighted. Finlayson, by way of compensation, thought that Gordon would be impressed with the splendid scenic environment of Victoria, and with pride asked what he thought of it. "I would not," said the captain in reply, "give one of the bleakest knolls of all the bleak hills of Scotland for twenty islands arrayed like this in barbaric splendor." History also records that a detachment of this same expedition had visited the country along the Columbia river and returned equally as disgusted with what they saw as was Gordon with Vancouver Island. These incidents undoubtedly gave credence to what after all may have been only an amiable fiction, with a world-wide circulation, that Oregon was lost to the British because the salmon in its waters refused to rise to a fly. The remote or the immediate causes of this would take too long to discuss, and be a useless labour in any event. Doubtless the British governments of the long days through which the controversy in all its phases dragged from first to last lacked imagination as well as information respecting the country, and, perhaps after all cannot be blamed for not being wiser than they knew. Few, if any, in those days could appreciate the possibilities that lay dormant in Oregon or pierce the veil of its mighty future. It goes without saying of course, that British Columbia with Washington and Oregon included would have been vastly greater than it is; but even shorn as it has been of its widest possibilities it has still an area of 381,000 square miles, an area large enough for, and larger than that of many, a kingdom.

It has already been stated that in 1857 the white population west of the Mississippi did not exceed half a million. As a matter of fact, the population of the western division of America—the Pacific slope—is given as 179,000 in 1850, to which may be added for the country north of the line 30,000 or 35,000, almost exclusively Indians. The population for the same area in 1906 is given officially at 4,100,000, to which may be added at least 250,000 for British Columbia. An official statement of the wealth of the Pacific Coast states in 1904 places it roundly at $10,-000,000,000. We have no similar statement of an official nature for British Columbia, but it may be fixed approximately at $350,000,000. In 1906 the exports and imports of the western ports of these states reached the respectable total of $217,500,000, whereas in 1890 they only reached $99,000,000. To this add $38,500,000 for British Columbia in 1906. In the case of Puget Sound, the increase in sixteen years was 14-fold, of Seattle

48-fold, and of Tacoma about 5-fold. The mileage of railways, which in 1860 was 23 miles, in 1906 was nearly 18,000 miles. Bank loans and discounts in the latter year amounted in volume to $175,000,000, and savings banks deposits to $264,000,000. This is a record of really much less than fifty years, and is eloquent of what we in British Columbia, still in the swadling clothes of development, are capable of.

Turning now to the exclusive consideration of this our own province, there have been many things affecting its destinies since 1849 when the colony of Vancouver Island came into existence— the mining excitements, the loss of the San Juan group of islands, the acquisition of Alaska by the United States, the entering into Confederation, the agitation for the speedy construction of the C.P.R., the Settlement Act, and, perhaps most marked in its effects, the completion of a transcontinental line. The last spike was driven in 1885 by Sir Donald A. Smith, now Lord Strath- cona, and the following summer the first through train from Montreal, after a continuous journey of 3,000 miles, arrived in Port Moody—a memorable event, the consummation of the great task of welding the scattered provinces of Canada together, but after all only the forging of the initial link in that mightier chain to unite the Motherland with Canada, the Orient and Australia on the all-red line of Empire.

There is no record of what was produced in British Columbia in 1871—the total was small—but from census returns of the output of manufacturers, of the forest, of the miners, of furs, of agriculture, and of the fisheries, we are enabled to follow up the progress since that time. By decades we have the following:

1881	$ 8,116,355
1891	22,213,575
1901	83,804,862

The returns for 1911 will undoubtedly show a still greater percentage of increase. The mines, which in 1901, produced values to the extent of $3,500,000, in 1906 produced in values $25,000,000. We have had even more remarkable progress in agriculture, whose products increased 11=fold between 1891 and 1901, and without doubt the most promising of all our great industries, notwithstanding the relatively limited areas of agricul- tural lands. Coming to exports and imports, we find totals as follows:

1872	$ 3,648,402
1881	4,721,197

1891 11,736,041
1901 32,187,545
1906 38,401,998

Taking these figures, which might be multiplied in great volume, and the statistics for the entire Pacific Coast—a territory which as I have stated has a great deal in common and is analagous in its general characteristics—and viewing them in the light of the surmises made over fifty years ago by the historian Greenhow or the not less distinguished British authorities to whom I have referred, one realizes how very unsafe it is to prophesy. What these wise men thought or wrote then is of no real importance now except, perhaps, to accentuate the facts which the future actually revealed. The moral of these facts may be readily drawn. The entire Pacific Coast has been singularly productive and progressive, notwithstanding its many obvious physical disadvantages. Its potential assets are climate, fertility of soil, scenery, ocean, timber, minerals, in almost prodigal combination. The country north of the boundary line, I wish to repeat again as the moral of my story, is similar in most respects to that south, with very many of the essential features emphasized in an especial degree. South of the line the development of the natural assets has been more rapid and fuller, for the reason that there has been a population behind it larger in the ratio of 15 to 1. The tide of population and prosperity having turned in the direction of Canada, British Columbia as its western shore line must share in that prosperity in abounding measure. It is the last of the undeveloped areas of the continent, the last west as a field for the pioneer, the seeker of fortune, and the settler in search of a home. I am not unmindful of the danger of prophesying, to which I adverted a moment ago, but looking at the future in the light of available data and reasonable possibilities, all the factors in the situation favour the belief that British Columbia will henceforth make relatively more rapid progress than any other part of the Pacific slope, remarkable as that progress has been in the past, and is likely to be in the future.

Let us examine carefully the reasons for making this bold proposition. The states of the Pacific slope, though still developing, are approaching the zenith of their achievements. British Columbia is still nascent. Throughout its entire extent it has been shown to be metalliferous, and it will not be denied, so far as events have carried us, that neither Washington nor Oregon can compare with British Columbia as mining countries. Whatever may be our future in this respect, up to the present only a fringe of the Province has been touched by transportation, and consequently only a fringe of our mineral resources has been made available. In railway construction the Pacific Coast states have been far in advance of us, having nine or ten times the mileage of British Columbia; but in addition to the Canadian Pacific railway, already a most important factor, we have the immediate promise of three other transcontinental lines—the Grand Trunk Pacific, the Canadian Northern and the Great Northern Railways, with, of course, the usual ramification of branch and local lines. One can hardly estimate the effect of such a stimulus to all the activities as will here be afforded. Again, British Columbia has admittedly the largest compact timber areas on the continent, and it is, therefore, unnecessary to dwell upon the importance of that fact. By far the most valuable deep sea fisheries are found north of the 49th parallel, and from as far north as Alaska the United States fishermen are getting their supplies for the American market. It may be freely admitted that in point of agricultural resources we are outclassed in the comparison, that is, as to extent of arable land; but even here we have nine or ten millions of acres, capable, by intensive fruit and small-farm culture, of yielding enormously, with a ready and most profitable market locally, in the middle Canadian provinces, and in Great Britain. While our output can never be as large, as that of the States south of us within corresponding areas, the industry is, for obvious reasons, of vantage in respect to market, likely always to be more profitable here than there. We possess another great advantage over our neighbours to the south in the nature of our coast line and the excellent facilities afforded for shipping. From San Francisco to Puget Sound there is no harbor of any size. Our coast line is full of harbours, many of them suitable as railway and steamship termini, so that in time if our anticipations are realized as to the developments to take place we have in this fact the basis of a great mercantile marine and commercial power. There is still the further advantages, in a sense not less important, in the abundance of coal, iron and pulp wood, which they do not possess. Many problems have been and still are connected with the development of the iron industry on this Coast, but it seems almost certain that sooner or later these will be solved. There are new processes in the smelting of iron and steel already in operation and likely to be applied to the situation here, which will make the magnetic iron ores, which prevail on this coast, convertible into products comparable with the best qualities of iron and steel turned out in the world. The pulp and paper industry, although never likely to asssume the importance it has in the east of Canada, is nevertheless likely to be very successful. Shipbuilding, too, ought to be from our very situation one of the leading industrial enterprises of the future. I have only touched upon a few of the leading factors in making my comparison and drawing conclusions. Manufacturing on the coast is still in its infancy, though steadily growing. We have peculiar natural advantages for manufacturing on an extensive scale. With iron and coal and lime and timber and sea all in close contiguity—things upon which Great Britain founded its supremacy—we have undoubtedly the essential elements of a vast industrial fabric. As soon as the prairies fill up there will be at least ten millions at our back door, and an Orient, and Australia and South America at our front doors, to consume our products. I was going to quote Lord Gray's remarks while in the Province last year, but space forbids to reproduce more than one short sentence, which seems to be particularly opportune: "I shall have failed in my object if I have not communicated to you my own profound belief in the present and potential advantages you can enjoy because of your great natural resources and of your unique geographical position."

This vast and in some respects still unknown country has possibilities in store for it not yet, perhaps, dreamed of. It has without peradventure, great possibilities as the home for the British emigrant and as a field for the investor; possibilities as the point of convergence of trade and commerce along the All Red Line to the utmost development of which the statesmen of the Empire are pledged; possibilities as an educational centre as famous as any in Europe; possibilities of great industrial wealth; possibilities in short as a greater Britain on the Pacific, where British arts and institutions will expand under fresh impetus, "where the British flag will forever fly, where British laws and justice will be respected and enforced, and where British men and women will be bred equal to the best traditions of the race."

5. The Settlement and Progress of British Columbia, 1871-1914
F. W. Howay

FREDERIC WILLIAM HOWAY *(1867-1943), was a lawyer and judge by profession and an historian by avocation. This article epitomizes Howay's interests in the first part of his career as an historian. He was later to turn to an intensive examination of the maritime fur trade.*

Confederation effected a complete change in the status of British Columbia and in the political power of its people. With the step from colony to province came responsible government. There were many who believed that the country was not ripe enough in settled population to justify the measure; but influential supporters of confederation had resolved that union and responsible government should synchronise.[1]

With confederation, too, came renewed faith. The burden of debt had been lifted. And yet the province was very much as Governor Frederick Seymour had described it—a wagon road, with a gold mine at one end and a seaport at the other. As Cariboo continued to wane, other sources of wealth—other forms of employment—were sought. Agriculture, spreading from the vicinity of the Cariboo Road to the valleys of the Thompson and the Fraser, drew to itself many of the miners, tired of following fickle fortune. The coal mines of Nanaimo were producing 30,000 or 40,000 tons annually and employing two or three hundred men. Salmon packing had commenced, and lumber was being exported to Australia, China, and South America.

The Lieutenant-Governor selected as Premier John Foster McCreight, a prominent lawyer. He was in no sense a politician and, moreover, had opposed the introduction of responsible government, so that the choice was a disappointment to its ardent supporters, who had hoped that the test of the system might have been inaugurated under one of its advocates. The Legislative Assembly, as constituted by the Act of 1871, consisted of twenty-five members: thirteen from the mainland and twelve from

Source: The Cambridge History of the British Empire, vol. 6, *Canada and Newfoundland* (Cambridge, England, 1930). Reprinted by permission of the publisher.

Vancouver Island.[2] This balancing of the two divisions, without regard to relative population, prevailed down to 1894. In 1871 the census of the province was 37,247: being, mainland 5627, island 5959, with 25,661 Indians, undistributed.[3] In the new order of things it was difficult to find a dividing line between Government and Opposition. However, as the island with twelve members had two salaried ministers, while the mainland with thirteen members had only one, a cleavage along the line of mainland against island resulted. It was, indeed, an old and easy line of fracture. To this nucleus other local and personal differences attached themselves.

The McCreight Government lived through only one session; yet that afforded the opportunity to enact many laws necessitated by the new conditions. The legislation which touched the vital spot was the cancellation of the tolls on the Cariboo Road.[4] These had been imposed to repay the cost of construction; but, as with confederation the debt had vanished, the reason for their existence was gone. The greatest forward step McCreight made was to abolish tuition fees and local levies and to substitute free education, placing the whole cost of the public schools upon the public revenue, where it remained until 1891.[5] McCreight also planned to substitute vote by ballot for the old-fashioned open voting; but before he could carry his intention into effect, he was defeated, and his Government resigned.

About this time came the end of the San Juan boundary trouble with the United States which had dragged on since 1853. The Treaty of Washington, 1846, fixed the boundary between British and American possessions along the 49th parallel "to the middle of the channel which separates the continent from Vancouver's Island and thence southerly through the middle of the said channel and of Fuca Straits to the Pacific Ocean."[6] The interpretation of these words was difficult, for between the continent and Vancouver Island lay the Haro Archipelago, comprising San Juan and other islands with a total area of about one hundred and seventy square miles. On the northern side was Haro Strait, which the Americans asserted was the channel; on the southern side, Rosario Strait, claimed by the British as the channel. The question was which, if either, of these waterways was "the channel" of the treaty. To prevent trouble the two claimants ordered their representatives to refrain from any acts in the disputed area that might provoke conflict.[7] The Hudson's Bay Company had large herds of cattle on San Juan Island, where, also, many Americans had squatted. A dispute between the Company and one of the squatters regarding the value of a pig furnished, in July 1859, an excuse for a fire-eating officer, General Harney, to order the occupation of San Juan by American troops.[8] British men-of-war were immediately despatched to the scene; but they landed no men, being content with the display of immensely superior force.[9] General Winfield Scott, the head of the United States army, soon arrived. He reprimanded Harney for his precipitate action, withdrew all the troops except one company, and arranged for a joint occupation by them and a company of British marines.[10] Numerous attempts were made to settle the question, but it was not until 1871 that the two nations requested the German Emperor to decide, which of the two— Haro Strait or Rosario Strait—was "most in accordance with the true interpretation of the treaty." The question in this narrow form the Emperor, on 21 October 1872, decided in favour of the Haro Strait and the contention of the United States.[11]

Amor De Cosmos, a brilliant but eccentric man, who succeeded McCreight as Premier, was also a member of the Dominion Parliament. He endeavoured to avoid the mainland against island cry by appointing two salaried ministers from each section. This not only failed to stifle that cry but raised another—that of inconsistency, inasmuch as, while preaching retrenchment and economy, he had added the expense of a new minister. To the credit of the short-lived De Cosmos Government are: the introduction of vote by ballot and the abolition of dual representation.[12] The latter compelled De Cosmos to choose between the two fields. He chose the larger, and on 9 February 1874 resigned his seat in the Provincial Legislature.

George A. Walkem, who had been Chief Commissioner of Lands and Works in the McCreight Government and Attorney-General under De Cosmos, now became Premier. Much of his administration touches the railway difficulties with the Dominion Government. The franchise under which Confederation had been accepted had been limited to British subjects having certain property qualifications; but in 1874 the Walkem Government introduced manhood suffrage. At the same time Chinese were excluded from voting, a privilege which they had exercised, if otherwise eligible, from the earliest days of elections on the mainland.[13] The province was passing through a period of depression, accentuated by the failure to commence railway construction and by the steady decrease of gold mining. Cariboo continued to dwindle; and search where they might in Omineca or in Cassiar the miners could find no diggings with promise of large and long-continued production. The population of the towns was at a standstill. The vast areas of vacant land still remained

vacant. Even for the produce of lands already occupied no sufficient market existed. To tide over the situation, to prevent a
recurrence of the conditions of 1866-8, the Government in 1875
entered upon a programme of public works much in advance of
the requirements.

The debt-free condition resulting from union lasted for six
months. Then began an era of deficits. By the end of 1874 these
amounted to more than $300,000; and in consequence the Wal-
kem Government floated the first provincial loan.[14] The great
expenditure of 1875 created a further deficit of $260,000. The
Opposition declared that this expenditure had been incurred with
an eye to the approaching election. Perhaps the charge was
justified, for the Walkem Government now repealed manhood
suffrage and substituted a statute under which the qualifications
varied in different sections of the province.

The elections occurred in 1875. The Government appeared to
have been placed securely in power, but early in the session of
1876 it met defeat. One of the first measures of the new—the
Elliott—Government was to re-enact manhood suffrage. This
Government had a short and stormy life, for the acute form of
railway trouble, known as "Carnarvon Terms or Separation",
caused intense friction, as appears from the fact that, when Lord
Dufferin, Governor-General of the Dominion, visited Victoria,
he was expected to drive under an arch bearing the motto "Separation." Hearing of this, he tactfully requested the mayor to
change "S" into "R," but, as this was not done, he drove round
the arch.[15] But, further, the Government suffered from the
looseness, or rather the absence, of ties between it and its supporters. Andrew C. Elliott had been so unwise as to admit into
his Cabinet a minister with whom he soon found it impossible to
work, and who, on being dismissed, not only joined the Opposition, but took his personal friends with him. Crippled by this
defection, the Elliott Government hobbled along with a majority
of two.[16] In this precarious situation Elliott was injudicious
enough to introduce a bill enlarging the Legislature to thirty-
three. A bitter fight began. For more than a month he tried, but
failure met him at every turn. His incapacity as a leader was plain
in this struggle. In the end he was forced to abandon his bill, and
accept a compromise whereby, supply having been voted, a new
election should be held.[17]

In that election Elliott was defeated and his opponent formed
the second Walkem Government, which held office from 1878 till
1882. Much of this period was occupied with railway troubles:
first, the failure to commence the construction of the Canadian

Pacific Railway; and, secondly, the refusal to build what was called the "Island section" from Esquimalt to Nanaimo. Until 1882 Walkem had usually a majority of seven or eight in a House of twenty-five. The rock on which he came to grief was the Esquimalt graving dock. This had been estimated to cost £100,000, and grants equalling that amount had been promised by the Imperial and Dominion Governments. It soon became plain that the cost would exceed the estimate. More than $180,000 was spent by the local government for site and plant. The people of the mainland complained of this expenditure at a time when roads and trails were a crying necessity. It was another phase of "mainland v. island." Walkem, thinking that the promised grants would complete the undertaking, stated in reply to a direct question that the dock "would not cost the people one cent more". At that time the Government had agreed to supply the cement, which was supposed to be merely a matter of $3500. When it was known that this item would probably reach $150,000 the excitement became intense. A Parliamentary Committee reported against the Government.[18] The House divided twelve to twelve; the Government was saved only by the vote of the Speaker.

The census of 1881 showed: on the island a population of 17,292, on the mainland, 32,167, making a total of 49,459—an increase of about 13,000;[19] but the House still contained only twenty-five members. Though it had been agreed that the readjustment of seats should be considered in 1882, Walkem, perhaps remembering the experience of his predecessor, evinced no intention of so doing. There was need for adjustment: Kootenay, which in the election of 1878 had polled only 15 votes, had two members; Esquimalt with 160 voters had two members; New Westminster District with 800 votes had two members. A resolution condemning the inaction of the Government was rejected by the casting vote of the Speaker.[20] Elliott with a majority of two had been unable to control the House; Walkem did so on the Speaker's vote. He was bold and resourceful; he succeeded in winning over one of his opponents, and, after voting supply, steered the ship of state safely into prorogation. Soon after the close of the session he was appointed to the Supreme Court of the Province.

Robert Beaven, the Minister of Finance, then formed a government, and in June 1882 went to the country. When the polls had closed the Beaven Ministry was seen to be in full rout: only eight of its supporters were to be found amongst the twenty-five. Nevertheless Beaven and his one colleague retained office. The

Opposition members presented to the Lieutenant-Governor a "round robin" to show that the Government had been defeated. He refused to act, for he regarded the party ties—if such they could be called that were but personal—as too loose to justify any serious action. The Opposition clamoured for the resignation of Beaven, or for his dismissal, or for the summoning of the House. Beaven would not resign; and the Lieutenant-Governor would not act. So affairs drifted along for months with Beaven and his one minister as a sort of skeleton government. Finally, in response to a memorial signed by three-fifths of the members-elect, the Lieutenant-Governor directed that the House be summoned for 25 January 1883.[21] Beaven, with a majority of eight against him on the floor, went through the solemn farce of laying down the policy of his so-called Government in the Speech from the Throne. But the House was in no humour to endure the mockery and at once condemned the ministers for violating the spirit of responsible government in failing to advise its prompt meeting.[22] So died the Beaven Ministry. As regards the finances of the province up to 1883, each year, except 1879 and 1881, saw a deficit, ranging from about $50,000 in 1880 to about $340,000 in 1876. The gross debt in 1882 was $800,566.[23]

The Government that came into power in 1883 existed under changing names—William Smythe, A. E. B. Davie, John Robson, Theodore Davie, and John H. Turner—and varying personnel until 1898. Smythe, the new Premier, determined to clear away the discord that had arisen over the Island Railway, and to relieve the province from the incubus of the graving dock. Negotiations with the Dominion Government secured the accomplishment of both these objects. The Island Railway, now called the Esquimalt and Nanaimo Railway, was to be built: the province granting in aid 1,900,000 acres and the Dominion contributing a bonus of $750,000. The graving dock was to be taken over by the Dominion, which gave to the province $250,000 and repaid the money already expended, $182,000. A large area, 3,500,000 acres, in the Peace River country was also granted to the Dominion in lieu of lands alienated within the railway belt. In 1883 and 1884 these arrangements were crystallised into Acts and declared to be a complete settlement of all claims between the two Governments.[24]

The province now entered upon a period of material development. On the mainland railway construction proceeded apace; on the island, too, the long-looked-for Island Railway approached completion. These works offered the market so fervently desired. The fertile valley of the Fraser and the rich farming and grazing lands of the interior were being occupied and cultivated; Saanich, Cowichan and other farming districts on Vancouver Island were receiving population. The country was at last filling up. Between 1881 and 1891 the number of inhabitants in Victoria, New Westminster and Nanaimo increased three-fold.[25] New lumber and grist mills, salmon canneries and manufactories were being established; railway construction brought a great increase of population, families coming where only individuals had come before. Settlement spread out from the railways as a base. The lengthening lines of rails gave to farmer, grazier, and manufacturer the means of access to new markets.

In this development the Indians shared. They entered slowly into the new economic life, taking their parts as farmers, fishermen, or unskilled labourers. Unfortunately they, too frequently, yielded to the vices of civilisation. Miners and settlers, especially on the Nass and Skeena Rivers, came into conflict with their tribal rights and ancient hunting and fishing privileges. These difficulties, however, were always adjusted by firm, yet sympathetic, treatment.[26]

At this time came the downfall of the Metlakatla mission. This station, established in 1857 by William Duncan, a layman, for the Church Missionary Society, had proved that the Tsimshian Indians, one of the fiercest of the coast tribes, could be trained in the arts of civilisation and brought under the influence of Christianity. The village of contented, civilised, and Christianised Indians, with its neat homes and well-built streets, its imposing church, its community organisation, cannery, saw-mill, and store, attracted the attention and won the admiration of everyone interested in the improvement of native races. For nearly twenty-five years it flourished, then a disagreement concerning church services and ritual led to turmoil, riot, and factional dissension which became so intense that a war-vessel was sent to the scene. In the end the community was rent in twain, and Duncan and his followers left the village to establish a new Metlakatla in Alaska.[27]

The membership of the Legislature had stood steadily at the original twenty-five; but in 1885 the Smythe Government added two members. In doing so the balance between island and mainland was preserved: each section received an additional representative.[28] In this period of expansion, the Government, with constantly recurring deficits, entered upon a policy of giving bonuses to transportation and development schemes.[29] Fortunately many of them fell by the wayside. Those that were carried through, e.g. the Eagle Pass Wagon Road and the Kootenay and Columbia Canal, benefited their promoters, but brought nothing of permanent value to the province. Under the terms of union the Canadian Pacific Railway ended at tide water on Burrard Inlet, but the Smythe Government granted 6000 acres for its extension to Coal Harbour. There in 1885 began the City of Vancouver, a city of marvellous growth, which in thirty years had reached a population of over 100,000. The completion of the railway in November 1886 was followed by the inauguration of the trans-Pacific trade, first to China and Japan, and later to Australia and New Zealand. The effect of rail connection with Eastern Canada is shown by the census of 1891. From 1871 to 1881 the increase was about 30 per cent., but in the next ten years, being the period of building and early operation of the railway, the population increased 100 per cent., and in each subsequent decennial census a similar growth has appeared.[30] The coal mines of Nanaimo reflected this growth: in 1874 the produced 81,000 tons; in 1879, 241,000; and in 1887, 413,360.

In 1890 the Robson Government increased the membership of the Legislature from twenty-seven to thirty-three; still retaining the vicious, but seemingly imperative, balance of power: seventeen on the mainland and sixteen on the island.[31] This action was the main point of attack in the elections of 1890; but in the changed conditions caused by the influx of population the cry was not: mainland against island. The newcomers had no interest in, or knowledge of, the facts that had fostered and fomented the sectional feeling. Criticism was directed to the varying unit of representation: for example, 7111 voters on the island elected sixteen members; while 6566 on the mainland elected only six members. The demand was for "Fair Representation"; but Robson, able, astute, and far-seeing, disarmed his opponents by admitting that the bill was only a temporary measure, intended to give a modicum of relief pending the decennial census of 1891. Robson had usually a majority of eight or ten, but after the elections of 1890 this was increased to about seventeen in a House of thirty-three.

Meanwhile the sealing industry had developed apace. In 1866 the Indians informed a trader of the facility with which fur-seals could be obtained thirty or forty miles off the coast of Vancouver Island. This was the germ of pelagic sealing. Year by year the number of schooners engaged in it increased. Year by year the Victoria schooners followed the seals northward farther and farther, until about 1883 they entered Bering Sea.[32] The herd was making for the rookeries on the Pribylov Islands, which were under lease to the Alaska Commerical Company. In 1886, without warning, United States revenue cutters seized British sealing schooners in Bering Sea, though seventy miles from the nearest land. The Americans claimed that sea as territorial water of Alaska. Until 1899 these seizures continued, though occasionally they were varied by an order to leave. In all fifteen British vessels were seized and confiscated and five others were ordered out of Bering Sea.[33] This high-handed conduct became the subject of many protests and much correspondence between Great Britain and the United States. Ultimately a tribunal of arbitration was established and sat in Paris in 1893 to decide what exclusive rights Russia had had in Bering Sea; how far they had been recognised by Great Britain; to what extent they had been transmitted to the United States; and what, if any, rights of protection or property the United States had in the seal herd beyond the three mile limit. If their findings were adverse to the United States the arbitrators were authorised to frame regulations for the government of pelagic sealing.[34] The arbitrators decided that Russia, and consequently the United States as her successor in title, had no jurisdiction beyond the three mile limit; that Bering Sea was a part of the Pacific Ocean; that the United States had no rights of protection or property in the seal herd after it had passed out of territorial waters—that is, beyond the three mile limit. Under the authority to enact regulations the Board prohibited sealing within a zone of sixty miles around the Pribylov Islands and also forbade, between 1 May and 31 July in each year, any sealing east of 180° longitude and north of 35° latitude. The remainder of the regulations dealt with the weapons and vessels to be used and the records to be kept.[35] The persons interested in the twenty schooners, that had been seized or interfered with, pressed their claims for damages which in 1896 were judicially investigated and fixed at $463,454.[36] The regulations did not affect the Asiatic side of Bering Sea and the Pacific Ocean, and sealers resorted thereto under an agreement made in 1893 between Great Britain and Russia, whereby British vessels were permitted to take seals in those waters except within a zone of thirty miles around the Russian seal islands.[37] This was the state of affairs down to June 1911 when, by agreement between Great Britain, the United States, Russia and Japan, all pelagic sealing ceased north of the 35th parallel. The United States, Russia, and Japan, all of whom had territory on which were seal rookeries, granted to Great Britain a certain percentage of the returns therefrom. Then the sealing fleet, which for forty years had been the pride of Victoria and had brought wealth to many of her citizens, was dispersed in every direction and into all classes of service. The owners, however, still share under the ageement which expired in 1926.[36]

In 1893 magnificent Parliament Buildings were constructed at Victoria. In 1894 the old idea of the balance of power between island and mainland tottered to its fall. The redistribution of the seats in that year left the number at thirty-three, but the traditional policy of allowing one member more to the mainland than to the island disappeared. Instead there were nineteen members on the mainland to fourteen on the island.[31] In 1895 Davie, the Premier, became Chief Justice, and again the Government was reorganised as the Turner Government. From 1883 when its predecessor, the Smythe Government, came into power, down through the A. E. B. Davie, Robson, Theodore Davie, and Turner Governments there was in each year a deficit varying from $28,912 in 8191 to $561,408 in 1898, and to the enormous sum of $1,010,899 in 1891. In those fifteen years the accumulated annual deficits reached $4,734,782. To provide for capital expenditures and these deficits the Governments were forced into continual borrowings. In 1884 the gross debt of the province was $770,812; by 1898 it had grown to $7,425,262.[40]

The demand now became insistent that the country must live within its income and that these repeated borrowings must cease. This feeling of dissatisfaction was evident when in preparation for an appeal to the people the Turner Government introduced a redistribution measure whereby the number of legislators was increased to thirty-eight.[41] In the votes on this bill its majority fell to seven; and then to five. It was plain that despite every effort the Turner Government was losing ground. In July 1898 the elections were held. The result was doubtful, but it appeared that the Government had been defeated, having only fifteen supporters in a House of thirty-eight. Twenty-nine election petitions were launched increasing the uncertainty. In August 1898, before any of these had been heard, and before a deferred election had been held, the Lieutenant-Governor (Thomas R. McInnes) dismissed Turner and, after some vacillation, called upon Charles A. Semlin.[42]

Internal difficulties in the Semlin Government led, in 1899, to the resignation of the Attorney-General, Joseph Martin, the "stormy petrel" of Canadian politics, who, following the custom of those days, joined the Opposition. During the session of 1900 the Semlin Government, though weakened by his defection, battered by his attacks, and crippled by the capricious support of one of its adherents, staggered along, sometimes with a majority of one and sometimes on the casting vote of the Speaker, until on 14 February 1900 it was defeated by a vote of 19 to 18. The

Lieutenant-Governor then informed Semlin that he must within a fortnight either resign or ask for a new election. Semlin did neither; he arranged for support, and reported that he could control the House. The Lieutenant-Governor, notwithstanding, dismissed him and called upon Martin to form a ministry.[43] The Legislature at once resolved that it had no confidence in Martin.[44] Shortly afterwards, when His Honour arrived to prorogue the House, every member, with one exception, rose and left the chamber, and the brief Speech from the Throne was read to empty benches. The scene was unparalleled in a British Legislature, but it was deemed necessary to mark the intense disapprobation of the course taken by the Lieutenant-Governor. As he left the hall the members filed in again, singing "God save the Queen!" and an uproarious scene followed: resolutions condemnatory of his conduct were mingled with patriotic songs and general disorder.[45]

All this boded ill for Martin. However he went bravely to work and formed a ministry, if such it can be called, composed of men quite unknown in the public life of the province. More than three months elapsed between the dissolution and the election. That interval Martin used in an aggressive campaign. Loud were the complaints that a body of men, five-sixths of whom had never been members of the Legislature, should for three months govern the country without the authority of the people. Such a condition, it was said, had no parallel in the history of responsible government.[46] The elections were decisive; out of thirty-eight members only thirteen were supporters of Martin. His opponents pressed for the dismissal of the Lieutenant-Governor, who, it was urged, had acted unconstitutionally in dismissing a minister with a working majority and calling upon a man who had no following—who led no party. Upon his refusal to resign Lieutenant-Governor McInnes was dismissed.[47]

James Dunsmuir, a wealthy coal mine operator, without political training, experience, or aptitude, formed a ministry, that in reality was a coalition, in which the only bond of union was opposition to Martin. For a year all went well; in some of its legislation the Government even had Martin's support. Dunsmuir, in September 1901, took into the Cabinet one of the Martin party. This move, so subversive of the *raison d'être* of his ministry, led to disruption; and he was only saved from defeat by the support of four members of the Martin wing.[48] In that year the Dunsmuir Government, in fulfilment of its promise to introduce a fair measure of representation, increased the membership of the Legislature to forty-two, of whom twelve were from island constituencies.[49] And so it remained until 1915 when the number became forty-seven.[50]

Dunsmuir resigned the leadership in November 1902. His successor, Colonel E. G. Prior, faced a difficult task; the original majority of seven had dwindled to two or three; there was little coherence amongst his supporters. By-elections reduced this small margin of safety. Clouds darkened deeply in 1903 upon the Prior Government. A committee was ordered to investigate the circumstances connected with the grants of coal and oil lands to a railway company and their subsequent cancellations.[51] While the enquiry was proceeding, Prior requested and obtained the resignations of two ministers who had been closely connected with these strange transactions. As usual they joined the Opposition. The Government no longer controlled the House and existed only by the indulgence of its opponents. Then came the final blow. The Premier had a controlling interest in a certain company. The charge was made that he had awarded to it a contract under circumstances arousing a suspicion that the figures of other tenderers had been known to the company before the submission of its tender. A parliamentary enquiry was ordered; the evidence obtained was placed before the Lieutenant-Governor; and on 1 June 1903 he dismissed Prior.[52]

Richard McBride, an energetic young man of thirty-three, the leader of the Conservatives, now formed a ministry. He resolved to introduce Dominion party lines into local politics.[53] In the thirty-two years since confederation, the non-party system had been fully tried. There being no bond of affiliation the support was personal, and, in consequence, on a breach of relations the dismissed minister or disgruntled supporter went over to the enemy, taking with him his personal following. The strongest argument was the practical failure of the non-party system during the past five years: in that time there had been five governments —Turner, Semlin, Martin, Dunsmuir and Prior. The history of the decline and fall of the Semlin, Dunsmuir and Prior Governments had been markedly similar.

Those five years had been black financially. Like the preceding fifteen they had been marked by constant deficits, varying from $287,077 in 1900 to $1,348,552 in 1903. The gross debt in 1898 had been $7,425,262; in 1903 it was $12,542,086: an increase of over five million dollars in five years.[54] In the decade from 1891 to 1901 the population had increased from 98,173 to 178,657.[55] From 1872 down to 1903, with the exception of 1879 and 1881, the financial story had been one of continual deficits, regardless of population, social conditions, or the government in power. In that interval the province had piled up a gross debt of twelve and a half million dollars. Even the surpluses for the two excepted years vanish when examined: the figures for 1879 only cover six months, and the deficit of the ensuing year swallowed up the supposed surplus; as to 1881, while that was a real surplus, it was obtained by the simple expedient of starving the public works.[56] This continual failure to keep expenditure within income, regardless of the pilot, gave rise to a feeling, which soon crystallised into a conviction, that the revenue had been and always would be insufficient to meet the expenditure; that the effort to govern with such limited income had, while causing extremely high direct taxation, exhausted the credit of the province, and yet had failed to balance the budget; and, in short, that it was impossible for British Columbia to carry on her ordinary expenditure under the existing terms of union.[57] Hence the demand for "Better Terms." Dunsmuir and Prior had both brought the situation before the Dominion Government and had argued that the failure of twelve finance ministers steadily through thirty years of varying conditions to produce a real surplus must be due to permanent causes. These, they suggested, were: (1) The cost of administration, owing to the physical character of the country. (2) The distance from the commercial, industrial, and administrative centres of Eastern Canada. (3) The non-industrial character of the province, as compared with Eastern Canada, whereby a larger percentage of goods was imported and consumed, increasing the contributions to the Federal treasury in the way of taxes in a ratio of three to one. (4) The disadvantage of the province in relation to markets for its special products.

The contention was that the financial arrangements in the terms of union were in reality a leap in the dark on both sides; that there was no unalterable quality in the terms; and that a state of affairs, not anticipated by either the Dominion or the province, had arisen as a result, which established a moral right to, and a sound constitutional claim for, an increased grant.[58] The subject of "Better Terms" was discussed year after year in the Legislature, and again and again with the Dominion Government, but no result was obtained. In 1906 a conference of Dominion and provincial representatives was held at Ottawa. McBride, armed with a unanimous resolution of the Legislature in favour of "Better Terms," attended and pressed the claim for special treatment. He asked for an impartial judicial tribunal to examine the question and report its findings. The other provinces refused to recommend that course and, after protest, McBride retired from the meeting. The remaining representatives then resolved that, owing to its large area, geographical position, and very exceptional physical features, British Columbia was entitled to special treatment, which they fixed at $100,000 a year for ten years.[59] The conference also recommended certain increases in the subsidies applicable to all the provinces. The Dominion Government embodied the findings in an amendment to the British North America Act, which, as drafted, provided that these payments should be, as the conference requested, "a final and unalterable settlement" of the claims of the various provinces. British Columbia protested against the insertion of those words and sent McBride as a special delegate to London to support the protest. As a result the obnoxious words, which in any event had no binding force, were omitted from the statute.[60] No further steps have been taken to press the claim for "Better Terms."

We turn to the burning question of the coastline. In 1824 there still remained three out of the original four claimants to the northwest coast of America. The portion belonging to Russia was delimited by the treaty of 1825. The line of boundary was to commence at the southernmost point of Prince of Wales Island and

> ascend to the north along the channel called Portland Channel as far as the point of the continent where it strikes the 56th degree of north latitude; from this last mentioned point the line of demarcation shall follow the summit of the mountains situated parallel to the coast, as far as the point of intersection of the 141st degree of west longitude;

and thence along that meridian to the Frozen Ocean. The treaty, after providing that Prince of Wales Island should belong entirely to Russia, went on to state:

> That whenever the summit of the mountains which extend in a direction parallel to the coast, from the 56th degree of north latitude to the 141st degree of west longitude, shall prove to be at a distance of more than ten marine leagues from the ocean, the limit between the British possessions and the line of coast which is to belong to Russia as above mentioned shall be formed by a line parallel to the windings of the coast and which shall never exceed the distance of ten marine leagues therefrom.[61]

In 1867 the United States purchased Alaska from Russia. The discoveries of gold in Omineca and Cassiar caused British Columbia to urge repeatedly the necessity of ascertaining the meaning of the language of the agreements and the exact position of the boundary line on the land.[62] But nothing was done. For twenty-five years the question drifted on, with occasional discussions; then it sprang into great and practical importance with the discovery of the Yukon gold-fields. Something had to be done, for there were thousands of adventurers "mucking" over the Chilcat and Chilcoot passes towards the latest river of gold. In 1898-9 a Joint High Commission considered a number of matters in dispute between Canada and the United States. No agreement was reached, though the contentions on each side were clarified, but a conventional boundary was fixed on the Dyea and Skagway trails at the summits of Chilcoot and White passes.

At last, after more than thirty years, a tribunal was created in 1903 to interpret the treaty and fix the course of the line. It was to consist of "six impartial jurists of repute who shall consider judicially the questions submitted to them."[63] Those questions were somewhat complex; but the important point in the controversy was whether the boundary should be drawn ten marine leagues from the heads of the inlets, so as to shut British territory off completely from the ocean, or parallel to and ten marine leagues from the general trend of the coast. Next in interest was the question whether the water boundary ran north or south of four uninhabited islands near the mouth of Portland Canal. The tribunal met in London in September 1903 and in the following month made a majority award deciding that the boundary line should be drawn so as to give two out of the four islands to each claimant, and that the line extended around the heads of the inlets, shutting out British possessions from the ocean.[64] In England the award was calmly received as a settlement of a disturbing question; but in Canada the belief that the American "impartial jurists" had been selected because of their fixed views created a feeling of intense dissatisfaction. The boundary, so obtained, greatly limits the possible development of the extreme northern portion of British Columbia.

Returning to internal politics we note that, when McBride took office in July 1903, the gross debt was more than $12,500,000 and there were besides floating liabilities of about $1,500,000. A loan of one million dollars to meet the pressing claims could only be had at 5 per cent and upon the agreement to repay it in ten annual instalments. The condition was so bad that the banks refused further credit. The new Government faced the problem firmly. The people, too, saw that sacrifices must be made to regain financial safety. There was a feeling that stable government had come at last.

Yet, despite the financial position of the Government, the province was advancing in wealth and population and was developing her natural resources. The lode mines of the Kootenays had been steadily increasing in importance and widening in extent, embracing the gold mines of Red Mountain (Rossland), the silver of Toad Mountain (Nelson), the silver-lead of Slocan and East Kootenay, and the copper of the boundary country. With the advent of railways the trade and transportation which had flowed to and through the neighbouring states were, in great part, secured to the province. The vast coal measures of the Crow's Nest were opened; and, a supply of coke therefrom being assured, smelters were erected at numerous places in the Kootenays. Towns, dependent upon the mines and the smelters, sprang up in every direction, throve with those industries, and languished as they waned. Agriculture and fruit-growing spread to the Kootenays and thence into the Okanagan, which had theretofore been, principally, a grazing country. The building of the Grand Trunk Pacific opened up the great northern part of the province and, besides giving rise to numerous small towns, brought into being the City of Prince Rupert at its western terminus. The fisheries of the coast expanded to include the herring and the halibut; whaling stations were established. Lumbering spread along the lines of the railways. The vast supplies of paper-making woods led to the establishment of pulp and paper plants at a number of places along the coast; and around them sprang up neat towns supported entirely by that industry. The population of the agricultural districts increased steadily. Coal mining on Vancouver Island continued to extend the area of its operations. All of these forces reacted upon trade and trade centres, stimulating new manufactories and forms of industry.[65] The population in 1901 was 178,657; and in 1911, 392,480.[66]

The McBride Government, in an effort to balance the budget, practically doubled taxation and at the same time reduced expenditure. In 1903 the deficit had been $1,348,552; in 1904 it was $224,534. Then came an era unprecedented in the history of the province: an era of surpluses, commencing in 1905 with one of $618,044 and reaching in 1910 the enormous sum of $2,417,748. In seven years, 1905 to 1911, a surplus of $10,-925,346 was accumulated. In 1910 the net debt stood at $8,969,778. Thus in seven years a surplus exceeding the net debt had been secured.[67] Then unfortunately the old era of deficits returned. Beginning in 1912 with about $400,000, it grew in 1913 to $2,976,295; but in 1914 the deficit was $5,283,653; and so it went on through 1915, 1916 and 1917. In the result the surplus accumulated between 1905 and 1911 was engulfed by the deficits from 1912 to 1918 and the days of borrowing returned.[68]

With the first influx of miners came the Chinese. During the prosperous days of Cariboo their numbers increased unnoticed. Content with a small but sure return they usually worked ground that was thought too poor to attract the white miner. In 1864 they numbered about 2000.[69] With the decrease of mining they plodded along, gleaning, or became traders, packers, farmers, gardeners, or domestic servants. In 1875 it was estimated that there were 949 Chinese in Cariboo as against 1800 whites. Their simple needs and low cost of living gave them a great advantage in competition. The agitation against them began in 1864[70] and continued unsuccessfully for more than twenty years, rising with dull times and falling with prosperous ones. Between 1872 and 1885 anti-Chinese legislation was frequently debated. The resolutions or bills usually authorised a special tax on Chinese or prohibited their employment on public works. They invariably failed to become law, or were disallowed, or declared unconstitutional.[71] Between 1876 and 1880 the increase in the Chinese population was 2326;[72] in 1879 the Legislature stated that there were 6000 Chinese in the province; the contractors for the Canadian Pacific Railway brought in about 6500.[73] The Chinese were alleged to be subject to loathsome diseases and demoralising habits; were charged with evasion of civic responsibility and of tax contributions; in short, were said to be an unassimilable people whose presence retarded the settlement and prosperity of the land.[74] In 1884 the Legislature passed three Acts against the Chinese: to prevent their immigration; to impose an annual poll tax of $10; and to forbid their acquisition of Crown lands.[75] The first was disallowed as an interference with Dominion rights of legislation over immigration; and the second was declared unconstitutional by the courts.[76] As a result the Dominion Government appointed a Commission to enquire into Chinese immigration. The report exonerated them from the charges of bad morals, public burdens, and criminal tendencies. It opposed exclusion and recommended moderate restriction.[77] In pursuance of the recommendation the Dominion Parliament in 1885 imposed a tax of $50 on every Chinaman entering Canada.[79] The province then legislated against their employment on public works and in coal mines. Much of this legislation was declared unconstitutional as being aimed at a particular race. They continued to arrive in large numbers. In 1891, 1893, 1894, 1895, 1897, and 1899 the province urged the increase of the tax.[79] The constant demand bore fruit; in 1900 the tax was raised to $100. This was only a temporary measure. A Commission investigated the whole subject, and upon its recommendation the Dominion Parliament increased the tax to $500.[80] At that amount it stood until 1923 when the immigration of Chinese (unless merchants, students, government representatives or persons born in Canada) was forbidden.[81]

The Japanese, though perhaps more dangerous competitors than the Chinese, passed unnoticed until about 1900 when the Legislature enacted that all immigrants must be able to read in some European language. Aimed at the Japanese, this plain trespass upon the field of Dominion legislation was promptly disallowed. It was re-enacted in 1902, 1904, 1905, 1907 and 1908, but in every case either failed to secure the assent of the Crown or was disallowed.[82] The Dominion Government had an understanding with the Emperor of Japan that he would forbid the emigration of his subjects to Canada; but the Japanese evaded the prohibition by obtaining passports to Hawaii and continuing their journey to British Columbia. Anger at this subterfuge underlay the Asiatic riots that occurred in September 1907 in Vancouver. In 1908 the Japanese Government agreed to limit the number of passports to Canada and the Canadian Government undertook to admit the holders of such documents, while refusing entry to all others. As a result Japanese immigration fell from 7601 in 1908 to 495 in 1909; and with one or two exceptions the annual entries remain about that figure.[83] Of all the problems of the province there is none whose solution calls for more courage, sacrifice, saneness, and breadth of view than this question of oriental immigration. Despite tax barriers and agreements there were in 1926 probably 40,000 Chinese and 18,000 Japanese in the province.[84] Their invasion of provincial industries continues. The remedy lies in the Dominion's power over immigration. The province is alive to the danger, but powerless; the Dominion powerful, but unable to appreciate fully the inroads that Chinese, Japanese and East Indians are making upon the industrial life of British Columbia.

The aboriginal population at confederation was supposed to be 25,661; forty years later the census gave 24,581.[85] The Indians are the wards of the Dominion Government who by the terms of union undertook to follow as liberal a policy towards them as had been pursued by the colony of British Columbia.[86] The province agreed to set apart the necessary lands for their reserves; in 1876 a Commission fixed the areas. Chiefs and councillors are elected by the bands and have power to enact bye-laws in trivial matters. Metlakatla showed that the Indian could be civilised and Christianised. Industrial, boarding, and ordinary day schools have, following that example, been established amongst them, sometimes by the Dominion Government and sometimes by religious denominations. And thus slowly the Indian is advancing along the path toward civilisation. In 1914 there were more than 8000 who could speak English or French. The income from their agriculture, fishing, hunting, and other industries reached in that year the sum of almost $2,000,000.[87] In recent years the Indian Title Question has appeared. The claim is that their possessory rights have never been extinguished, except as regards the southern part of Vancouver Island. The fact is not denied. Yet the provincial Government has consistently refused to recognise such title, claiming that the setting apart of ample reserves and their occupation by the Indians is a virtual equivalent or extinction of any title they may have possessed.[88] The question is one of the unsettled problems of the province.

Notes

[1] Tupper, Sir C., *Recollections of Sixty Years in Canada*, p. 127.

[2] *Acts passed by the Leg. Counc. of British Columbia*, 1871, no. 3, sec. 71.

[3] *Can. Census*, 1891, 1, Table 6, p. 366.

[4] *Statutes of B.C.* 1872, no. 2.

[5] *Ibid.* no. 16; 1891, chap. 40.

[6] Milton, Viscount, *A History of the San Juan Water Boundary Question*, p. 42.

[7] *Affairs in Oregon. House of Repres. 36th Congress, 1st Session.* Ex. Doc. no. 65, pp. 6 f.

[8] *San Juan Water Boundary*, p. 258.

[9] *Affairs in Oregon.* Ex. Doc. no. 65, pp. 28 ff.; Egerton, Mrs. Fred, *Sir Geoffrey P. Hornby*, pp. 64 ff.

[10] *Island of San Juan. House of Repres. 39th Congress, 2nd Session.* Ex. Doc. no. 24; *Message from the President of the U.S. December 21, 1866*, pp. 192 ff:, 229 ff.

[11] Cushing, C., *Treaty of Washington*, etc, pp. 204 f., 221 ff.; *Correspondence respecting the award of the German Emperor*, 1873, pp. 2 f.

[12] *Stats. of B.C.* 1873, no. 16, p. 81, *Can. Stats.* 1873, no. 2, p. 4.

[13] *Stats. of B.C.* 1871, no. 12; 1874, no. 12; 1875, no. 2.

[14] *Ibid.* 1874, no. 21.

[15] Lyall, Sir A., *Life of Lord Dufferin*, chap. 7; Hamilton, Lord Frederic, *The Days before Yesterday*, 1920, p. 249.

[16] *Journals of Leg. Ass. of B.C.* 12 Mar. 1877; 12 Feb. 1878.

[17] Kerr, J. B., *Dict. of well-known British Columbians*, p. 89, *Journals*, 9 Apr. 1878.

[18] *Sessional Papers of B.C.* 1882, p. 485; *Journals B.C.* pp. 65 ff. and pp. i ff.

[19] *Census of Canada,* 1891, 1, Table 6, 366.

[20] *Journals B.C.* 1882, pp. 25 f.

[21] *The British Columbian,* New Westminster, 9 and 29 Dec. 1882.

[22] *Journals B.C.* 26 Jan. 1883.

[23] Cowan, G. H., *B. C.'s Claim for Better Terms,* pp. 16 f.

[24] *Sess. Pap. B.C.,* pp. 453 ff., *Stats. of B.C.* 1883, chap. 14; 1884, chap. 14.

[25] *Canada Year Book,* 1914, p. 50.

[26] *Sess. Pap. B.C.* 1887, pp. 251 ff.; 1884, pp. 277 ff.

[27] *Metlakathlah Inquiry,* 1884: *Report of Commissioners,* in *Sess. Pap. B.C.* 1885, pp. 131 ff., 277 ff., *Depositions,* in *Sess. Pap. B.C.* 1885, pp. 317 ff.

[28] *Stats. of B.C.* 1885, chap. 3.

[29] *Ibid.* 1883, chaps. 25, 35, *Sess. Pap. B.C.* 1887, pp. 315 ff.

[30] *Canada Year Book,* 1913, p. 51.

[31] *Stats. of B.C.* 1890, chap. 7.

[32] *Fur Seal Arbitration: Proceedings of the Tribunal of Arbitration at Paris,* 1893, II, pp. 187 f.

[33] *Ibid.* 1 (Award and Declarations), 83, IV (Schedule of Claims), pp. 133 ff.

[34] *Ibid.* I, pp. 9 ff. (note).

[35] *Fur Seal Arbitration: Proceedings of the Tribunal of Arbitration at Paris,* 1893, 1 (Award and Declarations), pp. 78 ff.

[36] Howay and Scholefield, *History of B.C.* II, p. 465.

[37] Foster, J. W., *Diplomatic Memoirs,* II, p. 47.

[38] Howay and Scholefield, II, pp. 465 f.

[39] *Stats. of B.C.* 1894, chap. 26.

[40] *B.C.'s Claim for Better Terms,* pp. 16 f.

[41] *Stats. of B.C.* 1898, chap. 38.

[42] Gosnell, R. E., *Sixty Years of Progress: British Columbia,* Part 2, p. 144.

[43] *Ibid.* p. 146; *Journals B.C.* 14, 22, 23, 27 Feb. 1900.

[44] *Ibid.* 1900, p. 79.

[45] Gosnell, R. E., *History of British Columbia,* p. 144.

[46] Letter of Hon. R. W. Scott, to Lieut.-Gov. McInnes, 2 June 1900, in *The Daily World,* Vancouver, 5 July 1900, and in *The Daily British Columbian,* New Westminster, 6 July 1900.

[47] Gosnell, *Sixty Years* (Part 2), pp. 147 f.

[48] *Ibid.* (Part 2), p. 150; *Journals B.C.* 1902, pp. 56, 57, 64, 67.

[49] *Stats. of B.C.* 1902, chaps. 42 and 58.

[50] *Ibid.* 1915, chap. 14.

[51] *Journals B.C.* p. 61 and Appendix.

[52] *Journals B.C.* 1903, pp. 62 ff.

[53] *Ibid.* 1903, p. 66, 2 June 1903.

[54] Howay and Scholefield, II, pp. 526 f.

[55] *Canadian Year Book,* 1913, p. 51.

[56] Howay and Scholefield, II, pp. 538 f.

[57] Procter, F. J., *The Financial Crisis in British Columbia,* pp. 8 f.; *B.C.'s*

Claim for Better Terms, p. 18; Report of the Delegates to Ottawa, 1903, in *Sess. Pap. B.C.* 1903, pp. K 3 ff.

[58] Report of Delegates in *Sess. Pap. B.C.* 1903, p. K 6; *ibid.* 1907, pp. 28 ff.

[59] *Ibid.* 1907, p. D 12.

[60] 6 Ed. VII, cap. 11.

[61] *Proceedings of the Alaskan Boundary Tribunal*, II, pp. 12 ff.

[62] *Journals B.C.* 12 Mar. 1872, p. 36; 7 Jan. 1874.

[63] *Corresp. respecting the Alaska Boundary*, 1904, pp. 41 ff., 45 ff.; cf. article in *Can. Hist. Rev.* VI, pp. 332 ff.

[64] *Proc. Alaskan Boundary Tribunal*, I (Award), pp. 29 ff.; Foster, J.W., *Diplomatic Memoirs*, II, pp. 197 ff.

[65] Gosnell, *Sixty Years*, p. 161.

[66] *Canada Year Book*, 1913, p. 51.

[67] *Year Book of B.C.* 1911, 1914, pp. 278 ff., 391 f.

[68] *Canada Year Book*, 1925, p. 792.

[69] Macfie, M., *Vancouver Island and B.C.: their History, Resources, and Prospects*, p. 386.

[70] *Report of Royal Comm. on Chinese Immigration*, 1885, p. 109.

[71] *Journals B.C.* 1872, pp. 15 f.; 1874, p. 18; 1876, p. 48; 1878, p. 82; *Stats. of B.C.* 1878, chap. 35; *Journals B.C.* pp. 20, 47, 55 and p. xxiv; *Chinese Immigration Report*, Appendix G.

[72] *Chinese Immigration Report*, p. 5.

[73] *The British Columbian*, 22 Apr. 1882; 10 May 1882.

[74] *Journals B.C.* 1879, pp. 20, 47, 55 and p. XXIV.

[75] *Stats. of B.C.* 1884, chap. 3, chap. 4 and chap. 2.

[76] *Dominion and Provincial Legislation*, 1867-1895, 1896, pp. 1092 ff.

[77] *Chinese Immigration Report*, pp. lxxxii, lxxxvii, cxxx ff.

[78] *Stats. of Can.* 1885, chap. 71.

[79] *Journals B.C.* 1891, pp. 50 f., 53, 56; 1893, pp. 77, 91; 1894, p. 10; 1895, p. 55; 1897, pp. 12, 14; 1899, pp. 10, 99.

[80] *Stats. of Can.* 1900, chap. 32; 1903, chap. 8.

[81] *Ibid.* 1923, chap. 38.

[82] *Journals B.C.* 1902, p. 79; *Sess. Pap. B.C.* 1902, p. 1314; 1903, p. J I; 1909, p. G 36.

[83] *Canada Year Book*, 1925, pp. 181 ff.

[84] Nelson, J., *The Canadian Provinces: their Problems and Policies*, p. 188.

[85] *Canada Year Book*, 1913, p. 604.

[86] Clause 13, Terms of Union, in Howay and Scholefield, *History of B.C.* II, 697.

[87] *Canada Year Book*, 1914, pp. 640 f.

[88] *Year Book of B.C.* 1911, pp. 164 f.

6. The Introduction of Intoxicating Liquors Amongst the Indians of the Northwest Coast.
F. W. Howay.

FREDERIC WILLIAM HOWAY *(1967-1943), was a lawyer and judge by profession. He devoted his leisure to the writing and collecting of British Columbia history. This article is an example of his meticulous work on the maritime fur trade.*

One of the earliest proclamations of James Douglas dealing with peace and order on the mainland of British Columbia was issued at Fort Hope on September 6, 1858, immediately after the Indian trouble of that summer and more than two months before he became Governor of the Colony of British Columbia. It recited that

It has been represented to me that Spirituous and other intoxicating Liquors have been sold to the Native Indians of Fraser River and elsewhere, to the great injury and demoralization of the said Indians; and also thereby endangering the Public Peace, and the lives and property of Her Majesty's subjects and others in the said Districts.

And then proceeded to make it

Known unto all men that the Sale or Gift of Spirtuous or other Intoxicating drinks to the said Native Indians is contrary to Law, and is hereby strictly prohibited, and that persons charged with such offences will be proceeded against accordingly, and on conviction thereof before a Magistrate, will be mulcted in the penal sum of not more than Twenty Pounds, nor less than Five Pounds.

Et cetera. In view of this stern enactment, based on the protection of the Indian and the preservation of peace and order, it is well to trace the steps whereby the Indian of the Coast became acquainted with, and acquired a taste for, intoxicating liquor—"fire-water."

Source: A paper read before Section *II*, The Royal Society of Canada, at Toronto, May, 1942 and later published in *The British Columbia Historical Quarterly, VI*, 3 (Victoria, 1942), pp. 157-70. Reprinted by permission of the publisher.

The first European to see any part of the Pacific Coast north of California was Vitus Bering, a Dane in command of a Russian exploring expedition. He records, under the date of September 5, 1741, that being anchored near one of the Schumagin Islands, he sent an officer to interview the natives. On his return the officer reported that he had offered one of the natives "a glass of liquor, but as he tasted it he spat it out and returned the glass."[1] Other records of the incident are to the same effect. We have no information as to the "drink" further than Bering's statement that before leaving Kamchatka, for lack of anything better to take along on a sea voyage, they distilled liquor from a sweet grass by a process known in that country. Steller's *Journal* identifies the grass as *Sladkaya trana*. Probably we are justified in assuming that liquor so obtained required at least an educated taste.

This plain story was a bit embroidered by G. P. Muller in his Collection of Historical Materials. The French translation of Professor Muller's account runs as follows:

Waxel [the officer] lui présenta une tasse d'eau-de-vie. Mais cette boisson lui parut aussi désagréable qu'étrange. Il cracha ce qu'il en avoit dans la bouche, & se mit à crier, comme pour se plaindre aux siens qu'on en agissoit mal avec lui. Il n'y eut pas moyen l'appaiser. On lui offrit des éguilles, des verres à collier, un chaudron de fer, des pipes; il refusa tout[2].

When the great Captain James Cook reached Nootka Sound in March, 1778, he, the first European to tread the soil of British Columbia, found no intoxicating liquor, or any taste for it, amongst the natives. He writes that the Indians required that all of their food "should be of the bland or less acrid kind"; they would eat neither the leek nor garlic, "and when offered spirituous liquors, they rejected them as something unnatural and disgusting to the palate."[3] None of the other accounts contains any reference to the matter, although Ellis says, "Their drink is water and train-oil."

Mozino, the Spanish botanist who was at Nootka in 1792, gives similar evidence in his *Noticias de Nutka*. He states:

I doubt if they care for garlic, as although they come to sell it to us in their canoes, it appears to cause them some disgust when they see it on our tables. They had no fermented drink, and had satisfied their thirst with water only, until they began to trade with the Europeans. Since then they have become fond enough of wine, whiskey, and beer, to all of which they give themselves to excess when some one provides it liberally. Until now the thought does not seem to have occurred to them to procure these liquors through the medium of commerce.... They love excessively tea and coffe.... [4]

This contemporary evidence establishes what later visitors support: the Indian of the Northwest Coast had no inborn desire for or knowledge of intoxicating liquor, and his first reaction to it was one of disgust. A few years of the maritime trade completely changed him: he became inordinately fond of such liquor, indulging in it to excess and becoming under its influence a perfect demon. It reminds us of Pope's lines:

Vice is a monster of so frightful mien,
As to be hated, needs but to be seen;
But seen too oft, familiar with her face,
We first endure, then pity, then embrace.

The pioneer maritime fur-trader, James Hanna, arrived at Nootka Sound in the year 1785, seven years after Captain Cook's visit. In the interval Spanish exploring expeditions had ranged along our coast, but none had landed. It appears that at first the maritime traders did not use liquor as a trade medium. Sea-otter skins were then very plentiful, and the trading goods were of the simplest: bars of iron, sheets of copper, kettles, pots and pans, besides blue cloth blankets, beads, buttons, and trinkets. The aim of the trader then was to seek out some Indian village not before known, where the display of his wares would be like the casting of an attractive fly upon the surface of a trout-filled lake. The avidity of the natives for European manufactures, the absence of opposition, and the carrying-on of the trade with the canoes alongside whilst the vessel was hove to, miles from shore, combined to prevent the use of intoxicating liquor as an article of trade or even as an inducement. Apparently the only liquor that Hanna, Meares, Strange, Portlock and Dixon, Colnett and Duncan—the earliest maritime traders—had on their ships was for the personal use of the officers and crew, and it was strictly confined to such purpose.

The Spaniards, who were settled at Nootka Sound from 1789 until 1795, to their credit be it said, offered the Indians only tea, coffee, and chocolate. Martinez in his manuscript diary states that when he was about to leave Nootka Sound, on August 25, 1789, Maquinna, the head chief, came aboard the *Princesa* and begged for a drink of "Cha," that is tea, of which he had become quite fond. Malaspina, on August 27, 1791, on the eve of his departure from Nootka, had a visit from Maquinna, whom Roquefeuil calls "an importunate beggar," and records that, "He took some cups of tea abroad the *Atrevida*, a custom already established amongst his relations and subordinates."[5] Valdes, when at Neah Bay, in June, 1792, was visited by Tetacus, the head chief of the vicinity. He writes:

> When they presented him with a cup of chocolate, he gave proof of the affection which he had for his wife, since, having found at the first sips which he took that the taste was pleasant, he immediately moistened a piece of bread with it and was insistent that she should share in the treat.[6]

The first record of a change in the natives' attitude towards intoxicating liquor that I have met is dated July, 1790. Manuel Quimper, in the *Princesa Real*, the Spanish name of Meares's captured sloop *Princess Royal*, was lying at anchor in Neah Bay when to his surprise arrived one of his Indian friends from Clayoquot who had come all the way, about 80 or 90 miles, to visit him. The Indian embraced Quimper with great joy, saying that he had left home two days before, merely to see him. "I was most obliging to him," says Quimper, "and to prove how true was my former friendship, I entertained him with wine and biscuit of which he is very fond, proving by this that he had much intercourse with other nations."[7]

Marchand, in 1791, wrote:

> It is not known that the Tchinkitanayans [Tlingit] make use of any fermented drink or any strong liquor, and the brandy of which they were prevailed on to make a trial, appeared not to be to their liking.[8]

In 1805, Langsdorff met in the neighbourhood of Sitka some Tlingit Indians, of whom he says:

> Though they would like brandy very much, they reject it because they see the effect it produces, and are afraid that, if deprived of their senses, they should fall into the power of the Russians.

And again:

> Brandy, which is sometimes offered them by the Russians, they reject as a scandalous liquor, depriving them of their senses.[9]

And Ross Cox said:

> All the Indians on the Columbia entertain a strong aversion to ardent spirits, which they regard as poison. They allege that slaves only drink to excess; that drunkenness is degrading to free men.[10]

It appears, however, that the Indian's natural dislike of strong liquor very quickly broke down under the constant temptation to accept a drink in the spirit of *bonne camaraderie*. Marchand expressed the pious hope that the "fatal liquor" which had made such ravages amongst the natives of the eastern part of the continent might not find entry on its western shores; and his countryman, La Pérouse, declared that if to their own vices the Indians of the Coast should add "a knowledge of the use of any inebriating liquor", he feared that the race would be entirely annihilated. Having become acquainted with liquor by gift from a trader friend, the Indian at first regarded good fellowship as its proper environment. In 1791, when John Hoskins, the clerk of the ship *Columbia*, of Boston, visited Wickananish, the chief at Clayoquot, the latter expressed regret that he could not welcome Hoskins with liquor, and said that if he had been forewarned of the visit the deficiency would have been met.[11] Evidently the Spaniards followed the practice of the other Europeans and began to offer liquor, usually wine, to the chiefs. Thus, Galiano, in 1792, says that Maquinna "drank wine with pleasure and in order that his mind might not be fogged left others to determine the amount which he should drink of that which he called 'Spanish water.'"[12]

In 1792 we find the first vessel that brought intoxicating liquor to the Coast as a part of her trading media. The discredit belongs to the French nation. In that year the French ship *La Flavie* arrived at Nootka Sound, loaded with brandy "with design of disposing of it in Kamschatka, to trade in skins and to search for the Count de la Pérouse," as Quadra says in his manuscript journal. In reference to the alleged intention to search for La Pérouse the *Viage* remarks that "It seemed to us that this purpose was very secondary"—a very pertinent remark, for La Pérouse was last heard of at Sydney, Australia. It may be that the brandy was intended to find its principal market in Siberia, but Haswell tells us that at Nootka Sound *La Flavie* "sold a considerable quantity of spirituous liquors and clothing for sea-otter skins."[13] This is the first recorded sale of liquor by the maritime traders to our Indians, and it will be observed that it was brandy —strong stuff. In the same year the Boston ship *Margaret* anchored in Friendly Cove, Nootka Sound, in front of the quaint Spanish settlement. Her captain, James Magee, was very ill, and Quadra, the kind-hearted *Comandante*, granted him the use of a house during his illness.

"But before we were here long we found," says Edward Bell, the clerk of the *Chatham*, one of Vancouver's ships, "that ill-health was not Mr. Magee's only motive for remaining on shore here, for he was carrying on a most profitable trade with the Spaniards & Seamen in Spirituous Liquors, generously charging only four Dollars a gallon for Yankee Rum that cost him most probably about 2/-or half a crown per gallon."

Bell then continues:

Indeed, the ill effects of this shameful trade were soon too great to pass without taking notice of it, and endeavouring to put a stop to it. Our Seamen were continually drunk which from the badness of the liquor threw them into fits of sickness; and Captn. Vancouver was at last oblig'd to take measures that prevented any further trade of that nature with our people.[14]

It will be noticed that the writer of the above journal is silent regarding any sale of this awful liquor to the natives, for whom it was undoubtedly intended; nevertheless, it is difficult to believe that some part of it, at least, did not reach them. Frequent indulgence had conquered the original and inherent aversion. We are now at the headwaters of the liquor traffic; the Indian is started on his downward path.

When Vancouver anchored in Friendly Cove, in August, 1792, Maquinna came to pay him a formal visit, but his superior rank not being known to the sentinel, he was refused admittance to the *Discovery*. The mistake being discovered he was invited on board, complaining angrily of the affront to his savage dignity. Quadra, who was also on the ship as a visitor, obligingly took upon himself the task of explaining the error and smoothing the ruffled feathers of the chief. Suitable presents placated him and he was at last satisfied of the friendly intentions of the British commander.

. . . but no sooner had he drank a few glasses of wine, than he renewed the subject, regretted the Spaniards were about to quit the place, and asserted that we should presently give it up to some other nation; by which means himself and his people would be constantly disturbed and harassed by new masters.[15]

This is one of the first recorded instances of the effect of liquor on the Indian, arousing in him forgotten grievances and latent animosities.

The maritime traders did not, at first, realize the great hold that liquor had obtained on the natives, and until about 1800 did not include it in their trade goods, but only used it as a means of encouraging trade. In 1793, Captain Roberts, of the Boston ship *Jefferson*, says of the Haidas of Queen Charlotte Islands:

Jusqu' ici les liqueurs fortes sent peu désirées par eux; le cuivre, le fer, sont ce qu'ils recherchent davantage: particulièrement le cuivre en feuille.[16]

But six years later R. J. Cleveland says that when the *Caroline* was lying at anchor near Rose Point, Queen Charlotte Islands, the son-in-law of Conehaw, a Haida chief of Kaigani, approached the cutter and at his earnest solicitation was invited on board.

We invited him into the cabin, and gave him a glass of wine, which pleased him so much that he soon asked for another.[17]

The evidence shows that in the 1790's the Indian everywhere on the coast had acquired a taste for intoxicating liquor. In August, 1793, when Vancouver was near Cholmondeley Sound, Clarence Strait, in southern Alaska, he gave the Haida chiefs bread and molasses—always a great treat to the Indians. In return they presented to him a bladder of whale-oil, extolling its superior qualities and claiming that it was the equal of treacle; but the odour was so obnoxious that Vancouver excused himself from taking even a spoonful. To clear himself from this seeming impoliteness he offered them "a large glass of rum, a luxury to which they seemed by no means strangers."[18] Again, in 1794, at Cook Inlet—a place long frequented by Russian and other traders—Vancouver was visited by a young man and a girl, in a skin canoe. Both showed by their conduct that they were acquainted with European liquors and customs. They came on board the *Discovery* without the least hesitation.

The man took his dinner without the least ceremony, drank brandy, and accepted such presents as were made him, but seemed to prefer snuff and silk handkerchiefs to everything else.[19]

A few days later, in the same vicinity, three natives paddled to the ship, and on coming aboard made signs for snuff and tobacco; on receiving them they expressed regret that they had nothing to offer in return.

At dinner they did not make the least scruple of partaking of our repast, with such wine and liquors as were offered to them; though of these they drank very sparingly, seeming to be well aware of their powerful effect.[20]

In June, 1795, Captain Charles Bishop, in the *Ruby*, was at Banks Island, where he met the chief Shakes, and regaled him, as he informs us in his manuscript journal, with "biscuits and butter, and a few glasses of wine, and the trade commenced."

Up to this point, with the exception of the French ship *La Flavie* and the Boston ship *Margaret*, the maritime traders had used liquor, not as a trade medium, but as a concomitant of trade, and as a means of ingratiating themselves with the natives. By about 1800 the keen competition for sea-otter skins had led to the general introduction of intoxicating liquor as an article of barter, for which the ground had been well prepared. In the fifteen years that had intervened since Hanna's arrival in 1785 the whole system had changed: no longer was the trade carried on while the ship lay-to anywhere from 3 to 6 miles offshore; no longer was entry upon the vessel's deck confined to the chiefs or prominent persons—every native had come to regard it as his *right* to be on board when disposing of his skins; no longer was trade confined to iron bars, sheets of copper, cloth, blankets, beads, buttons, bangles, and trinkets. The trading ships now carried an assorted cargo of European manufactures; they were a combination of liquor store and modern department store, aiming to supply every need, every fancy, of the fickle native. They even dealt in the products of the Coast iself: clamons (native armour of tanned elk or moose hide), shrowton (grease extracted by the natives of the Nass River from the small fish, oolachan), haiqua (the dentalium shell), and slaves. All these the traders obtained from tribes having them in quantity, and carried for sale to distant tribes. On board every trading vessel as a part of her goods for barter were arms and ammunition, and casks—many casks—of New England and West Indian rum, whether shown on her manifest or not. Dr. S. E. Morison, a very accurate and reliable authority, fell into a sad error when he wrote:

New England rum, that ancient medium for savage barter, is curiously absent from the Northwest fur trade. Molasses and ship-biscuit were used instead of liquor to treat the natives.[21]

After 1800 the only vessels in the maritime trade were American, usually from Boston; and so notorious was the fact that they were carrying large stocks of liquor that as early as 1808 the Russian Government complained of their traffic with the natives in firearms and "fire-water"—certainly a dangerous combination. The *Columbia*, of Boston, on her second voyage had on board three hogsheads (311 gallons) of New England rum, two hogsheads (225 gallons) of West Indian rum, and, possibly, four more hogsheads (451 gallons) of New England rum, together with half a ton of powder and about 200 muskets. Jewitt informs us that the *Boston*, at the time of her capture in 1803, had as part of her trading-goods nearly twenty puncheons of rum, about 2,000 gallons. Fortunately the *Boston* was burned before the Indians had secured more than a case of gin and one tierce (about 35 gallons) of rum, "with which," says he, "they were highly delighted, as they have become very fond of spirituous liquors since their intercourse with the whites." And they drank so freely of it

> . . . that in a short time they became so extremely wild and frantic that Thompson and myself, apprehensive for our safety, thought it prudent to retire privately into the woods, where we continued till past midnight.[22]

The Indian women, who he says then drank nothing but water, concluding also that discretion was the better part of valour, had fled before the orgy commenced. When Jewitt and his companion returned they found the Indians stretched out on the ground in a state of complete intoxication. Jewitt seized the opportunity of protecting himself by boring a hole in the cask, and in the morning it was empty. He had saved a case of port wine, "which the Indians are not fond of," he says, probably because it was not ardent enough to produce intoxication quickly.

The Columbia River region, being infrequently visited by the maritime fur-traders and thus free from any struggle for trade, was the last part of the Coast to be reached by the traffic in intoxicating liquor. James G. Swan, who came to Shoalwater Bay in 1852, writes:

> They are all extravagently fond of ardent spirits, and are not particular what kind they have, provided it is strong, and gets them drunk quickly. This habit they have acquired since the visit of Lewis and Clark in 1805, for they state that they had not observed any liquors of an intoxicating kind used among any of the Indians west of the Rocky Mountains. . . .

An old woman told him that liquor was introduced amongst the Chinooks by a person whom from her description Swan thought to be Lieutenant Broughton, of H.M.S. *Chatham*, who was in the Columbia River in 1793—sixty years before Swan arrived. The old woman must have been but a small child at the time. However she said that

> They drank some rum out of a wine-glass—how much she did not recollect; but she *did* recollect that they got drunk, and were so scared at the strange feeling that they ran into the woods and hid till they were sober.

This is just another example of the introduction of liquor in the spirit of good comradeship: for if the person were Broughton he had nothing to gain by the act, and nothing to sell to the natives. Swan continues:

> They have been apt learners since that time, and now will do any thing for the sake of whisky. Old Carcumcum [the old woman] said they had but a very little rum from the traders till the settlement of Astoria, when they began to get a little more used to it.[23]

We have now traced the stream of liquor amongst the natives of the Coast from its source in the friendly glass of wine given by the explorer simply for good fellowship, or by the maritime trader to ingratiate himself and enable him more easily to do business with the Indian; we have seen the Indian's original antipathy and disgust change rapidly to fondness for and intense desire for intoxicants; and we have seen the casual friendly glass replaced by thousands of gallons of liquor sent out as the best trade medium. The deleterious and dangerous effects upon the Indians are shown by Jewitt's description of the wild debauch that followed the looting of the *Boston*. Everywhere the effect was the same. But the unrestrained maritime traders, seeking only present gains, utterly oblivious of the terrible results, finding it a potent trade medium continued to bring the "fire-water."

The land fur-traders on the contrary, having permanent trading-posts and a continuing interest in the fur-harvest which the ephemeral maritime traders lacked, saw the necessity of refraining from the use of liquor in their relations with the Indians. In 1812 the representatives of the North West Company and the Pacific Fur Company entered into a compact "to abstain from giving the Indians any spirituous liquors, to which both parties strictly adhered."[24] And thirty years later the Russian American Company and the Hudson's Bay Company agreed not to use liquor in any way in the fur-trade with the natives, unless made necessary by the presence of "opposition" on the Coast, which meant in reality the trading vessels from Boston, the "Boston pedlars," as they were sometimes deprecatingly called.

To complete the circle with a contemporary picture of the effect of intoxicating liquor on the Indian, I am reproducing, with the kind permission of the Provincial Archivist, Dr. W. F. Tolmie's eye-witness account of the wild debauch when in 1834 the Hudson's Bay Company, to ensure the safety of its people in abandoning the old Fort Simpson, gave rein to the Indian's acquired taste for that liquor.[25]

On Saturday morning [August 30, 1834] rum had been sold to

the Indians & some of them getting intoxicated were very turbulent & from noon till sunset when we embarked we were all under arms & in momentary expectation of having to fight our way on board [the *Dryad*] or being butchered on the spot. They attempted frequently to beat down the slight barricade raised on the site of the bastions, but were deterred on seeing us ready with firearms to send a volley among the intruders. About a dozen or twenty indians with muskets were posted on a hill immediately behind from whence they could fire with deadly effect into the Fort at any part. Outside the pickets they were numerous & armed with guns, boarding pikes & knives & endeavouring by their savage whoops & yells to intimidate us. Remained quite in this state for sometime but owing to a temporary lull in the clamor outside, ventured to send a few articles to the boats which were waiting at the beach one or two had passed down with wooden utensils unmolested—no indians appearing in sight—another man was proceeding with a barrel, full of miscellaneous articles, & unheaded [*sic*] when [all] at once several armed villains rushed out from amongst the bushes—& one more inebriated & thence more daring than the rest, seized the barrel & with drawn dagger drove the man from his charge—he returned to the fort & first meeting me I went out but seeing the savage advancing with his knife aloft in a menacing attitude I stepped slowly to the gate & procured a cutlass from the doorkeeper. Thus armed I walked towards the Indian who was surrounded by his friends persuading him to desist & at the same time Kennedy issued & addressed the savages while the barrel was rolled to the beach in the meantime without molestation. Soon after a gun was fired from the woods at one of the people employed at the strand, the ball whizzing past his ear. Every thing of value having been already embarked, no further attempts were made to ship what remained. Red Shirt the indian just mentioned, was, to prevent his doing mischief outside, admitted into the Fort & was immediately assailed by Caxetan the chief with a volley of abuse for his conduct. From words they soon came to blows. Red Shirt's dagger was prevented from doing mischief by two sober indians Jones & Couguele, but being a tough active fellow he still retained it in his grasp & managed with the other hand most cruelly to abuse Caxetan's visage who, on his part fought bravely tooth & nail, considerably damaging his opponents visual organs. Mr. Ogden at length got Caxetan & Jones to accompany him on board & once there retained them as hostages for our safety. Now prepared to abandon the Fort &

held a debate as to the propriety of leaving behind a cask
containing 25 gallons Indian Rum. It was left, Kennedy being
the only person who wished to take it along with us. Took the
precaution of drawing the priming from all the superfluous
muskets after each man had been provided with one. As soon
as the gate was open, the armed natives collected around. I
went out first & stood at the threshold until the last person had
issued. The natives then rushed in to pillage & we reached the
boats unmolested. Soon after to our astonishment, Caxetan &
Jones from the bank shouted to us, that they wished us to send
the boat for the Rum & on our refusing, offered [*sic*] to bring
it on board themselves. They were then told to appropriate it
to themselves & on this intelligence they brought the rum on
board the vessel to be divided by us. This act proved them to
be possessed of more prudence & foresight than we would have
given them credit for. Had the division been made amongst
themselves bloodshed would in all likelihood have ensued. All
night a constant hammering was kept up in the deserted fort &
dawn revealed several gaps in the pickets made by those who
were intent on procuring the iron spikes which attached the
pickets to the bars. It blew a NE We set sail [*sic*] soon after
daybreak bidding adieu without regret to the inhospitable
regions of Nass & in the evening after a pleasant sail, anchored
in McLoughlin's Harbour at the new establishment.

Notes

[1] F. A. Golder, *Bering's Voyages* (New York, 1922), I., pp. 147-148.
[2] *Voyages et Découvertes faites par les Russes* . . . traduits de l'allemand
de G. P. Muller (Amsterdam, 1766), I., pp. 271-272. On this is based the
version in Burney's *North-Eastern Voyages* (London, 1819), p. 168.
[3] Captain James Cook, *Voyage to the Pacific Ocean, 1776-1780* (Folio
ed.) (London, 1784), II., p. 323. (Book IV., Chapter III)
[4] José Mariaño Mozino Suárez de Figueroa, *Noticias de Nutka* (Mexico,
1913), p. 18. A translation was made for the writer by V. D. Webb, Esq.
[5] Alejandro Malaspina, *La Vuelta al Mundo* (Madrid, 1885), p. 193.
(Translation.)
[6] *Viaje hecho por las Goletas Sutil y Mexicana* (Madrid, 1802), p. 33.
English translation by Cecil Jane: *A Spanish Voyage to Vancouver and
the North-West Coast of America* (London, 1930), p. 29.
[7] Quimper's diary, quoted in Henry R. Wagner, *Spanish Explorations in
the Strait of Juan de Fuca* (Santa Ana, Calif., 1933), p. 124.
[8] Etienne Marchand, *A Voyage Round the World*, 8 vo. ed. (London,
1801), I., p. 340.
[9] G. H. Von Langsdorff, *Voyages and Travels* (Carlisle, 1817), pp. 396,
412.

10 Ross Cox, *The Columbia River*, 3rd edition (London, 1832), I., pp. 291-292.

11 Hoskins' narrative in F. W. Howay, *Voyages of the "Columbia"* (Boston, 1942), p. 260.

12 *Viage Hecho por las Goletas Sutil y Mexicana*, p. 17; *A Spanish Voyage* . . . p. 17.

13 Haswell's Second Log, in *Voyages of the "Columbia,"* p. 347.

14 "A New Vancouver Journal," *Washington Historical Quarterly*, V. (1914), p. 224.

15 Captain George Vancouver, *A Voyage of Discovery*, 8 vo. edition, (London, 1801), II., p. 337.

16 Rochefoucald-Liancourt, *Voyage dans les Etats-Unis*, Paris, An VII. [1800], III., p. 25.

17 Richard J. Cleveland, *Voyages and Commercial Enterprises of the Sons of New England* (New York, 1855), p. 107.

18 Vancouver, *op. cit.*, IV., p. 225.

19 *Ibid.*, V., p. 151.

20 *Ibid.*, V., p. 162.

21 Samuel Eliot Morison, *The Maritime History of Massachusetts*, 1783-1860 (Boston, 1921), p. 57.

22 Robert Brown, ed., *The Adventures of John Jewitt* (London, 1896), pp. 84 ff.

23 James G. Swan, *Three Years at Shoal-Water Bay* (New York, 1857), pp. 155 ff.

24 Cox, *op. cit.*, I., p. 180.

25 Quoted from the original *Private Diary* of William Fraser Tolmie, August, 1833 to December, 1835, MS., Archives of B.C.

7. British Columbia Becomes Canadian, 1871-1901
Walter N. Sage

WALTER NOBLE SAGE *(1888-1963), formerly professor and head of the history department at the University of British Columbia, is the first academic historian in the collection. This article can usefully be compared with the selection by Ormsby which covers the same period.*

In an impassioned speech against federation delivered in the Legislative Council of British Columbia in March, 1870, Dr. John Sebastian Helmcken uttered these prophetic words:

> No union between this Colony and Canada can permanently exist, unless it be to the mutual and pecuniary advantage of this Colony to remain in the union. The sum of the interests of the inhabitants is the interest of the Colony. The people of this Colony have, generally speaking, no love for Canada; they care, as a rule, little or nothing about the creation of another Empire, Kingdom, or Republic; they have but little sentimentality and care little about the distinctions between the forms of Government of Canada and the United States.
>
> Therefore no union on account of love need be looked for. The only bond of union outside of force—and force the Dominion has not—will be the material advantage of the country and the pecuniary benefit of the inhabitants. Love for Canada has to be acquired by the prosperity of the country, and from our children.[1]

The last four words are more than prophetic. They are a stroke of genius! Probably in his old age the good doctor was fated to hear the school-children of British Columbia singing:

Our fair Dominion now extends
From Cape Race to Nootka Sound.

The children and children's children were in the process of becoming Canadians. It was not a speedy evolution. At Confederation British Columbians were *not* Canadians. By 1901 Canadianism had spread and penetrated the province. But there were still

Source: Queen's Quarterly, LII, 2 (Kingston, 1945), pp. 168-83.
Reprinted by permission of the publisher.

many in the older age groupings who remembered the colonial period and were still definitely British Columbians. The youngsters were Canadians, but Canadians with a difference. The barrier of the Rocky Mountains had conditioned them. Their outlook was towards the Pacific and not towards the Atlantic nor even towards Hudson Bay. They were not well acquainted with Ontario and knew little of the prairies or the Maritimes, and probably still less about Quebec. None the less they were becomingly increasingly conscious that they were a part of Canada.

Dr. Helmcken was right. Love for Canada was at first not a spontaneous or a natural growth in British Columbia. It did not spring from the native soil of the provinces as did love for British Columbia. In the colonial days and even for a time after Confederation "Canadians" were unpopular. They were known as "North American Chinamen"—a tribute to their thrift. They sent their money home and did not spend it so freely as did the open-handed Americans. But British Columbia could not thrive without the aid of the rest of Canada. She was cut off from American markets by the tariff laws of the United States. Until the completion of the Canadian Pacific Railway in 1885 there was no direct link through Canadian territory between the Coast and Eastern Canada. It is true that during the critical years from 1866 to 1871 British Columbia might have followed "Manifest Destiny" and as the Territory of Columbia have become a weaker edition of Washington Territory—weaker because, in spite of her huge expanse, she had a smaller and more widespread population. But British Columbia had made her decision. She would remain British even though it entailed paying the high price of becoming Canadian. The only other course open to her was to remain a bankrupt British colony on the edge of nowhere!

A glance at the early history of the British colonies on the Northwest Coast and especially at the so-called critical period between 1866 and 1871 will show that British Columbia was much more British and American in outlook than it was Canadian. In fur-trading days before 1849 there was relatively little Canadian influence. There had been some when the North West Company was operating west of the Rockies, but the union of 1821 left the Hudson's Bay Company in complete control. Very few of the company's officers were from Canada, although there were many French-Canadians among the *voyageurs*. The Colony of Vancouver Island was a British, not a Canadian, venture. The gold-seekers of 1858 were from California. A few of them were Canadians who had been attracted to the placer mines of the Golden State and were now following the paystreak north. The miners' meetings stemmed from California and even "Ned McGowan's War" had its roots in the troubles between the Vigilantes and the Law and Order Group, rival California organizations, members of which had come north to Fraser River.[2] The United States was omnipresent. The British Isles were half the world away, and Canada, although geographically nearer than Great Britain, was even farther away in spirit. There was a sentimental tie with the Mother Country but as yet practically none with Canada. Joseph Despard Pemberton, former Colonial Surveyor, in a letter to the Victoria *British Colonist* early in 1870, summed up the situation neatly in verse:

> True Loyalty's to Motherland
> And not to Canada,
> The love we bear is second-hand
> To any step-mama.

At first sight it would seem that American influences preponderated in British Columbia. The economic tie was with California, and this tie remained until the completion of the Canadian Pacific Railway. As the late Marcus Lee Hansen has penetratingly observed:

> The new province of British Columbia, although firmly attached to the empire by political, naval and military bonds, was in commerce and population a part of the Pacific region which had its center at San Francisco.[3]

Hansen also states that

> Fully three-fourths of the fifteen thousand miners who in 1864 made up the principal element in the population were Americans, and half of the business houses were branches of American establishments.[4]

The only regular steamship communication which British Columbia possessed with the outside world was by American vessels.[5] The express companies were of American origin, although local express was carried by British Columbian companies which maintained American connections. Postal service was through San Francisco. It was necessary for letters posted in British Columbia, destined for Great Britain, Canada, the United States, or elsewhere, to bear United States stamps in addition to their local postage. Governor Musgrave protested against this practice, but it was found impossible to change it.[6] Telegraph service with San Francisco, by way of Portland, Oregon, was established in 1865. The completion of the Union Pacific Railroad in 1869 provided

British Columbia, through San Francisco, with railway connections with the Atlantic seaboard, and put an end to travel by the tedious, and often dangerous, Panama route.

From California the mining frontier spread eastward and northward to Nevada, Utah, Colorado, Wyoming, Montana, Idaho and British Columbia. The gold rushes of 1858 to Fraser River and of 1862 to Cariboo stemmed from San Francisco. Later rushes to Omineca, the Stikine, Cassiar, and finally to Atlin and the Klondike were closely connected with California. Mining methods in British Columbia were similar to those in vogue in California, and the miners who came north were accustomed to "frontier justice." In British Columbia, however, they found Judge Begbie, but not 'Judge Lynch'.

American influences were economic, and, to a less degree, social and cultural. British influences were political and institutional and also social and religious. The political and legal structure of British Columbia was entirely British. The colonial governors were all of British origin. Most of the government officials had been born in the British Isles. In the Legislative Council of British Columbia, which in 1870 discussed terms of union with Canada, the majority had come from the Motherland. The Royal Navy was another link with "Home." The part played by the Special Detachment of the Royal Engineers in the early development of the Crown Colony of British Columbia is too well known to demand more than a passing reference. The Church of England was also a link with the Mother Country. Bishop Hills, the first Bishop of Columbia, was consecrated in Westminster Abbey and set apart for his work in the far-off colony. In 1860 he arrived in Victoria, where he diligently upheld the traditions and dignity of his Church, but was unable to secure its establishment as the State Church of the colony. The first Presbyterian ministers came from Ireland, but the 'Scottish Kirk' flourished under their ministrations, and for many years retained a close connection with the Established Church of Scotland. The Roman Catholics and the Methodists, on the other hand, had Canadian connections. The first Roman Catholic priests came from Canada to the Columbia in the 1830's, and later in the 1840's came north to Fort Victoria and the Fraser River. The Methodists were sent from Canada, in the late 1850's, to establish a mission in British Columbia.

Canadian influences were at first relatively weak, but they strengthened as the battle for Confederation was fought. The leading Confederationists were chiefly British North Americans: *e.g.*, Amor De Cosmos, John Robson, Dr. R. W. W. Carrall,

Francis J. Barnard, and J. Spencer Thompson. Some Englishmen —*e.g.*, Robert Beaven and Alfred Waddington—also joined the cause of federation. George A. Walkem was Irish by birth but Canadian by adoption. Many of the Confederationist leaders had come to British Columbia by way of California. Their sojourn in the United States had, apparently, not dulled their affection for British institutions, but had strengthened rather than weakened their determination that British Columbia should join Canada.

A mining population is notoriously unstable. It is a case of "Here to-day and gone to-morrow." As a rule the American gold-seekers returned to the United States when they had "made their pile" or had become disgusted with the "Fraser River humbug." It was the British and the Canadians who remained and settled down in Cariboo, along the lower Fraser River, or on Vancouver Island. Unfortunately it is not possible to make an accurate check of the birthplace of British Columbians before 1871.[7] Some idea of the national origins of British Columbians at that date may, however, be obtained from a study of J. B. Kerr's *Biographical Dictionary of Well-Known British Columbians*, published in Vancouver in 1890. Of the 242 names listed in this publication, 178 were resident in British Columbia in 1871. An analysis of their birthplaces is rather enlightening: *British Isles*, 94, divided as follows: England, 57; Scotland, 21; Ireland, 16. *Dominion of Canada*: 45,—Nova Scotia, 7; New Brunswick, 3; Prince Edward Island, 1; Quebec, 5; Ontario, 29.[8] *British Columbia*, 7; *Other British possesions*, 5; United States, 12; Other Foreign Countries, 14; no birthplace, 1.

These figures clearly show that British Columbia was *British* in the broadest sense of the term. The Americans had come and gone. The British, including the Canadians, remained.

In the Canadianization of British Columbia from 1871 to 1901 three phenomena are clearly observable: political development, the building of the Canadian Pacific Railway, and the arrival as settlers of large numbers of Eastern Canadians. It must not be thought that British and American influences did not continue to be strong. What happened was that Canadian influence strengthened, especially after the completion of the Canadian Pacific Railway. The period divides naturally at 1886. The first regular transcontinental passenger train from Montreal arrived at Port Moody on July 4th of that year. Vancouver came into existence in April, and was burnt to ashes in June. But nothing could daunt the future Canadian metropolis of the West Coast. It arose triumphantly from its ashes and five years later had a population of 13,709 as compared with Victoria's 16,841. The census of 1901 showed that Vancouver had already surpassed Victoria in population—29,432 as against 20,919.[9] Since Victoria was the centre of the British-born (natives of the British Isles) Vancouver's rapid advance was a sign of Canadianization. The roots of its people strike deep into Eastern Canada.

The political phase of Canadianization is concerned chiefly with the establishment of the provincial government and with the relations existing between the Lieutenant-Governor of British Columbia and the Government of Canada. Before federation British Columbia had possessed representative but not responsible government. Her political education was, therefore, not so far advanced as that of the eastern provinces. On the other hand, British Columbia had been the only Crown Colony west of the Great Lakes, and was rather more experienced than Manitoba in the art of self-government. Yet British Columbians in 1871 were still politically immature.

The Terms of Union with Canada provided for "the introduction of Responsible Government when desired by the Inhabitants of British Columbia."[10]

It was not, however, until after the first provincial elections had been held in October, 1871, that Lieutenant-Governor Joseph William Trutch could claim to have "established a Responsible Cabinet."[11] Actually, it may be doubted whether responsible government was fully established during the régime of John Foster McCreight, the first Premier of British Columbia. McCreight was a distinguished lawyer, Irish by birth, who had no previous political experience. Probably Trutch selected him because he was "a 'safe' man, one whom the Lieutenant-Governor could direct and guide."[12] Trutch virtually ruled British Columbia during the McCreight régime, 1871-1872. When Amor de Cosmos became premier in December, 1872, Trutch found his power challenged. De Cosmos, with his Nova Scotian tradition and his long political experience in British Columbia, was not prepared to yield the reins of power to any Lieutenant-Governor, even though he had once held office in colonial days as Chief Commissioner of Lands and Works.

Trutch was in a unique position as regards Ottawa. He considered himself the accredited representative of the federal government in British Columbia. His letters to Sir John A. Macdonald and Macdonald's replies clearly indicate that he was definitely the *liaison* officer between Ottawa and Victoria during the period from July 20th to November 14th, 1871, that is, until the McCreight ministry was formally constituted. The real difficulty was that Trutch did not hand over full authority to McCreight. In his analysis of the situation R. E. Gosnell saw very clearly:

> During the transition from Crown Colony government to Provincial autonomy there was a brief inter-regnum in which it was necessary for him [Trutch] to administer affairs on his own initiative, but he continued this rule much longer than was necessary, or than was constitutionally defensible.[13]

Part of Trutch's difficulties arose from his selection of McCreight as premier. Neither he nor McCreight had any real acquaintance with responsible government. The leading opponents of Trutch and McCreight—Amor De Cosmos and John Robson—possessed this experience. Either of them could, in all probability, have headed a real responsible ministry. In a rather pathetic passage in a letter to Sir John A. Macdonald Trutch unburdened himself as follows:

> I am so inexperienced and indeed we all are in this Province in the practice of Responsible Govt. that we are initiating that I step as carefully and guardedly as I can—and whilst teaching others I feel constantly my own extreme need of instruction on this subject—which must account to you—if you please—for the trouble which I have put you to—and which I know I ought not to have imposed on you.[14]

De Cosmos, for his part, roundly denounced the Trutch-McCreight combination in an appeal addressed to "the Liberals of the Province":

> To rally round their old leaders—the men who have year after year fought their battles and have in no instance deserted the popular cause. To take any other course is to convict themselves of Treason to manhood, Treason to the Liberal party, that year by year for fourteen years have urged Responsible Government, Union of the Provinces, and Confederation with the Dominion. It is no Treason, no public wrong to ignore the nominees of Governor Trutch.[15]

The reference to the "Liberal party" is extremely interesting. Actually there were no political parties, in the federal sense of the term, in British Columbian provincial politics until 1903, when Richard McBride announced the formation of a Conservative ministry. De Cosmos, in his federal career, supported Macdonald and Mackenzie in turn. It is noteworthy, however, that as early as 1871 he could make his appeal to the 'Liberals'.

By the Terms of Union British Columbia was entitled to three senators and six members of the House of Commons. The senators were Dr. R. W. W. Carrall, Clement F. Cornwall and W. J. Macdonald. Carrall was from Ontario, but the other two senators were born in the British Isles. The six Members of Parliament were J. Spencer Thompson, Hugh Nelson, Robert Wallace, Henry Nathan, Amor De Cosmos, and Charles F. Houghton. Two of them, Thompson and De Cosmos, both Canadians, had been prominent Confederationists. In Ottawa all six were classed as supporters of the Macdonald administration.

In the federal elections of 1872 Sir Francis Hincks was elected by acclamation for Vancouver Island. Six years later, in the well-known National Policy election, Sir John A. Macdonald, defeated in Kingston, Ontario, was elected for Victoria City. His colleague was Amor De Cosmos.

During the Macdonald régime from 1878 to 1891 the British Columbian Members of Parliament were Conservatives. They gave their political allegiance to the party which had promised to build the transcontinental railway. It must be confessed that, with the exception of Amor De Cosmos, the British Columbians do not seem to have played any large part at Ottawa. But their presence there showed that the Pacific province was part of the Canadian federation.

As has been noted, federal parties as such took no part in provincial politics until 1903. Political divisions in the provincial area were local rather than national. Until the population of the Mainland had surpassed that of Vancouver Island the division was Mainland vs. Island. But local issues in the 1870's and early 1880's were closely intertwined with the all-important railway question.

The greatest single Canadianizing force in British Columbia during the period 1871 to 1901 was the Canadian Pacific Railway. Its construction had been promised in the Terms of Union. Delay in carrying out those terms almost led to the secession of British Columbia from the Canadian federation in 1878. The change of government in 1873 and the attitude of the Mackenzie administration were largely responsible for this delay, but there is no denying that George A. Walkem in British Columbia made political capital out of the difficult situation. The return of Sir John A. Macdonald and the Conservatives to power in 1878 put an end to the secession movement and led to the chartering of the new company which built the railway. Over that railway from 1886 to 1901 came thousands of eastern Canadians who were to become the cement binding British Columbia more closely to the rest of the Dominion.

The well-known story of the building of the Canadian Pacific Railway need not here be retold. Its terminus was fixed at Port Moody, not Esquimalt. The so-called "Island section of the main line" became the Esquimalt and Nanaimo Railway, constructed not by the Canadian Pacific Railway Company, but by Robert Dunsmuir, the 'coal king' of Vancouver Island, and the 'Big Four' of the Southern Pacific Railway—Collis P. Huntingdon, Mark Hopkins, Leland Stanford, and Charles Crocker. The Yellowhead Pass route through the Rocky Mountains was abandoned in favour of the Kicking Horse. In 1887 the "branch" line from Port Moody to Vancouver was built.

From the vantage-point of nearly three-quarters of a century after the event the real wonder is that the railway was ever built at all. The total population of the Dominion, including Prince Edward Island, in 1871 was 3,689,257. Of this total 25,228 are listed for Manitoba, 36,247 for British Columbia, and 48,000 for the Northwest Territories.[16] The white population of Western Canada was probably short of 25,000. The four "original provinces" of Eastern Canada had a population of 3,225,761. It was a tremendous undertaking for Canada to build a transcontinental railway, and it is not surprising that others than Edward Blake had misgivings. But Sandford Fleming blazed the trails before the Canadian Pacific Railway Company was formed and that great group of railway builders who made up the new company built the road. James J. Hill withdrew from the directorate in 1883 when it became evident that the company was determined to build the Lake Superior section. Hill then began to plan the Great Northern Railway, which would invade the prairies and southern British Columbia.

The completion of the main line in 1886 did not, however, end the activities of the Canadian Pacific Railway in British Columbia. There was American competition to be faced, especially in the Kootenays and the Boundary country. In the 1880's and early 1890's the chief American competition was the Northern Pacific Railway, but in the late 1890's the Great Northern had seriously invaded the field. The Canadian Pacific Railway began to buy up, or lease, local lines in the Kootenays, especially the Columbia and Kootenay, the Columbia and Western and the British Columbia Southern. Eventually the south line of the Canadian Pacific from Lethbridge, Alberta, through Crowsnest Pass and through the Kootenays and Boundary country was completed in

1916 by the construction of the Kettle Valley Railway. By that time the Great Northern had been worsted. The Trail smelter, which originally had been an American venture, was in the hands of the Consolidated Mining and Smelting Company of Canada, a subsidiary of the Canadian Pacific Railway. Thus did Canadian interests triumph over American in the Kootenays.

For many years there was a story current in British Columbia that an old-timer in Victoria addressed a newcomer from Eastern Canada as follows: "Before you Canadians came, you know, we never had to take the shutters down till ten o'clock." Whether apocryphal or not, the tale illustrates the clash between the early settlers, who usually had come from the British Isles, and the rather more hustling and energetic "Canadians." On the whole, this clash was more in evidence on Vancouver Island than on the Mainland. Cariboo had never been so "English" as Victoria and the lower Fraser Valley after 1886 rapidly absorbed the newcomers from "the East." Vancouver was, *par excellence*, the Mecca of the men and women from Ontario and the Maritimes.

In a study of this sort there is no accurate yardstick by which the growth of Canadianism can be measured. Still, it is possible to detect certain tendencies. In 1871 Canadians in British Columbia had made their presence felt. Many of them had come from California during the early gold rushes. Others had come direct to British Columbia by way of Panama and San Francisco. One devoted band—"The Argonauts of 1862"—had come "the plains across" through British Territory from Fort Garry. But it was not until after the completion of the Canadian Pacific Railway that eastern Canadians came in large numbers to "the West beyond the West."

During the decade from 1871 to 1881 the population of British Columbia increased from 36,247 to 49,459. Manitoba's went up from 25,228 to 62,260. The next decade, 1881 to 1891, witnessed an increase in British Columbia from 49,459 to 98,173, but Manitoba shot up from 62,260 to 152,506. British Columbia from 1891 to 1901 increased from 98,173 to 178,657 and Manitoba from 152,506 to 255,211.[17] But even as late as 1901 British Columbia possessed only 3.33 per cent of Canada's total population. In 1901 only 12.02 per cent of Canadians lived west of the Ontario-Manitoba border. The proportion in 1941 was 28.30 per cent, roughly 3,250,000 out of 11,500,000.

The first Census of Canada contained figures dealing only with the four "original provinces." It was not until the 1880-1881 Census that information was published regarding Manitoba, British Columbia and Prince Edward Island. The population of British Columbia is given as 49,459. According to birthplace this number was made up as follows:[18]

Born in British Columbia		32,175
Born in the British Isles		5,783
English	3,294	
Irish	1,285	
Scottish	1,204	
Born in other parts of Canada		2,768
Prince Edward Island	23	
Nova Scotia	379	
New Brunswick	374	
Quebec	396	
Ontario	1,572	
Manitoba	24	
Born in The Territories		14
Born in other British Possessions		211
Born in the United States		2,295
Born in other countries and at sea		5,462
Birthplace not given		751
Total		49,459

The Third Census of Canada, 1890-91, gave the population of British Columbia as 98,173, but apparently gave no statistics as regards the birthplaces of the people. It did, however, provide information regarding the numbers born in Canada and in foreign countries. In British Columbia 37,583 are classed as native, born of a native father; 19,268 as native, born of a foreign father; and 41,322 as foreign-born.[19] In this census, as in the previous one, the native Indians of British Columbia are included in the native-born totals. No attempt has been made to separate white men and Indians.

It is from the Fourth Census of Canada, 1900-1901, that most information is obtained regarding racial origins, nationalities and the birthplaces of the people. The population of British Columbia was now 178,657. According to racial origins 106,403 were of British birth (English, 52,863; Irish, 20,658; Scottish, 31,068), 25,488 were Indians, 532 Negroes, 19,482 Chinese and Japanese and the remainder of continental European origins or "unspecified". On the basis of nationality, 144,989 are classed as Canadian, 10,088 as American, 14,201 as Chinese, 3,516 as Japanese and the remainder from the continent of Europe. But it is Table XIII—"Birthplaces of the People"—which best tells the story. Of the 99,612 listed as born in Canada 59,589 were born in British Columbia; 2,203 in Manitoba; 2,839 in New Brunswick; 4,603 in Nova Scotia; 23,642 in Ontario; 1,180 in Prince Edward Island; 4,329 in Quebec; 991 in the North-West Territories and 236 in "Canada not given." The total of those born in the British Isles was 30,630 distributed as follows: English, 19,385; Irish, 3,957; Scottish, 6,457; Welsh, 710; Lesser Isles, 121. From the other British Possessions had come 1,843. The foreign-born totalled 46,110, of whom 17,164 were from the United States.

From the statistics given above it is obvious that by 1901 the Canadianization of British Columbia was fairly well complete. A new generation had grown up west of the Rockies since 1871. No matter where their parents came from these young people were Canadians. To be sure, they were British Columbian Canadians, not quite the same as Canadians from the other provinces, nevertheless Canadians. Many of them were destined to prove their loyalty to Canada and to the British Empire in 1914. By 1901 east and west in Canada were really joined and "the West beyond the West" had become Canadian.

Notes

[1] *Debate on the Subject of Confederation with Canada* (Victoria, 1870), p. 13.

[2] On this subject see F. W. Howay, *The Early History of the Fraser River Mines* (Victoria, 1926), pp. VIII-XVII.

[3] Marcus Lee Hansen and J. Bartlet Brebner, *The Mingling of the Canadian and American Peoples* (New Haven, 1940), p. 155.

[4] *Ibid.*

[5] For a discussion of this topic *cf.* F. W. Howay, W. N. Sage and H. F. Angus, *British Columbia and the United States* (Toronto: Ryerson, 1942), pp. 184-186.

[6] *Cf.* A. S. Deaville, *The Colonial Postage Systems and Postage Stamps of Vancouver Island and British Columbia, 1849-1871*, Archives Memoir No. VIII (Victoria, B.C.: King's Printer, 1928), pp. 137-143.

[7] *The Census of Canada, 1870-1871,* Volume I, does not give figures for British Columbia. In *The Census of Canada, 1880-1881*, the total population of British Columbia, in 1871, whites, Indians, Chinese and coloured is given, however, as 36,247. Of this number 25,661 were Indians. *Cf.* L. T. Marshall, *Vital Statistics of British Columbia* (Victoria, B.C.: Provincial Board of Health, n.d. [1932]), p. 192.

[8] Technically, of course, Prince Edward Island was not part of Canada till 1873, but this seems a hair-splitting distinction.

[9] *Canada Year Book, 1943-1944* (Ottawa: King's Printer, 1944), p. 125.

[10]*Journals of the Legislative Council of British Columbia, Session 1871* (Victoria, B.C., 1871), p. 6.

[11] J. W. Trutch to Sir John A. Macdonald, Nov. 21, 1871, *Macdonald Papers*, Trutch Correspondence, 1871-1873, p. 98. (Public Archives of Canada.)

[12] W. N. Sage, "John Foster McCreight, the first Premier of British Columbia," in the *Transactions of the Royal Society of Canada*, Third Series, Section II, Vol. XXXIV (1940), p. 177.

[13] E. O. S. Scholefield and R. E. Gosnell, *British Columbia, Sixty Years of Progress* (Vancouver and Victoria, 1913), Part II, p. 15, n.l.

[14] *Macdonald Papers*, Trutch Correspondence, 1871-73, pp. 101-102.

[15] Victoria *Daily Standard*, November 21, 1871.

[16] *Canada Year Book, 1943-44*, p. 79.

[17] *Canada Year Book, 1943-44*, pp. 79, 80.

[18] *Census of Canada, 1880-1881* (Ottawa: McLean, Roger & Co., 1882), Vol. I, pp. 396-7, Table IV.

[19] *Census of Canada, 1890-1891* (Ottawa: King's Printer, 1893), Vol. II, p. 228.

8. Party History in British Columbia, 1903-1933
Edith Dobie

EDITH DOBIE *is professor emeritus of history at the University of Washington and a specialist in British imperial history. This article, together with a companion piece on the years 1871-1903 (Pacific Historical Review, 1932, pp. 235-251), reviews the political history of the province up to the end of its sixth decade.*

The period 1903-1933 forms a significant unit in the party history of the province of British Columbia. In 1903 federal party lines, Liberal and Conservative, were introduced;[1] in 1933 both parties were put on the defensive by a third party which challenged not just their programs or policies but the theory of government from which they had sprung. Thus in a single generation the stream of party affairs in the province seems to have gone over a course upon which the Dominion and the United States both entered in the 1860's and which they are still pursuing. Since therefore the currents of this stream have moved swiftly and in a narrow channel, it may be possible to see more clearly their general direction and the forces that have determined that direction. It is possible, too, that such observation may aid in interpreting the course of events in other and larger political units because though the population of the province is small, the area is of such extent and character as to permit wide diversification of economic and social life.[2]

The story of the activities of the two "old" parties as they soon came to be called, is told in the newspapers and reveals the nature of the party as a political institution, how it functioned, how it met or failed to meet the social and economic demands of the period. The complexion of the government was as follows: 1903-1916, Conservative; 1916-1928, Liberal; 1928-1933, Conservative; and the Liberal government set up in 1933 seems likely to have at least five years in office.

An examination of party platforms, resolutions of local and provincial Associations, speeches from the throne, debates in the legislature reveal almost complete agreement between Liberals and Conservatives both in theory and in policies. Both urged

Source: Pacific Northwest Quarterly, XXVII (1936), pp. 153-66. Reprinted by permission of the author and publisher.

railway expansion, exclusion of Asiatics, increase of bonded indebtedness in order to bring population and business into the province. Likewise, both favored provision by the state of means for settling labor disputes, also government regulation and ownership of railways, telephones, and public utilities in general. Finally both supported government aid for those settling upon the land, abolition of property tax and extension of the application of income tax, health insurance, old age pensions, mothers' pensions.

These policies reflect the obligation of each party to all the important economic interests, and in the legislation proposed and enacted there is still further evidence that the political leaders endeavored to satisfy as many groups as possible. If land grants were made too freely—and they were—to those who wished to hold them for speculative purposes, the government also bought back large tracts from the railroads and made them available for settlers. High rates for government bonds worked to the advantage of the investor, but government funds were advanced for irrigation projects for the advantage of the agriculturist. While those engaged in the lumber industry gained timber leases that permitted large profits, the laborers in the woods were protected through laws regulating their working conditions. If employers, as was claimed, escaped a fair share of taxes, there was an effort to aid employees through such devices as Minimum Wage and Workmen's Compensation.[3]

Obviously each party then was a cross section of the population, and since just as in the Dominion and the United States, both represented the same economic groups, both were bound to seek the same ends. What does stand out, however, in the party programs and in the legislation of the time is the influence regularly exerted by two groups that have in many communities got the ear of party men only through revolt or threat of revolt, namely, farmers and laborers.

The agricultural group probably gained attention chiefly because it was so small. The census of 1901 reported only 16.88 per cent of those gainfully employed as engaged in agriculture. In 1911 the percentage was 11.86; in 1921, 15.99; in 1931 only 5.59. In a region in which during these same decades population had increased 119.68 per cent, 33.66 per cent, and 32.35 per cent respectively,[4] the demands of those engaged in producing food were not likely to go unnoticed. Moreover, in 1903 farmers were already learning the value of united action through Farmers' Institutes; and later through such additional bodies as the United Fruit Growers and the Stockmen's Association they effectively voiced their needs.

Labor on the other hand owed its influence to numbers and organization and to the fact that it was so largely recruited from Great Britain.[5] One measure of the size of the Labor group is the proportion of the population classed as urban. In the ten years preceding 1901, urban population had risen from 37.92 to 50.48 per cent of the total; in 1911 it was 51.9 per cent; in 1921, 47.19; in 1931, 56.84.[6] If we remember that a large part of the rural population—66 per cent in 1931—was engaged in such occupations as mining, lumbering, and fishing, we can see that workers other than agricultural composed the largest single interest.[7] Labor unions had been established in the province almost from its founding and they had become so influential by 1903 that fear lest the voters might align as labor and anti-labor was one of the factors in the move to introduce party lines.[8] While most unions followed the policy of the A.F.L. to which some of them were affiliated and gave support to whichever candidate—Liberal or Conservative—seemed most likely to promote their interest, there was a sufficiently well organized Labor party to present candidates in every provincial election and to elect members to the legislature in 1920, 1924, 1928, and 1933.[9] In the large number of immigrants from Great Britain were many who had had experience both in formulating and in agitating for measures to improve working conditions; and the long list of statutes passed before 1914 such as Factory Acts, Eight-Hour Day, Employers' Liability, also the social legislation of the 1920's, such as Old Age Pensions, all bear witness to the success of their efforts.

To see the parties in action it is necessary to observe what happened at the meetings of the Liberal and Conservative Associations, also at the sessions of their Executive Committees and to follow the proceedings of provincial conventions and of the legislative caucus. In addition there should be noted the annual tour of the province made by the Premier and some of his ministers, also the speeches of the minority leader in various parts of the province usually when a general election was not too far off, and finally the election campaigns. In all of this activity, whether of Liberals or Conservatives, one fact seems written plain—the office holders, the presidents of local and provincial Associations and their Executive Committees, members of Provincial and Dominion parliaments, district leaders were the party. It was they who came together in Association meetings and conventions to name candidates for office and to determine which party men must be given consideration, which might with safety be temporarily neglected. They were the general staff who chose the time and field of battle and summoned the rank and file to the fray. They had really but two objectives—to get out the vote that made office possible and to share and distribute the rewards of office.

After victory at the polls the matters that called for earliest attention were those connected with appointments. The places in the cabinet as one might expect were reserved for the generals— with due attention to geographic distribution—but unfortunately generals were always more numerous than cabinet posts. Minor offices the lesser strategist might fill or distribute.[10] When out of power each party waxed eloquent on the evils of such practice, but when in office each party likewise was determined to make the patronage serve its ends. In the lean years of 1903-1916 the Liberals were valiant in agitating for a merit basis for appointment to the civil service, and a law providing for this was enacted early in their term of office[11]; but in 1922 their leader, John Oliver, said at the provincial convention, "We in the innocence of our hearts passed over to a commission patronage rights that should have been exercised by the members of the government and the representatives elected by the people. The results are not satisfactory, therefore we will either have a change in regard to management of the Civil Service or know why."[12] The usual procedure when the party was charged with carrying on the government was to decide what action would ensure party solidarity or increase party influence and then adjust details of government accordingly. For example, in 1926 in an attempt to unite warring factions in the Conservative party, Dr. Tolmie was elected leader.[13] As he was not a member of the provincial legislature, a safe seat had to be found for him. Whereupon Mr. Coventry, the people's choice for Saanich riding, resigned for the good of the party and not long afterward was found to possess just the qualifications needed for the post of Fruit Sales Commissioner in London.[14]

The absorption of the general staff in matters of patronage always making for inefficiency was shown to be a serious obstacle to the very progress of democracy when in the course of these thirty years the government had assumed responsibility for enforcing elaborate labor laws, for operation and management of a railroad,[15] and for administration of social services.

Division of the rewards of office also led to party feuds that absorbed the energies of leaders and claimed from the Government attention that should have been directed toward general welfare. From this evil the province suffered more at the hands of the Conservatives than through the Liberals. As early as 1904, the very year that Richard McBride, the first official Conservative leader was chosen, there appeared a rift between him and no less a general than Sir Charles Tupper, former leader of the Dominion Conservatives.[16] Sir Charles was still hostile in 1909, and in 1916 he publicly attacked McBride's successor, W. J. Bowser, and urged voters to defeat every Conservative leader who showed his head.[17] The party associates of this recalcitrant chieftain were apparently back of the so-called "young Conservatives," who between 1916 and 1922 were frank to say that they had not got their share of the patronage in the past and who in 1922 with something less than perfect tact called for the resignation of their leader on the ground that he was a millstone round their necks.[18] This faction won out finally and in the 1926 convention, after a bitter contest which left wounds that have proved slow to heal, they deposed Mr. Bowser.[19] It was a costly victory, however, since the new Conservative leader was hampered in his conduct of Government 1928-1933 by the danger of the defection of these resentful "Bowserites."[20]

What of third parties the traditional means of disciplining "old" parties? Largely because the various agricultural interests have been organized and reasonably successful in gaining their demands upon the government third parties have not played so large a part in British Columbia as in the prairie provinces. Such groups as the Farmers' Party of 1920, the Provincial Party of 1922-24, and the People's Party of 1932 may be classed as Progressives. They seemed to see nothing in the nature of party as it had developed in the province to account for the conditions against which they were protesting. All that was needed they implied was the right kind of leadership. As one group put it, they were aiming at a party of "moderately honest people;"[21] and the slogan of the Provincial party in 1924 when John Oliver was the Liberal and W. J. Bowser the Conservative leader, was, "Turn Oliver out and don't let Bowser in."[22]

Since the instigators of such revolts often ceased to be concerned about reform as soon as they received some recognition from the organization they were attacking, the Progressives had left behind them a trail of disillusionment with regard to party; but fortunately the disillusionment was not sufficiently widespread nor complete to admit the demagogue. The fact that there was no sudden upward trend in the shirt business in British Columbia during the early thirties may have been due in part to the existence of two other parties which had more positive theories and programs—Socialist and Labor. These two parties, though small in numbers, were almost as old as the province itself and through election speeches and debates in the legislature, they had conducted a long campaign of education in socialist principles.

Unlike the Progressives, they attributed the failure of the Liberals and the Conservatives not simply to the wrong kind of leadership but to a dual cause; first, the assumption that government should serve the party, and, second, the weakness of the economic system which the old parties had been expected to bolster up through political action. When, therefore, continued hard times seemed to justify their condemnation of the economic order and political leaders continued to promote party interests rather than to use government to resolve some of the difficulties, the Socialists and the Labor party became rallying points for much of the steadily growing discontent.

But if economic disaster gave the Socialists ammunition for their attacks upon the whole political system, it also gave the Conservative premier, Dr. Tolmie who had taken office in 1928, a chance to show that within that same political system could be devised ways and means to meet the crisis. With 35 out of 47 seats[23] in the legislature he could have inaugurated some constructive policies—though at the expense of some sections of his party —and by omitting some rewards for party service rendered could have curtailed administrative expense. Instead, while hesitant to apply any drastic relief measures, he increased the number of his cabinet to eleven, thus taking care of three more of the faithful.[24] Moreover, by failure to win over malcontents in his own organization he allowed the general public to see that control of party rather than public interest was the paramount consideration. The "Bowserites" if they received any political plums must have found them hard and green for by 1931 they were demanding a convention.[25] This they knew would split the party and bring defeat in the next election; but it might make Mr. Bowser head of the general staff in place of Dr. Tolmie and that, it appeared, was what really mattered.

In April of 1931 a deputation requested the cabinet to appoint a committee to investigate the whole field of government finance. It represented 22 organizations, among them the Vancouver Board of Trade, Canadian Manufacturers' Association, Victoria Chamber of Commerce, the Retail Merchants' Association, and five service clubs of Vancouver. The committee was appointed and submitted its findings and recommendations in April of 1932. In their report commonly known as the Kidd Report they stated that "increased taxation being impossible" the only alternative was to reduce expenditure, and they proceeded to indicate the ways in which a reduction of six million was to be made in the annual budget of about 25 million dollars.

One-third of the entire saving was to be in the field of education. Free tuition was to be limited to children under fourteen with half the cost provided for those remaining in school until the age of sixteen. In addition to the economies accruing from this through reduction of the teaching staff and decrease in the number of buildings needed, the salaries of all teachers were to be cut 25 per cent. The appropriation for the University of British Columbia was to be discontinued and if as a result it could not carry on, the question of closing it should at once be raised. Among other economies advised was the reduction of the number in the legislature from 47 to 28 and the cabinet from 11 to 6. Service on the state owned railroad upon which some people in the region north of Vancouver were dependent was to be discontinued if the road were not sold in nine months. Further increase in state supported social services was to be halted.[26]

Perhaps the most significant feature of this report was the implication as to the status of that great triumph of twentieth century democracy—government social services. What the large section of the community made up of workers had come to regard as their rights were in the opinion of the committee, privileges, and therefore to be curtailed at the discretion of those who paid for them. A second important feature of the report was the condemnation of the party system. This system, said the committee, had been the means by which the difficulties due to excessive expenditure had been created and in the opening page of their list of recommendations they note that political life had become "largely a struggle between one party to retain and the other to recapture the benefits of office." From this point on nearly every aspect of party came in for criticism. It was urged that the efforts of party leaders to satisfy numerous interests prevented their saying "No" to unwarranted requests for government expenditures and that concentrating on party strategy led to inefficiency and multiplication of government positions.[27]

When the report was made public in August 1932, the life of Conservative Government was drawing to a close; and Dr. Tolmie, in preparing for the general election which Micawber-like he delayed to the last moment, seemed to show uncanny skill in fully substantiating this indictment of the old parties. With defeat for his party on any question of ability to cope with current problems inevitable, he made two attempts to persuade Mr. Pattullo, the Opposition leader, and Mr. Bowser, the demoted and hostile chieftain in his own organization, to join him in a union government.[28] When both refused he tried a second means of saving his party from defeat. The Executive of the provincial Conservative

Association announced that the Association would take no part in the election and later after polling the local associations, it was decided that these organizations should fight the coming battle along whatever lines seemed best.[29] In short, Conservatives were to win victories in their various constituencies under whatever name they liked—Union Conservative, Independent, Non-Partisan, Independent-Conservative. If they lost, there would be no burden of defeat upon the party. If they won, the Conservative chieftain might gather them into a nondescript group which after strife had ceased, could change its varied hues for the even color of Conservatism. Meantime the general staff safe at headquarters would suffer neither losses nor substitutions in personnel and unscathed by the provincial conflict could face the next Dominion contest with lines unbroken.[30] The followers of Mr. Bowser had already launched a "citizenship movement." Mr. Bowser in accepting the leadership of this movement, which he called "Non-partisan," claimed that the day of party in provincial politics was over and that henceforth governments must be made up of the "best brains, regardless of party."[31] It is possible, however, that one of his followers came nearer the truth when he wrote in a letter to a newspaper as follows: "For the last four or five years a number of us have been trying to build up a political movement behind W. J. Bowser that would give Conservatives an opportunity to vote for men of their own party and principles without having to be associated with the incompetent 'Tolmie crowd'."[32]

Meantime, groups of people throughout the province filled with the kind of disgust with political affairs which had found expression at earlier times in the various Progressive parties, joined with those who shared or had been influenced by the viewpoint of the Socialist party and sought membership in the Cooperative Commonwealth Federation, a movement organized at Calgary, Alberta, in August of 1932. This party, better known as the C.C.F., which proposed to establish a Socialist government by democratic means did not get its organization in British Columbia under way until late spring, but before the end of the summer, it had nominated candidates in 46 of the 47 ridings.[33] These candidates claimed that both old parties were bankrupt for lack of issues that squared with the needs of the time. They insisted also that since any adjustment of the social and economic order which Liberals or Conservatives might promise must be at the expense of interests upon which they depended for support, the fulfillment of their promises was unlikely in any case and most improbable in hard times. They, however, were prepared to establish a planned socialized order which would make possible the efficient development of natural resources and insure an equitable distribution of income.[34]

The Conservative party being in a state of suspended animation, it devolved upon the Liberals to meet both the challenge of the C.C.F. candidates and the charges of citizens in general that parties had failed as agents of government. The Liberals were in excellent shape for the contest. Their leader, Mr. Pattullo, was able and forceful and this being his first general election, he had accumulated none of the personal antagonisms that are part of the aftermath of any political contest. They had been out of power only five years; consequently their memory of the loaves and fishes was still vivid enough to persuade them that patient cooperation was the best way to get and keep this nourishment so necessary to the life of the party.

Disregarding the recommendations of the Kidd Report they answered the demand of the C.C.F. for a new social order by promising to achieve the results claimed for that order by extension of governmental social services. As they put it, they were offering practical idealism as against "visionary socialism." The charge that government set up by party was bound to take cognizance of the strongest interests in the party instead of the most pressing needs of the province, the Liberals countered by plans for an Economic Council in which all interests would be fairly represented. This body, they implied, would aid also in economic planning. To answer the accusation that party dominated the legislature through the caucus they agreed that their members could oppose and even defeat measures of the Government without overthrowing it; and finally they promised a cabinet, chosen not on the basis of party service but for administrative ability.[35]

The outcome of the election was a sweeping Liberal victory. Of the 47 seats the Liberals gained 34—within one of the number held by the Conservatives at dissolution. The C.C.F. secured 7, thus becoming the official Opposition; the Unionists—followers of Tolmie in the Conservative party, 1; Independent Non-partisan —followers of Bowser, 2; Independent 2; Labor 1. The popular vote probably registered more clearly the trend of public opinion. Out of a total vote of 357,534, the Liberals polled 159,131; C.C.F. 120,185; Independents 101,896. The new party thus in its first contest had polled 31 per cent of the popular vote.[36]

This election campaign with the appearance of what seems a new and genuine party alignment on the question of the fundamental structure of society may have wide significance. Coming as it has after thirty years' experience with the traditional two-party system of the 19th century, this type of political alignment may indicate eventualities in other regions undergoing a steady process of urbanization. The Conservatives, it is true, refused to face the issues, but if the C.C.F. lives and grows, the two old parties will have to unite to save the social and economic institutions with which they are so intimately related.

In meeting the challenge of the C.C.F. the Liberals appear to have pointed the way which the old parties must take if as instrumentalities in a democratic regime, they are to cope with current problems. First they recognized the importance of keeping party an aggregation of adequately represented interests; thus they may keep class feeling from playing too large a part in political life. In the Economic Council they seemed also to recognize that there can be no adequate consideration of all interests in a community without some planning which takes all resources into account.[37] In curbing or seeming to curb the caucus, they at least called attention to the danger of party encroachment upon other and equally important instruments of political life. Finally, their emphasis on the use of the best minds in government, which may have been a gesture to meet the claims of the Bowser Conservatives calling themselves Non-partisans, was a slight turning toward the use of the expert in government.[38]

Whether by accident or intention the Liberals have thus indicated some factors in the development of a party fitted to make a successful transition to really socialized democracy. It is for this reason that this culmination and the developments that led to it may claim the attention of the student of history, for it may well be that in our attempt to foresee the trend of the future, there is no more fruitful object of observation than the political party.[39]

Notes

[1] In the earlier part of this period the Conservative party was still known as Liberal Conservative, a name resumed again for a time during and after the World War; but in the interest of clarity the term Conservative will be used throughout.

[2] The area, which is approximately that of Washington, Oregon, California combined, includes coastal plain, mountain, valley, and plateau regions. The 1931 census shows 12.51 per cent of the people engaged in manufacturing; 12.31 per cent in transportation; 10.26 per cent in fishing, logging, and mining; 5.59 per cent in agriculture.

[3] Good accounts of the various party platforms and discussion of issues by candidates also of debates on measures on the floor of the provincial parliament are to be found in the press of Victoria and Vancouver.

Summaries of platforms and legislation enacted are given in the *Canadian Annual Review of Public Affairs.*

[4] *Seventh Census of Canada 1931* (Ottawa), II, p. 4.

[5] *Manual of Provincial Information* (Provincial Bureau of Information, Victoria, 1930), pp. 73, 67.

[6] It must be noted, however, that in the Canadian census "urban" includes all residents of incorporated cities, towns, and villages, irrespective of size. In British Columbia a locality with a population less than 1000 may be erected into a village and there are cities with population less than 200. *Census of Canada 1931*, II, p. 139.

[7] cf. W. B. Hurd and Jean Cameron, "Population Movements in Canada 1921-1931," in *Canadian Journal of Economics and Political Science* (May, 1935), I, p. 228.

[8] *Canadian Annual Review of Public Affairs,* 1901, p. 434.

[9] Party distribution in each legislature is given in the *Canadian Annual Review.*

[10] *The Vancouver Daily Province*, November 4, 1933.

[11] *Canadian Annual Review*, 1917, p. 824.

[12] *The Vancouver Daily Province*, September 29, 1922, p. 16.

[13] *Victoria Daily Times*, November 26, 1926.

[14] *The Vancouver Daily Province*, November 4, 1933.

[15] The Pacific Great Eastern.

[16] *Victoria Daily Times*, February 2, 1904.

[17] *Ibid.*, November 22, 1909, p. 9; March 3, 1916.

[18] *The Vancouver Daily Province*, April 11, 1922, p. 12; April 13, 1922, p. 15.

[19] *Victoria Daily Times*, November 26, 1926, p. 3.

[20] *Ibid.*, November 28, 1931, pp. 2, 4.

[21] *The Vancouver Daily Province*, January 15, 1923, p. 3.

[22] *Ibid.*, June 21, 1924.

[23] In redeeming a 1928 campaign promise to reduce the size of the legislature, the Conservative government had enacted a measure providing for the merging of the constituencies of Columbia and Revelstoke, also Alberni and Nanaimo, and creating a new constituency in the Peace River district, thus changing the number of legislators from 48 to 47.

[24] *The Vancouver Daily Province*, August 22, 1928.

[25] *Ibid.*, November 27, 1931; *Victoria Daily Times*, November 27, 28, 1931.

[26] *Report of the Committee Appointed by the Government to Investigate the Finances of British Columbia* (Victoria, 1932), pp. 13, 33-36, 48-49, 53-55.

[27] *Ibid.*, 16-17, p. 54.

[28] Victoria *The Daily Colonist*, September 13, 18, 1932; *Victoria Daily Times*, March 27, 28, 1933.

[29] Victoria *The Daily Colonist*, June 11, 1933.

[30] cf. *The Vancouver Daily Province*, August 5, 1933, p. 3. That this was sound party strategy seems evident in the returns of the federal election of 1935. While in the election of 1933 the Conservatives, calling themselves

Unionist, Independent Non-Partisan, and Independent, secured only 4 out of 47 seats in the Provincial Parliament, in the election of 1935 they secured 5 out of 16 seats in the Dominion Parliament.

[31] *Victoria Daily Times*, March 2, 3, 1933; Victoria *The Daily Colonist*, August 11, 1933.

[32] *Victoria Daily Times*, September 16, 1933.

[33] The C.C.F. did not nominate in Fernie where there was a strong Labor candidate.

[34] *The Commonwealth* Official Organ of the C.C.F. (B.C. Section) October 4, 1933.

[35] *Victoria Daily Times*, April 20, 1933; October 4, 1933; *The Vancouver Daily Province*, July 20, 1933; August 22, 1933.

[36] *Statement of Votes by Electoral Districts General Election 1933* (Victoria, 1934). Not all Independents were Conservatives.

[37] The history of the Economic Council to date is both interesting and important. This body made up of men chosen mainly because of their general knowledge of and interest in economic affairs in the province was reported in November 1935 to have discontinued its meetings six months earlier. The staff of the Council which is concerned with careful collection of data has continued to function, and apparently to prove useful to the Government, furnishing another example of the trend toward the use of the expert in government.

[38] As a matter of fact the appointment of Dr. G. M. Weir as Provincial Secretary and Minister of Education has proved most significant. The policies of Dr. Weir worked out in the interest of the whole province have demonstrated in effective fashion the advantage of the use of the expert. The experience of his department in devising a suitable Health Insurance bill may also throw much light on the way groups exert pressure to protect their own immediate interests at the expense of the common good.

[39] cf. Max Ascoli, "On Political Parties," in *Social Research* (May, 1935) II, p. 209.

9. Extract from the Introduction to *The Letters and Journals of Simon Fraser, 1806-1808* W. K. Lamb

WILLIAM KAYE LAMB, *was in turn British Columbia provincial librarian and archivist and the librarian of the University of British Columbia. He retired as national librarian and archivist. The extract typifies his extensive writing and editing in the areas of early exploration and the fur trade.*

[Simon] Fraser's fame relates chiefly to the brief period of three years, from the autumn of 1805 to August of 1808, in which he carried out . . . instructions to advance up the Peace River, cross the Rockies, establish trading-posts in what is now the interior of British Columbia, and endeavour to trace the Columbia River to its mouth.

Fortunately this is also much the best documented part of his career. In the pages that follow will be found the journals that he kept during his most important journeys of exploration in 1806 and 1808, and a series of letters written in the winter of 1806-7 that in great part fills the gap between the journals.

Harriet Fraser, the explorer's daughter, believed that the decision to extend their trade to the country beyond the Rockies was made by the partners of the North West Company in the summer of 1805. She was convinced that Simon Fraser attended the annual rendezvous that year at Fort William, received his instructions there, and left for the West in August. There are some inherent improbabilities in this story, but we know that in his later years Fraser discussed his travels with Harriet, and her version should stand until disproven on good authority.

We do know for certain that in the autumn of 1805 Fraser led a party of about twenty men up the Peace River and established a post at Rocky Mountain Portage, at the foot of the turbulent Peace River Canyon. This was intended to be both a trading-post and an advance supply base from which he could set off to cross the Rocky Mountains with a minimum of delay. With Fraser were two clerks, John Stuart and James McDougall. Stuart was

Source: The Letters and Journals of Simon Fraser, 1806-1808, edited and with an Introduction by W. Kaye Lamb (Toronto: Macmillan of Canada, 1960), pp. 15-30. Reprinted by permission of the author and publisher.

an exceptionally able and reliable man, and was to serve as Fraser's second-in-command throughout the adventurous three years that lay ahead. McDougall is a lesser character, but he carried out important preliminary explorations on several occasions, and deserves more notice than he has received. Chief amongst Fraser's voyageurs and engagés was one La Malice, whose prominence is difficult to explain, and who showed himself again and again to be a shifty and unreliable character, entirely worthy of his name.

Having set most of his men to work on the building of Rocky Mountain Portage House, Fraser left Stuart in charge and pushed on with McDougall and La Malice to explore the upper reaches of the Peace River. In so doing he was following in the footsteps of his famous predecessor, Sir Alexander Mackenzie, and, like Mackenzie, when he reached Finlay Forks he turned to the left and followed the Parsnip River. A few days later he entered the smaller Pack River, which Mackenzie had failed to notice, and this led him to a lake known for a time as Trout Lake, but eventually named McLeod Lake. The natives thereabouts, which Fraser refers to as the Big Men, were a band of the Sekani Indians. They were friendly, and Fraser decided that the lake would be a good site for a trading-post. On its shores he built Trout Lake Post, later Fort McLeod, the first permanent settlement west of the Rocky Mountains in what is now British Columbia. Leaving La Malice and two men to winter at the new post and trade with the Indians, Fraser and the rest of the part returned to Rocky Mountain Portage House.

A rough journal kept by John Stuart from December 20, 1805, to February 28, 1806,[1] enables us to follow events at the portage. Little of note occurred. Fraser and McDougall spent Christmas at Dunvegan, the important post farther down the Peace River, where consultations were held with Archibald Norman McLeod, a senior partner in the North West Company. Friction developed between La Malice and his men at Trout Lake Post; the men finally left him and found their way, through bitter winter weather, to Rocky Mountain Portage. McDougall was sent to investigate, and found that La Malice himself had also abandoned the post and the Company's property there, and La Malice eventually turned up at Rocky Mountain Portage.

Fraser's own journal begins in April of 1806, when preparations for a long journey of exploration to the West were in full swing. By that time James McDougall had made a notable reconnaissance trip from McLeod Lake into the lands to the West occupied by the Carrier Indians. He reached the "Carriers'

Lake"—a form of reference that has led some to suppose that he went only as far as the body of water known today as Carrier Lake; but it is clear that Stuart Lake was meant, a much larger and more important lake in the very heart of the Carrier country.

To reach this lake, and establish a post on its shores, was to be the first objective of Fraser's own journey. At first sight it is difficult to understand why he did not proceed directly overland to Stuart Lake from McLeod Lake, as McDougall had done. The trip had taken only three days and a half, whereas Fraser was to follow a long, difficult and round-about water route that took him more than a month to cover. The explanation is that his primary objective was to explore the Columbia River (as the Fraser was then thought to be) to the sea. As a first step, he would examine again the portion of the river that Alexander Mackenzie had followed in 1793. McDougall has ascertained from the Indians that Stuart Lake drained into the Fraser through a river of some sort, and Simon Fraser's plan, which he duly carried out, was to follow the Fraser until he reached this tributary (which turned out to be a combination of the Nechako River and its own tributary, the Stuart River) and then ascend it to Stuart Lake.

In making his preparations, Fraser was beset with great difficulties. John Stuart, his invaluable clerk, was the only competent canoe-builder at Rocky Mountain Portage, and he was too busy with other duties to devote much time to the work. As a consequence, the three canoes in which the exploring party finally set out were a sorry lot, constantly in need of repair, and the cause of innumerable delays along the way. The best of them was a veteran craft in which Fraser had travelled all the way from Lac La Pluie the previous year, and which he had used again in the autumn on his first journey to McLeod Lake. But even this soon began to disintegrate, and new canoes had to be built before the party could proceed beyond the Pack River.

The men available were on the whole an unsatisfactory lot. Few of them were capable canoe-men, and the majority suffered from physical ailments of one kind or another. Because La Malice was an experienced traveller, Fraser felt that it was essential to take him with him, and, true to his name, he turned out to be the most troublesome of the entire crew.

Fraser, Stuart and La Malice each took charge of a canoe, and each had a crew of three voyageurs. The names of these nine men happen to have come down to us and they deserve to be recorded here: Bazile, Ménard, La Londe, La Garde, St. Pierre, Saucier, Wananshish, Gagnon and Gervais Rivard. At the Pack River two new canoes were substituted for the original three, and a voyageur named Blais, from Fort McLeod, took the place of Saucier, who was too ill to travel farther.

Break-up was late on the Peace River in the spring of 1806; it was not until May 20 that the river was sufficiently clear of ice to permit a start to be made from Rocky Mountain Portage. By the 28th Fraser was at Finlay Forks, and on June 5 the canoes entered the Pack River. Because it was necessary to build new canoes there, the party did not get on its way again until June 23. A week later Fraser was approaching the height of land that divides the watersheds of the Arctic and Pacific Oceans. His route here lay through three little lakes, now appropriately named Arctic, Portage and Pacific, and these led him to the narrow, shallow and turbulent stream that Mackenzie called the Bad River (the present James Creek). The name was apt and descriptive, for the little river, filled with obstructions and broken by rapids, gave Mackenzie some of the worst moments of his long journey to the Pacific coast. Fraser had a similar experience; the week he spent descending it was exhausting in the extreme. But it ended at last, and having passed through parts of Herrick Creek and the McGregor River, Fraser came finally, at 10 a.m. on July 10, 1806, to the "Large River ... fine and navigable" that was later to bear his name, but which at the time he hoped and believed was the upper part of the Columbia. The Fraser was still in freshet, and its current carried the party along so swiftly that they were able to encamp next day at the mouth of the Nechako River.

Thus far Fraser had been following in Mackenzie's footsteps; the rest of his jorurney was a venture into the unknown. The Nechako is broken by rapids, and ascending it proved to be a tedious process. To make matters worse, a Carrier Indian who accompanied the party, and who was supposed to act as guide, knew so little about the country that Fraser concluded finally that he had probably never seen it before. On July 18, when Fraser's journal breaks off abruptly, the party was still four days distant from the Stuart River. Ascending it, they reached Stuart Lake on the 26th.

There Fraser was greeted by Toeyen, a Carrier Indian who had met James McDougall when he was in the vicinity earlier in the year. McDougall had told Toeyen that a party of white men would be coming to found a trading-post, and had given him a piece of red cloth as a means of identification. Years later Father A. G. Morice, who worked amongst the Carriers as a missionary, heard from them their own account of Fraser's arrival. The version printed in Morice's *History of the Northern Interior of British Columbia*[2] reads as follows:

> The 26th of July, 1806, was a rather windy day on what the Indians then called Lake Na'kal, the surface of which was being ploughed into deep furrows. The soap-berries were ripening, and most of 'Kwah's [the Indian chief's] people were camped at the mouth of Beaver Creek, to the south-west of the present Fort St. James, when what appeared to them two immense canoes were descried struggling aginst the wind, around a point which separated them from the outlet of the lake.
>
> Immediately great alarm arises in the crowd of natives. As such large canoes have never plied on Carrier waters, there is hardly a doubt that they must contain Toeyen's friends, the wonderful strangers from 'the country beyond the horizon' he had been told to expect back. Meanwhile, the strange crafts are heading for Beaver Creek, and lo! a song the like of which has never been heard in this part of the world strikes the native ear. What can that mean? Might not this be a war party, after all?
>
> "No," declares Toeyen, who, donning his red piece of cloth as an apron, seizes a tiny spruce bark canoe lying on the beach and fearlessly paddles away. On, on he goes, tossed about by the great waves, until he meets the strangers, who, recognizing him by his badge, bid him come on board. His fellow-tribesmen, now seeing in the distance his own little canoe floating tenantless, take fright.
>
> "They have already killed him," they exclaim. "Ready, ye warriors; away with the women!"
>
> At this cry, which flies from mouth to mouth, the men seize their bows and arrows, and the women and children seek shelter in the woods. But the curious crafts, which, on coming nearer, prove to be large birch-bark canoes, are now within hearing distance, and Toeyen cries out to the men on shore to be of good cheer and have no fear, as the strangers are animated by the most friendly dispositions. The fugitives are hastily recalled, and Simon Fraser, with John Stuart and his other companions, put ashore in the presence of a crowd of wondering Carriers. . . .
>
> On landing, Fraser's men, to impress the natives with a proper idea of their wonderful resources, fired a volley with their guns, whereupon the whole crowd of Carriers fell pros-

trate to the ground. To allay their fears and make friends, tobacco was offered them, which, on being tasted, was found too bitter, and thrown away. Then, to show its use, the crew lighted their pipes, and, at the sight of the smoke issuing from their mouths, the people began to whisper that they must come from the land of the ghosts, since they were full of the fire wherewith they had been cremated. Pieces of soap were given to the women, who, taking them to be cakes of fat, set upon crunching them, thereby causing foam and bubbles in the mouth, which puzzled both actors and bystanders.

All these phenomena, however, were soon explained away, leaving no suspicion in the native mind, but a most pronounced admiration for the foreigners and their wares. . . .

Fraser's letters show that this paints much too rosy a picture of conditions at Stuart Lake. "It is a fine large Lake," he told the Gentlemen Proprietors of the North West Company in his first report, "But since we arrived here, my ideas are far short of what Mr. McDougalls account would lead [one] to expect." His stock of provisions was low; he was very scantily provided with trade goods; the Indians—whom he later characterized as "a large, indolent, thievish set of vagabonds"—were not numerous, and showed little inclination to part with either food or furs. The salmon run was late, and, as it turned out, was not to begin for another six weeks. As a result, the party was soon in a state of semi-starvation.

Fraser nevertheless set his men to work building the post on Stuart Lake that was later to be famous under the name Fort St. James. As soon as he could collect sufficient provisions, he intended to resume his major task—the exploration of the Fraser River—and to follow the main stream to the south at least as far as Mackenzie had done in 1793. As it turned out, lack of provisions made this impracticable. Weary and vexatious weeks were spent in waiting for the salmon run, which in the Carrier country conditioned many things. It became clear at last that Fraser must abandon his plan; "it would have been little short of madness," he explained to the North West Company, "to attempt going down the Columbia [i.e., the Fraser] in a starving state, without an ounce of any kind of provisions."[3]

Instead, he turned to the other task assigned to him—the founding of still another post west of the Rocky Mountains. On August 28 he sent Stuart and two men to visit a lake that he had heard about, and which might be a suitable site. This was Fraser Lake, which Fraser thought lay to the west, but which was actually south of Stuart Lake. After seeing it, Stuart was to meet Fraser at the mouth of the Stuart River, and Fraser left on September 3 to keep this rendezvous. Stuart's account of Fraser Lake was so favourable that Fraser went to see it, and there he built the future Fort Fraser.

In the last weeks of the year Fraser's plans suffered another major setback. In his letters to the Company he had stressed the fact that reinforcements were essential if the new posts were to become firmly established and profitable. When he returned to Stuart Lake from Fraser Lake on December 18, it was to find that no supplies or additional men had been sent to him; and this, as he explained to McDougall, was "a considerable loss to the Company, and a severe blow to our discoveries".[4] In spite of this, a letter written to Stuart in February 1807 is full of plans and projects, the most important being the building of a supply depot of some sort on the Fraser River at the mouth of the Nechako. Like Rocky Mountain Portage House, this would be both a trading-post for the immediate area, and a base from which an exploring expedition could set off down the Fraser with a minimum of delay.

In the autumn of 1807 two canoes carrying men and supplies finally arrived from across the mountains, and Fraser set about carrying his plan into effect. A post, later named Fort George, was established at the mouth of the Nechako, and Hugh Faries, one of the two clerks who had arrived with the supply canoes, was placed in charge of it. Fraser decided that the other clerk, Jules Quesnel, should accompany John Stuart and himself on the expedition down the Fraser River that was planned for the late spring and summer of 1808.

The great journey of 1808 speaks for itself in the pages that follow, but a few observations regarding it are none the less called for.

The exploring party was 24 in number: Fraser tells us that it consisted of 19 voyageurs, two Indians, his two clerks (Stuart and Quesnel) and himself. The names of eight of the French-Canadians are mentioned in the journal: La Chapelle, Baptiste, D'Alaire, La Certe, Waka or Wacca (the nickname of Jean Baptiste Boucher), Bourboné (whose name should probably be spelled Bourbonnais), Gagnier and La Garde. The latter had been with Fraser on his 1806 expedition, and it is possible that Gagnier is the man whose name appears as Gagnon in the earlier journals.

It was a youthful contingent: Fraser was 32 at the time, Stuart was 29, and Quesnel only 22. Both Fraser's assistants were men of character, with important careers ahead of them. John Stuart was to succeed Fraser in 1809 as officer in charge of New Caledonia, and was to retain the post for no less than fifteen years. He became a partner in the North West Company in 1813, and a Chief Factor in the Hudson's Bay Company in 1821, following the amalgamation of the two concerns. Able and highly respected, he seems to have been somewhat reserved and serious-minded; he enjoyed theological discussions, and frequently indulged this bent in the company of friends, notably Daniel Williams Harmon. Stuart retired to his native Scotland in 1839 and died there in 1847.

Jules Maurice Quesnel was one of the thirteen children of Joseph Quesnel, of Montreal, a poet and musician of some note. He left the fur trade in 1811, and eventually became prominent in Quebec political life. He was a member of the Special Council of Lower Canada from 1838 to 1841, and was then appointed to the Legislative Council of the United Province of Canada. He died in Montreal in 1842.

The first entry in the "fair copy" of Fraser's journal is wrongly dated, and this has given rise to some doubt about the expedition's point of departure. The date given in the manuscript (May 22) does not correspond with the day of the week (Saturday). It has usually been assumed that the date was correct; but this would leave five days unaccounted for in the journal, whose second entry is dated Sunday, May 29. If the first entry is corrected to Saturday, May 28, all details fall neatly into line. There is no adequate reason to think that Fort George, which, as we have seen, was built specially as an advance base for Fraser and his party, was not the spot from which they set out.

The journey down the Fraser was hazardous in the extreme, but one reason for its perilous nature is seldom made clear. The "tremendous gulphs and whirlpools . . . ready every moment to swallow a Canoe with all its contents and the people on board" were not only dangerous in themselves; what multiplied the perils was the virtual impossibility, in many places, of getting out of the river to avoid them. Fraser mentions many instances of this in his journal. "The current throughout the day ran with amazing velocity," he wrote on June 5, "and on this and [the] last course our situation was really dangerous, being constantly between steep and high banks where there was no possibility of stopping the canoe, and even could it be stopped, there would be no such thing as going up the hills, so that had we suddenly come upon a cascade or bad Rapid, not to mention falls, it is more than likely that all of us would have perished, which is much to be apprehended." A century and a half later, the men who set out to duplicate Fraser's journey encountered the same difficulty; "in most of the length of the river," they reported, "the greatest single problem is that once you are in it, you cannot get out."[5]

Fraser faced two other major problems that did not trouble his modern successors: uncertainty about the attitude of the Indians along the river, and a total lack of information about its course and character.

The Indians, who were surprisingly numerous, were on the whole friendly, and Fraser showed great skill and courage in his dealings with them. But he was well aware that they were a constant hazard, and in spite of appearances he was under no illusions about the grave dangers that surrounded his little party. "Here we are," he wrote at a time when all was outwardly peaceful, "in a strange Country, surrounded with dangers, and difficulties, among numberless tribes of savages, who never [before] saw the face of a white man. Our situation is critical and highly unpleasant; however we shall endeavour to make the best of it; what cannot be cured must be endured.[6]

The great crisis of the journey came in the first days of July, when Fraser reached the delta of the river and there encountered the hostile and aggressive Cowichan Indians. He brought his men safely through the ordeal, but it momentarily shattered their morale, and it took all his eloquence and prestige to give them heart and determination to undertake the long and fatiguing journey back up the river to Fort George.

When he sought information about the river from the Indians, their reports were almost always vague and discouraging. In part this was probably due to a desire to dissuade the travellers from going further, in the hope of gaining gifts and other benefits from their continued presence. But in many instances, though Fraser did not realize it at the time, they spoke the simple truth about the dangers and difficulties that lay ahead. The river was in places unnavigable, especially when in freshet, and this Fraser discovered for himself in due time. The Indians found it easier in many places to travel by land, and they could not be expected to understand that to survey the actual river, and to travel down it whenever humanly possible, was the purpose of Fraser's journey. As it turned out, even Fraser was compelled to travel considerable distances by land. Between Leon Creek, north of Lillooet, near which he cached his canoes, and Yale, at the foot of the Fraser Canyon, the whole party rarely travelled by water. In some places all had to proceed overland; in others some of the party could use canoes, and the rest followed Indian trails along the hills.

The actual distance down the winding course of the river from Fort George to the Strait of Georgia has never been accurately measured, but it is appreciably more than 500 miles. Fraser completed the journey in 36 days (May 28 to July 2), and made the return trip in one day less (July 3 to August 6). It has been said that he turned back before he actually reached the Strait, but his journal makes it quite clear that this is not so. The Musqueam area, where he made his last recorded landing, extends along the shore beyond the mouth of the North Arm of the Fraser River, and Fraser certainly saw the open Strait and the mountains on Vancouver Island across its waters. Indeed, it is clear that he paddled along the shore for some distance beyond Musqueam, in the direction of Point Grey; and he would have gone farther still had not the hostility of the Indians thereabouts made it prudent to return before nightfall.

Like Mackenzie before him, Fraser completed his great journey in a state of frustration and disappointment. He had discovered a great river and traced it to the sea, but it was not the Columbia, as he and everyone else had assumed, and its character made long stretches of its useless as a travel and supply route for the fur trade. All that was left to comfort Fraser was the realization that he had performed a journey of immense difficulty with speed and efficiency, and without loss of life or serious injury to any of his men. An occasional sentence in his journal suggests that he was aware that, whatever view his hard-headed colleagues in the North West Company might take, his accomplishment was in its way extraordinary. To quote an instance: "I have been for a long period among the Rocky Mountains," he wrote while in the vicinity of Hell's Gate, in the Fraser Canyon, "but have never seen any thing to equal this country, for I cannot find words to describe our situation at times. We had to pass where no human being should venture."[7]

The absence of familiar place-names will strike any reader of the journals and letters who is acquainted with the interior of British Columbia. It is often assumed that Fraser, Stuart and Quesnel made a sort of triumphal progress through the country, naming lakes and rivers and trading-posts after themselves as they went their way. The documents in the case show that this is not so. Fraser notes in his 1808 narrative that he has named the Thompson River after David Thompson and the Quesnel River after his third-incommand, Jules Quesnel, and he refers to Carp

Lake and the West Road River (the latter a name bestowed by Alexander Mackenzie in 1793); but these are the only present-day names of features west of the Rocky Mountains that appear in his papers. Fort McLeod is referred to as Trout Lake Post, Fort St. James is called Nakazleh, Fort Fraser is Natleh, and Fort George is given no name at all. The Nechako, Stuart and Chilcotin rivers were all named later, and so were Stuart, Fraser and McLeod lakes.

The earliest use of the name New Caledonia, which was applied to the large area in the northern interior of British Columbia in which all these post, rivers and lakes are located, would seem to have been in 1808. As we shall see, Daniel Williams Harmon refers to New Caledonia in an entry in his journal made at Fort Chipewyan on September 21, 1808. According to family tradition, Fraser chose the name New Caledonia because the country recalled to his mind his mother's descriptions of the Highlands of Scotland.

As Fraser had named the Thompson River, it is fitting that it should have been David Thompson who named the Fraser River. On Sir Alexander Mackenzie's map, printed in his *Voyages* in 1801, the Fraser is called the "Tacoutche Tesse or Columbia River". Some notes by John Stuart indicate that it was sometimes referred to as the Jackanet River.[8] The first entry in the "fair copy" of Fraser's 1808 narrative shows that the name Fraser River was at one time given to the Nechako; but this must have been a purely local usage, and no other reference to it has been noticed.

Thompson first used the name Fraser River on a "rough chart" of what is now Western Canada, prepared in 1813. He had moved to Terrebonne the previous year, and there set about compiling the famous "map for the North West Company" that was completed in 1814. Some "remarks" dated April 1813, prepared to accompany the preliminary version of the map, include the note: "The River Mr. Fraser followed down to the Sea, I have named after him . . ."[9] Other notes by Thompson show that his delineation of the river was based on John Stuart's notes, not on those of Fraser himself. This recalls the fact that although many courses and distances are recorded in the surviving fragment of Fraser's rough journal of 1808, it was Stuart who was charged with the duty of keeping the official log of the expedition. Unfortunately Stuart's survey has long since disappeared.

The search for a supply and travel route from New Caledonia to the Pacific Coast did not end with Fraser's great journey to the sea. The effort was continued by others, notably by John

Stuart, who succeeded Fraser as officer in charge of the New Caledonia posts. Eventually a solution was found by linking the explorations of Fraser and Stuart with those carried out by David Thompson in the valley of the Columbia River. In 1811 Thompson descended the Columbia to its mouth and found that, though broken here and there by rapids and falls, it provided a satisfactory route to the Coast. In 1813 Stuart worked out a practicable link between the Columbia and New Caledonia. This followed the Fraser River as far south as the vicinity of Alexandria, and then veered to the south-east and ran overland to Kamloops, at the junction of the North and South Thompson rivers. Thence the route continued on southwards through the Okanagan Valley to the Okanagan River, a tributary of the Columbia. Here the fur brigades took to the water again, and followed the Okanagan and Columbia rivers to the ocean.

Supplies carried by ship from England to the mouth of the Columbia River, and brought inland over this route, first reached the New Caledonia posts in the fall of 1814. Thereafter it was used regularly by the North West Company, and, after the amalgamation of 1821, by the Hudson's Bay Company. A few years later, however, it became clear that permanent British possession of the lower valley of the Columbia was by no means assured, and the search for an alternative supply route farther to the north was therefore resumed. In 1828 Governor George Simpson of the Hudson's Bay Company decided that the Fraser must be re-examined, and he and his party set out to follow the actual course of the river, regardless of obstacles. Simpson enjoyed one great advantage compared with Fraser: he was descending the river in the autumn, when water levels were relatively low, and most of the rapids and whirlpools were much less swift and formidable than during the summer freshet. Because of this, Simpson and his expert crew were able in great part to accomplish their objective: except for occasional short portages they did in fact contrive to travel down the river virtually the whole way. But the experience was a terrifying one, and Simpson emerged from the ordeal with a healthy respect for Fraser and convinced that the river was useless as a travel route. The 1808 expedition, he wrote in his journal, reflected "infinite credit" on both Fraser and Stuart; he described their journey as "an undertaking, compared to which, in my humble opinion, the much talked of and high sounding performances of His Majesty's recent discovery expeditions in the Arctic regions, were excursions of pleasure." As for the river itself, he had this to say: "Frazers River, can no longer be thought of as a practicable communication with the interior; it was never wholly passed by water before, and in all probability never will again: . . . and altho we ran all the Rapids in safety, being perfectly light, and have three of the most skilful Bowsmen in the country, whose skill however was of little avail at times, I should consider the passage down, to be certain Death, in nine attempts out of Ten. I shall therefore no longer talk of it as a navigable stream."[10]

Simpson was thus reluctantly compelled to confirm the verdict that Fraser had passed upon the river twenty years before.

What manner of man was Simon Fraser?

His journals furnish less evidence than one would expect, because they are more in the nature of official logbooks than personal diaries. The chief qualities they reveal are the determination with which he pushed on in the face of great difficulties, his physical courage and stamina, and the firmness, tempered with restraint, with which he handled his men. Not even the thoroughly exasperating behaviour of the rascally La Malice made him either lose his temper or act unfairly.

Fraser's fairly frequent and somewhat disparaging references to Sir Alexander Mackenzie roused the ire of H. H. Bancroft, who has few kind words for him in his *History of the Northwest Coast.* "Fraser," Bancroft wrote, "was an illiterate, ill-bred, bickering, fault-finding man, of jealous disposition, ambitious, energetic, with considerable conscience, and in the main holding to honest intentions."[11] And lest the reader should be too impressed with the final phrases, Bancroft hastened to add that no man could be truly honest who was as unjust and blinded by prejudice as he conceived Fraser to be.

This is certainly a badly distorted conception of the man. Much nearer the mark is a character sketch written in 1908 by E. O. S. Scholefield, who had spent long hours studying both Fraser's letters and journals and all available pictures of him. Scholefield saw in him "a well-built active man, with a heavy, almost dour, face, whose distinguishing features are a determined chin, firm, large-lipped mouth, prominent somewhat snubbed nose, light-blue eyes, broad receding brow, overhung with a mass of tousled hair of reddish tinge —a strong, honest face, indeed, but one giving more the idea of determination and physical robustness than of intellectuality or refinement. A man inured to hardship; versed in woodcraft and the lore of the savage; strong in danger; of inconquerable will and energy; unlettered, not polished, it may be, but true to his friends and honourable in his dealings; somewhat eccentric if we judge aright; a man typical of his age and calling. An heroic spirit truly, if cast in the not altogether heroic mould of a fur-trader. He stands there a commanding figure."[12]

Notes

[1] Original manuscript in the Archives of British Columbia; photostat copy in the Public Archives of Canada.

[2] 3rd edition, Toronto, 1905, pp. 60-2.

[3] Fraser to the Gentlemen Proprietors, December 21, 1806.

[4] Fraser to McDougall, December 1906.

[5] *The Report of the British Columbia Centennial Committee*, Victoria, 1959, p. 187.

[6] Narrative, June 15, 1808.

[7] *Ibid.*, June 26, 1808.

[8] The name is used in notes by Stuart appended to A. C. Anderson's *History of the Northwest Coast*; manuscript in Archives of British Columbia.

[9] David Thompson, "Remarks on the Countries westward of the Rocky Mountains with reference to the rough Chart of David Thompson". Manuscript in the Library of the Royal Commonwealth Institute, London; photostat copy in Public Archives of Canada.

[10] E. E. Rich (ed.), *Part of Dispatch from George Simpson, Esqr . . . 1829* (Toronto and London, 1947), pp. 38-9.

[11] H. H. Bancroft, *History of the Northwest Coast*, vol. II, San Francisco 1884, p. 89.

[12] *Westward Ho! Magazine* 111 (1908), p. 222.

10. Canada and the New British Columbia
Margaret A. Ormsby

MARGARET A. ORMSBY *recently retired as professor and head of the department of history at the University of British Columbia. Ormsby, with Lamb and Ireland, belongs to the first generation of British Columbia historians to receive their undergraduate training at the University of British Columbia. This early article presents views differing from those in her major work* British Columbia: a history *and contrasts interestingly with the Sage selection.*

The completion of railway communication between British Columbia and eastern Canada is often considered to mark the beginning of the absorption of the Province into the Dominion of Canada. The bonds of race, custom, and economic interest, it is true, were strengthened after 1885 as Canadian population and capital moved westward, but it should not be forgotten that integrating factors existed from the commencement of Canadian settlement on the Pacific coast. The political and social concepts of eastern Canada were transplanted to British Columbia by the first Canadian settlers, and by 1871 the sense of sharing a common nationality was sufficiently strong to offset the economic attraction of the United States and to break the direct political tie with England. In spite of strained relations between the provincial and the federal government following the entrance of the province into Confederation, Canadian sentiment among British Columbians was materially strengthened by the joint endeavour of Canadians from all parts of the Dominion to build the section of the national railway which lay within the province's limits.

Canadians at first formed a minority group in British Columbia.[1] Although their individuality attracted little notice in gold-mining days, their influence in the maintenance of law and order came to be appreciated as the colony developed. In a society where economic monopoly and governmental paternalism were being replaced by the competitive acquisition of wealth and by anarchical tendencies, Canadians upheld morality and respect for authority. They became permanent residents in the colonies, and

Source: The Canadian Historical Association Annual Report (1948), pp. 74-85. Reprinted by permission of the author and publisher.

the builders, if not the surveyors and planners, of New Westminster and the smaller towns of the Fraser Valley and Cariboo. They supplied the professional and other services required in a pioneer community. And they led the way in political reform; for, from an old colonial environment, they had transferred to a new, a deep resentment of political disqualification and its off-shoots, economic discrimination and social slighting.

Almost from the beginning of Canadian settlement in the late fifties and early sixties, there was a manifestation of democratic tendencies which had emerged earlier in older British North American colonies. As on the American and the Upper Canadian frontiers, in British Columbia, the backwoodsman, the small farmer, and the day labourer instinctively abhorred class privilege. The agitation for the recognition of the people's rights was led by Canadians who revived the old formula of autonomy, free lands, separation of church and state, and opportunity for unhampered economic activity. Their struggle for these ideals forms one of the chapters in the history of the evolution of democratic institutions on this continent.

Change was already in the air when Canadian settlement commenced in the British colonies on the Pacific coast. In the older colony of Vancouver Island, British colonists had just succeeded in helping to persuade the British government to end the liaison between colonial administrators and Hudson's Bay Company officers. The colony's system of government was to be modernized so that control would be exercised directly by the Crown, and the sponsorship of the Hudson's Bay Company ended. The attention of the British authorities had been called to various grievances: the division of the governor's attention between governmental and Company affairs, nepotism in the filling of offices, the executive's irresponsibility, the high property qualification for office-holding, and the deterrent to settlement in the high price of crown lands. The curbing of the Company's power, which the imperial government proposed as a method of redress, was not wholly satisfactory to the British colonists, or to the Canadians who began to arrive in 1858 and 1859. Although such action implied that settlers would enjoy greater economic freedom, it did not necessarily mean that the people's power in government would be increased. Only fully representative and responsible government would give political freedom.

In the colony of British Columbia, organized on the mainland after the discovery of gold on the bars of the Fraser in 1858, conditions were still less satisfactory. Imperial considerations, and the expense involved in sending a military force to protect and police the gold colony and to assist in the development of its resources, necessitated a plan for the economical management of its affairs. On condition that he sever his connection with the Hudson's Bay Company, James Douglas, governor of Vancouver Island, was offered the dual position of governor of the two colonies. Convinced that gold-miners were not qualified by experience or by temperament for office-holding, Douglas delayed fulfilling his instructions to set up an assembly on the mainland, and appointed officials as members of an executive council. The colonists of British Columbia resented their exclusion from government, the colony's lack of a separate governor, and the residence of officials in Victoria. For five years they battled to obtain recognition of their rights only to find in 1863, when the separate existence of the mainland colony was acknowledged, and a legislative council set up, that the people's representatives could be checked by the relatively superior strength of the official element and the exercise of authority by the new governor.

Three years later, as depression spread in the colonies and retrenchment became necessary, the imperial authorities decided to unite the colonies, extend the jurisdiction of the executive and legislature of British Columbia over the Island, and abolish Vancouver Island's assembly. Union satisfied neither islander nor mainlander. As might have been expected, there were disputes about the location of the capital, the amount of representation allowed to each section in the council, and the unequal debt-load which the united colony assumed from the two colonies. There was, too, the inevitable bickering about the burden of taxation and the distribution of government monies. One school of thought in Victoria favoured the demand for "the immediate restitution of our political rights, with full measure of responsible government" or permission from the British authorities for the colony to become annexed to the United States.[2] Another group of colonists felt that the suggestion of annexation was a counsel of despair, and that British Columbia's merging in a union of eastern Canadian colonies would be the best means of obtaining popular government and economic salvation.[3] In the year 1866 the first attempt was made to obtain permission from the Colonial Office for recognition of British Columbia's right to be admitted into Confederation.[4] At this time the British North America Act was before the imperial parliament. Obstacles, such as the Hudson's Bay Company's control of territory intervening between British Columbia and the Upper Canada, and Governor Seymour's lack of enthusiasm for union, prevented the immediate materialization of the plan for union.

Meanwhile, journalist agitators aroused interest in the establishment of self-government in British Columbia. They loudly denounced the political iniquities of the local administration, hoping to bring about reform through the education of opinion and indoctrination of the general public. It was to be reform through evolution; militant radicalism was impossible in a colony where there was a racial mixture and where a great many of the settlers were politically uninformed. The gold-miners tended to be strong individualists, living from day to day, and becoming so discouraged by hardship that many of them left the country.[5] Speculators in lands and mines were more concerned with making quick profits than in combining efforts for the building of a stable society. Only those who had a real stake in the country, the farmers, the merchants, the traders, and the wage-earners who hoped to improve their condition, were seriously concerned about a more equitable distribution of political power.

The most serious problem facing the reformers was that of uniting classes and racial elements. British officials on Vancouver Island did not relish the prospect of premature retirement from their posts.[6] Victoria also contained an influential group of Britishers who were active or retired Hudson's Bay men, and who enjoyed an indirect voice in colonial government. They, too, were not anxious for change. In addition, a merchant class of Germans and Jews in Victoria had business connections with San Francisco and thought in terms of possible annexation of the colony to the United States.[7] Population was even more mixed on the mainland. There, a conservative British element, composed partly of officers and men retired from the Royal Engineers was satisfied with keeping the *status quo*, while Irish and Scots who desired increased prestige, were inclined to favour the Canadian cause. A group of European settlers, Germans, Austrians, Frenchmen, and others, lacked interest in local political issues and failed to throw weight behind the reform movement. This was also true of the French Canadians who were isolated socially and given little encouragement to take part in political life. The large Chinese element remained completely segregated from other groups. It was therefore difficult to obtain identity of interests. The only two groups sharing the same political tradition were the English and the Canadians. Many of the former considered their residence in the colony as constituting an interlude in a professional career, and, like Judge Matthew Baillie Begbie, continued to think of England "as if it were just outside the door."[8] Some of them might have been willing to support the reform movement, had they not, with some justice, suspected Canadian leaders of under-lying ambitions to hold office.

The sparse settlement of British Columbia also made for difficulty in getting concerted action. In Cariboo, the mobility of population caused fluctuation in the size of the towns. New Westminster, which had the greatest aggregation of reformers, was distant from Cariboo, as well as from the new mining areas in the Okanagan and the boundary country. It was also tied by proximity and by economic bonds to the agricultural districts of the lower mainland, where the agrarian element was not united in demands for governmental change. At Langley, where the Hudson's Bay Company had long been established, a group of farmers was nervous about the proposed inclusion of a demand for responsible government in the terms of union to be negotiated with Canada. In 1870, they expressed the opinion that:

> Responsible Government at present would only enable the unscrupulous politicians of Victoria to plunder more effectually the interests of the Mainland, and impede the progress of the country generally.
> The people of Langley cannot help believing that the past Government of this Colony has lent its influence in enabling the people to demand and obtain unjust concessions to the very great detriment of the other parts of the united colony and should any more of this foul treatment appear to be furthered, we shall do everything in our power in conjunction with the rest of the Mainland to rid ourselves of all connection with that part of the united colony known as Vancouver Island.[9]

As economic organization developed from the stage of private endeavour to joint enterprise, the reform movement gained momentum. By 1866, the tapping of the tremendous resources of the forests, mines, and rivers had commenced,[10] and projects had been started which necessitated large-scale investment of capital as well as a labour supply. Neither the government nor the banks gave financial assistance to the promoters of these enterprises. After 1866, the burden of the government's indebtedness increased with each passing year. Both the Bank of British North America and the Bank of British Columbia followed extremely conservative policies, and were reluctant to make credit available either to the government or to individuals.[11] Lack of cheap land also hindered economic development. Until 1867 the Hudson's Bay Company retained sovereignty over crown lands on Vancouver Island,[12] and in many cases, sites which would have been favourable for centres of trade or new industries, formed part of the Company's holdings[13] or were set aside as government reserves. In addition, the large areas in good farming districts which had been acquired by former Hudson's Bay men, were not subdivided. Many Canadians felt that the shift from an economy based on the staples of fur and gold to one based on coal-mining, lumber-milling, salmon-canning, and flour-milling, would result from political union with Canada. Only in this way, they thought, could capital and labour be imported, and a railway built. In anticipation of prosperity, some of them eagerly participated in speculative activities after 1871, investing their savings in lands near the probable route or terminus of the Canadian Pacific Railway.[14]

In addition to a desire for a greater voice in politics and for greater economic opportunity, Canadian reformers were motivated by antipathy for Englishmen. Knowing that many of the British officials and settlers belonged to the upper middle class or country gentry, Canadians who emigrated to British Columbia were of the first generation born in Canada, and many of them had come from Ontario where they had been raised on farms or in country parsonages or in the small-town homes of merchants and professional men. They lacked sophistication, and even the journalists, doctors, and lawyers among their number who took an active part in political life, were not always admitted to the closed social circle the Englishmen had created.

To a certain extent, the British element constituted an aristocracy of wealth and talents. In addition to economic security, arising from sound investment in land or guaranteed income from office, it had a feeling of cultural superiority. Many of the British settlers cultivated a taste for the arts and for letters, and carried on scientific investigations.[15] They still read *The Times* and ignored colonial newspapers; and they published their literary works in England. Furthermore, on the fringe of the forest, and against the encroachment of the backwoodsman, they maintained the standards of polite society in Victorian England. In contrast, many of the Canadian settlers were young men who had not become established in professional or business careers when they left the East, and they still had little financial reserve. Those who turned to farming, usually had little education, and they knew only the social life of rural areas. Disinclination as well as the exigencies of frontier life with its lack of interchange of ideas, prevented their intellectual development.

At the same time, they did not relish the exclusion of friends and relatives from the professions. It was insulting to all Canadians, for example, to have Judge Begbie recommend the temporary granting of licences to Canadian barristers, "there being no English barristers or attornies [*sic*]," and it being "expedient to take the best that can be got."[16] George A. Walkem, later premier of the province, who had been admitted to the bars of Upper and Lower Canada, had to wait until 1863, before Begbie would recognize his right to practise law. Such action convinced Canadians generally that the English "clique" was snobbish and tyrannical.

Diatribes in the press helped to widen the channel between Canadian and Englishman. Conscious that he "stood outside the Fort—the great Company,"[17] Amor de Cosmos, a Nova Scotian who belonged to the Howe tradition, in the columns of the *Colonist* flayed Douglas during his governorship for lack of liberalism and for too great concern for the Hudson's Bay Company's business interests.[18] After Douglas's retirement, de Cosmos took up the cause of representative and responsible government. On the mainland, de Cosmos's counterpart was John Robson, a reformer from Upper Canada who had a Wesleyan Methodist background and who edited the *British Columbian.* Robson's brush with Judge Begbie increased his antagonism for English officialdom, and probably for all Englishmen, and made him an energetic fighter for the introduction of a more popular element into the Legislative Council.[19]

In the latter phase of the colonial period, these two Canadian journalists poured forth political polemics and vituperative denunciation of the British oligarchy. Each of the editors had an excellent grasp of constitutional issues and a first-hand knowledge of local conditions, but neither of them had a great interest in political or economic theory. To a certain extent, they were both demagogues, and neither was unmindful of advantages which (once they had succeeded in securing British Columbia's entrance into Confederation) might accrue to himself. Temperamental differences and rivalry for attention made them political enemies. When in 1871, de Cosmos advocated the establishment of party government and the creation of a "Liberal" party,[20] he acted, according to Robson, "in the insane belief that he [de Cosmos] will be first Premier."[21] In short order Robson called for a legislature of independents, working for the good of the country at large.[22] Yet their combined efforts, and their conviction that change was necessary, made them important leaders of the reform movement in the period before 1871.

The influence of two medical men was also of considerable importance in the late colonial period. One of them was Dr. I. W. Powell, the son of a Canadian legislator[23] whose family sometimes had Macdonald's ear. A man of high principle, Powell was a sincere democrat. At the same time, too, he was not completely without interest in obtaining a federal appointment. The centre of his influence was Victoria. In the Cariboo, Dr. R. W. W. Carrall, a native of Woodstock, kept Macdonald informed about the progress of the Confederation movement, and carried out the prime minister's injunction to "keep the union fire alight until it burns over the whole Colony."[24] Carrall became one of the three British Columbia delegates who negotiated the terms of union and was rewarded for his efforts by being made one of British Columbia's first three senators.

Governor Musgrave indicated that he had some knowledge of the personal ambition of these men, when he wrote the colonial secretary, "The more prominent agitators for Confederation are a small knot of Canadians who hope that it may be possible to make fuller representative institutions and Responsible Government part of the new arrangements, and that they may so place themselves in positions of influence and emolument."[25] No doubt Macdonald relied on their private interests to help in the defeat of what he termed the conspiracy of "government officials, the Hudson's Bay agents and the Yankee adventurers"[26] to delay union. If he encouraged their ambitions, he had to pay the price later, for British Columbians hounded him for appointments.

In the end, external as well as internal pressure brought about British Columbia's entry into Confederation. By 1870, the imperial government lacked enthusiasm for continued support of an indigent and distant colony, which might be menaced by American expansionist activity in the Pacific. It encouraged the ambitions of the Canadian government to round out the national boundaries. For his part, Macdonald put "the screw on Vancouver Island,"[27] by arranging for the appointment of Governor Musgrave, who previously had worked for the cause of Confederation in Newfoundland. De Cosmos, a "western confederationist," had spent the summer of 1867 speaking in eastern Canadian cities in favour of British Columbia's union and on his return to the Colony he continued the fight. His work was supplemented by the efforts of John Robson, Dr. Carrall, Dr. Powell, Francis J. Barnard, and J. Spencer Thompson. Negotiations were conducted with Sir Georges Cartier in 1870 and an enlarged Legislative Council debated the terms of union in the spring of 1871. The generosity of treatment accorded British Columbia in fiscal arrangements, promise of railway communication, and freedom of choice in the setting up of responsible government and the application of the Canadian tariff, carried the day for union. Provincial status was formally attained on July 20.

Already the prime minister was besieged by applications for

appointments. Within a fortnight of British Columbia's entry into Confederation, Macdonald replied to a request from Dr. Carrall in these words:

> I have your note of the 5th instant introducing Mr. Robson of the British Colonist. I have heard a good deal of Mr. Robson from Mr. Trutch and others as well as from yourself and shall be very glad to forward his views in any way in my power. The only difficulty will be the modus operandi as most of the important offices in the Province belong to the Provincial Government. We have only Post Offices, Customs, Excise to give, and are of course bound to retain the present office-holders in those Departments so long as they choose to remain & perform the duties efficiently. Still vacancies do occur occasionally, & I shall gladly keep Mr. Robson in mind. We think here that the Colonist deserves encouragement, and I have no doubt that a full share of any Government patronage there may be in that line will be extended to it. Mr. Langevin who visits British Columbia will see to that and other cognate matters.[28]

Soon the prime minister had to consider Dr. Powell's request that he be made Indian commissioner. Powell had reminded him that "At present there is not a single Canadian official in B.C. and being Confederationists too from the first, to Canadians is mainly due the credit of finally carrying Union against both English and official influences."[20]

Walkem was offended when the first federal appointment to the judiciary was given to John Hamilton Gray of New Brunswick, one of the Fathers of Canadian Confederation, who had been disappointed in his aspiration to become first speaker of the House at Ottawa. In pleading the case of Premier McCreight, Walkem but thinly disguised his own interest:

> You have wounded our feelings by passing over Mr. McCreight . . . in the matter of the judgeship. I assure you that the murmur of displeasure has extended beyond our local Bar. What has a barrister to hope for in the future if he doesn't enter the H. of Commons? I have heard all you said to Carrall and De Cosmos on the subject and while admitting the justice of the bar principle involved, I sincerely regret in common with others that lesson No. 1 in Canadian politics reminds one too much of the taskmasters of Egypt. We all serve, but are to be treated like serfs—Downing St. earned for itself the most bitter animosity, simply because merit in this *quondam* Colony was overlooked & some empty-headed favourite wanted a place. The latter remark doesn't of course apply

to Col. Gray who, I believe, is a good lawyer & most estimable man. In his appointment you simply ask us to overlook the slight to McCreight and accept the bon-bon that is offered or in other words to swallow a spoonful of honey with a quart of bad vinegar —and look pleased. I know there is no use grumbling. . . . [30]

The following spring, although Walkem was a provincial cabinet minister, he tried to obtain the solicitorship at Victoria of the Canadian Pacific Railway.[31] But Macdonald would only go as far as making him Queen's Counsel.[32]

At least as long as dual representation lasted, de Cosmos appeared to be content with his role in public life, and did not press his suit on Macdonald.

As far as his relations with British Columbia were concerned, one of the prime minister's chief aims was not to single out favourites from either Canadian or British factions. His choice for the office of first lieutenant-governor of the province was Joseph W. Trutch, who was not sufficiently identified with the ruling caste of the colonial period to be anathema to Canadians, and not too friendly with Canadians to be objectionable to Englishmen. Trutch, a civil engineer, who had been commissioner of lands and works in the colonial government, would probably have preferred employment in a professional capacity, to service as an officer of the crown.[33] In any case, he had been one of British Columbia's delegates who had arranged the terms of union, and before their acceptance by the House of Commons, he had given a pledge that the province would be reasonable about the fulfilment of the railway commitment. For Macdonald, there were several advantages in having him in the post of lieutenant-governor. Trutch could be offered political tutoring since he did not understand the working of cabinet government; he had some influence with local politicians and could prevent them from being too wayward and headstrong; and he might induce the people of the province to adopt a reasonable attitude, if it were necessary to modify the terms of union. When Trutch chose as the first premier, John Foster McCreight, a Britisher who was not too close to the former oligarchy, Macdonald did not demur. It was possible that McCreight could be useful in uniting Canadian and British opinion.

So successful was Macdonald in winning popularity in British Columbia, and so general his support, that he was able by 1872 to use British Columbia as a pocket borough when Sir Francis Hincks was defeated in the election of that year. At that time, there was a strong desire in British Columbia for cabinet representation, so Trutch did not press the question of Hincks's eligibility under provincial regulations. Instead, he suggested to Macdonald that "if nothing is said on this point you can if you think fit make some adjustments at the opening of the next session."[24] Neither did Walkem adopt too critical an attitude. Complimenting Macdonald on Hincks's success. Walkem wrote:

> I should have liked to have taken a hand in your election matters, but in the language of Bret Harte,
>> In the game that ensued
>> We did not take a hand
>> But the cards they were strewn
>> Like leaves o'er the sand.
>
> I should really like to tell you some good and original stories, but the silent language of a letter spoils them. Before I left, I heard many of yours, but as you are aware, the "faculty" is confined to the few. Order me, command me, give me an embassy in order that I may be one Hour in Ottawa. No pay *in coin*.[35]

Six years later, in 1878, Macdonald himself was glad to accept a Victoria seat, after his defeat in Kingston.

By that time, the same standard of political ethics prevailed at Ottawa and Victoria. Patronage was expected to be the reward for loyalty, and provincial premiers liked to dispense largesse themselves. As premier, Walkem attempted to obtain control over the appointment of county court judges. To induce Macdonald not to stand in his way, he warned him that "an *opposition* member from this Province: could give you a great deal of annoyance on this & Railway expenditure."[36] Later, when the Liberals were in office at Ottawa and his relations with Mackenzie were far from friendly, Walkem tried in 1874 to obtain legislation giving the provincial government control over the placing of county court judges. It must have given Edward Blake, who had had other experience of Walkem's manoeuvring, considerable pleasure to be able to checkmate him through disallowance.[37]

In the province's early years, both the strength and weakness of democracy were discernible. The secret ballot was introduced, and the franchise was extended to all but Indians and Chinese; but the spoils system existed, and the machinery of government worked slowly. There was inefficiency in government financing, and hints that prominent men were guilty of bribery and corruption. When British Columbia became a discontented province as the result of the slow prosecution of the railway project, negotiations for the settlement of differences were sometimes concluded abruptly, threats of secession were raised, as well as the first faint cries for "better terms." Mainland and Island interests continued to compete in pressing claims for the railway terminus, and learned their first lessons in lobbying. A crowd of hungry would-be politicians and their friends importuned Ottawa for government employment or contracts for railway construction. Political strategy in vogue in Ottawa, had its replica in Victoria.

Only in the failure to introduce party government did British Columbia depart from eastern practice. As Goldwin Smith observed, government appropriations were a more serious thing in British Columbia than party affiliations. Yet in the early seventies before the full implication of the loss of favour of the Conservative party at Ottawa was realized, there was some talk of drawing party lines. In 1873, Walkem told Macdonald that "a very strong *Grit* element has been transplanted from Ont: & taken root here,"[38] and Judge Gray considered de Cosmos "*a Grit in every pulsation of his heart.* McKenzie [sic] or Geo. Brown are no more thoroughly so."[39] After 1873, however, it would have meant political suicide for any leader in British Columbia if he had made open declaration of affiliation with the Liberal party of the east.

While political conformity between province and Dominion developed, cultural ties also grew stronger. By 1872 educational principles and practice in the Province, for example, were drawn in line with those in Ontario. During Douglas's governorship, common schools, supported by the government but charging tuition, had been established on Vancouver Island.[40] Church schools and private schools had also made their appearance. The establishment of a system of free education was largely the work of Dr. Powell, who succeeded in obtaining an act in 1865 for the establishment of common schools on Vancouver Island. The "admirable system of Canada West" was the model for the first free non-sectarian school in Victoria established by John Jessop in 1864.[41] Free education helped to break down class distinctions, and it was no longer necessary to provide separate schooling for what Douglas had termed "laborers' children."

Religious ties also developed between eastern and western communities. From the time of the arrival of the four pioneer Methodist missionaries in 1859, a strong Methodist thread ran through the fabric of early British Columbia history. Methodism, with its emphasis on temperance and honesty in business, was a reforming influence on the frontier, and did much to improve relations between white men and natives. It could be exclusive, as it was at Chilliwack, where at one time land purchase depended on religious conformity.[42] Like Puritanism in the early New England colonies, it did not frown too much on the core of hard materialism to be found in many of the early settlers. New Westminster was the centre of the Methodist following. A city laid out by Royal Engineers, its spiritual as well as its political heritage was Canadian.

Apart from the Methodists, only the Roman Catholics had close affiliations with eastern Canadian centres. Roman Catholic influence was tremendously strong with the Indians as the result of proselytizing activities, and important where there were French and French-Canadian settlers. There were few Irish in the fold, however, for British Columbia's Irish element was chiefly Protestant.

Anglicanism was not too popular in the lower mainland where it was regarded as being the faith of the Englishman; and on the Island its strength was dissipated because of factional feuds.

Interest in the common man was expressed by provincial politicians as well as by federal leaders in the eighties. Most British Columbians at that time would have accepted the measuring-rod adopted by J. B. Kerr later in assessing the worth of pioneer settlers: he "was very successful in his business, making a great deal of money."[43] For most British Columbians, as well as for most Canadians, the man of virtue was the successful farmer or business man. John Robson's early stand on the Oriental question, which is in such contrast to Douglas's liberal attitude when a negro colony on Vancouver Island was being planned, was thought by some, to spring from an interest in the lot of the working man.[44] Robson, however, was just as naive as John A. Macdonald, when it came to comprehension of the theory of class conflict. Scientific socialism was a field in which he could hardly claim to be a specialist. It was not until the industrial capitalist came to British Columbia in the nineties, that the craft union movement, which had started in 1862, marshalled its strength. Revolutionary socialism made its appearance in the early years of the twentieth century, gaining its support from the well-read British workingmen, coal-miners, and smelter-workers, who were the product of an intellectually more mature community than existed for native British Columbia workers.

Canadians who came to British Columbia between 1858 and 1885, were not theorists, but practical men of affairs, who had a deep respect for property and believed in the merit of hard physical work. They fought vigorously for constitutional reform, and expected benefit if it were accomplished; they knew that the maintenance of law and order was in their business interests; they introduced manners and standards of behaviour which they had known in the east; and they followed the social pattern they had known at home. Gradually they inched closer to British society, adopting some of its customs, and some of its outlook. Their enterprise and their energy gave to British Columbia, political, religious, and educational institutions which were Canadian. By the time of the completion of the trans-continental railroad, British Columbia was manifestly Canadian in spirit and custom.

As his last entry in his diary of the Confederation negotiations in 1870, Dr. Helmcken had written: "I am to tell from Sir George Cartier that it is necessary to be Anti-Yankee. That we have to oppose their damned system—that we can and will build up a northern power, which they cannot do with their principles, that the Govt. of Ontario, or rather of the Dominion is determined to do it."[45] Surely it was Dr. Helmcken, and not Cartier, who identified the government of Ontario with the government of the Dominion. As a product of the old colonial environment of Vancouver Island, Dr. Helmcken knew only too well the change that the "Ontario" men had made in government, as well as in the political and social life of British Columbia.

Notes

The number of miners who came from California to the Fraser River mines in 1858 is variously estimated at 20,000, 25,000 and 30,000. Britishers were among those who came, but no contemporary reference is made to Canadians. For information concerning overland expeditions from Canada, see M. S. Wade, *The Overlanders of '62* (Archives of British Columbia, Memoir IX, Victoria, 1931), pp. 2-7.

[2] Resolution of a meeting called by Leonard McClure in Victoria, Sept., 1866, as reported in the *Colonist*, Sept. 29, 1866.

[3] The question of Confederation was debated in the first meeting of the legislature of the united colony and unanimously approved. *Journals of the Legislative Council of British Columbia* (New Westminster, 1867), p. 72.

[4] This request was either mislaid or not sent. Seymour again communicated with the Colonial Office on September 24, 1867. F. W. Howay in his article, "The Attitude of Governor Seymour towards Confederation" (*Transactions of the Royal Society of Canada*, 3rd series, XIV, sec. ii, 1921, pp. 31-51) contends that Seymour was unfriendly to the plan. After a Confederation League was formed in Victoria in May, 1868, branches were set up in New Westminster, Yale, and Lytton. A rally at Yale in September, 1868, has been referred to as "British Columbia's counterpart of the Charlottetown and Quebec Conferences," Walter N. Sage, "Amor

de Cosmos, Journalist and Politician" *British Columbia Historical Quarterly*, VIII, July, 1944, p. 196).

5 S. D. Clark, *The Social Development of Canada* (Toronto, 1942), p. 309.

6 Lisgar wrote to Kimberley on April 27, 1871, that special consideration should be given to the subject of pensions, since "it had been distinctly understood on all sides that it would be very difficult to obtain the assent of British Columbia to the proposed terms of Confederation unless satisfactory assurances were given in reference to the question . . ." (Public Archives of Canada, G 365, no. 96).

7 Williard E. Ireland, "The Annexation Petition of 1869" (*British Columbia Historical Quarterly*, IV, Oct., 1940, p. 281).

8 Sydney G. Pettit, "Dear Sir Matthew: A Glimpse of Judge Begbie" (*British Columbia Historical Quarterly*, XI, Jan., 1947, 14).

9 *Daily Standard* (Victoria), Dec. 1, 1870 .

10 See the articles by F. W. Howay, "Early Shipping in Burrard Inlet, 1863-1870" (*British Columbia Historical Quarterly*, I, Jan., 1937, 3-20); "Early Settlement on Burrard Inlet" (*ibid.*, I, Apr., 1937, 101-14); and "Coal-Mining on Burrard Inlet, 1865-1866" (*ibid.*, IV, Jan., 1940, pp. 1-20); also the article by W. Kaye Lamb, "Early Lumbering on Vancouver Island, Part II, 1855-1866" (*ibid.*, II, Apr., 1938, pp. 95-144).

11 See R. N. Beattie, "Banking in Colonial British Columbia" (M.A. Thesis, Department of History, University of British Columbia, 1939), for a discussion of banking policies during the colonial period.

12 Leonard A. Wrinch, "Land Policy of the Colony of Vancouver Island, 1849-1866" (M.A. Thesis, Department of History, University of British Columbia, 1932, p. 70).

13 F. W. Laing, "Hudson's Bay Lands on the Mainland" ((*British Columbia Historical Quarterly*, III, Apr., 1939, pp. 75-101).

14 De Cosmos held property at Bute Inlet, the route proposed for the railway if the island railway was built as part of the national railway system. Dr. Powell had holdings at Burrard Inlet to which he added after Vancouver was chosen as the terminus of the Canadian Pacific Railway.

15 G. M. Sproat's anthropological work is discussed in T. A. Rickard's article, "Gilbert Malcolm Sproat" (*British Columbia Historical Quarterly*, I, Jan., 1937, pp. 21-32); W. F. Tolmie's interest in botany is mentioned in S. F. Tolmie, "My Father: William Fraser Tolmie: 1812-1886" (*ibid.*, I, Oct., 1937, pp. 225-40). Books written by Britishers describing living conditions in the colonies include the following: R. C. Mayne, *Four Years in British Columbia and Vancouver Island* (London, 1862); D. G. F. Macdonald, *British Columbia and Vancouver Island* (London, 1862); Matthew MacFie, *Vancouver Island and British Columbia* (London, 1865); J. D. Pemberton, *Facts and Figures Relating to Vancouver Island and British Columbia* (London, 1860).

16 Sydney G. Pettit, "Judge Begbie in Action" (*British Columbia Historical Quarterly*, XI, Apr., 1947, p. 132).

17 Beaumont Boggs, "What I Remember of Hon. Amor de Cosmos" (*British Columbia Historical Association, Fourth Report and Proceedings*, 1929, p. 58).

[18] W. N. Sage, "Amor de Cosmos, Journalist and Politician" (*British Columbia Historical Quarterly*, VIII, July, 1944, p. 189).

[19] Pettit, "Judge Begbie in Action," p. 134.

[20] *Daily Standard*, July 19, 1871.

[21] *British Colonist*, July 18, 1871.

[22] *Ibid.*, July 28, 1871.

[23] B. A. McKelvie, "Lieutenant-Colonel Israel Wood Powell, M.D., C.M." (*British Columbia Historical Quarterly*, XI, Jan., 1947, p. 34).

[24] P. A. C., Macdonald Papers, Letter Book 12, 367, Macdonald to Carrall, Jan. 5, 1869.

[25] G 365, Musgrave to Granville, Oct. 30, 1869.

[26] Macdonald Papers, Letter Book 12, 874, Macdonald to Musgrave, May 25, 1869.

[27] *Ibid.*, 972, Macdonald to Sir John Young, May 25, 1869.

[28] *Ibid.* Letter Book 16, pp. 120-f, Macdonald to Carrall, July 31, 1871. Robson at this time was editor of the *Colonist*.

[29] *Ibid.*, General Letters, 1871, 319, Powell to Macdonald, Sept. 8, 1871.

[30] *Ibid.*, Macdonald-Walkem Correspondence, 5-6, Walkem to Macdonald, July 27, 1872.

[31] *Ibid.*, General Letters, 1877, 101, de Cosmos to Macdonald, Apr. 11, 1873.

[32] *Ibid.*, Macdonald-Walkem Correspondence, Walkem to Macdonald Apr. 17, 1873, acknowledging the appointment.

[33] *Ibid.*, Letter Book 19, 770, Macdonald to Trutch, Feb. 13, 1873, "As the Railway is to be built through the intervention of a Company, the Government will have nothing to do directly with the engineering. They will of course appoint an Inspector who will report on the progress of the work, and on whose certificate alone the subsidy in money or land will be granted. I do not suppose that such an appointment would in any way suit your views. I have gathered from you that your ambition is to be charged with the very interesting work of constructing the Railway through British Columbia and the Rocky Mountains. I have no doubt of being able, from my influence, with the Board to secure you this appointment and I have no little doubt that the remuneration will be fixed at a satisfactory rate."

[34] *Ibid.* Macdonald-Trutch Correspondence, 191, Trutch to Macdonald, Aug. 28, 1872.

[35] *Ibid.*, Macdonald-Walkem Correspondence, 13, Walkem to Macdonald, Sept. 14, 1872.

[36] *Ibid.*, 20, Walkem to Macdonald, Dec. 11, 1872.

[37] Provincial Archives of British Columbia, Executive Document 29/75, Copy of a Report of a Committee of the Hon[oura]ble the Privy Council, approved Oct. 16, 1875.

[38] Macdonald Papers, Macdonald-Walkem Correspondence, 25, Walkem to Macdonald, Apr. 17, 1873.

[39] *Ibid.* General Letters, 1873, 60, J. H. Gray to Macdonald, Jan. 27, 1873.

[40] D. L. MacLaurin, "Education before the Gold-Rush" (*British Columbia Historical Quarterly*, II, Oct., 1938, pp. 248-9).

41 George W. Spragge, "An Early Letter from Victoria, V.I." (*Canadian Historical Review*, XXIX, Mar., 1948, p. 55).

42 J. E. Gibbard, "Early History of the Fraser Valley, 1808-1885" (M.A. Thesis, Department of History, University of British Columbia, 1937, p. 244).

43 J. B. Kerr, *Biographical Dictionary of Well-Known British Columbians* (Vancouver, 1890).

44 Adam Shortt and Arthur G. Doughty, *Canada and Its Provinces* (Toronto, 1914), XXI, p. 253.

45 Willard E. Ireland, "Helmcken's Diary of the Confederation Negotiations, 1870" (*British Columbia Historical Quarterly*, IV, Apr., 1940, p. 128).

11. British Columbia's American Heritage
Willard E. Ireland

WILLARD E. IRELAND. *recently retired after a 34-year career as British Columbia provincial archivist, also served most of that time as provincial librarian. His stress on the contribution of the United States, especially of California, to colonial British Columbia was in its day a new emphasis. For a view of the British Columbia-California connection in a later period, see the Ralston article.*

One of the most interesting anomalies in the history of British Columbia arises from the fact that the strongest single impellant in the creation of what eventually became Canada's Pacific province was the fear of American expansionist tendencies west of the Rocky Mountains and yet that tendency, although established in fact by population movements, never seriously transferred itself into the arena of practical politics.

The role of American expansionism in the evolution of the physical boundaries of British Columbia is relatively easy to demonstrate. When the boundary line between British and American territory in the Pacific Northwest was defined by treaty in June, 1846, north of the forty-ninth parallel there was no organized British settlement, only a few widely dispersed parts of the fur-trading monopoly—the Hudson's Bay Company. That the Colonial Office was fully cognizant of the serious implications of this situation is demonstrated by a *minute* written by the colonial secretary, Lord Grey, on September 10, 1846. "Looking to the encroaching spirit of the U.S. I think it is of importance to strengthen the B[ritis]h hold upon the territory now assigned to us by encouraging the settlement upon it of B[ritis]h subjects. . . . "[1] Moreover, His Lordship was convinced that any colonization scheme could only be carried out effectively by the Hudson's Bay Company and, in consequence, despite tremendous opposition from "colonial reformers" and "Little Englanders" alike, the Crown Colony of Vancouver Island came into being under the terms of the royal grant of January 13, 1849. The subsequent history of the Company's trusteeship is not pertinent to this discussion, but the threat of American expansion, whether real or imagined, had resulted in more concrete efforts to safeguard British sovereignty.

Source: The Canadian Historical Association Annual Report (1948) pp. 67-73. Reprinted by permission of the author and publisher.

Nor was this activity long to remain confined merely to Vancouver Island, for shortly thereafter rumours of gold discoveries in the Queen Charlotte archipelago aroused the interest of American adventurers who laid plans to investigate the new finds. Governor Douglas was convinced that if their gold seeking should prove successful, American colonization would follow and that they would seek "to establish an independent government until by force or fraud they became annexed to the United States."[2] While, in reality, his fears proved to be unfounded, nevertheless, they carried sufficient weight with the Colonial Office to result in his appointment as lieutenant-governor of Queen Charlotte Islands, thus bringing the region within the orbit of a regularly constituted colonial jurisdiction.

The Queen Charlotte Islands incident at least gave some forewarning of situations that were to develop when the great rush to the Fraser River developed in the spring and summer of 1858. It is not necessary here to detail the origin and progress of that rush, the effects of which were almost as serious and perturbing for San Francisco as for Victoria. According to the San Francisco *Alta California* of June 5, 1858, "throughout the entire length and breadth of the State the 'Frazer river fever' " had seized the people and threatened "to break up, or at least seriously disarrange for the time being the entire mining business of the State."[3] Victoria itself was completely transformed and became, in effect, San Francisco in miniature. Of the thousands of persons joining the exodus from California, many had no inclination to embark on the hazards of mining on the bars of the Fraser. Artisans, clerks, professional and business men—in fact a representative cross section of society— joined in the rush and many hoped to pursue in Victoria their customary occupation. Merchants moved in "lock, stock and barrel." Indeed the old iron storefronts still to be seen on Wharf Street in Victoria bear mute testimony to the completeness of the transfer.

Needless to say numerous indications of the so-called Americanization of Victoria could be cited but only a few will be mentioned in passing. On June 25, 1858, the first issue of the *Victoria Gazette* made its appearance. This newspaper, the first to be published in British territory west of the Great Lakes, was owned by James Towne and Company of San Francisco and edited by H. C. Williston and C. Bartlett, prominent San Franciscan newspaper men. It was an excellent publication and not until the establishment of the *British Colonist* in December, 1858, by the former Nova Scotian, Amor de Cosmos, did it encounter any real competition and even this did not in any way impair its popularity. The sudden demise of this newspaper in November, 1859, is significant to this discussion.

Despite the heavy preponderance of the newer elements in the population of Victoria in dealing with local political issues, this newspaper, though not averse to criticism of Governor Douglas, had, on the whole, maintained a scrupulously neutral position. Its collapse was swift and complete when it abandoned that policy and began to express what might be called the American point of view. Apparently in Victoria at this time American sentiment was neither sufficiently strong nor interested to sustain a well-established mouth-piece. Throughout the gold-rush period, however, it is important to remember that although the original British population was submerged by the great immigration of 1858, the administration of the government continued to remain firmly in the control of pre-gold-rush British officials.

It is perfectly true that key American public holidays were usually celebrated with as complete gusto in Victoria as in communities down the Sound but British holidays were also commemorated with equal fervour by all elements of the community. The establishment and development of the fire companies in Victoria is perhaps one of the best illustrations of the imprinting of the American pattern upon a British base. Governor Douglas had planned a fire brigade acting under the jurisdiction of the police, but public sentiment swept this aside and brought into being independent volunteer brigades, manned more often than not by men with long experience in the fire companies of San Francisco and using equipment procured from that city. So firmly entrenched did this system become that in 1879 when the city contemplated taking over the companies they refused to consider such a transfer of their equipment and it was not until 1886 that a civic-paid fire department came into existence.[4]

Still another indication of the infiltration of American sentiment into the structure of colonial life is to be found in the history of the Masonic order. The first lodges were organized under warrant of the Grand Lodge of England but the work practised by these lodges was unfamiliar to the many Masons arriving in the colony. In consequence an agitation arose for the organization of a lodge using American work and a dispensation from the Grand Lodge of Washington was sought. This plan was abandoned and in the end warrants were secured under the Grand Lodge of Scotland the work of which was more similar to that of American lodges. Indeed by 1871 there were five lodges operating under the Scottish and only four under the English constitution.[5]

In the main such examples of Americanization are probably more obvious and superficial than significant. There is one aspect of the gold-rush, however, that is all too frequently ignored. It is true that Governor Douglas was overwhelmed by the rush of newcomers and wrote to the Colonial Office in May, 1858:

> ... if the country be thrown open to indiscriminate immigration the interests of the Empire may suffer from the introduction of a foreign population, whose sympathies may be decidedly anti-British.
>
> Taking that view of the question it assumes an alarming aspect, and suggests a doubt as to the policy of permitting the free entrance of foreigners into the British territory for residence without in the first place requiring them to take the oath of allegiance and otherwise to give such security for their conduct as the Government of the country may deem it proper and necessary to require at their hands.[6]

But in that same despatch Douglas took some pains to analyse the passenger list of the American steamer *Commodore* which had arrived on April 25 with 450 on board, 400 of whom went to the gold fields. Douglas reported: "About 60 British subjects, with an equal number of native born Americans, the rest being chiefly Germans, with a smaller proportion of Frenchmen and Italians, composed this body of adventurers."[7] Whether or not this particular group can be considered representative of the whole gold-rush immigration, it is impossible to say, but at least it gives some foundation to the contention that the British element in the population of the colony was strengthened at least to a degree by the rush. In addition many individual cases could be cited of British subjects having followed the lure of gold through California and Australia only to seek and find permanent residence in British Columbia and Vancouver Island.

In addition it is obvious that Douglas realized the essential difference between previous population pressure from the south and that resulting from the gold-rush. He had witnessed at first hand the flood of immigration that burst through the Rocky Mountains in the early eighteen-forties to populate Old Oregon and put an end to the monopoly of the Hudson's Bay Company. This immigration was composed mainly of families whose roots ran deep into the soil of American civilization as found on the Atlantic Seaboard. It was but a part of the amazing westward advance of the agricultural frontier which was at once dangerous because of its tremendous driving power and its deep-rooted appreciation of the pattern of American life. In 1858, however, Douglas realized that the gold-rush was not a repetition, and consequently he took care to differentiate between "native born Americans" and that complex mass that seems inevitably to form the population of a gold camp. No longer does he stress the fear of a pro-American sentiment but rather of the "anti-British."

Up to this point attention has been concentrated mainly on conditions in Victoria, but what of the situation on the mainland where the gold fields were located. If there has been a "critical period" in the history of British Columbia it surely must have been during the greater part of 1858 when large numbers of foreign miners and others were located on the bars of the Fraser River at a time when no legally constituted authority existed on the mainland. The original regulatory "proclamation" issued by Governor Douglas had, in effect, no validity for his commission as Governor did not run on the mainland. How then did it come to pass that the mob violence which disgraced the California gold regions finds no repetition in British territory although often even the same personnel were present?

For one thing mining on the bars of the Fraser was a more hazardous undertaking and the delay involved in waiting for the high water to recede discouraged many of the "hangers on" who never did reach the gold fields. It is true that in American newspapers "Manifest Destiny" propaganda was rampant. The sentiment expressed in the following jingle printed in the Washington *Pioneer and Democrat* is typical.

Up above, among the mountains,
Men have found the golden fountains;
Seen where they flow! Oh joy transcendent!
Down, down, in noiseless stream transplendent,
    Then, hurrah, and set your riggings—
    Sail above, to richer diggings.

When news gets where Buch and Cass is,
Johnny Bull can go where grass is,—
He may rave and rant to foaming,
It will never stop our coming.
    Then, hurrah, nor wait for papers,
    The license men may cut their capers.

Soon our banner will be streaming,
Soon the eagle will be screaming,
And the lion—see it cowers,
Hurrah, bosy, the river's ours.
    Then, hurrah, nor wait for calling,
    For the Frazer's river's falling.[8]

But in the mines the situation was different. It was generally recognized that the regulations laid down by Douglas were restrictive but not discriminatory. There was no foreign licence fee such as had been required in California. Everyone came under the same licensing system and in consequence the many foreigners involved in the rush soon came to realize in practice the meaning of fair play, and as a result there was less unrest and agitation. Likewise, Douglas never allowed a situation to get out of hand, nor did he allow the law to be overridden. This is possibly best indicated in his method of dealing with the attempt of local groups of miners to set up their own regulations sometimes in conflict with the general law. Douglas was willing to compromise within certain limits, as for example by increasing the size of claims. Moreover, he recognized the latent desire and ability for some local government in his creation of local mining boards under a gold commissioner but he firmly insisted that their activities be confined to improving conditions in the gold fields and not maintaining law and order. Once constitutional authority was established in November, 1858, and with the advent of a judge like Matthew Baillie Begbie, all elements in the population came to have a healthy respect for British justice and realized that there was no necessity for the "six shooter," the bowie knife, the vigilantes, or the posse in British Columbia.

With the decline of the gold excitement and the accompanying trade depression there was naturally much heart searching as to the future prospects of the colonies. Consolidation might be carried out; but would a united colony of British Columbia be in any relatively stronger condition? Subsequent history of the union did not engender much optimism. Canadian Confederation was being consummated in the East. What was the prospect of British Columbia's participation therein? Was annexation to the United States either feasible or desirable? Much has been written on the annexation movement in British Columbia and in the main its significance has been overplayed.[9] It was primarily an expression of economic discontent and in that respect merits much the same interpretation as the parallel agitation in Montreal twenty years earlier. Within the colony it had a very precarious base for the leaders were for the most part not Americans but foreign born, and it was confined almost entirely to Victoria for there is no evidence of a parallel movement on the mainland nor even elsewhere on the island.

Annexation was from the beginning a forlorn hope. The British government had endorsed the federation plan and was astute enough to recognize that an annexation movement had high propaganda value as a means of plundering the imperial treasury. Canada was willing, if not able, to see Confederation extended, and within the colony there was a considerable and active group supporting Confederation, although admittedly from a variety of motives. The

Victoria *British Colonist* summed up the situation tersely, as follows: "Knowing, as we do, that annexation is impossible, even if it were desirable, and that Confederation is inevitable, even if it were undesirable would not all of us be more profitably employed in seeking to secure the best possible terms for the Colony as a province of the Dominion."[10] It is curious that despite the large American and foreign element in the population of British Columbia in the late sixties and seventies, politically it was neither active nor vocal. In consequence there has been no political heritage. Even events such as the purchase of Alaska and the Alabama claims failed to arouse any great attention in the colony. The only newspaper to advocate annexation was short-lived.[11] There was no semblance of a party or group nor any leadership, which was certainly not the case for the supporters of Confederation or its opponents. Few, if any, references to annexation are to be found in the Confederation debate of 1870. Anti-confederation sentiment there was in abundance, but annexation was never the alternative. J. S. Helmcken forthrightly stated the province's case:

> The sum of the interests of the inhabitants is the interest of the Colony. The people of this Colony have, generally speaking, no love for Canada; they care, as a rule, little or nothing about the creation of another Empire, Kingdom, or Republic; they have but little sentimentality, and care little about the distinction between the form of Government of Canada and the United States.
>
> Therefore no union on account of love need be looked for. The only bond of union outside of force—and force the Dominion has not—will be material advantage of the country and the pecuniary benefit of the inhabitants. Love for Canada has to be acquired by the prosperity of the country, and from our children.[12]

Confederation was a question of terms, and the price Canada was prepared to pay was acceptable to the people of British Columbia. The fulfilment of the terms of union proved to be another story. On many occasions preceding the completion of the Canadian Pacific Railway the situation was often difficult and occasionally critical. But as a further indication of the absence of American political sentiment, in the numerous arguments and resolutions regarding fulfilment of the terms of union the right of secession was often discussed and once formally requested, but, as in colonial days, annexation was never put forward as the alternative. Newspapers in the United States might frequently misinterpret this state of affairs and indeed the imminent annexation of British Columbia was as widely heralded in 1883[13] as it had been in 1869. But the true state of affairs was summed up editorially by the Victoria *Colonist*:

> For many years, at stated periods, and generally during the tourist season, when the town is filled with strangers, principally citizens of the United States, the residents of Victoria have been met with the enquiry, "Is there any desire for annexation in this province?" Nine men out of every ten thus addressed, if they spoke the truth, have answered, "Scarcely any." The large majority of the people are not satisfied with Canadian rule. They feel that they have been treated badly; but however disaffected they may be towards the Dominion they would not consent to sever the connection with Great Britain.[14]

Indeed on this particular occasion annexation sentiment may be said to have swung full circle. The premier, Mr. William Smithe, availed himself of the opportunity presented by an after-luncheon speech to the journalists touring with the Villard Northern Pacific Railway party, not only to deny flatly the existence within the province of annexationist sentiment but went on to suggest that the United States might not long remain united and that part of the State of Washington might become annexed to British Columbia.[15]

Of the three main strands in British Columbia's heritage—British, Canadian, and American—the American has been politically the least vocal and significant and yet perhaps in other ways it has left its impression.[16]

Notes

[1] Public Record Office, C. O. 305, vol. 1, Minute, Sept. 10, 1846, on Pelly to Grey, Sept. 7, 1846.

[2] C. O. 305, vol. 3, Douglas to Grey, Jan. 29, 1852, printed in *Parliamentary Papers, House of Commons*, 788 of 1853, 2.

[3] San Francisco *Alta California*, June 5, 1858.

[4] For details see F. W. Laing and W. Kaye Lamb, "The Fire Companies of Old Victoria," *British Columbia Historical Quarterly*, x (1946), pp. 43-75.

[5] For details see Willard E. Ireland, "A Further Note on the Annexation Petition of 1869," *British Columbia Historical Quarterly*, v (1941), pp. 69-72.

[6] Douglas to Labouchere, May 8, 1858, MS, Archives of British Columbia, printed in cmd 2398, *Correspondence Relative to the Discovery of Gold in the Fraser's River District in British North America* (London, 1858), p. 13.

[7] *Ibid.*

[8] Olympia *Pioneer and Democrat*, Nov. 5, 1858.

[9] On this point see W. N. Sage, "The Annexationist Movement in British Columbia" *Transactions of the Royal Society of Canada*, 3rd series, xxi, sec. ii, 1927, pp. 97-110; Hugh L. Keenleyside, "British Columbia—Annex-

ation or Confederation," *Canadian Historical Association Report* (1928), pp. 34-40; and Willard E. Ireland, "The Annexation Petition of 1869," *British Columbia Historical Quarterly*, IV (1949), pp. 267-87.

[10] *British Colonist*, Nov. 20, 1869.

[11] This was the Victoria *Evening News* which suspended publication in June, 1870 after a precarious existence of fourteen months.

[12] British Columbia, Legislative Council, *Debate on the Subject of Confederation with Canada* (Victoria, 1870), p. 5 (March 9, 1870).

[13] As, for example, the dispatch of August 14, 1883 of a correspondent of the Chicago *Tribune* reprinted in the Victoria *Colonist*, Aug. 29, 1883. See also New Westminster *Mainland Guardian*, Sept. 12, 1883.

[14] *British Colonist*, Sept. 25, 1883.

[15] *Ibid.*, Sept. 25, 1883, Oct. 10, 1883.

For the reaction of various American newspapers to this proposal see *Victoria Standard*, Oct. 1, 3, 8, 10, 1883.

[16] The standard history of British Columbia is E. O. S. Scholefield and F. W. Howay, *British Columbia* (4 vols., Vancouver, 1914). The more recent study, dealing more specifically with American inter-relations, is F. W. Howay, W. N. Sage and H. F. Angus, *British Columbia and the United States* (Toronto and New Haven, 1942).

12. A Colonial Administration: An Analysis of Administration in British Columbia, 1869-1871
Isabel Bescoby

ISABEL BESCOBY *(1913-1969) was the holder of Bachelor's and Master's degrees in history from the University of British Columbia and had a long career in the federal public service. Her lengthy article, here abridged, provides a detailed summary of events leading to British Columbia's entry into Confederation and a close analysis of the various interests involved.*

...Seven days after Governor Frederick Seymour's death at Bella Coola on 10 June, 1869, the Secretary of State for the Colonies, Earl Granville, communicated to Anthony Musgrave, Governor of Newfoundland, his appointment as Governor of British Columbia. On the same day, the residents of British Columbia were informed of the appointment through their newspapers. Granville requested Musgrave to leave for Victoria at the earliest convenient moment. "The state of British Columbia is such as to make the presence of the governor very necessary." Musgrave's special "Commission" and instructions under the royal sign manual were not completed until October 16, 1869. Yet, in the first direct communication to him on June 17, Granville wrote:

> Among the questions which will immediately press on your attention is that of the incorporation of British Columbia with the Dominion of Canada. On this subject I shall probably have occasion to address you shortly. Meanwhile I think it prudent to inform you that although H. M. government would wish you to use no expressions which would indicate intension on their part to over-rule the wishes of the community, yet they attach importance to the early adhesion of British Columbia to the North American confederation, and would wish your language and policy to be such as are likely to conduce to that end.

Source: Abridged from *Canadian Public Administration*, X (1967), pp. 48-104. Reprinted by permission of the author and publisher.

Musgrave arrived in Victoria on August 23. On August 14, from Downing Street, Granville wrote at length to Musgrave on the subject of the "incorporation of British Columbia with the Dominion of Canada." The Secretary explained the earlier negative attitude of the British government, the changed situation, the continuing obstacle to confederation, the close connection between British Columbia and the British government, and the unusual personal responsibilities of the Governor of British Columbia.

Granville left no doubt regarding Musgrave's special task in British Columbia and the British Government's appreciation of the forces to be handled in accomplishing it:

> The question therefore presents itself whether this Single Colony should be excluded from the great body politic which is thus forming itself.
>
> On this question the Colony itself does not appear to be unanimous. But as far as I can judge ... I should conjecture that the prevailing opinion was in favour of Union. I have no hesitation in stating that such is also the opinion of Her Majesty's Government. ... You will therefore give publicity to this despatch ... and you will hold yourself authorized, ... to take such steps as you properly and constitutionally can, for promotion of the favourable consideration of this question. ...

In fulfilling the normal continuing tasks of a Governor of a British colony, Musgrave received from the Colonial Office no particular advice or instruction other than his Commission, dated October 16, 1869, gazetted November 8. It pertained principally to his relations with his Executive Council. He could presume, therefore, that he was to manage the administrative machine so that (a) the colony was safe from external attack (Russian, American, Fenian), (b) the financial debt caused no serious embarrassment to the British government, the investors in colonial enterprises, or the colonists, (c) the native Indians remained tranquil, (d) the colonists did not become aggressively hostile to British administration, (e) the Colonial Office stature in relation to other departments was not diminished, and (f) the administrative staff met his requirements and did not antagonize the population.

On procedural matters, Musgrave was left to rely either upon colonial files and officials' memories to discover instruction and precedent or upon his own memory of practice in other colonies. This led to awkwardness. For example on December 8, 1869, Musgrave explained to Granville the comments in the Executive Council minutes relative to the cases of three Indians convicted of murder. The first Indian, George, was to be executed; because of questionable evidence from the accuser, the only witness, the sentence of the second was commuted and the accused granted a reprieve; the third, a young boy, was accused of attempted murder of a white man and Musgrave, on Judge Begbie's advice, had commuted his sentence to life imprisonment. Musgrave then explained that he was not sure whether or not to report such cases. He thought he remembered in other colonies that no report was required. "British Columbia seems always to have made one." So he decided to follow British Columbia precedent and send one "until otherwise instructed." The Colonial Office later instructed Musgrave that a report to London was always required in a case of capital murder.

What of the expectations of the colonists whose affairs he administered? In general, they were men of superior education, mental and physical strength, and determination. They sought circumstances in which to improve their economic and social positions and to advance the colony as a progressive community—roads and public services, educational, health, and recreational facilities. They realized that these goals could be achieved only with capital, population, and economical and businesslike public administration. One expression of the public expectation of government appeared in the *Colonist* newspaper, Victoria, January 10, 1871:

> ... [T]he main source of criticism of the 1871 Estimates seems to be no funds set aside for immigration and none for education ... [T]here is the old disagreeable fact ... that far too large a portion of the revenue is still swallowed up in the expense of administering the affairs of the country, leaving, comparatively speaking, a trifle to be expended upon reproductive or necessary public works. . . .

There was no popular agreement for or against self-government, for or against confederation or annexation or continued colonial status. But there was agreement on the need for economic and social progress and on willingness to pay the price as long as public funds were efficiently administered.

As for the officials, clerks, and other public servants whom he was to command, they expected responsible leadership from Musgrave, as well as gentlemanly relations according to the rules of the civil service, sufficient reward for willing followership, fair representation to their administrative superiors of subordinates' problems, protection from public abuse, if any, and freedom from emotional, political, or other pressure.

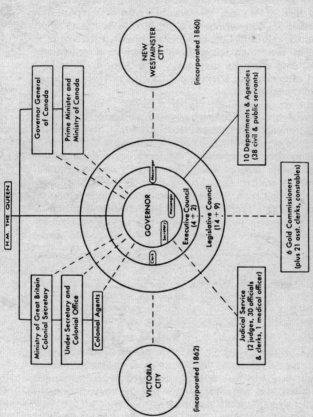

Figure 1. Government of British Columbia, 1870.

Finally, Musgrave did have to meet an obligation to the Prime Minister of Canada, to steer British Columbia into the Canadian orbit with all haste and at only reasonable cost to Canada.

Did or could Musgrave meet reasonably well the conflicting and overlapping expectations of these four parties "interested" in his Governorship? Already he had experienced some success in fulfilling the special task assigned by the Secretary of State, some failure in satisfying the demands of British Columbians and public servants. A closer look at his operations and techniques will reveal the specific strengths and weaknesses of his administration.

The Machine

The vehicle for colonial government comprised five parts: the British connection, the office of Governor, the British Columbia public service composed of the appointed officers and support staff engaged in executive, legislative, judicial, and administrative duties, the non-official legislative and executive officers, and the public. (See Fig. 1)

During the Gladstone ministry (December 1868-February 1874), the Queen was advised regarding colonial affairs by her Secretary of State (Lord Granville, December 1868-July 1870; Lord Kimberley, July, 1870-February 1874), who in turn was served by a permanent Under Secretary (Sir F. Rogers, May 1860-May 1871; Sir R. G. W. Herbert, May 1871-February 1892), two undersecretaries, and, by 1871, a substaff of fifty. Relative to other departments the prestige of the Colonial Office was low in the Cabinet, in Parliament, and in public opinion. It was continuously attacked for ignorance of colonial conditions and incompetence. The small staff dealt with matters of policy, operations, and personnel. It did in fact tend to process Governors' communications "as soon as the mails came in," to use telegraphic services effectively, and to approve everything except actions in conflict with British statutes or regulations. Faulty drafting was not used as a reason to veto a colonial act. All colonial legislation was subject to disallowance by the Crown, i.e., in practice, by the Colonial Office, but the authority was seldom used.

Attached to the Colonial Office were Crown Agents who conducted in Britain, for fees, the financial and commercial business of the colonies. The Agents raised loans, paid the interest thereon, managed the sinking fund for redemption of loans, supervised repayment of loans, made contracts for public works, paid the

salaries of officers home on leave, made steamship reservations, et-
cetera.

As part of the British connection, the colony's meagre but
adequate defence establishment must be mentioned. By the time
Musgrave arrived, the only immediately available defence force in
British Columbia was the shore base and ships of the British
Navy at Esquimalt, near Victoria. Ships of the Royal Navy had
been stationed regularly in Esquimalt harbour as early as 1846.
The Navy had surveyed the harbours, helped the Governors with
police duties in relation to native Indians, been a supply base for
the British Pacific Squadron during the Crimean War, and
assisted Governor Seymour substantially during Fenian scares. In
1865, Esquimalt became the Navy's North Pacific base.

On the mainland, 165 Royal Engineers had surveyed land and
townsites, built roads, designed buildings, escorted early gold
shipments. The force had been withdrawn in 1863, practically all
the non-commissioned officers and sappers taking their discharges
in British Columbia. Detachments of British and American
troops jointly occupied San Juan Island in the Gulf of Georgia
and fraternized there. They were charged with specific occupation
duties while the claims to right of possession were being arbi-
trated. The three volunteer rifle and artillery companies in the
colony were inactive. Since 1867 they had received no financial
support. The aim of the British government had been for British
Columbia to be self-supporting in military as well as financial
matters. The plan had not materialized, principally because of the
relatively large Indian population. So, for armed defence, ceremo-
nials, and extraordinary police duties, Musgrave was entirely
dependent upon the Royal Navy.

The total cost of Vancouver Island and British Columbia to the
British treasury in 1867-68 had been £1295, for naval charges
and miscellaneous aids. At no time, as appears from a report
tabled in the British House of Commons on February 24, 1870,
did the British treasury pay for Vancouver Island or British
Columbia the following expenditures which in other colonies were
charged to Great Britain: salaries of governors, justices, secretar-
ies, clerks, police; charges for pensions, jails, prisoners, hospitals,
public works, survey equipment, medical and surgical services,
schools and education, Indian administration, ecclesiastical costs,
steamers.

The British government and the Colonial Office in 1869 were
entirely favourable to the union of the remaining British Colonies
in North America. As to British Columbia's joining the new Canadian federation, Lord Granville explained to Musgrave the view of

members of Her Majesty's government as follows on August 14, 1869:

> They believe that a Legislature selected from an extended area and representing a diversity of interests is likely to deal more comprehensively with large questions, more impartially with small questions and more conclusively with both than is possible when controversies are carried on and decided upon in the comparatively narrow circle in which they arise, questions of purely local interest will be more carefully and dispassionately considered when disengaged from the larger politics of the Country, and at the same time will be more sagaciously considered by persons who have had this larger political education.
>
> Finally they anticipate that the interest of every province of British North America will be more advanced by enabling the wealth, credit and intelligence of the whole to be brought to bear on every part, than by encouraging each in the contrasted policy of taking care of itself, possibly at the expense of its neighbour. Most especially is this true in the case of internal transit. It is evident that the establishment of a British line of communication between the Atlantic and Pacific Oceans, is far more feasible by the operation of a single Government . . . than by a bargain negotiated between separate . . . Governments and Legislatures. The San Francisco of British North America [Victoria] would under these circumstances hold a greater commercial and political position than would be attainable by the Capital of the isolated Colony of British Columbia. . . .
>
> The constitutional connection of Her Majesty's Government with the colony of British Columbia is as yet, closer than with any other part of North America. . . .

This statement was an all-important influence upon Musgrave while he dealt with the conflicting pressures in British Columbia.

Once settled in the colony, Musgrave, like every other British Columbia colonial Governor, found himself with virtually absolute and exclusive responsibility for the administration of government. He did have a nominated Executive Council selected from the senior administrative officers, a council which he consulted at his own discretion. Normally, by 1869, a governor was required to seek, for money bills, the approval of an elective and representative Legislative Assembly but, as we have seen, British Columbia had no Legislative Assembly before confederation. She had a Legislative Council, or senate or upper house but, until the final election before confederation, this council did not have a majority of elected members. Of the position of Governor of

British Columbia, Governor Frederick Seymour had written on May 9, 1868, to the Duke of Buckingham:

> The present system of government . . . imposes in a colony like this enormous responsibility on the Governor not alone as a legislator but he stands so entirely removed by his extraordinary powers from the public officers that that he has occasionally . . . to appear in the character of an armed volunteer and in others . . . to assume the duties belonging to a constable for the maintenance of public peace. . . .

His term as Governor of Newfoundland almost expired, Anthony Musgrave had chosen to go to British Columbia where he would assume virtually absolute powers. During his unsuccessful effort to bring Newfoundland into Canadian federation, he had become acquainted with Sir John A. Macdonald. So, when it became known that Seymour intended to take extended sick leave, Musgrave applied to the Colonial Office Secretary for the British Columbia post. At the same time, May 12, 1869, he wrote confidentially to Macdonald, " . . . [I]t is my ambition to be allowed to pilot in British Columbia. . . . At all events, *between ourselves*, I have asked for it. . . . " Macdonald proceeded to recommend Musgrave to Granville and to inform Musgrave that his appointment to the new post "would be highly satisfactory to the Government of the Dominion. . . . " On the day of Seymour's death, June 10, Musgrave protested to Macdonald that the May 12 letter had not been intended as a hint, that it would not do for the Colonial Office to think that Musgrave asked Macdonald for a recommendation but that he did thank Macdonald for offering to send one.

When appointed, Musgrave was a handsome widower. He was gentlemanly, though less so than his predecessor. Musgrave could be indelicate, Seymour never. Musgrave had been born in Antigua in 1828 of English parents. He had studied at the Inner Temple to be a lawyer. Almost his entire career had been spent in the colonial service as colonial secretary, administrator, lieutenant governor, and governor in Antigua, Nevis, St. Vincent, and Newfoundland. He was well oriented in civil service clerical methods and personnel regulations. As Governor, he personally respected the bureaucratic rituals of acknowledging, reporting on schedule, providing copies as required or to offer courtesy and seek attention, applying for leave in advance, following instructions even when they were personally very inconvenient. He had more than average ambition for a successful career in the colonial service. So he observed public service rules flawlessly before, during, and after each appointment. He believed that the machinery of government existed to benefit the governor. Subsequent to his British Columbia service, he received promotions in South Africa, South Australia, Jamaica, and Queensland. He was knighted while Governor of South Australia.

The members of the Executive Council which Musgrave inherited from Seymour were English permanent officials: H. P. P. Crease, Attorney General (1864-1870), J. W. Trutch, Chief Commissioner of Lands and Works (1864-1871), W. Hamley, Collector of Customs (1864-1871), P. J. Hankin, Colonial Secretary (1869-1871). The first three were a closely knit pioneer group the first a lawyer, the second an engineer, the third an enforcement and financial specialist. Hankin, formerly Royal Navy, was a social outcast whose appointment had caused local consternation early in 1869. On January 1, 1870, under authority sought by and accorded to Seymour when he was Governor, Musgrave added two unofficial members to the Executive Council: J. S. Helmcken, another British pioneer, the Hudson's Bay Company medical doctor who remained one of the most influential citizens of Victoria, and R. W. W. Carrall, a Canadian medical doctor from Barkerville, Cariboo. Dr. Helmcken and Dr. Carrall were elected members of the Legislative Council. The Queen approved the appointemnts on March 7, 1870. By his Commission, Musgrave was to consult his Executive Council in all matters

> excepting always in cases which may be of such a nature that in your judgment our service would sustain material prejudice by consulting our Council; or if the matters to be decided are too unimportant ... or too urgent ... provided that in all such urgent cases you do ... communicate to the said Council the measures you may so have adopted and the reasons thereof. ...

The Commission then instructed the Governor to report to the Colonial Office all his actions in opposition to the advice of the members of the Council:

> ... We do further direct and appoint that no question shall be brought before our said Executive Council for their advice or decision excepting only such questions as may be proposed by you for that purpose, providing nevertheless that if any member shall by application in writing request you so to propose any question, it shall be competent to any such member to record upon the said minutes of the said Council such written application together with the answer returned by you to the same.

The Legislative Council of 1868-69 met with five officials, eight magistrates, and eight representatives elected by open vote of all males including Chinese pursuant to an Order-in-Council of June 11, 1863. This Order was revoked on the advice of Musgrave and a new Order on August 9, 1870, constituted a "Legislative Council for the Colony of British Columbia." By it, the Council was to consist of fifteen members, nine elective and six non-elective. The non-elective members were to be named by the Governor and confirmed by warrant under the Royal Seal. The elective members were to be chosen by open voting in the eight existing electoral districts, with two members allowed for Victoria City. Every male of 21 years, able to read English, was "qualified to vote and to be elected unless convicted. . . ."The Governor was empowered to make proclamations regarding qualifications of electors, electoral districts, and the conduct of elections. He could by proclamation prorogue or dissolve the Legislative Council "when he shall think fit but in the absence of such dissolution the elected members of the said council shall hold their seats for four years. . . ." The Order then outlined a procedure for council meetings patterned on the British upper house. Finally:

21. Council shall not pass nor shall the governor assent to any bill appropriating any part of the public revenue for any purpose which has not first been recommended to the Council by the Governor during the session in which such bill was proposed and in fact the said revenue shall not be issued except in pursuance of warrant under the hand of the Governor.

22. The Governor may transmit by message to the Council a draft of any laws which may seem desirable by him to introduce and all such drafts shall be taken into consideration by the Council in such convenient manner as shall be by the rules and orders provided for that purpose.

23. Whenever any bill shall be presented to the Governor for his assent thereto he may return the same by message for consideration by the Council with such amendments as he may think fitting.

24. No bill . . . to take effect until the Governor has assented to same. . . .

25. Her Majesty by Order-in-Council may disallow any law passed by the said Governor-in-Council at any time within two years after such law shall have been received by the secretary of state and every law so disallowed shall become null and void as soon as the disallowance is published in the colony by the Governor. . . .

The entire administrative service of British Columbia in 1869 was reduced to (1) the Governor's staff and the Council staff, (2) ten departments and agencies, namely the Colonial Secretary with three clerks and one messenger, the Printing Branch with a superintendent and three printers, the Treasurer with three clerks and one messenger, the Assay and Refining Office with one assayer and one melter, the Auditor General with two clerks, the Commissioner of Lands and Works with four clerks and one messenger, the Collector of Customs with nine officers besides clerks, boatmen and pilots, the Postmaster with two officers and one clerk, the Registrars General (one each for Vancouver Island and for British Columbia) and a Harbour Master, (3) six Gold Commissioners with twenty-one clerks and constables, (4) two Chief Justices to whom were assigned four clerks and a messenger, (5) the Attorney General with one clerk, (6) the High Sheriff, and (7) the Police and Gaol Attendants (twenty-three officers, wardens, constables, guards, a cook, and a medical officer). Officers and clerks had passed British civil service competitive examinations in England and had the usual academic and social qualifications. Salaries ranged from $250 annually for a messenger, to $800 for a department head, to $4000 ($3000 plus $1000 travelling) for the Governor, a reduction of $1000 from Seymour's $500 annually. All were under strict rules to preserve integrity. Hours of work were somewhat casual. Vacation leave at half salary was granted at the rate of two months a year plus six months after ten years. The Colonial Office provided or attempted to have provided from colonial funds generous pensions amounting to two-thirds the annual salary plus a retiring grant of one month's salary for each year of service, given after ten years' service. It may be noted that no opportunity to win support by patronage was available to the Governor of British Columbia.

Except for the Gold Commissioners, the administrative duties of the various officers and clerks were established by British colonial tradition. Special tasks were assigned by the Governor. The assignments caused no jealousy or bickering. Work was done in a leisurely fashion. During the recession of Seymour's time, as separations occurred, jobs were combined or remained vacant. There was no Treasurer and no Postmaster-General, for instance, when Musgrave assumed office. There were still two Chief Justices in 1869, one on Vancouver Island and one on the mainland, administering justice under two different sets of laws.

At the local level, the Gold Commissioners administered the entire area of the mainland, other than the incorporated city of New Westminister. It has been said that Douglas became aware of their usefulness from studying the record of administration in the New Zealand and Australian mining fields. For the posts, he selected Anglo-Irish gentlemen, a confident and colourful group. In a report to Lord Lisgar, Governor-General of Canada, on November 22, 1870, Musgrave describes their duties thus:

> These magistrates are not only Justices of the Peace, but County Court Judges, Indian agents, Assistant Commissioners of Lands and Works, Collectors of Revenue in the different Departments of the Public Services at the several Stations hundreds of miles apart and in very extensive Districts. I think that these appointments are singularly well filled, and I regard the successful administration of this government and the remarkable maintenance of Law and order as compared with the neighbouring territories as mainly due to the services of these officers. . . .

Finally, as parts of the machinery of colonial government, must be mentioned the politicians and other representatives of the public and indeed the public themselves. For Musgrave had been charged with consummating confederation only if he could do so and not "overrule the wishes of the community."

Vancouver Island in her Legislative Assembly, and later in her Legislative Council, and British Columbia in the Legislative Council had been fortunate in their unpaid political representatives. Their duties were merely to advise or approve and their numbers were until the final session of the Council in 1871, always in the minority. They, too, had no patronage to dispense. It is difficult to know what might have been their legislative and executive competence under representative and responsible government. Under colonial conditions, they individually displayed independence and thoughtfulness in public matters, a mixture of conservative and liberal tendencies. Canadians, who were pro-confederation, held the mainland seats. The leader, Dr. R. W. W. Carrall, was opposed to local self-government, i.e., responsible government without confederation. The others were pro-confederation under any political arrangement. The island representatives were split. At one extreme was the conservative, anti-confederation, old-time Britisher and reluctant politician, Dr. J. S. Helmcken, at the other an unstable reformer from Nova Scotia, Amor de Cosmos.

Officially, the public was not enabled to have a hand in administering its own affairs. We shall see that unofficially, during the 1869-1871 period, many obvious and some less obvious devices were employed by the populace to influence the course of administration: petitions, public meetings, lively and lengthy newspaper debates, private representations in Ottawa and London, special pressures at the points of influence in Victoria as well as in Ottawa and London. Mechanical means of communication were used to the utmost: mail service by steamer and stage coach from Victoria to Cariboo taking four or five days with a charge of twenty-five cents per letter; mail service to London by steamer, railroad, and steamer, taking six weeks to two months; telegraph via San Francisco and Detroit to Ottawa; cable via San Francisco to London; railroad from the Pacific to the Atlantic across the United States of America.

The overall view is that British Columbia's "government machine" of 1869-1871 was outdated. It needed repair. Moreover, its wheels were fixed in deep ruts; the driver could move the vehicle in only one direction regardless of the destination or route desired by the passengers or shippers; they could not cease to use it; its fuel supply was low; its fuel consumption was uneconomical; all its operating parts lacked adequate maintenance service and some were dangerously damaged; its control and safety devices were outworn. *The five operating parts of the British Columbia government vehicle were unequally defective and, as a whole, were incapable of performing their essential functions.* Anthony Musgrave thus stepped into a malfunctioning vehicle aimed on a crash course. He drove at peak speed.

The Action

1. The Colonial Office prepared Musgrave for his major role in British Columbia no better than it had prepared his predecessors. He received no special orientation into conditions on the northwest coast, though he had requested permission to proceed to London from St. John's, Newfoundland, for a briefing. He was left to his own resources, the colonial records, and the memory of present and former officials on the spot to discover the basic legal, financial, procedural, and social facts. Throughout his term, he frequently found that he lacked essential background information about the situation in British Columbia.

The Colonial Office did, as was already mentioned, instruct Musgrave completely and promptly regarding his special assignment. He knew the viewpoint of the British government on confederation, the reasons therefor, and the limit and extent of his authority in the matter. What is more, the Colonial Office at no time failed to support him to the utmost, using all available facilities for communication. For example, by letter from Victoria, on February 23, 1870, he notified Lord Granville of his proposal to change the constitution of the Legislative Council to nine elective and six appointed members. An Order-in-Council was passed on August 8, 1870, to enable him to alter the membership as requested. It was received in Victoria on October 13. This was normal request and response time. Again, in November 1869, Attorney General Crease submitted to Lord Granville through the Governor (the directive that all official outgoing and ingoing correspondence for a colony be transmitted through the Governor being rigidly practiced by this date in British Columbia) a scale of fees payable to him, the Attorney General, for professional services rendered to the Crown. His predecessor had charged nominal fees when appearing in the courts as barrister. Musgrave forwarded Crease's communication and in a covering letter on November 26, noted (1) that he was unaware that an Attorney General was entitled to anything more than his fixed salary for duties rendered, (2) that the salary of the Attorney General in British Columbia was low for his rank and the importance of his office, and (3) that instruction was required. The Colonial Office replied on January 22, 1870, naming seven colonies in which the Attorney General received only a fixed salary, and quoting those salaries. Musgrave was advised to fix fees at a medium rate so that the Attorney General's total emolument would correspond with the salaries for Attorneys General in other colonies and "to afford the least possible inducement to make or escape work." As one further example of the Colonial Office's cooperation, on December 27, 1869, Musgrave sought permission to take leave "to visit New York for a personal matter of importance in April or May," stating that he "would meet with the government of Canada on the subject of confederation thereafter." On the margin of the letter, a Colonial Office official noted "matrimony." The office did grant leave but withheld permission to draw full salary, considering it wiser for Musgrave to follow the established practice and draw half salary.

While the Secretary of State supported Musgrave well in pursuit of the special objective of confederation, the Colonial Office provided no effective stimulus or direction for his management of the domestic administrative affairs of the colony. The officials checked him when periodic reports or routine applications for leave were late in arriving in London. The office expected him to acknowledge and comment upon every circular sent to colonial governors. But, except as they affected the confederation issue, the Colonial Office during the entire period of Musgrave's governorship showed no substantial interest in Indian, Fenian, financial, commercial, industrial, agricultural, mining, civic, or other major concerns in British Columbia. If Musgrave had been asked, "What is the major objective of your management of British Columbia?" he could not have replied, "political stability," "the economic welfare of the colonists," "the social welfare of the natives and colonists," "the profit of investors in British Columbia industry and commerce," or "the growth of the British Empire." He would have had to reply weakly, "Conformity with the administrative requirements of the Colonial Office."

   2. The Governor and the senior officials. Musgrave diligently pursued his special assignment to realize confederation. (See the analysis in Table I.) British Columbia was his field of combatting forces which he would manoeuvre toward the preconceived end. His strategy for moving British Columbia into Canadian union may be outlined step by step. Figures 2-6 illustrate these steps by which Musgrave brought the various conflicting driving and supporting forces to reach an equilibrium and accept confederation. The phases graphically illustrated in the Figures may be narrated as follows.

Phase I (assess situation; plan)
   1. Aug. 23-Sept. 3, 1869. A social time in Victoria to become acquainted with officials and influential citizens. On August 25, writing to the Colonial Office and referring to threats of Fenian invasion, he reported "all well."
   2. Sept. 4-Oct. 14, 1869. Musgrave toured the mainland to check first-hand the attitude of the colonists and assess the forces for and against confederation.
   3. Oct. 15, 1869. He reported to Granville on his return to Victoria the expressions of cordial loyalty encountered, the increasing stability and economic prosperity of the colony, but the lack of unanimous pro-confederation feeling.
   4. Oct. 30(?), 1869. He published Lord Granville's pro-confederation despatch in the *Gazette*, to offset a grapevine from Canada which had "communicated the contents to unofficial persons in British Columbia."
   5. Oct. 30, 1869. He reported at length to Lord Granville that "it is not by any means clear that the majority of the community are prepared for Union with the Dominion except on terms which are not likely to be possible, or with a view to political arrangements for which this community is by no means ripe. . . . " The "agitators for confederation" were "a small knot of Canadians who hope that it may be possible to make fuller representative institutions and Responsible Government part of the new arrangements, and that they may so place themselves in positions of influence and emolument." They had support from Victoria merchants who believed that a free port would be part of the confederation arrangements.
   Opposed or indifferent to confederation were the many Americans in the colony, farmers who feared both the Canadian tariff and

TABLE I

MUSGRAVE'S DESIGN OF THE CONFEDERATION PROJECT, OCTOBER 1869

Participants	Relation to Issue	Base of Attitude	Action Expectation	Governor's Strategy to Influence
Imperialists				*respect* opinion and advice, *weaken resistance, rush acceptance:* make leader of opposition, a negotiator of scheme; withhold local self-government; deny free port; arrange generous financial terms representation, and transport with Canada; ensure military and social services and works; publicize all negotiations; protect farmers; arrange pensions for officials
Officials	anti – medium	fear of minority status social superiority	support if pensions guaranteed	
Banks and British investors	anti – strong	inadequate and costly government services	neutrality if financial terms generous	
Commercial interests	anti – strong	growing financial insecurity	support if transport to Canada, fair tariff	
Farmers, British and Canadian	anti – medium	military insecurity Canadian trickery	neutrality if tariff concessions	
Annexationists				*disregard* officially: exclude from franchise; if necessary, use as counter-force to stimulate pro-confederation action
American commercial interests, Victoria	anti – weak	favourable social and business relations with western United States	none effective	
Confederationists				*weaken* but keep *active:* eliminate grapevine between members of this group establish liaison between Canadian politicians and official negotiators of confederation; include a wagon road in terms
Elected members	pro – strong	knowledge of "secure" political position anxiety to exercise "rights" of self-government	smug demands	
Canadian businessmen	pro – strong	discrimination in professional employment isolation from own social group	intrigue for personal benefit	
Politicians in Canada	pro – strong		loud detrimental agitation until stopped	
Reformers				*weaken* to offset opposition and then *regain lost force:* declare against self-government and later, if necessary, grant it to operate only after confederation; have confederation vote made by majority of elected members; declare a liberal franchise
Elected members	pro – strong	Imported political values	unstable support, opposition when unwise reform withheld; exaggerated reports of pro-confederation support and criticism of government action	
Newsmen	pro – strong			
Non-Participants				*retain neutrality:* gain support if possible; exclude from franchise; enhance British prestige *exclude* from active participation in negotiating terms
Non-British miners and white settlers	neutral	British law enforcement and orderliness tradition in British colonies	disinterest in politics unless aggravated	
Chinese	excluded			
Native Indians				
Negroes			none	

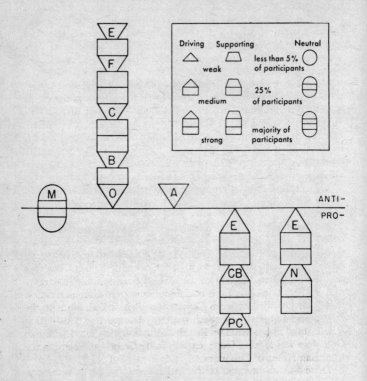

Figure 2. Confederation scheme: force field analysis. Phase I (assess, plan), August-October, 1869. Code: A = American commercial interests. B = Banks and British investors. C: = Commercial interests. CB: = Canadian businessmen. E: = Elected members (legislature). F: = Farmers, British and American. M: = Non-British miners and settlers. N: = British Columbia newsmen. O: = Officials. PC: = Politicians in Canada.

the free port, and the British. The latter reacted negatively because the Canadian immigrants "have not contrived to impress their fellow colonists with a prejudice in their favour." Public officers would cease to oppose confederation if pensions could be provided for them upon their retirement.

Musgrave then outlined in detail his plan to sever the negative fringe forces, to retain the support but lower the agitation of positive forces, to lower or neutralize the resistance of central negative forces. Communication with Canada and advantageous financial terms were the issues on which opposing forces could agree. Responsible government and a free port were to be delayed and if possible rejected.

Musgrave prepared the despatch on October 30, intending to forward it on November 2. While training a filly on November 2, he sustained a compound fracture of the leg. Although British Dr. Helmcken was first on the scene, Musgrave permitted a Canadian, Dr. Powell, to treat the injury. This he later regretted; he suffered a lameness all his life. The despatch was mailed on November 10. Meanwhile, there had been a leak of its contents to the local press. On November 5, the *Colonist*, in an editorial entitled "Self Government," attacked the Governor's stand on responsible government as "unjustifiable" and a "gross libel upon an intelligent people."

Phase II (draft terms; weaken both support and opposition)

6. Nov.-Dec., 1869. With aid from members of the Executive Council, Musgrave drafted the terms for confederation. They were: (a) For financial arrangements the population of British Columbia should be taken as 120,000 for she would be relinquishing the revenue of 120,000 in other parts of the Dominion. (b) Communication should be provided between Canada and British Columbia, partly by railroad and partly by coach road. (c) The existing constitution should stand until altered by British North America Act. (d) British Columbia was to have four members in the Senate and eight in the Canadian House of Commons.

There was no mention of the Indians, responsible government, tariff, or free port concessions. During November and December, newspapers in New Westminster and Victoria protested against the Governor's disregard of the desire for responsible government and a free port.

7. Jan. 1, 1870. Musgrave recommended that the Executive Council be enlarged to include two "popular" non-official members, provisionally appointing Dr. Carrall, who was pro-confederation, anti-self-government-before-confederation, and Dr. Helmcken, who was anti-confederation. It is interesting to note that Musgrave forced Dr. Helmcken to accept the appointment, writing him on November 24, 1869, "My predecessor received authority to enlarge the Executive Council. . . . I shall be glad if you will now help me . . . by accepting appointment as a member of the Board, and so obliging. . . . " Helmcken graciously declined on the same date in these words: " . . . I am pleased with your

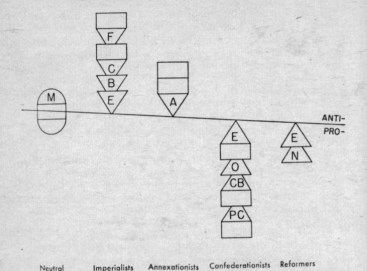

Neutral   Imperialists   Annexationists   Confederationists   Reformers

Figure 3. Confederation scheme: force field analysis. Phase II (draft terms), November 1869-March 1870.

kind offer to decorate me with the honour of being a member of the Executive Council, but strange as it may seem, it is nevertheless true, that I have really no ambition whatever for political distinction.... I being unfriendly to the scheme [confederation] and indeed pledged to oppose its consummation..., a pledge I intend to keep,... could lend you but little assistance.... I have really no time to attend to the duties.... I do therefore sincerely hope that you will consider the offer as not having been made leaving to me *only* the pleasant remembrance and feelings of gratitude." The other member of the Legislative Council for Victoria City, Mr. M. W. T. Drake, was considered for the appointment but was persuaded to withdraw his acceptance. Musgrave notified Helmcken of Drake's withdrawal on November 29 and concluded, "I shall therefore consider that you accept appointment to the Council." And further in a letter dated "Monday, 1869," "I have put your refusal into the fire, and depend upon you to stand by me now. You must not get me into any more difficulties."

8. Jan. 1, 1870. Musgrave recommended that a military guard be retained at Government House, Victoria, though no longer necessary to secure the personal safety of the Governor. Mus-

grave felt it "should be left here as a recognition of and mark of respect to the position of the governor as the Queen's representative. . . . "

9. Jan. 7, 1870. Official members of Legislative Council were won over to the confederation cause when the Governor discussed the pension rights of a former colonial official, W. A. G. Young, and the ease of passing any measure "if the official members are ordered to vote as the governor directs." As five of the official members had been appointed by Downing Street and the Magistrate members held two-year incumbencies, Musgrave discarded as too slow a plan to select and appoint a new pro-confederation Council.

10. Jan. 12-March 31, 1870. He "accepted" public declarations favouring annexation to the United States of America which he followed by a vigorous opposition to annexation. On January 28, 1870, the editor of the *Colonist* reported, "Annexation may now be said to be rampant in this community." On February 15, Musgrave forwarded to the Colonial Office a second memorial from over forty residents of Vancouver Island to the President of the United States seeking annexation of British Columbia to that country. On February 3, he had received a confidential despatch from the Colonial Office including copies of confidential messages on the subject from the British ambassador in Washington. When Musgrave forwarded the pro-annexation memorial, the Colonial Office took no action except to mark it "put by." On February 23, 1869, Miss A. Burdett Coutts, who was concerned with the endowment of archdeaconries in British Columbia, enquired of the Colonial Office about the truth of the rumour that British Columbia would "cease to form part of the British Empire." She received no reply.

11. Feb. 15-Feb. 21, 1870. The Legislative Council met and accepted with minor modifications the confederation terms drafted by Musgrave. Musgrave's opening speech was read for him. Council defeated a motion to introduce responsible government simultaneously with confederation. All the official members opposed the motion.

12. Feb. 21, 1870. Musgrave repeated his declaration against responsible government and noted that the influential, broad-minded citizens were reassured that self-government was not to be proposed and that time would be allowed to consider the terms thoughtfully. Simultaneously he forwarded copies of the proposed confederation terms to Lord Granville, Secretary of State for the Colonies, and to Sir John Young, Governor General of Canada.

13. Feb. 23, 1870. Musgrave requested an Order in Council to

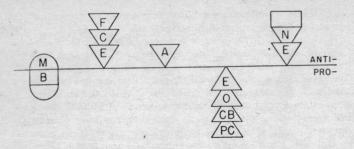

Neutral   Imperialists   Annexationists   Confederationists   Reformers

Figure 4. Confederation scheme: force field analysis, Phase III (negotiations), April-July, 1870.

alter the constitution of the Legislative Council so as to provide a majority of elected members—nine elected and six appointed. Suffrage would be limited to British subjects. Permitting "foreigners" to vote would defeat confederation.

14. March 8, 1870. He asked permission, before the transfer of the Crown fund of Vancouver Island to the general revenue, to apply the sum of £400 to buy furniture for Government House in New Westminster. He liked to "go and visit once in a while."

Phase III (negotiations)

15. April 5, 1870. Musgrave appointed as "his" delegates to negotiate a confederation agreement with Canada J. W. Trutch, the able pioneer engineer who was conservative and politically reliable, J. S. Helmcken, now the ex-spokesman for the anti-confederation group, and R. W. W. Carrall, an able politician from Canada, not overly interested in "political place and power." Helmcken was again pressured into accepting a distasteful political responsibility. Musgrave wrote him on April 18, 1870: " . . . As to the Delegation . . . you *Must* go. Even the Mayor, and the Committee from the Public Meeting could not help admitting that I could not select a better man to work for the interests of the Colony than yourself. . . . I told them plainly that I should certainly try to persuade you. I mean to stick to my Delegation if my Delegation will stick to me. Let me have a positive answer . . . in the affirmative." Radicals were excluded from the negotiating party. Three senior journalists, being dissatisfied with "his" delegates and still championing the responsible government cause, sent a newsman, H. Seelye, as " "Your Spe-

cial Delegate" to influence the Canadian government in favour of responsible government for British Columbia.

16. May-July, 1870. Musgrave communicated frequently by telegraph with Canada and "his" delegates to Ottawa regarding the discussions with Sir George Etienne Cartier, Sir Samuel Tilley, and others. For financial purposes, the British Columbia population was to be taken as 60,000; but Cartier had the federal grant increased by proposing an annual subsidy of $100,000 for a belt twenty miles wide on each side of the railway. Canada proposed a railway to the coast to be completed within ten years, so British Columbia dropped the wagon road requirement. Representation was to be reduced to three senators and six members of the House of Commons. British Columbia was to be free either to accept the Canadian tariff upon union or to retain her own until completion of the overland railway. Seelye influenced the Canadians sufficiently to force addition of Article 14 stating that Canada agreed to responsible government whenever British Columbia should so request. The Privy Council of Canada approved these confederation terms on July 5, 1870. It was agreed that they would be published first by Governor Musgrave. Ontario newspapers opposed the terms as being too generous to British Columbia. On July 27, Musgrave wrote to Governor General Young that the terms were "not only satisfactory but liberal to this Colony." On August 4, from Downing Street, Earl Kimberley wrote to Governor General Sir John Young expressing his pleasure that the "British Columbia negotiations have made so much progress." In September, acknowledging a despatch of July 28 reporting confederation terms, Kimberley reported to Musgrave the August 4 letter to Young.

A personal note was that on June 20 Musgrave married in San Francisco an American lady related to Cyrus Field. They were welcomed to Vancouver Island in early July by the citizens represented by the manager of the Hudson's Bay Company, the American consul, and "other leading citizens." No official was named in the news story.

Phase IV (acceptance)

17. Oct. 13, 1870. A Government Gazette Extraordinary was issued at P.M. proclaiming a new constitution for the Legislative Council of nine elected and six appointed members. Writs for an election were issued, electoral districts specified, and a liberal franchise proclaimed, extending to British subjects able to read English, with no registration of voters. On October 17, Musgrave expressed to Kimberley the hope that all writs would be returned

by the end of December so that the new Council could be convened early in January.

18. Oct. 20-Nov. 4, 1870. Musgrave toured the east coast of Vancouver Island on H.M.S. "Sparrowhawk" to test confederation feeling and to investigate the conditions of the Indians, agriculture, and coal mining.

19. Nov. 8, 1870. He declined the invitation of Sir John A. Macdonald to travel to Ottawa to help gain passage of the confederation terms in the Dominion Parliament. He proposed instead to send Trutch, and emphasized the need to provide pensions for public officers who would be affected by union. "It is important to remember that I cannot work the scheme through successfully without the loyal support of the officials, and I wish them to be satisfied that they will be dealt with justly."

20. Nov. 22, 1870. He informed Lord Lisgar, Governor General of Canada, that the returning British Columbia delegates had reported the Canadian government anxious to avoid the necessity of paying retiring allowances to British Columbia officials. Naming the officials and assessing their capacity one by one, he made recommendations respecting their employment in another colony, in Canada, or in British Columbia, and suggested salaries. His conclusion was that the Canadian government might be relieved of the necessity to pay pensions but that nevertheless they should be provided at two-thirds the rate of present salaries. On February 6, 1871, the Executive Council of British Columbia requested that pensions should be provided in all cases and that each officer should have the option of employment or pension. Musgrave

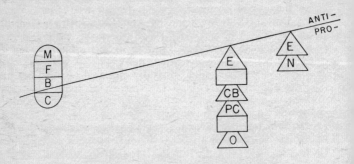

Neutral   Imperialists   Annexationists   Confederationists   Reformers

Figure 5. Confederation scheme: force field analysis. Phase IV (acceptance), October-December, 1870.

registered his belief that "none of the officers would have cared at present to have been removed even in way of promotion, except possibly, to some station of considerably increased honour and emolument, in some equally good climate." On Febeuary 9, 1871, in a letter to Lord Lisgar, Musgrave vigorously supported the officials' "just claims."

21. Nov. 24, 1870. He wrote at length to Macdonald regarding his difficulties in engineering the election of a group of representatives to support confederation: "I am a little anxious as to the result, though still hopeful, because if things go against us . . . we shall have as a majority of the elected members men without brains and without principle who think nothing, for any selfish motive or for no reason at all, of upsetting all that I have been labouring to accomplish. I am not going to be beaten, however, if I know it. . . . Notwithstanding all the boasted eagerness of the Community for Confederation the only men I can depend upon are the officials. DeCosmos and the leading Demagogues like their fellows in Newfoundland would throw Confederation to the winds tomorrow if without it they could obtain Responsible Government which with them does not mean rational self government as in a larger community, but official plunder and possession of the public offices . . . ; if I were weak enough to yield this point we might whistle to no purpose for Confederation for years to come." Musgrave urged Macdonald to settle quickly the question of pensions for public officers, to grant him a retiring allowance of half salary until his posting elsewhere ("one ought scarcely to be expected cheerfully to cut his own throat for the glory of the thing and other people's satisfaction"), and to extend the guarantee of the dock at Esquimalt to twenty years instead of ten.

22. Dec. 5, 1870. Musgrave transmitted to Governor General Lisgar a petition from 550 influential citizens of Victoria, delivered on Saturday, December 3, seeking to have Esquimalt named as the western railway terminus, rather than a point on the mainland. To the delgation Musgrave appeared negative but he did not commit himself. Lord Lisgar answered from Ottawa on December 31 that the route of the Pacific railway could be settled only after confederation. A survey party, appointed by Canada and on which British Columbia would be repesented, would make a recommendation.

Phase V (consummation)

23. Jan. 11, 1871. Musgrave opened the Legislative Council meeting, which was prorogued March 28, 1871. He praised the generosity of the terms which the Canadian government was

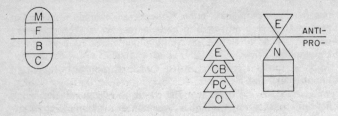

Neutral   Imperialists   Annexationists Confederationists   Reformers

Figure 6. Confederation scheme: force field analysis. Phase V (consummation), January-July, 1871.

prepared to support in the House of Commons and urged their immediate acceptance. A bitter debate on local responsible government ensued. All official and some conservative elected members opposed its introduction before confederation; after confederation all major issues would be under federal control. All proposed amendments to the terms were defeated. On January 17, Musgrave sent a "favourable" progress report to Macdonald by telegram.

24. Jan. 20, 1871. By telegram from Musgrave to Kimberley and in accordance with the provisions of the British North America Act, 1867, British Columbia presented an address to the Queen, seeking union with Canada on terms passed unanimously that day by the Legislative Council. Her Majesty's assent was given on May 16. On the same date, the public was advised that the estimated debt of British Columbia on July 1, 1871, would be $1,068,040, to be assumed by Canada. The Dominion might expect to provide British Columbia with a net revenue of $170,450 plus subsidies of $212,908 for a total annual revenue of $383,358. The estimate of expenditure was $236,073, so British Columbia might expect an annual favourable balance of $147,285.

25. Jan. 25, 1871. A telegram from Musgrave to Lisgar transmitted a resolution of the Legislative Council seeking consent of the Canadian government to reduce the British Columbia tariff on spirits, flour, and wheat to the Canadian rate. Musgrave recommended assent. Since the summer of 1870, Helmcken had urged lower duties on spirits and wheat as a sop so that agriculture would be protected by retention of other duties. Musgrave, fearing risk to his political reputation, had at first vigorously opposed Helmcken's suggestions directly to Helmcken in a letter of September 8 and to other members of the Executive and Legislative Councils by letter of July 28 to Trutch. At length he

surrendered to popular opinion. By telegram, Lisgar replied on February 1, stating that "the terms of union are in the nature of a treaty.... The Canadian government think they have no right to alter those terms...." On February 16, Musgrave wrote to Kimberley, pointing out that British Columbia opposed accepting Canadian tariff rates on cereals as being too hard on farmers and brewers, and urging that the tariff clause should stand and that the date for British Columbia acceptance of Canadian rates should be left open. On March 9, Musgrave forwarded to Kimberley for royal assent a copy of an Act to Repeal the Customs Amendment Ordinance, 1870. The 1870 ordinance had temporarily added fifty cents a gallon to the duty on spirits to provide funds to re-establish the telegraph to Cariboo; the 1871 act removed the extra tariff.

26. Feb. 18, 1871. Musgrave forwarded to Kimberley for royal assent an Act to Alter and Amend the Constitution, together with the Attorney General's comments. Musgrave and the Executive Council agreed "that the concession now of what is desired ... would conduce much to the future tranquility of the colony.... I still believe that the system of responsible government is in advance of the development of the colony and that the existing legislative constitution would be sufficient for all local purposes after the union if it were allowed to work without factious opposition. But on the other hand, that opposition would be instant and incessant, no cordial support would be rendered outside of the official circle...." Musgrave and the Executive Council drew up a constitutional act, modelled on that of Ontario, with a single legislative assembly. There were to be twenty-five representatives, thirteen from the mainland and twelve from Vancouver Island, thus allowing for the expected influx of population to the mainland, though Vancouver Island had the larger population in 1871. The Executive Council was to be appointed as in Ontario and Quebec. When the act became operative, members were for the first time to be paid. By Section 47, operation of the act was to be suspended until after Her Majesty's assent had been given and the effective date fixed by proclamation of the Governor, being a date prior to union. Musgrave advised that assent should not be given unless confederation was certain within a specified time, otherwise, the act should be "laid aside." On April 20, Kimberley asked Lisgar if he had any objection to the act. On May 5, Lisgar replied that he had "no objection to the immediate sanctioning by Her Majesty...." The act was assented to on May 12.

27. Feb.-March, 1871. Musgrave frequently wrote to Kimber-

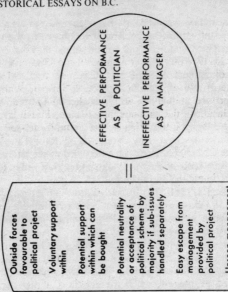

PERFORMANCE

EFFECTIVE PERFORMANCE AS A POLITICIAN

INEFFECTIVE PERFORMANCE AS A MANAGER

=

THE SITUATION

Outside forces favourable to political project

Voluntary support within

Potential support within which can be bought

Potential neutrality or acceptance of political scheme by majority if sub-issues handled separately

Easy escape from management provided by political project

Unseen management opportunities

×

THE MAN

Past experience in other colonies

Skilled politician, experienced bureaucrat with knowledge of situation, driving ambition

Lack of management skill

Threat to special project

DEMAND AND EXPECTATION

Public servants expect strong leadership within the administrative machine

Superiors demand political strategy and suggest bureaucratic management

Public expects vigorous management of colony's business

FIGURE 7. Governor Musgrave's administrative performance in British Columbia, 1869–1871.

ley and Macdonald regarding pensions for the officials prejudicially affected by confederation and not employed by the Canadian government.

28. Feb. 1871. Trutch was sent officially to Ottawa to help the Canadian government to win acceptance of the confederation terms in the House of Commons. Seelye, Powell, Waddington, and other private individuals also travelled to Ottawa to lobby. At the conclusion of the parliamentary debate, Trutch travelled to London. Pensions for the officials were among his special concerns.

29. March 22, 1871. Musgrave asked permission of Kimberley to leave British Columbia as soon as possible in order to obtain treatment for the injury to his foot.

30. March 31, 1871. He forwarded to Kimberley an Act to Provide for a Permanent Civil List, an act which did not enjoy popular support. It was intended to prevent jobbery. Assent was recommended by Kimberley on May 12.

31. April, 1871. The proposed British Columbia confederation was debated before the House of Commons and Senate in Ottawa. There was strong opposition to the government motion but it passed at the end of April and was approved by Her Majesty at Windsor on May 16, 1871.

32. April 5, 1871. Musgrave forwarded to Kimberley for royal assent an Act to Regulate Elections of Members of the Legislature. The two supreme court judges, Begbie and Crease, opposed the measure, which provided for disputed elections to be settled by the courts. Musgrave commented that he thought "the only reason they object is that they will have more work to do."

33. April 15, 1871. Musgrave was appointed an ordinary member, third class, of the Order of St. Michael and St. George. When the news reached Musgrave, he passed it on to Trutch. "Lord Kimberley has given me the Order of St. Michael and St. George, but I think you deserve it more and I hope you may have it before the end of the year when we have finished our work. . . ."

34. May 10, 1871. Musgrave wrote Lisgar for permission to leave Victoria soon after August 1, as Mrs. Musgrave wished "her expected confinement to be in London: . . . why I have been so pressing to have the Union completed and get away from British Columbia." On April 12, Musgrave gave another reason to his confidant and mouthpiece, Trutch, in these words: "I have received a letter from Sir George Cartier in which he mentions the wish of the Canadian Government that I should remain for a time, but I have written in reply . . . to explain why I regard it as

a duty not to do so at the expense of postponing treatment of my foot. . . . Helmcken, although he wishes me to stay, tells me that he thinks delay would be imprudent. I have made up my mind, therefore, to go on as soon as I can after Union is declared. . . ." On May 10, Lisgar advised both Musgrave and Kimberley that July 20 was the earliest convenient day for union.

34. June 17, 1871. Kimberley notified Musgrave by telegraph that an Order-in-Council on May 27 had fixed the date of union as July 20. Musgrave was congratulated and thanked for his endeavours.

35. July 6, 1871. J. W. Trutch was appointed as first Lieutenant-Governor of British Columbia. It had been expected that the appointment would go to Sir Samuel Tilley. Helmcken succeeded at last in his effort to escape from public life.

36. July 20, 1871. British Columbia became a Canadian province.

37. July 25, 1871. Musgrave and his party left Victoria on H.M.S. "Zealous," meeting briefly in San Francisco with Trutch, who was returning as Lieutenant-Governor of British Columbia.

38. Sept. 14, 1871. From Piccadilly, Musgrave, then on leave, wrote to Trutch, the Lieutenant-Governor, "[The Colonial Office] seem much pleased about B.C. affairs and like your appointment as Lieutenant-Governor. . . . I shall look out with interest for a letter from you, as I am anxious to know how the new machinery works. No man can 'run' it better than you. . . ." Trutch had written to Musgrave on September 3, to which Musgrave in naked self-revelation replied on October 28: " . . . But I was much pleased to get so satisfactory an account of the state of public affairs. Yet it is not more than I expected. I had full confidence in your discretion and management. You have done exactly what I should in your place. And it seemed impossible that any serious objection could be raised to a course so obviously judicious. It is not the less gratifying, however, that matters should be running so smoothly. Your reply to the Municipal Address was first rate; in perfect temper, a manly, plain, straightforward exposition of the policy which, I think, ought to govern your proceedings. . . . Of course you won't forget to let me hear from you after the Elections when you have settled upon your Ministry. That will be the Crowning matter; and afterwards with a little management you will not have much trouble with the machine. You will make your 'Responsible Advisers' the buffers. . . . I saw Hankin . . . he belonged to the machinery which was broken up. . . ."

39. May 17, 1872. Musgrave wrote Sir John A. Macdonald

from London introducing his brother and seeking employment for him: "If you think that your government owes me anything for work in the B.C. affair I shall take it as more than compensation if you can do anything for him. . . ."

40. October 15, 1879. Musgrave wrote to Macdonald from Westminster, "I still take great interest in Canadian affairs and progress and am glad to know that your administration will do something for our B.C. friends about the Railway. . . ."

13. An Outline of the Economic History of British Columbia, 1881-1951
R. E. Caves and R. H. Holton

RICHARD E. CAVES, *of Harvard University and* RICHARD H. HOL-
TON, *of the University of California at Berkeley, are American
economists who produced this capsule economic history of British
Columbia as a part of a study of Canada for the Canadian
Pacific Railway.*

British Columbia in 1881

British Columbia was united with Canada in 1871 and was not
included in the census of Canada for 1871. A census of the colony
in 1870 gives a crude idea, however, of the make-up of the
economy for there were some 2300 men in mining, 1800 in
agriculture, 1300 in trade, and but 400 in manufacturing.[1] Data
on exports from the province are available for 1872 and these
show unmistakably the importance of the export staple. "Products
of the Mine" accounted for $1,389,585 worth of exports, 75 per
cent of the total exports of the province. The fisheries exported
about $38,000 worth of goods, and animals and animal products
accounted for another $215,000.[2] About $214,000 worth of forest
products were also exported.

By 1881 mining was of considerably less importance in the
export picture, accounting now for just under 60 per cent of the
total. The big increase had occurred in the export of fisheries
products, which were more than ten times as great in 1881 as a
decade earlier. Nor was 1881 a unique year for the British
Columbia fisheries. In 1882 and 1883 and again in 1888, fisheries
products exports exceeded $1,000,000, compared with $400,000
in 1881. The exports of forest products were rising slowly but
1881 was an abnormally low export year for this sector. The exports of animals and animal products had increased about 50 per
cent. In short, the exports from the mines had done little better
than hold their own over the period in absolute terms, while the

Source: Richard Earl Caves and Richard Henry Holton, *The Canadian Economy, Prospect and Retrospect* (Cambridge, Mass., 1959),
pp. 218-232. Reprinted by permission of the authors and publisher.

exports of fisheries products and animal products were rising rapidly.[3]

In 1881 there were between 2600 and 2800 persons engaged in each of the main export industries—mining, fishing, and agriculture. Agriculture had been altered a bit since the days when its sole function was to serve the mining camps, and it now produced a substantial amount of livestock. By 1881, too, the manufacturing sector had grown to the point where nearly 2900 persons were reported as employed in industrial establishments. Nearly half of these were reported in the "preserved articles of food" industry, mostly fisheries products.[4] About 400 more persons were working in the sawmills and the remainder were scattered among the various types of small scale manufacturing which one expects to find in a new economy, such as boots and shoes, foundries, carpentering, blacksmithing, flour and grist mills, and so on. Between 1870 and 1881, then, we find the kind of change in the structure of the economy which has been apparent in some of the other regions: a relative shift from the export staple which was the original cause for the region's growth, accompanied by the development of a new export staple and the emergence of a manufacturing sector of some importance.

British Columbia in 1911

Between 1881 and 1911 the population of British Columbia jumped nearly 700 per cent, from 50,000 to 392,000, while the country as a whole grew by about 67 per cent. This was not as rapid an expansion as that experienced in the prairies, but it is impressive nonetheless. What caused this rapid growth?

First, the completion of the transcontinental railroad and the expansion of the prairies were themselves partly responsible, for British Columbia served as a gateway through which some of the trade of the prairies passed. In 1911 more than 14 per cent of the work force in the province was engaged in transportation as compared with but 10 per cent for all of Canada. But British Columbia was still relying primarily on the extractive industries. Of the extractive industries, lumbering apparently expanded the most. The 1881 and 1911 occupational data in the Census are not comparable, but the information on manufacturing establishments provides some evidence. In 1881 there were but 27 sawmills reported but by 1911 there were 224 firms indicated in "log products." Employment in these firms had risen from 393 to nearly 15,400.[5] Despite the fact that there were five times as many miners in 1911 as in 1881 in British Columbia, lumbering had expanded so much more rapidly that both industries accounted for between 15,000 and 16,000 workers in the latter year. Employment in agriculture had apparently expanded considerably faster than in mining, rising from about 2600 to over 24,000. The fisheries recorded the least rate of increase in employment among the extractive industries, with but a 65 per cent increase. Although one can raise questions about the dissimilarity in classification methods in the two censuses, the data are at least satisfactory in indicating the rough magnitudes of change. In brief, the rise of lumbering between 1881 and 1911 was spectacu-

TABLE 28

Ten leading industries in British Columbia by value of products and by number of employees, 1881, 1911, and 1951.

Industry	Value of product (thousands of $)	Industry	Number of employees
	1881		
Preserved articles of food	592	Preserved articles of food	1,449
Sawmills	550	Sawmills	308
Fittings and foundry working	183	Boots and shoes	112
Flour and grist mills	179	Dressmaking and millinery	95
Boots and shoes	151	Fittings and foundry working	70
Carpenters and joiners	115	Carpenters and joiners	78
Bakeries of all sorts	113	Tailors and clothiers	62
Sash, door, and blind factories	88	Blacksmithing	60
Tailors and clothiers	87	Bakeries of all sorts	44
Opium factory	79	Flour and grist mills	47
Blacksmithing	70	Printing offices	41
	1911		
Log products	19,753	Log products	15,379
Smelting	11,715	Fish, preserved	5,788
Fish, preserved	4,469	Lumber products	1,862
Lumber products	3,827	Smelting	1,282
Foundry and machine shop products	2,100	Car repairs	1,148
Car repairs	1,801	Foundry and machine shop products	881
Liquors, malt	1,519	Housebuilding	464
Electric light and power	1,302	Ships and ship repairs	443
Coke	1,302	Brick, tile, and pottery	517
Confectionery	1,260	Confectionery	387

Industry	Value of product (thousands of $)	Industry	Number of employees
		1951	
Sawmills	347,147	Sawmills	29,462
Nonferrous metal smelting and refining	215,329[a]	Nonferrous metal smelting and refining	4,849[a]
Pulp and paper	141,503	Fish processing	4,168
Fish processing	84,122	Pulp and paper	5,778
Slaughtering and meat packing	50,080	Shipbuilding	3,484
Veneers and plywood	43,202	Veneers and plywood	3,416
Petroleum products	41,903	Printing and publishing	2,752
Sash, door, and planing mills	41,331	Sash, door, and planing mills	2,770
Miscellaneous food preparation	36,614	Bread and bakery products	2,621
Fertilizers	30,810	Fruit and vegetable preparations	2,355

[a] Because there are fewer than four establishments in this industry, data for the province are not published in the DBS, *General Review of Manufacturing, 1951*. The employment figure is the occupational figure from the *Census of Canada*, 1951. The gross value of product estimate presumes British Columbia to have the same share of the country's gross value of output as of employment in this industry. There may be a substantial error involved here, but probably not great enough to alter its rank in the list.

Source: *Census of Canada, 1880-81*, Vol. III, Table 61; *Census of Canada, 1911*, Vol. III, Table 1; and *General Review of the Manufacturing Industries of Canada, , 1951*, Table 14.

lar, leaving lumbering on a par with mining in terms of employment; but agriculture employed about half again as many workers as lumbering or mining, and the fisheries about one-third as many as mining.

The change in the relative importance of the various extractive industries is reflected in the change in the make-up of the manufacturing sector between 1881 and 1911. As Table 28 shows, the canneries had slipped in relative importance, for now preserved fish was outranked in value of product by log products and smelting. In terms of employment, however, it was second to log products. The role of Vancouver and Victoria as transportation terminals is also apparent in the data. The industries which had disappeared from the ten leading industries list, including (alas!) the opium factory, had all been producing for the local market. By 1911 British Columbia's manufacturing had become much more involved in trade with other areas.

The province's agriculture by 1911 had shifted away from beef cattle somewhat and toward wheat and dairy cattle, The number of beef cattle rose by nearly 60 per cent but the number of dairy cattle more than tripled. Wheat acreage doubled. One really spectacular change in British Columbia's agriculture reflected the livestock economy, however: the production of oats, according to the census, was thirty times as great in 1911 as in 1881, while the hay acreage was about seventeen times as great. In the former years only about 10 per cent of the field crop acreage was in hay, but in 1911 nearly 60 per cent was in hay. The pressure of a growing cattle population on the available open range land was apparently the cause of this shift. The second significant development in British Columbia's agriculture was the expansion of fruit and vegetable production. In 1911 there was about six times as much acreage devoted to this use as in 1891, and in 1910 the value of fruit and vegetable production was about one-third as great as the value of all field crops and about two-thirds as great as the value of all livestock sold. The bulk of this expansion in fruit and vegetable production occurred between 1901 and 1911.

The character of mining in the province, too, had been altered considerably by 1911. Gold mining was most prominent in 1881, for the Vancouver Island coal mines, which had been producing at least since 1850, yielded but 268,000 tons in 1881 according to the census. In 1911, however, over 2,500,000 tons were produced and the value of output was roughly half again as great as for gold.[6] Copper, first mined in quantity in the late 1890's, ranked with gold in terms of dollar value of output by 1911 and employed about five times as many workers. Lead and silver were of lesser importance.

In 1911, then, we see that British Columbia was no longer dependent on the exports of the single commodity but had diversified its mineral production. Nor was it so dependent on imported manufactured goods, for now the province had quite a respectable manufacturing sector of its own. Some 35,000 persons were reported in manufacturing employment; this was more than were employed in mining, forestry, and fishing combined and about 10,000 more than were employed in agriculture. Over 17,000 workers, or nearly half of the manufacturing employment, were reported in log products and lumber products. The preserved fish industry accounted for another 5800 and smelting for 1300. The manufacturing sector in 1911 was so large, then, because of the processing of goods for export rather than because of the production of goods for local consumption.

British Columbia, 1911-1951

The most spectacular growth during this period was recorded in lead and zinc and in pulp and paper production. Again it was production of an export staple which seemed to accelerate the province's growth. The population rose from 392,000 to 1,165,000, the work force from 206,000 to 444,000.[7] How was this increase in the work force divided up among the various sectors of the economy and what seems to have been the nature of the growth in more detail?

Table 29 shows the growth of employment in the extractive industries. It is apparent that only about 5 per cent of the increase in the work force can be attributed directly to the extractive sector. The really huge increases in employment occurred in manufacturing, in the services, and in trade. Of the increase in total work force of 238,000, manufacturing accounted for 68,000, the various services (excluding government but including public utilities) accounted for 66,000, and trade accounted for 48,000.[8]

TABLE 29

Distribution of the labor force among the primary industries in British Columbia, 1911 and 1951.

Industry	1911	1951
Agriculture	24,442	27,659
Forestry	11,831	24,911
Mining	15,569	11,442
Fishing and hunting	4,580	4,836

Source: *Census of Canada, 1911*, Vol. vi, Table I; and *Census of Canada, 1951*, Vol. iv, Table 16.

Expressed in relative terms, the work force more than doubled but the services (defined as above) and the trade sectors more than tripled in size and the manufacturing sector nearly tripled. Employment in government nearly tripled, also. The economy appears to have "filled up" in the sense that the secondary and tertiary sectors expanded in response to the growth of the local market and the availability of raw materials.

Let us examine these changes in more detail. In mining, coal output had fallen by about 40 per cent and the number employed in coal mining dropped even more drastically, from about 7000 to 2000. Due mostly to the price increase but partially to a quantity increase, the value of gold output rose over this period so that it was about equal to that of coal in 1951.[9] But the star performers in mining in British Columbia over these four decades were, of course, lead and zinc. The expanding automobile and electrical goods industries during the 1920's helped pull lead production in the province up from about 40,000,000 pounds in the early 1920's to 320,000,000 pounds in 1930. After a depression dip, lead production rose to a wartime peak of about 480,000,000 pounds, but it has since fallen back to about the 1930 level. Zinc output followed a similar path, since it is found with lead. In dollar terms, lead output was no less than 50 times as great in 1951 as in 1911 and zinc output was more than 500 times as great. In 1951 the value of output of these two metals was on the order of 5 and 6 times the value of output of gold and of coal. These changes were accompanied by an absolute decline in the number of persons reported in mining, from 15,600 in 1911 down to 11,400 in 1951. The doubling of the work force, then, was not caused by the minerals.

Forestry production in British Columbia over this period was undergoing quite a different type of experience. Employment in this sector more than doubled. The most spectacular growth in this sector was recorded by pulpwood production, which rose from 150 cords in 1911 to 860,000 cords in 1951. The former year's output was unusually low, however; total pulpwood used in the province in the four years 1909-1912 was (in cords) 1316, 440, 150, and 35,000. Pulpwood production was just getting under way during the first decade of the century and output, or at least the recording of output, was erratic. Nonetheless in 1951 the bulk of the timber cut still was used for purposes other than pulp; only about 12 per cent of the production by quantity was cut for pulpwood.

In agriculture two types of change had taken place side by side over these forty years. One would anticipate that the growth of population would have given rise to the usual kind of shift toward more dairy and poultry products as well as more beef and pork relative to the grains. However, the data for the province indicate that among the field crops barley and wheat acreage increased most rapidly. Barley acreage rose by a factor of nearly 12 and wheat by a factor of 7. The explanation of this phenomenon is that the Peace River country in the northeastern part of the province had been opened up after 1911. This region is agriculturally an extension of Alberta, and so a type of prairie agriculture expanded in British Columbia during the 1911-1951 period. In 1951, 25 per cent of the improved farm area of the province was in Division 10, the Peace River country, but about 70 per cent of the wheat acreage, 56 per cent of the oats acreage, and nearly 70 per cent of the barley acreage in the province lay in this one division. The southern part of the province was engaged in an entirely different sort of agriculture, oriented much more toward cattle and fruit. In the area around Vancouver in 1950 nearly 90 per cent of the value of all field crops was accounted for by fodder crops. Fruit and vegetable production in that year was about two-thirds as valuable as the output of all field crops. Farther east, the tree fruits become of overwhelming importance. The province's cattle are in the central and southwestern regions rather than in the Peace River country, with the dairy cattle concentrated around Vancouver.

In the manufacturing sector, employment grew over the 1911-1951 period at nearly twice the rate of total employment in the province. This growth in manufacturing was not so much the result of the processing of new staples but rather a growth of the processing of the old staples plus the development of a very substantial amount of smaller scale manufacturing scattered among several industries. Table 28 reflects at least the first of these two aspects. In 1951 the leading manufacturing industries were still based on lumber, fishing, and smelting, just as in 1911. Pulp and paper had come of age and more wood-using industries had developed. However, the forest products industries as a group recorded a substantially smaller percentage increase in employment than did manufacturing as a whole. Due to the large absolute employment in this group of industries, however, its relatively small percentage increase nonetheless represented more than one-third of the total increase in manufacturing employment over the 1911-1951 period. The food processing industries showed the second largest increase in employment in absolute terms, but here, too, the percentage growth was slower than for manufacturing as a whole. The manufacturing industries which grew at particularly high rates during four decades were transportation equipment (the census defines this industry to include garages), iron and steel products, smelting, shipbuilding, printing and publishing, commercial bakeries, clothing, chemical products, and leather products. The growth of manufacturing in British Columbia, 1911-1951, was accounted for in large part by this "filling out" of the manufacturing sector by means of the growth of industries which were, for the most part, market oriented rather than materials oriented.

Table 30 helps give a clearer picture of the province's manufacturing sector compared with that of Canada as a whole. If we assume that a region showing a greater proportion of its work force engaged in a particular industry than is true for the country as a whole must be on an export basis with respect to that industry, we see that British Columbia is on an export basis only in food and beverages, wood and paper products, nonferrous metal products, and petroleum and coal products. So, despite the fact that the highest rates of growth in the 1911-1951 period were in the other manufacturing industries, the province is still on an import basis with respect to those products. This supports the view that in recent decades the most rapid rates of growth have been in those types of manufacturing catering to local demand.

We have seen that the extractive industries accounted for but 12,000 of the 240,000 increase in the work force over the 1911-1951 period and that manufacturing, which accounted for an-

TABLE 30

Number of employees in manufacturing industries per thousand persons in the labor force, Canada and British Columbia, 1951.

Industry	Canada	British Columbia
Food and beverages	28.9	30.9
Tobacco and tobacco products	1.6	
Rubber products	4.2	.1
Leather products	7.4	2.6
Textile products	15.8	1.8
Clothing	23.1	5.2
Wood products	28.1	91.4
Paper products	17.4	17.8
Printing, publishing, and allied industries	12.1	12.1
Iron and steel products	38.7	20.2
Transportation equipment	36.0	25.2
Nonferrous metal products	10.0	14.1
Electrical apparatus and supplies	13.7	2.4
Nonmetallic mineral products	6.8	3.1
Products of petroleum and coal	2.6	2.9
Chemical products	10.0	4.2
Miscellaneous manufacturing	6.0	3.4

Source: Census of Canada, 1951, Vol. V, Table 16.

other 67,000 of the increase, grew not only because of the processing of the old staples but also because of the expansion of those types of manufacturing which produced for the local market. The really huge increases occurred in trade, transportation, and the services. Excluding construction from the tertiary sector of the economy, employment in British Columbia in this sector rose from about 90,000 to over 230,000 over the 1911-1951 period.

More than one-half of this increase occurred in the distributive trades alone. The census classifications differed in 1911 and 1951 and so it is impossible to tell exactly how the increase in employment in trade was distributed among the different types of retailing and wholesaling. Even so, it is easy to see that the major increases were in such lines as automobiles, food, apparel, lumber, and drugs. The growing importance of most of these types of business reflected either the increase in the standard of living or the increased proportion of consumer goods going through the market place (rather than being produced and consumed at home) or both.[10] The increase of more than 11,000 in employment in transportation, storage, and communication is explained primarily by the increase in employment on the railroads and in truck transportation.[11] Government employment skyrocketed from about 10,000 to 30,000, but about half of the increase is explained by increases in the number of people in the armed forces. Although the census categories in the 1911 and 1951 censuses are not strictly comparable for our present purposes, it appears that the number of persons engaged in medicine and in various aspects of medical care accounted, too, for a substantial proportion of the increase in the work force, as one would expect.

But even in 1911 British Columbia reported quite a high proportion of its employment in the tertiary sector. Whereas the country as a whole devoted almost exactly one-third of its workers to this sector, in British Columbia the proportion was 44 per cent. The difference then could be attributed mostly to the greater (relative) employment in transportation and in government in British Columbia. By 1951 the difference had narrowed but was still substantial, the proportions being 45 per cent for all Canada and 53 per cent for British Columbia. The percentage difference in employment in transportation was no longer as great as earlier; the province showed a quite consistent tendency in all tertiary industries to show an employment percentage greater than did the country as a whole. The difference was greatest in the services and in trade, the latter being a large sector in part because of the export trade.

The causes of growth since 1939

From 1939 to 1955 the population of Canada rose by 39 per cent. The population of British Columbia rose by an astronomical 70 per cent. This raises an interesting question, for we have been made aware of the oil boom in Alberta, yet there the population rose only at the national rate. In British Columbia, which experienced no single new resource development, what pushed the population up so rapidly?

A piece of the answer lies in the ratio of the population to the work force. Since it was a younger region, British Columbia for a long while showed fewer persons being supported per member of the work force than was true for the country as a whole. But this figure has been creeping upward. It was but 2.27 in 1931, compared with 2.64 for the whole country, whereas in 1955 it stood at 2.97 in contrast with 2.83 for the country. Had the province's ratio but come up to the national one by 1955, the 1939-1955 population increase would have been 60 rather than 70 per cent.

For a fuller explanation, however, one must look at the nature of the particular industries which expanded most rapidly during the 1939-1955 period. Beyond this, we must consider, too, certain unique features of the province's economy as it existed in 1939.

Table 31 shows the percentage increase in the value of product of the major primary and secondary sectors of the economy.

TABLE 31

Percentage increase in undeflated value of product and in number of employees in selected sectors, British Columbia, 1939-1955.

Sector	Value of product	Number of employees
Forestry	616	60
Manufacturing	569	115
Fisheries	243	a
Agriculture	237	a
Mining	166	10

aNot available.

Source: British Columbi, Bureau of Economics and Statistics, Department of Industries Development, Trade and Commerce, *British Columbia Facts and Statistics,* Vol. X (1956), *passim;* and DBS, *Annual Review of Employment and Payrolls, 1951 an 1955,* Table 7.

Unfortunately the employment data are based only on firms employing fifteen or more persons and are not available for some sectors. The increase in the output of forestry products is immediately apparent, but the repercussions of that increase are not quite so obvious from the above data alone. In 1955 there were over 13,000 persons employed in logging in the province.[12] But there were several times that many people in the manufacturing sector engaged in various wood products industries. There were 31,300 in sawmills, 6700 in pulp and paper, 5400 in veneers and plywood production, 3600 in sash, door, and planing mills, and 1970 in furniture plants, to mention only the major wood-processing industries. In these industries alone, then, there were about 370 workers for each 100 workers in logging. This ratio stands in marked contrast with the corresponding one for Alberta's oil industry, where the long-term prospects are for only about 33 workers in processing oil and gas per 100 workers in primary production of oil and gas. To put the proposition in other words, in British Columbia's wood processing industries there are about ten times as many workers per worker in the primary industry as is true of Alberta's oil and gas products industry. This is one major reason why British Columbia's population has expanded so much more rapidly than has Alberta's over the 1939-1955 period.

But a second reason is at least as important as the first. In British Columbia the total employment in manufacturing industries expanded by only 41 per cent in 1939-1955, as compared with a 74 per cent increase in Alberta. This fact taken by itself seems out of keeping with the increase in total population, which favored British Columbia so strongly. The answer to this enigma can be found in the structure of the two economies in 1939. Alberta was devoting nearly one-half of its work force to agriculture, whereas in British Columbia only one-seventh or one-eighth of the work force was so engaged.[13] Alberta's manufacturing sector, on the other hand, was far smaller than British Columbia's.[14] In Alberta, then, the farm population was able to provide workers to the manufacturing sector over the ensuing years in substantial numbers. In British Columbia, the farm population was too small relative to the industrial work force for the labor requirements of the latter to be filled in the following years from the rural labor group. A quick look at the 1941 and 1951 census work force data shows what was happening. In Alberta the persons engaged in agriculture dropped by nearly 33,000, or 22 per cent. The labor force in manufacturing increased by no less than 40 per cent over this period, but in absolute terms this amounted to only about 10,000 workers. In British Columbia, on the other hand, the agricultural sector shrank much more than in Alberta percentage-wise (37 per cent as compared with 22 per cent) yet this provided only about 16,000 workers to a manufacturing sector in which employment increased by over 30,000. Mining, quarrying, and oil wells employment dropped by 25 per cent in British Columbia in the 1941-1951 decade, but this provided fewer than 4000 workers to the expanding sectors of the economy. Clearly British Columbia had to attract immigrants in order to fill its labor requirements. Alberta, with its much greater agricultural sector and much smaller manufacturing sector, could staff its rapidly expanding manufacturing industries primarily with people leaving agriculture.

One other contrasting feature of the two economies helps explain the much greater rate of population growth in British Columbia. For every 100 workers in the primary and secondary sectors in British Columbia in 1951 there were about 113 in the tertiary sector. In Alberta there were but 79 in the tertiary sector for every 100 workers in primary and secondary industries.

To summarize, British Columbia's 70 per cent increase in population, 1939-1955, was the result of at least four forces: (1) an increase in the number of people dependent on each member of the work force; (2) the expansion of the export market for forest products, which not only increased employment in primary production but also generated more jobs in wood processing than in primary production itself; (3) the limited "slack" in the economy in 1939, meaning that the sectors of the economy in which employment could shrink were too small to provide the growing sectors with enough workers, thus necessitating immigration to fill the labor force requirements; and (4) the relatively large number of persons British Columbia has in the tertiary sector, due in part to the export trade, relative to the primary and secondary sectors, thus giving a higher employment multiplier than would be expected in Canada as a whole.

Certain inadequacies in the data on the manufacturing sector have necessitated our stressing the forest products industries more than is probably justified. The disclosure rule prohibits the publication of data for the nonferrous smelting and refining industry, in which employment was increased substantially by the opening of a new aluminum plant at Kitimat. The company has reported that the work force was about 1300 in 1956.[15] But this kind of development, like the oil development in Alberta, has but limited repercussions in the economy because of the small employment multiplier. British Columbia's primary export staple is one which lends itself to extensive processing prior to export, and this processing is fairly labor intensive. It is this feature of the economy, so in contrast with that of Alberta, which largely explains the very rapid growth since the beginning of World War II.

Notes

[1] *Census of Canada, 1870-71*, Vol. iv, p. 377.

[2] The forestry sector was an important one at an early point in the history of British Columbia not only because of the export market but also because of the lumber needs of the mining towns. This source of demand for lumber was especially great after shaft mining developed in the Kootenay region, generating a need for pit props. See H. A. Innis, *Settlement and the Mining Frontier* (Toronto, 1936), especially chs. v-vi.

[3] Economic Council of British Columbia, *Statistics of Industry in British Columbia, 1871 to 1934* (Victoria, 1935), Table T-1 to T-8 (not paged).

[4] See Bancroft, p. 748.

[5] "Log products" in the 1911 census apparently included little else than sawmills since "lumber products" constituted a separate industry. It seems apparent that even after any conceivable adjustments in the data to assure comparability, one would still find employment in the industry in 1911 being roughly thirty times as great as in 1881.

[6] Economic Council of British Columbia, Table M-5. In 1910 and 1912, production exceeded 10,000,000 tons, the 1911 the output being affected by a strike. See E. Jacobs, "Mines and Mining," in *Canada and Its Provinces*, ed. Adam Shortt and Arthur G. Doughty (Toronto, 1914), p. 574.

[7] Note the change in the number of persons, besides himself, which each worker had to support: from 0.9 in 1911 to 1.6 in 1951.

[8] The employment data in the census of 1951 are not strictly comparable with those of 1911. We have not attempted any reconciliation of these two series since we are interested only in the approximate magnitude of the changes.

[9] In 1951, about 280,000 ounces of gold were produced. After World War I output fluctuated between 100,000 ounces and 250,000 ounces until about 1933. Output then rose to a peak of nearly 600,000 ounces in 1939-40 but fell down to the 200,000 ounce level and below by the end of the war. British Columbia, *Annual Report of the Minister of Mines, 1951*, p. A21.

[10] See George J. Stigler, *Trends in Employment in the Service Industries* (Princeton, 1956), ch. viii, for a fuller discussion of the forces increasing employment in the service industries.

[11] Automobile repair services are not included in this sector in the census but rather are considered as a manufactring industry under "transportation equipment."

[12] British Columbia, Department of Industrial Development, Trade and Commerce, Bureau of Economics and Statistics, *British Columbia Facts and Statistics*, Vol. x (1956), p. 19.

[13] Detailed employment data by province and by sector are not available for 1939. In the 1941 census, however, the proportion of the work force reported

in agriculture stood at 47 per cent in Alberta and but 13 per cent in British Columbia.

[14] In 1941, the census reported about 21 per cent of the British Columbia work force in manufacturing compared with but 8 per cent in Alberta.

[15] Aluminum Company of Canada, Ltd., *Submission to the* RCCEP (Montreal, 1956), p. 14.

14. Patterns of Trade and Investment on the Pacific Coast, 1867-1892: The Case of the British Columbia Salmon Canning Industry
H. Keith Ralston

H. KEITH RALSTON, *one of the editors of this volume, teaches history at the University of British Columbia. His article treats the same period covered by the Howay, Sage and Ormsby selections, but examines the growth of one of the province's resource industries.*

After noting the indisputably important part played by California and Californians in the Fraser River gold rush of 1858, historians have tended to emphasize the continued predominance of California, and more especially San Francisco, in the economic and social life of British Columbia. San Francisco, it is agreed, was the metropolis of a region that included British Columbia in its hinterland. This situation is considered to have lasted through the succeeding rushes to Cariboo, Wild Horse Creek, and the Big Bend, and to have continued in face of the rapid decline of the gold fields after 1865, ending only in the decade after the completion of the Canadian Pacific Railway in 1886.[1]

It has been further argued that not only was San Francisco the commercial metropolis of the region, but entrepreneurs with United States backgrounds predominated in the new resource-based industries that began, albeit slowly, to give the area a new economic base. Political life might be reserved for Britishers and Canadians, but Americans were the leaders in economic life.[2] It seems, therefore, worthwhile to examine, in general terms, the growth of one of the resource industries—salmon canning—to test the validity of this hypothesis.

The development of canning was decisive in the growth of commerical fisheries in far-away western North America, the very outward edge of European expansion. The distance of this coast from large population centres ensured that canning would be the dominant method of processing. Prior to its introduction fishing was almost exclusively for the local fresh market, and attempts to export salted salmon in barrels had met with only limited success.

Source: B. C. Studies, I (1968-69), pp. 37-45. Reprinted by permission of the author and publisher.

Trial shipments to Britain did not arrive in palatable condition, and even exports to Australia often spoiled before reaching their destination.

Commercial fisheries have an inherent drive to expand, and any particular fish population tends to become overexploited and thus unprofitable to catch.[3] The fishing captain is always on the prowl for new grounds, but in any given period the range of his catch is limited. The limitation lies partly in the size of the boat and the catching efficiency of the gear, but mostly in the distance over which the catch can be transported and still be acceptable to the consumer. The problem of palatability is complicated by the nature of the bacteria of decay in fish. Meat is "aged" to improve its flavour, but fish, once caught, soon become offensive to both the sense of taste and the sense of smell. The pioneering role of the commerical fisherman in the northwestern Atlantic has been eloquently expounded.[4] The fisherman did not play a similar role in the northeastern Pacific simply because he could not get his catch to any large market without spoiling. Until canning began on the Pacific coast, the chief commercial sea products of the area came not from fishing, but from the hunting of mammals —sea-otters, fur-seals, and whales. This was precisely because pelts and oil could be transported over long distances without deterioration.

The nineteenth century added canning to the older methods— drying, salting, smoking, and pickling—of extending the range over which fish could be transported. Canning, the placing of the fish product in an airtight container, usually of metal, was a byproduct of new industrial processes that permitted the rolling out of very thin, uniform sheets of metal. Fish canning was just a small part of a much larger canning industry. As well as canning meat, this industry canned many varieties of fruit and vegetables, both to facilitate transport and avoid the seasonal gluts associated with marketing fresh produce.

Canning is in many ways a particularly North American industry, having its greatest growth on this continent, perfecting its techniques here, and diffusing them to other countries. In yet another sense it is a peculiarly United States industry. Long before the first Tin Lizzie was ever conceived by Henry Ford, tins in their hundreds of millions were rolling out of canneries, using those methods of mechanization—minute division of labour, repetitive operation, and line assembly—that are usually considered the hallmark of United States industry.

In the past hundred years fish canning has been dominated by two or three kinds of fish, the salmons being one. Part of the adaptability of salmon to canning is based upon its life cycle. Whatever the differences in the family of salmons, the main species are all *anadromous*, beginning their lives in rivers or lakes, descending to spend the middle span of years in the sea, and returning upriver to spawn in the place of their birth—not only in the same river system but in the very tributary where their ancestors spawned. Thus the salmon entering any river system, especially the large Pacific coast rivers, may be not only of separate species—chinook or spring, red or sockeye, silver or coho—but of distinct groups of a single species, each differentiated by the time and the place of spawning. On the Fraser River, for example, there are spring salmon, summer chums, and fall pinks, as well as Early Stuart River sockeye and Late Stuart River sockeye. These separate groups are called races by the fisheries scientist. The fisherman calls them "runs," since they return to the river together as a school.[5]

The return of the salmon to the river in great numbers over a short time makes it in some ways ideal for factory processing. The fish can be caught in the estuary or in the river itself, close to the processing plant, and river and estuarial fishing require less elaborate boats and gear. The more-or-less uniform size of the fish, especially of some species such as the sockeye or the pink, also lends itself to factory operations. The chief problem in salmon canning is that it is a seasonal industry, a characteristic it shares with fruit and vegetable canning, and, like them, it can suffer from crop variations: the runs of salmon may vary widely from year to year. The Fraser River in British Columbia is especially affected by this variation. Sockeye, its most prolific species, has historically had a reasonably regular four-year cycle of abundance: one very good year, one not as good, and two poor.[6]

Salmon canning derived its basic processes from the larger canning industry, making various improvements in machinery or adapting it as required. Only one machine, the so-called "Iron Chink," an ingenious device for beheading, gutting, and de-sliming the fish, is peculiar to salmon canning. Otherwise it is essentially the same as other forms of canning—a specialized, factory-type, mass production of uniform products. The salmon canning factory, a land operation, preceded the factory ship, its ocean-going counterpart in fish processing, by at least seventy-five years.

Salmon canning began in Europe in the rivers flowing into the North Atlantic. Atlantic salmon were native to most rivers of northwest Europe but by the nineteenth century had either been fished out or shut out of their spawning grounds by man-made alterations to the river environment. They survived only at the edge of their former habitat in countries removed from the main population densities, such as Norway, Scotland, and Ireland. Canning as a means of transporting the fish to market seems to have begun on a very small scale in Scotland in the 1820s. By the 1840s it had moved to take advantage of the larger opportunities across the Atlantic in New Brunswick and Maine, which were also distant from the centres of population, and which had larger, relatively unexploited stocks of salmon.[7]

From Maine and New Brunswick the salmon canning industry made the big leap in 1864 to the eastern rim of the Pacific Ocean, and it too "found gold"—bigger rivers, much larger fish populations (although with differences that were to plague pioneer scientists familiar with the Atlantic salmon), and fish stocks not yet affected either by alterations in the natural environment or by the overfishing that soon limited its growth in northeastern North America. With these opportunities, salmon canneries spread in about twenty years from the southern limit of salmon habitat in the rivers that flow into San Francisco Bay to the northern limit in Alaska, leapfrogging in a frenzy of development from the Sacramento to the Columbia, from the Fraser to the Skeena, and finally into the rich salmon streams of Bristol Bay, Alaska.[8]

The market for canned salmon was industrial Europe, primarily Great Britain. Britain, in 1867 the world's leading industrial state, was the manufacturing country least able to feed itself because of its limited land area and rapidly growing population. Canning was only part of a general process by which such industrial states extended the area of the world from which they drew their food and raw materials. Canned salmon, like canned meat, was particularly important in the years before the successful use of refrigerated ships, because it provided a source of cheap protein. In the latter 1860s, when canned salmon came on to the British market, canned meat sold for about sixpence a pound, half the cost of fresh meat. Canned salmon was soon able to hold its own in both price and palatability with canned meat, which was rather unappetizing.[9] One of the pioneers of Pacific coast canning tells of groups of workmen pooling their pennies to get a tin of salmon for their midday meal. The tin was opened at the shop, thus providing a ready check on the quality of the contents.[10]

Another circumstance helped the marketing of canned salmon. As Charles Wilson has pointed out, the last third of the nineteenth century saw the introduction in Britain of brand names, many of them still familiar in British households.[11] New types of retail trading also characterized late nineteenth-century Britain and the old-style grocer, who weighed out commodities from a bulk stock, began to get competition from the fixed-shop retailer who specialized in prepackaged goods.[12] The tin of salmon, with its brightly coloured label (coloured labels were used on British Columbia salmon before 1877), was very well adapted to this new outlet.

Where does the British Columbia canning industry fit into this generalized picture? The first point to be made is that its beginning was independent of the beginnings on the Sacramento and Columbia rivers. The Fraser River was the biggest of the British Columbia coastal streams and the first to be exploited. Initially, canning techniques did not come to the Fraser either directly or indirectly from the United States Pacific coast. They were first applied by men whose experience, whether first-or second-hand, derived from the two earlier salmon canning areas, Scotland and New Brunswick.

A faster rate of growth in the United States industry, however, soon over-shadowed the British Columbia industry. Salmon canning began on the Columbia and Fraser rivers in the same season, 1867, but by 1877 the Columbia pack was 380,000 cases, whereas the pack on the Fraser had reached only 55,000 cases.[13] For these first ten years, influence from the United States was indirect, although the American industry did become a source of techniques. For instance, labels were printed in San Francisco, and one Cariboo miner, who had struck it rich in the gold fields, spent three seasons on the Columbia learning how to operate a cannery before setting up on his own on the Fraser.[14] In 1877 direct United States investment began in the Fraser River canning industry. A San Francisco-based company also tried in that year to exploit a new stream in northern British Columbia, the Skeena River. By 1881 a Canadian government survey showed that American firms controlled about 30 per cent of the total fixed capital invested in the British Columbia industry, and other American entrants in 1882 raised this proportion.[15]

With United States capital came American marketing agencies. The typical marketing agency on the Pacific coast in this period was the commission merchant. Firms of commission merchants were not specialized, usually handling both imports and exports and dealing in a variety of commodities. The earliest Fraser River canneries marketed their pack through commission merchants in Victoria. The Victoria firms, established in the days of the Fraser River and Cariboo gold rushes, had first been in the business of importing goods for the infant colonies of British Columbia and Vancouver Island. Since there were no overland connections with Canada until after 1885, they built up a direct trade with Great

Britain. These Victoria merchants in effect financed the early Fraser River canners by a system of advances, secured by chattel mortgages, which carried the canners through the eighteen-month cycle from the ordering of the tinplate in Wales until the sale of the pack in England. A similar system prevailed in San Francisco, the financial headquarters of the United States industry. Canners who moved in from the United States retained their San Francisco connections, and many of them were financed by W. T. Coleman and Company of that city.

In the mid-1880s the expansion of the industry on both the Columbia and Fraser rivers slackened. The Fraser River pack of 1882, nearly 200,000 cases, was not surpassed until 1889. The Columbia River pack of chinook salmon reached its highest point in 1883 and then began to decline.[16] There were cries that overfishing was responsible, and an agitation began for conservation measures. But the reasons seem to lie elsewhere, since both rivers produced larger packs in the 1890s. Part of the problem was markets. Market expansion did not keep pace with the growth of the pack, and there was a glut of unsold salmon in the hands of British agents. The other reason was a transfer of fishing effort to new areas. The 1880s saw the rise of the Alaska industry, and canners on the Fraser River opened plants on the Skeena, the Nass, and other salmon-producing streams of the north coast of British Columbia.

With the revival of the trade in the late 1880s came changed relations between the British Columbia industry and that in the United States. The industry on the Pacific coast had begun as an export industry and BC canners were even more dependent on offshore markets than American canners. A home market did begin to develop in the eastern United States, but the home market opened to BC canners with the completion of the Canadian Pacific Railway was very much smaller. For British Columbia, Britain was still the chief market, and it seems to have been this close connection which attracted British capital directly into salmon canning in the province.

Acting in each case on the initiative of local people, two British-backed limited liability companies were formed—the British Columbia Canning Co. Ltd. in 1889, and the Anglo-British Columbia Packing Co. Ltd. in 1891. They acquired existing canneries, Anglo-British Columbia buying out all the American-owned concerns on the Fraser. The acquisition of American interests was facilitated by the difficulties of W. T. Coleman and Company, who had acted as broker for the American-owned firms. Years of litigation, charge, and counter-charge ended in Coleman's bankruptcy in 1888. Most of the remaining locally owned canneries banded together under the leadership of their Victoria agent, R. P. Rithet and Company, into the Victoria Canning Company Ltd. By 1891, then, the whole Fraser River was organized into five groups: two British companies, one local company, and only two independents.[17] The Fraser River canning industry, and British Columbia canning generally, had broken its ties with United States interests, and future development was to be marked by a strong competitive feeling.

The development of the British Columbia salmon canning industry does not, then, support the hypothesis that relations between San Francisco and British Columbia in the years 1867-92 were simply those of metropolis and hinterland. There was no simple transfer of an industry from Maine to San Francisco Bay and then northward under the aegis of the commercial and financial agents of the dominant centre. Salmon canning in BC began independently. If was financed primarily by local commission merchants with direct trade connections with Great Britain. The bulk of the pack was exported directly, not via San Francisco. American canners on the Fraser and Skeena rivers were not the advance representatives of a takeover by United States industry but a minority interest that was unable to sustain itself and was bought out by British- and Canadian-backed companies.

The wider economic relationships in this period between California, especially San Francisco, and British Columbia cannot be usefully considered unless the relationships of both with Great Britain are examined. In the latter third of the nineteenth century Great Britain was the buyer for the Pacific coast's largest export —wheat. In the years 1870-1900 the grain trade accounted annually for 50 to 70 per cent in value of total exports from the United States Pacific coast. The wheat fields of the region shipped from one-quarter to three-quarters as much as was exported from the United States east coast and usually stood second only to the east coast among world suppliers of wheat to Britain. Great Britain was also the world's great exporter of capital, and the grain trade attracted both British shipping and British mercantile enterprises to California. British firms, such as the San Francisco commission merchants Falkner, Bell and Company, became agents of British insurance and shipping interests. Other British firms—such as Balfour, Guthrie—were established by their parent Liverpool houses to handle the needs of the grain trade. These trade connections also undoubtedly help explain the astonishingly rapid rise in canned salmon exports from the Pacific coast. The salmon trade rode along on the back of the grain trade, and British capital followed this trade. Not only did Balfour, Guthrie invest in California, but banks with British capital and British charters established themselves in San Francisco and played a leading role in the financial community. These British ventures have already been discussed by others, but one dimension can be added to the picture which may further illuminate it.[18]

An alternative channel of British financial and mercantile entry into the United States Pacific coast was through British Columbia. The Bank of British Columbia, which received a royal charter in 1862 and had its headquarters in London, found that it could not profitably employ its capital in the limited opportunities of the British Pacific colonies. It therefore established branches down the coast, beginning with San Francisco in 1864. The historian of the bank estimates that it was second in San Francisco only to the Bank of California and, after 1875, to the Nevada Bank. Considering the chequered careers of these two, it may fairly be said to have been the most stable of the larger banks in the city. Certainly, in the panics of 1877 and 1893 it proved itself to be. The Bank of British Columbia's period of operation in California under its own name, from 1864 to 1900, almost coincides with the period of the California export grain trade. This is not just coincidence, for it was heavily involved in that trade, advancing money against wheat in warehouses and buying bills of lading on overseas shipments of wheat in transit when other banks would not take the risk. It also had a large share of exchange operations with London and New York. In boom years, the San Francisco and Portland branches made more money than Victoria, the nominal head office in North America, although losses in depression years were also correspondingly greater. In the 1870s San Francisco profits were three times those of Victoria. In 1888 and 1889 they were more than Victoria and all the other branches in British Columbia put together.[19]

The Bank of British Columbia also provided an umbrella for ambitious entrepreneurs to move out of British Columbia into the wider area of the Pacific coast. One such firm was Welch, Rithet of Victoria, the predecessor of R. P. Rithet and Company. By the late 1880s it was the biggest of the mercantile firms in British Columbia and the leading agent for salmon cannery operators. In San Francisco it operated as Andrew Welch and Company with a branch in Liverpool. Andrew Welch and Company was a large customer of the San Francisco branch of the Bank of British Columbia, did a commission merchant's business, and had sugar interests in the Hawaiian Islands. When Welch died in 1889, it was said of him that he had "acquired his wealth on the Pacific coast, having come to Victoria as a bookkeeper."[20]

These bits of evidence, admittedly fragmentary, suggest that relations between California and British Columbia were more complex than those simply of metropolis and hinterland. Rodman Paul notes that the grain trade made "rural California and mercantile San Francisco almost a colonial appendage of Victorian Britain."[21] It might also be said that British Columbia in the same period was another such appendage. For both the triangle of trade involved direct and independent links with Great Britain, as well as cross-connections with each other.

Notes

[1] F. W. Howay, W. N. Sage, and H. F. Angus, *British Columbia and the United States* (Toronto: Ryerson, 1942), pp. 184, 190, 217.

[2] J. C. Lawrence, "California's influence on the industrial and commercial development of British Columbia, 1858-1885," paper read at the 1968 meeting of the Pacific Coast Branch of the American Historical Association.

[3] Michael Graham, a United Kingdom fisheries scientist, states the "Great Law of Fishing" as "Fisheries that are unlimited become unprofitable" (*The fish gate* [London: Faber & Faber, 1943], p. 155).

[4] Harold A. Innis, *The cod fisheries: The history of an international economy* (New Haven: Yale University Press, 1940).

[5] This account is based chiefly on Philip Gilhousen, *Migratory behaviour of adult Fraser River sockeye*, 1960, International Pacific Salmon Fisheries Commission, Progress Report (unnumbered), pp. 2-6.

[6] F. J. Ward and P. A. Larkin, *Cyclic dominance in Adams River sockeye salmon*, 1964, International Pacific Salmon Fisheries Commission, Progress Report no. 11, pp. 4-12.

[7] Charles L. Cutting, *Fish saving* (New York: Philosophical Library, 1956), p. 191.

[8] The best general account is in Homer E. Gregory and Kathleen Barnes, *North Pacific fisheries* (New York: Institute of Pacific Relations, 1939).

[9] Jack Cecil Drummond and Anne Wilbraham, *The Englishman's food* (London: Jonathan Cape, 1939), p. 381.

[10] Henry Doyle, "Rise and decline of the Pacific salmon fisheries," University of British Columbia manuscript, vol. 1, pp. 29-30.

[11] Charles Wilson, "Economy and society in late Victorian Britain," *Economic History Review*, 2nd series, v. 18 (August 1965), p. 191.

[12] James B. Jeffreys, *Retail trading in Britain, 1850-1950* (Cambridge University Press, 1954), pp. 128-30.

[13] John N. Cobb, *Pacific salmon fisheries* (4th ed.; US Department of Commerce, Bureau of Fisheries, Fisheries Document No. 1092, 1930), pp. 562, 579.

[14] J. B. Kerr, ed., *Biographical dictionary of well-known British Columbians* (Vancouver: Kerr and Begg, 1890), pp. 216-17.

[15] Canada, *Sessional Papers*, 1882, no. 5 supp. 2, p. 223.

16 Cobb, *op. cit.*

17 For a fuller account see my "The 1900 strike of Fraser River sockeye salmon fishermen" (unpublished MA thesis, University of British Columbia, 1965), pp. 23-7 and Doyle, *op. cit.,* v. 1, pp. 156-80.

18 The two preceding paragraphs are based mainly on Rodman Paul, "The wheat trade between California and the United Kingdom," *Mississippi Valley Historical Review,* v. 45 (December 1958), pp. 391-412 and Morton Rothstein, "A British firm on the American west coast, 1869-1914," *Business History Review,* v. 37 (Winter 1963), pp. 392-415.

19 Victor Ross, "The Bank of British Columbia," *The history of the Canadian Bank of Commerce* (Toronto: Oxford University Press, 1920), v. 1, pp. 251-350.

20 Victoria *Colonist,* July 26, 1889, p. 4.

21 Paul, *op. cit.,* p. 412.

15. The Business Community in the Early Development of Victoria, British Columbia
J. M. S. Careless

J. M. S. CARELESS, *professor of history at the University of Toronto and one of Canada's foremost historians, is best known for his formulation of the "metropolitan" thesis which examines Canadian history in terms of the relation of major cities—Paris, London, Montreal, Toronto—to their hinterlands. This article represents a change of focus in its study of the growth of specific urban centres.*

The rise of Victoria from the Hudson's Bay fort of the 1850's to the substantial commercial city of the later nineteenth century may be readily associated with striking events like the Fraser and Cariboo gold rushes, the political course of able Governor Douglas and the somewhat colourful officialdom about him—or the still more colourful doings of Amor de Cosmos, a kind of dedicated opportunist in politics, working toward the crucial decision of federal union with Canada. Far less likely is Victoria's growth to be associated with the more prosaic, lower-keyed activities of the city's businessmen. Nonetheless, their quieter, continuing operations played an essential part in making the Vancouver Island community the chief entrepot of young British Columbia. Nor was the process lacking in colour or in noteworthy figures of its own. To trace that process, the development of the business community in conjunction with Victoria itself, is thus the object of the present study.[1]

Before 1858, and the onset of the gold rush to the Fraser on the neighbouring mainland, Victoria was a tranquil little hamlet of some three hundred inhabitants clustered about a fur trade depot. For Victoria, founded in 1843, did have the distinction, of course, of being the Hudson's Bay headquarters on the coast, as well as seat of government for the colony of Vancouver Island that had been erected in 1849, still in the keeping of the fur trade company. As a part of a great British commercial and imperial

---

Source: David S. Macmillan, ed., *Canadian Business History: Selected Studies, 1497-1971* (Toronto, 1972), pp. 104-23. Reprinted by permission of the author and publisher.

enterprise, and on the open Pacific within the world reach of British seapower, Victoria was by no means wholly isolated or unchanging. Parties of colonists had arrived from the United Kingdom to settle among the Company's officers and employees. The mild climate and fertile soil of the adjacent districts produced good crops. The Company had opened valuable coal mines up the coast at Nanaimo in the early fifties, and the timber wealth of the Island's heavy forests was initially being tapped. Finally, there was an increasing trade southward in coal, lumber, and sometimes fish or potatoes to San Francisco, the bustling Californian gold metropolis, from where most of the colony's necessary imports were derived.

Nevertheless, Victoria had remained an outpost community of small endeavours and limited opportunities. It was not one to invite much business enterprise when the fur company dominated the major economic activities—not to mention political—and when markets were either local and scanty or far off and uncertain. True, the Hudson's Bay interests had worked at developing farms, mines or sawmills, and had diversified their trading operations on the coast well beyond the traffic in furs. Yet problems of access to market and to sufficient shipping plagued them too, while the established, hierarchical ways of the old fur monopoly inevitably made new adjustments harder. Outside of the quasi-bureaucratic world of the Bay Company, moreover, there scarcely was a business community, other than well-to-do tavernkeepers like James Yates (a former Company employee), some artisans, and a few independent settlers engaged in trade.

John Muir, formerly a Company coal-miner, sent spars, piles and lumber to Victoria from his small mill at Sooke, for shipment to the California market. Captain William Brotchie had pioneered in opening the spar trade, but found it hard to get adequate transport, and subsequently became Victoria's Harbourmaster. And Captain James Cooper, who had commanded Hudson's Bay supply vessels, had set up as an independent trader, bringing the little iron schooner, *Alice,* out from England in sections, then shipping cargoes like coal, cranberries and spars to San Francisco and the Hawaiian Islands. The role of sea captains in early business development on Vancouver Island was notable, in fact. But shipmasters then had long been roving businessmen, used to trading where they could, seeking cargoes, and commissions in their own or others' service. They were particularly prominent in early lumbering on the Island. Of fourteen subscribers to the Vancouver Steam Saw Mill Company five were ship captains, the rest Hudson's Bay officials or associates.[2] The Company itself introduced the first steam saw mill machinery to Victoria in 1853, but the venture failed from lack of sufficient capital, and the mill did little before it was destroyed by fire in 1859.

This, then, was the restrictive climate for business enterprise in early Victoria: lack of funds outside the Company for any but the smallest scale of operations, and lack of stimulating demands generally. The San Francisco market itself was far from satisfactory, when the products of Washington or Oregon were competitive and closer, and also did not face duties there. During the California boom that reached a peak in 1853, demands had been high enough to make the Vancouver Island lumber trade important; and of the nineteen lumber ships that left Victoria that year eighteen were bound for San Francisco.[3] When the boom faded, however, so did much of the Island's wood trade. Coal did better, earning a place in the California market as good steamer fuel; but again it could suffer from price fluctuations and the competition of coal from Britain, Australia or the eastern United States. In short, down to 1858, Victoria had not yet found a trade pattern that could encourage much business growth. Then came gold, to change the picture almost overnight.

In the spring of 1858, news of gold strikes in British territory along the lower Thompson and Fraser valleys reached San Francisco. The mass hysteria that makes gold rushes surged within the city, and thousands prepared to leave for a new El Dorado. Some might make their way to Puget Sound or by rough overland trails up through the mountainous interior, but most chose the quickest, surest route by sea, the four-day passage to Victoria. For here was a port of entry to the British far western domains, the one place of settlement in all that wilderness. It offered a base of supply and a point of transhipment for the river journey up the treacherous Fraser, unnavigable by large ocean-going vessels. The importance of already existing patterns of transport in focussing this flow of traffic is fully evident here. The mass of shipping that was now swept into highly profitable runs to Victoria was simply following a recognized lane to an established harbour that lay beside the entrance to the Gulf of Georgia, from where the fur trade had long maintained contact with the mainland posts of the interior by way of the Fraser route.

For Victoria, however, the flow of ships brought golden inundation by waves of eager miners, who needed food and shelter, transport to the interior, supplies beyond what they had carried with them, and had money to spend for it all. The first four hundred and fifty arrived in April on the American steamer

Commodore. They came in ever-mounting numbers through the summer, until, it was estimated, the town's population had climbed to seven thousand.[4] Most of the newcomers soon had to be housed under canvas; Victoria became a veritable tent city. But construction proceeded rapidly, brick as well as wooden buildings going up, while land values soared—rising for choice lots from an initial fifty dollars to three thousand dollars and more.[5] For with the miners had come entrepreneurs with capital, store and hotel keepers, commission merchants and real estate buyers, who were ready to invest in the business which they envisaged would accrue to Victoria from its services to the gold fields.

Some, of course, were essentially speculators, planning to grab a quick return and move on. Others were agents of established San Francisco firms, seeking profitable new branches, and still others were more vaguely attracted by the thought of commercial opportunities in another California-like boom. Many would leave, especially after the initial enthusiasm of the rush ran out in disillusionment by the winter, and contraction and depression followed. But enough of the new commercial element remained, along with miners in the hinterland, to bring an enduring change to Victoria. And when the next year sufficient finds further up the Fraser kept the mining frontier going, then its main outlet continued to grow also as a town. Though Victoria's population had fallen back under three thousand by 1860,[6] it had indeed become an urban centre with a trading pattern of its own, supplying a considerable market on the mainland and exporting quantities of gold to San Francisco.

The pattern was strengthened in 1860, when Governor Douglas declared the town a free port. New Westminster, established near the mouth of Fraser in 1858 as capital of the new mainland province of British Columbia, faced the burden of customs duties as well as the problems of Fraser navigation. It became little more than a river-steamboat halt, while Victoria remained the terminus for ocean shipping. The Vancouver Island town, indeed, had the best of both worlds: free external contact with an international, maritime traffic system, customs and licenses on the mainland to check encroachments on its inland trade from over the American border. Accordingly, although Victoria's business life, like its population, ebbed and flowed with the fortunes of gold mining, it nevertheless acquired substance and solidity as an entrepot, building a merchant group alongside the older Hudson's Bay and official elements that would steadily gain in stature.

Its business community grew particularly with the new rush to the Cariboo goldfields in 1862. Over the next two years, as Barkerville and other mining towns grew up far in the interior, as the Cariboo Road was opened to serve the fields, and as their deeper-driven mines increasingly needed capital and a greater volume of supplies, Victoria once more grew apace. But this time its business operations were necessarily on a bigger scale, in provisioning, transporting and financing for the larger enterprises of the Cariboo—where, moreover, farming and ranching were soon widening the bases of hinterland activities. It was good evidence of growth when Victoria was incorporated as a city in 1862, and its Chamber of Commerce was organized in 1863. That year, indeed, *The British Columbian and Victoria Guide and Directory* could say of the new city, "Her true position as the center and headquarters of commerce north of the Columbia has been placed beyond a doubt."[7]

In these early years of growth, Victoria's business community of several hundreds had acquired some significant characteristics, as well as many individuals worthy of note. One frequently remarked feature was the high proportion of Americans in the rising merchant group; another, its strongly marked cosmopolitan flavour as well. The former was to be expected from the commercial ties that made Victoria an outpost of San Francisco. The latter reflected the multi-national nature of gold rush society, whether among miners or those who would mine the miners, and whether in California or the British possessions to the north. But if Victoria had become "in effect, San Francisco in miniature,"[8] it none the less had features of its own. There were the continuing elements of the older settler society and the Hudson's Bay-official elite. Some of their members did quite well by the Victoria boom, in hotels, stores and real estate; James Yates, for instance, piling up sufficient fortune to retire. Besides, other businessmen of British or British North American background arrived to share in the town's expansion, and later more generally stayed on, when Americans tended to withdraw. Finally, some of the "American" business migrants were better included in the multi-national category, since a number of them had earlier been immigrants to the United States; and, having moved on temporarily to San Francisco, had now moved on again.

In this regard, it has been noted that of the first 450 newcomers who arrived in 1858 aboard the *Commodore* from San Francisco, only about 120 were either British or Americans (about equally divided), the rest being mainly German, French or Italian.[9] There was also a notable Jewish admixture in the cosmopolitan influx of the gold-rush era, not to mention a significant contingent of American Negroes, and additional numbers of Slavs, Hawaiians and Chinese. The commercial community that took shape in Victoria was more Anglo-American in its upper ranks, more varied on the level of small shopkeepers or skilled tradesmen. Yet French, German and Jewish names figured prominently on the higher levels, while two Negroes, Mifflin Gibbs and Peter Lester, set up the first large general store to compete effectively with that of the Hudson's Bay Company.[10]

Adolph Sutro, a cultivated German Jew, arrived in 1858 to extend the wholesale and retail tobacco business he and his brothers had established in San Francisco. The Sutro warehouse in Victoria continued under brothers Gustav and Emil, though Adolph shortly afterward returned to San Francisco, to make a fortune in the Comstock Lode and became one of the Californian city's most lavish benefactors.[11] In similar fashion David and Isaac Oppenheimer, also German Jews, arrived from California to develop a wholesale dry goods business in Victoria. After flourishing for years, they were to move to the newly founded town of Vancouver, where they became two of its wealthiest citizens and David a celebrated mayor.[12]

And in the days of the rising Victoria business community there were, besides Sutros and Oppenheimers, men like Selim and Lumley Franklin, English-born Jews, who again came in the early wave from San Francisco. They were two of Victoria's first auctioneers, prospered in real estate and as commission agents, promoted shipping and cattle sales. Selim, moreover, sat for Victoria in the Vancouver Island legislature from 1860 to 1866, while Lumley was mayor of the city in 1865.[13] Still further, there were names like Ghiradelli and Antonovich, commission merchants, Jacob Sehl, furniture dealer from Coblentz, and P. Manciet, who kept the Hotel de France (a leading establishment in the sixties), all to demonstrate the variety of this new little urban business world.[14]

As for Ameicans, almost the most significant for the future was William Parsons Sayward, of New England origin. In 1858 he came up from a lumber business in San Francisco to found a similar one in Victoria. His wharf and yards grew over the years; but, more important, he went into sawmilling at Mill Bay in 1861, and ultimately became one of the chief figures in lumbering on the North Pacific coast.[15] Then, there was C. C. Pendergast who opened an office for Wells Fargo in Victoria in 1858. From the start, Wells Fargo played a major part in banking, in exporting gold to San Francisco, and for some time in handling mail for the business community: all of which made "Colonel" Pendergast a man of wide regard.[16] Equally well regarded was T. N. Hibben, a South Carolinian whose stationery and bookselling firm, begun in 1858, would have a long existence in Victoria. Still others prominent in the American segment of the community were Edgar Marvin, hardware and farm machinery importer (an 1862 arrival who became United States consul), and J. A. McCrea and P. M. Backus, both auctioneers.[17] Theirs was an important occupation at the time, when so many cargoes as well as properties inland were disposed of through auction sales.

There were also agents of San Francisco shipping lines, wholesalers and forwarding houses in the Victoria trade; for example, Samuel Price and Company, Dickson, De Wolf and Company, or Green Brothers. Sometimes their local representatives were Americans, but often instead they were Victorians of British background, serving as local partners in their firm—which itself might reach back far beyond San Francisco in a chain of interlocking partnerships to New York, Liverpool and London. Dickson De Wolf, for example, was (locally Dickson and Campbell), was based on H. N. Dickson's of London, and also had houses or correspondents in Liverpool, Boston and Halifax.[18] Yet from the time of the Fraser gold rush, a good deal of Victoria's expanding wholesale trade was handled by local commission agents and general merchants, who of course had San Francisco correspondents. And in this field it seems evident that the British segment of the business community became particularly important.

The relative prominence of British wholesale merchants in the basic import trades no doubt related to the fact of operating in British territory, and the likelihood of their securing better contacts with colonial authorities or the still influential Hudson's Bay Company—not to mention the possibility of their having useful business ties back to Great Britain herself, where some of them returned to visit. A good illustration is that of J. J. Southgate, an Englishman who had been a commission merchant and shiphandler in San Francisco, but moved to Victoria in 1858 with a letter of introduction to Governor Douglas. Southgate soon prospered there, gaining, for example, a contract to provision His Majesty's warships lying in nearby Esquimalt harbour.[19] He built a fine brick store (still standing), with financial backing from Commander H. D. Lascelles, R. N., dealt in real estate, took the lead in organizing a Masonic Lodge, and was elected to the legislature in 1860.[20] Another example is that of the Lowe brothers, Thomas and James, two Scots commission merchants in San Francisco, who similarly transferred their business to Victoria in

1861-2. Thomas was an old Hudson's Bay man who had close links with the Company trading network along the coast, and in the fifties had pioneered in selling coal from the Company's Vancouver Island mines in the San Francisco market.[21] It was notable, incidentally, that the Lowe firm wrote the letter of introduction that Southgate carried to Douglas.[22] Subsequently the brothers took over the latter's wholesale business when he was absent in England; and James Lowe became President of the Chamber of Commerce in 1866, though he failed to win election to parliament in 1869.

Among many other leading early British businessmen one may mention R. C. Janion, with Liverpool and Honolulu connections, J. Robertson Stewart, Robert Burnaby and G. M. Sproat— President of the local St. Andrew's Society in 1863. Born in Kirkcudbrightshire, Gilbert Sproat had come to Vancouver Island in 1860 in the service of Anderson and Company, a big London firm of shipowners and shipbrokers who were developing a large steam sawmill at Alberni on the west coast of the Island. He became manager of the mill himself when its initiator, Captain Edward Stamp, resigned; but he also built up his own importing and insurance business in Victoria.[23] Another Anderson employee was to become Sproat's partner, Andrew Welch, an Englishman with a distinguished business career ahead of him. And Thomas Harris, also from England, Victoria's first butcher, grew to be a well-to-do provisioner and the city's mayor in 1862.

The British element was also found in banking, for the wealthy London-based and chartered Bank of British North America had opened a Victoria branch in 1859. A few months previous, however, the town's first private bank had already been established by Alexander Macdonald, an enterprising Scotsman who had come up from California with the gold rush in hopes of living by it. He did well at first, making advances in gold dust for sale in San Francisco. But in 1864 his bank was burgled (through the roof) of well over $25,000, which ruined him, and sent him fleeing back to California.[24] The Bank of British Columbia, again London-based with a royal charter of 1862, proved more substantial and reliable, helping to finance wholesale operations, and soon, indeed, the government itself.

"British" at this period quite properly could cover subjects of the Queen who came to Victoria from the eastern colonies of British North America. It is of interest to note that there was some (prospective) Canadian content in contemporary Victoria business and professional circles, as evidenced by Thomas Earle, wholesale grocer and later member of parliament, an Upper

Canadian who arrived in 1862.[25] Gradually more eastern British Americans did appear, usually still by way of California; but one of the earliest significant indications of their coming was in journalism. The first newspaper, the *Victoria Gazette,* established in June, 1858, may have been an extension of American press enterprise, but it is worth observing that its publisher, James W. Towne of California, was born in Nova Scotia.[26] And the far more important David Higgins, who arrived in 1860 and subsequently would edit Victoria's enduring *Colonist* for many years, was similarly of Nova Scotian birth, if American upbringing.[27] Above all, there was the founder and first editor of the *British Colonist* (begun late in 1858), Amor de Cosmos, also a native Nova Scotian, who also came via California. His vehement and erratic career in press and politics may not suggest too close an analogy with Joseph Howe; but at least there was some Nova Scotian ingredient added to early Victoria, through this transplanting of Bluenoses from one coast to another.

The character of this business community, strongly associated with the American Pacific metropolis but also with the older British metropolis of the Atlantic, did not greatly change for years the stamp it had received in the gold boom era of the early 1860's. New men were to come forward, additional interests to develop; but the men largely emerged out of older firms and partnerships, and the broader economic developments did not alter Victoria's basic role as a maritime commercial entrepot serving a simple extractive hinterland. Of course, declining gold production from the mid-sixties onward, the coming of Confederation with Canada in 1871, and the mounting influence of Canadian metropolitan power thereafter—signalized by the National Policy of 1878 and the building of the Canadian Pacific in the next decade—all brought significant changes that inevitably affected Victoria business more and more. Yet well into the 1880's, and perhaps even to the nineties, the patterns of Victorian commercial society set between 1858 and 1864 continued as a basis; even while American or continental European elements within it decreased or were assimilated, and British and Canadian elements were enlarged. This, then, is the general framework for the next two decades. It remains to dicuss the newer activities and the newer men that did emerge inside it.

The falling output of the gold mines after 1864, and the failure to find rich, easily workable new fields, did not seriously harm Victoria at first, still living on the momentum, so to speak, of the expectations of more finds, and with some stimulus to trade derived from the American Civil War. Falling gold revenues and heavy colonial debt burdens, however, did lead in 1866 to the union of Vancouver Island and British Columbia as an urgent move of retrenchment. And this union sharply affected Victoria by removing its privileges as a free port. It was almost the hand-writing on the wall; continental costs of development and need for customs duties had defeated the interests of maritime free trade. At the public proclamation in Victoria of the new united province of British Columbia, so the *Colonist* noted, members of the crowd variously informed the sheriff that he was reading his death-warrant, warned a red-nosed bystander that port was no longer duty-free, and urged "a seedy-looking individual" to hurry up Government Street and buy a suit while he could still save fifteen per cent.[28] At least there was the consolation that Victoria remained provincial capital—to New Westminster's chagrin.

Activity in lumbering had offset in some degree the lessening role of gold. At Alberni, Gilbert Sproat's steam saw mill had reached a splendid peak in 1863, producing over eleven million feet of lumber, until the rapid exhaustion of timber close to water, accessible to the hand or ox-logging of those days, forced its closing by 1865.[29] However, the saw mill that W. P. Sayward had opened in 1863 up the Island's east coast near Cowichan thrived on a more accessible timber supply. In 1864 his mill alone brought two million feet to Victoria, and by the close of the decade put him into the export trade.[30] At the time of the union of 1866, moreover, there were six Vancouver Island saw mills in operation, much of their produce being marketed by way of Victoria. Furthermore, during the depression of the later sixties, they and the Burrard Inlet mills, that had now appeared on the mainland at Moodyville and Hastings, ended the former dominance of American Puget Sound mills over the import market.[31] While for some years following, Island lumbering failed to grow markedly, an important productive basis had been laid for future development, in which the Sayward milling and lumbering interests would play full part.

Then there was coal. In 1858 the Hudson's Bay Company had returned control of Vancouver Island to the Crown, and the next year its trading rights on the mainland had ended. Thereafter the Company had sought to concentrate on its original concern, the fur trade, divesting itself of other complicating ventures, such as its coal mines in the Nanaimo area. Thus in 1862 it sold these holdings to the Vancouver Island Coal Mining and Land Company, which was based in England and backed by British capital. (It also seems to have had an oddly literary connection, since T.

C. Haliburton was its first chairman and among its investors were Agnes Strickland and the father of John Galsworthy.[32] In Victoria, the thriving firm of Dickson, Campbell and Company served as its agents, George Campbell being made a director. Much of the Vancouver Coal Company's output went directly from Nanaimo to market, to San Francisco or the Royal Navy based at Esquimalt. But some as well went via Victoria, where Charles Wallace, also of Dickson and Campbell, managed the two ships that the Company bought for its trade in 1864.[33] The next year coal production rose to 32,000 tons; and to 44,000 in 1868.[34] But by 1870 it seemed to have reached a plateau, and in the following decade the Company ran into trouble, owing to lack of further capital to develop new mines, and competition not only in the American market but within Vancouver Island itself.

The latter competition came from Robert Dunsmuir, the son of a Scottish coal master, who had first been employed at Nanaimo in the Hudson's Bay Company mines, but had been engaged in his own independent workings there since 1855. In 1864 another English coal mining venture, the Harewood Company, was launched, backed by the Hon. H. D. Lascelles, commanding H.M.S. Forward and Dunsmuir became its resident manager.[35] Though he drove his miners rigorously (which did not stop them entertaining him to a public tea that year),[36] he could not overcome the fact that the Harewood Mine, after starting well, began to peter out. Dunsmuir withdrew. In 1869, however, he discovered the truly rich Wellington Mine, and set up a company to work it, with financial aid from another naval officer, Lieutenant W. N. Diggle of the Grappler.[37] The Dunsmuir Company soon flourished, having one of the best coal seams on the coast and thus well able to stand the competition in the San Francisco market. Moreover, it undertook dock and railway developments at Nanaimo that ministered to that town's growth. And some of the benefit would redound to Victoria, since it kept much of the supply trade of the area. Hence, by the seventies, at least, growth in this coal hinterland could help balance decline in the older one of gold.

And then there was shipping. During the 1860's Victoria became the centre of shipping and shipbuilding interests of its own. It started, of course, with the rush of mining traffic to the Fraser. At the outset the Hudson's Bay Company had commanded the transport service; its pioneer steamers, the Beaver and Otter, would long be famous around the coasts and up the lower reaches of the river. But because of the demands for transport during the gold rush, Governor Douglas had recognized the need to allow American steamboat captains to enter the river navigation. A number of veterans of Puget Sound or Columbia River steamboating thus came in, and largely found it practicable to make Victoria their base of operations, as the main terminus of the Fraser trade. Captain William Irving became the most prominent and enduring of them—but here again the description of "American" is misleading, since he was a Scot, with much seagoing experience behind him before he pioneered with the first steamboat in Oregon.[38]

Irving joined with another Scottish steamboat pioneer from the Columbia, Alexander Murray, to build the stern-wheeler *Governor Douglas* at Victoria in 1858, her engine being brought from San Francisco.[39] This "first steamer built in the province for the inland trade" was soon joined by a sister ship, the *Colonel Moody*.[40] The previously mentioned merchants, Thomas and James Lowe, invested in the vessels; James for a time was an agent for the line, as were the also-mentioned Samuel Price and Company.[41] Irving built still more ships at Frahey's yard in Victoria, the *Reliance* in 1862 and the *Onward* in 1865.[42] The Hudson's Bay Company also acquired new craft to meet their competition and that from American steamboats. But the fall in gold-mining activity after 1864 led American captains to leave the Fraser, so that for the rest of the decade Irving's and the Bay Company's ships between them controlled the river.[43] Indeed, this situation virtually continued until Captain Irving's death in 1872, and afterwards his son, John Irving, built a still larger shipping domain.

Joseph Spratt was significant also, because the Albion Iron Works, the foundry and marine machinery works he established in Victoria in 1862, became central to the subsequent growth of the city's shipping activities. After having had some training as a marine engineer in England, Spratt had gone to San Francisco, where he had opened a foundry and reputedly built the first steam locomotive on the Pacific coast.[44] As well as running his iron works, he went into shipbuilding, later salmon-canning and whaling, and organized a shipping line up the island's east coast. In any case, by the end of the 1860's he had added the beginnings of industrial enterprise to Victoria. And by that time, too, nine of the seventeen steamers trading to British Columbia and eighteen of the twenty-eight schooners were Victoria-built.[45]

As the sixties drew to a close, however, the city was in a state of depression. The newer activities in lumber, coal or shipbuilding had not yet hit full stride, and what was still far more apparent was the passing of the gold frontier, with its consequent effects on the wholesale trade, real estate and financial interests of the

Victoria entrepot. Business in the city in 1869 was so slow, in fact, that thistles grew in the gutters along Government Street, while the population was falling back again to little more than three thousand.[46] In this condition, it is not surprising that the business community was considerably despondent, or that, in the midst of continuing discussions on joining the new and far-off Canadian Confederation, some of its members might look to the simpler, sharper release of annexation to the United States. At any rate, the Annexation Petition of 1869 appeared in Victoria in November, signed with 104 names in all.

It is true that this was a limited number; that many of the signers were small men, not leading merchants; and that they included a large element of foreign born who had no strong political positions, either anti-British or pro-American, but voiced what was indeed "primarily an expression of economic discontent."[47] It is also true that the essential issue in Victoria was union with Canada or no union; that annexation was never a real alternative. Yet it is possible, besides, that doubts and fears expressed in anti-unionism among Victorians found a sharper focus in some of those businessmen who did subscribe to annexation: a matter of choosing the devil you knew at San Francisco to the distant unknown one at Ottawa, especially when the former so obviously commanded power and fortune. And certainly one might see concern for the wholesale trade or property values in such substantial signatories as Isaac Oppenheimer and David Shirpser, dry goods merchants, W. H. Oliver and W. Farron, heavy investors in Victoria real estate, or Emil Sutro, tobacco merchant, and T. N. Hibben, the prominent stationer.[48]

At all events, the flurry passed with little consequence; and within a few months Confederation was settled policy. By the time it took place in July, 1871, a brighter Victoria was ready to welcome it, hopeful indeed of the terms that had been agreed upon, including a railway to link East and West. For it well might be expected that a Pacific railway would have its terminus in or near Victoria, crossing to Vancouver Island over the narrows at its northern tip. Certainly the fact that a survey party for the projected Canadian Pacific were present in Victoria for the celebrations that accompanied the proclamation of British Columbia's entry into Confederation did not lessen the festivity.[49] And Victoria's businessmen could thus anticipate that change would also mean improvement for their community.

As the 1870's opened, it was a good thing that Victorians did have expectations from Confederation, for times continued slow in many respects: their city's population only passed 4,600 by 1874.[50] However, they could look to some federal relief from the provincial debt burden, some aid from a broader union in meeting the high costs of developing transport in the rugged hinterland. And there was the prospect of the railway, which raised new visions of Victoria as the San Francisco of the North, with its own transcontinental rail link like the newly opened Union Pacific, and its own Pacific oceanic empire of trade. Politically, at least, the city had been connected into a new continental system. Now it looked for the necessary communication network to be constructed also, to put it on the highroads of world development.

Gradually, moreover, its basic hinterland trades improved. Gold production, after reaching a low point in 1870, went up in 1871, and up still further in 1874-5, although it never came near the scale of the early sixties.[51] Coal output also began a steady climb from 1873 to 1879, though bigger years of growth would come in the next decade.[52] And if lumbering on the Island experienced no great advance yet, a new hinterland enterprise of considerable export potential made its appearance: salmon-canning. The salmon-canning industry had reached the American Pacific coast in the 1860's, from earlier beginnings in Maine and New Brunswick; but it was first established on the lower Fraser in 1870, independent of any American connection.[53] Victoria commission merchants effectively financed the Fraser river canneries and acted as agents in exporting their product directly to Great Britain.[54] For the canning process offered a means of overcoming the barrier of distance between a rich North Pacific food resource and a hungry industrial market. Furthermore, it produced a valuable trade that did not face the impediment of ever-rising American tariff barriers.

British Columbian salmon-canning grew slowly at first in the seventies, faster in the eighties, by which time the industry had spread northward to the Skeena (in 1877) and to the Nass and beyond. Victoria businessmen continued to play a major role in the enterprise: J. H. Todd provides a good example. Born in Brampton, Upper Canada, he had gone to Barkerville in 1863, speculated in mines and operated a successful merchandising business before moving to Victoria in 1872 to undertake another. Through profits from mining properties, and through acting as agent for canners on the Fraser, the Todd wholesaling firm was able to acquire two canneries there and another at Esquimalt. Subsequently it added a much larger one on the Skeena obtained from another prominent Victoria house of the day, Turner, Beeton and Company. Todd and Sons, in fact, continued to operate from Victoria as late as 1954, its fishing interests ultimately going to B.C. Packers.[55]

Furthermore, the redoubtable Joseph Spratt of the Albion Iron Works early entered the business. He developed the oilery (for pressing out herring oil) that he had opened on Burrard Inlet in 1868, at the site of the present city of Vancouver, into a floating salmon cannery.[56] Popularly termed "Spratt's Ark," it was a pioneer in the area's canning industry. More important in the long run, however, was R. P. Rithet, a Victoria wholesale merchant of widespread interests and enterprises. After acting as an agent for local Fraser river canners, he organized a number of them into the Victoria Canning Company in 1891, to meet the competition of two British-backed companies, British Columbia Canning and Anglo-British Columbia Packing, who had acquired virtually all the other canneries on the river.[57] That story, however, runs beyond this study, and it is more important here to examine the advancing career of Robert Paterson Rithet as an exemplification of Victoria business in itself.

Born in Scotland in 1844, he was in the Cariboo in 1862; but after a few years came to Victoria, still in his early twenties, to find employment in the wholesale trade. In 1868 he was working for Sproat and Company; indeed, was running its Victoria office, since Gilbert Sproat, a man of many parts—merchant, insurance agent, sawmill manager, lobbyist, author and ethnologist—was then mainly in London, directing the Committee on the Affairs of British Columbia that he had organized.[58] The next year Rithet moved to San Francisco, to deal with the firm's interests there; evidently a promotion, for Sproat had sent him "kind words of confidence" by letter.[59] And here he came in close contact with Sproat's San Francisco partner, Andrew Welch. Welch, who had begun as a bookkeeper from England and worked with Sproat in the Alberni sawmill before entering into partnership in his wholesale business, was already emerging as a wealthy and prominent member of the San Francisco commercial elite. Before his death in 1889 he was to become a millionaire several times over, do much to develop the shipping trade between Victoria and that city, gain control of the Burrard Inlet mills at Moodyville, and thus build up a large-scale lumber export business.[60] Rithet could hardly have made a better connection. It resulted, eventually, in his own partnership with Welch.

Before that transpired, he returned to Victoria, still in Sproat's service; and there in 1870 had a stiff little encounter with a Mrs. Sutton, who did not approve of his attentions to her daughter. In fact, he broke his engagement to Miss Sutton by formal note to her mama—a Victorian touch in the wider sense of the term.[61] That year, moreover, Rithet left Sproat's firm to join that of J. Robertson Stewart, one of the old original British merchants in Victoria, who carried on insurance business for British and American companies, and helped direct the British Columbian Investment and Loan Society, as well as operating a large wholesale warehouse.[62] In May of 1871, Rithet was "at present managing his business" because of Stewart's illness.[63] The latter soon decided to dispose of his interests and retire to Scotland. Andrew Welch bought him out, with Rithet's cordial approval.[64] In fact, that August a new firm was announced in the press, Welch, Rithet and Company, successors to J. Robertson Stewart. "We began," wrote Rithet, "under very favorable auspices, when the colony seems to be about to enter an era of improvement and progress. . . . with houses in San Francisco and Liverpool we should be able to make a business, and our outside connections are also tip-top."[65]

Thereafter through the seventies, and on into the eighties, Rithet's interests continued to grow: in wholesaling, shipping, insurance, lumbering, canning, grocery importing, and generally financial investment in a wide range of enterprises. With Welch, he became engaged in the sugar trade of the Hawaiian Islands; they acquired control of plantations there.[66] He invested in the mills at Moodyville, the Albion Iron Works, in sealing, whaling and in farming. He became president of the Board of Trade and a justice of the peace in the 1870's, mayor of Victoria in 1885, then was elected to the legislature in the 1890's.[67] And on Welch's death he took over as head of both Welch and Company, San Francisco, and R. P. Rithet and Company, Victoria.[68] There is no space to deal with his later ventures in the mining and railway development of the British Columbia interior, nor in the building of deepwater dock facilities at Victoria through his Victoria Wharf and Warehouse Company. All that can be noted is his connection with the continued growth of the city's shipping interests through the founding of the Canadian Pacific Navigation Company in 1883. And this brings in another of the leading Victorian entrepreneurs of the era, John Irving.

Irving had assumed control of his father's steamship company in 1872, although only eighteen years of age. Gold discoveries in the Stikeen and Cassiar districts in the seventies revived the coastal shipping trade, and Irving moved vigorously into competition, adding new boats to his fleet. At the same time growing settlement on the mainland and its expanding needs produced more traffic to the Fraser, while soon plans for the Pacific railway's construction brought a further stimulus. In 1878 Irving obtained a contract to carry the first shipment of rails from Esquimalt to Yale, and from then on increasingly left all rivals behind.[69] His chief competitor was still the Hudson's Bay Company's fleet. In 1883 he successfully arranged to merge it with his own.

It might not be without significance that a year earlier John Irving had married the daughter of Alexander Munro, Chief Factor of the Company in Victoria—nor that two of the bride's brothers worked for R. P. Rithet, who himself had married one of the Munro girls in 1875.[70] At any rate, the Canadian Pacific Navigation Company that now emerged to combine the lines under his management had Rithet as one of its directors and chief shareholders, along with Munro and that other noted business figure, Robert Dunsmuir of colliery fame.[71] Understandably, one of the line's fast ships was the *R. P. Rithet*. Irving's shipping empire (a far cry from Captain Cooper's little schooner, *Alice*) took over minor companies at the end of the eighties, and increasingly went into inland navigation on the lakes of the interior. It was ultimately bought out by the Canadian Pacifc Railway as its coastal service in 1900. That, in itself, marked the passing of Victoria's as well as Irving's steamboat hegemony; but it had been a very good run indeed.

Meanwhile Robert Dunsmuir's coal operations had grown steadily. In 1873 his one mine, the Wellington, had turned out 16,000 tons (just entering full production) to 45,000 for all those of the Vancouver Island Coal Company's.[72] In 1880, his holdings alone produced 189,000 tons, and three years later he bought out his partner for $600,000.[73] He was well on his way to being the province's outstanding industrial capitalist, with a fleet of cargo vessels, a mine railway and a large part of the Albion Iron Works besides.[74] As if to fit the classic picture of the nineteenth-century capitalist, he had a hard reputation with labour. He faced strikes at the mines in 1877 and 1883, brought in strikebreakers, and on the former violent occasion, a gunboat and the militia also. Apart from this, Dunsmuir now settled in Victoria, was also moving into railway promotions and construction. In 1883, the Esquimalt Railway Company of which he was president (it included the powerful figures, Leland Stanford and Charles Crocker of San Francisco, and C. P. Huntington of New York) obtained a contract from the federal government to build the Esquimalt and Nanaimo line, on terms that included a lavish grant of land.[75]

Begun in 1884 under Dunsmuir's direction, it was finished in 1886, for the first time giving Victoria overland access to the coal hinterland.

Yet the seventy-mile Esquimalt and Nanaimo was a rather small consolation prize for Victoria not securing the Canadian Pacific—which was essentially what it had turned out to be. Through much of the seventies the city had envisioned and urged the transcontinental line by way of Bute Inlet and Seymour Narrows to Vancouver Island, and hotly protested proposals for a Fraser valley route to tidewater instead. In 1874 the railway on the Island was at least promised anew by the Mackenzie federal government, but the bill for it was defeated in the Senate, leaving Victoria bitterly disappointed, and much angry talk of secession in political and business circles. But though the dispute rose and fell in the ensuing years, with recurrent swells of separatism again, the fact was that the capital or the Island did not necessarily speak for the province as a whole; and the British Columbian mainland communities saw far more benefit to be gained from a Fraser valley rail route. Here was, indeed, still further indication that the island community of Victoria had been brought into a continental system, and now had little weight to bear against the whole thrust of Canadian metropolitan designs. The best that could be done was look for consolation prizes.

The Esquimalt dry dock and the E. and N. itself were two of these. And by the time that Dunsmuir undertook to build the latter (seeking truly magnificent consolation for himself and friends in terms for subsidies, coal fields and lands), Victoria interests were ready to make the best of the inevitable. Hence, in 1884, when the C.P.R. was already well advanced in its building, both up the Fraser and into the Rockies from the east, a final settlement of terms was harmoniously achieved. Victoria still had a sizeable and prosperous maritime trading domain; its population stood at twelve thousand that year,[76] and the city was thriving and hopeful. For at least it would have its own Island railway now.

Not only was the Island railway opened in 1886, but the C.P.R. that year also carried its first through trains to the Pacific —to Burrard Inlet. And this really marked the ending of an era for Victoria, for now Vancouver's meteoric rise was under way, as the true beneficiary of the transcontinental railway, the National Policy, and the forces of Canadian metropolitanism in general. The little lumber settlement on the Inlet had been launched into its role as Canada's chief western outlet and Pacific port of entry. Not till 1898 did the import trade of the upstart city pass that of Victoria's; yet the trend was there before that was to make Vancouver the new British Columbian entrepot and distributing centre.[77] In the later eighties and nineties Victoria would further develop its coal, salmon and lumber trades, along with new growth in deep-sea fishing, sealing and also in grain exports. But a reorientation of commercial patterns from sea to land was in process, in which Victoria could not hope to dominate great new hinterlands of deep-rock mining in the interior ranges or of agriculture on the prairies. A phase was over for the maritime city; and the completion of the transcontinental railway signalized it better than anything else.

There had not been want of energy or initiative in the Victorian business community. Men like Rithet, Dunsmuir and Irving demonstrated that fact, as did W. P. Sayward, who had built a large new lumber mill at Victoria in 1878—which by 1890, was cutting nearly eleven million feet a year itself, while Sayward's logging camps were scattered up the Island, feeding his large-scale export trade.[78] Others, perhaps, in the community had showed less enterprise, being more content with things as they were, in a pleasantly civilized little world readily open to greater worlds in San Francisco or London, but remote from the harder, cruder surroundings of the continental interior. Yet it would be difficult to prove such a point; and in any case it was not so much lack of enterprise as lack of situation and economic leverage that had placed it beyond the power of Victoria's businessmen to deal with changing patterns of trade. They had responded successfully to various favourable factors in the climate of enterprise; there was not much that could be done when the unfavorable overtook them.

There are many other names that could be singled out in the period of the seventies and eighties that would show the general stability and substance of this business community. Many firms from gold rush days continued in being, carrying on names like Southgate, Hibben, Dickson and Campbell, Sehl, Pendergast, Heisterman and others. Some early merchants indeed had died, retired or left, the Lowes going, one to Scotland, one to San Francisco, in the seventies; David Oppenheimer shrewdly moving to Vancouver in 1886, to become "the father of Vancouver's jobbing trade."[79] Yet there were still others who had known Victoria's earlier days actively on hand, like William Ward, manager of the Bank of British Columbia since 1867 and clerk before that, or A. H. Green of Garesche and Green, whose large private bank had taken over from Wells Fargo in 1873 but who had worked for that agency previously.[80] A notable feature of the

Victoria commercial community, in short, was still its continuity; new leaders largely rose from within its own ranks. But no doubt this was a result of there having been no spectacular advances since the gold rush to bring new groups of entrepreneurs. Victoria was already an "old," settled, quietly-growing town, after less than three decades of urban existence.

Its ties with San Francisco and Britain remained fully evident. In 1886, the bulk of its external trade was still directed to the former, though British goods continued to be of as much significance as imports, and exports of salmon to Britain (and eastern Canada) were fast rising. Offsetting San Francisco influence, of course, was British influence through politics, capital investment, business personnel, and the very dealings with major firms in San Francisco that were themselves part of a London-Liverpool and Glasgow metropolitan network; like Welch and Company, Dickson, De Wolfe, Falkner Bell, and several others.[81] Noticeable, too, was the growth of eastern Cnadian agencies and imports in Victoria by this time, behind the national tariff wall; but nothing comparable to the change effected in a few years through the C.P.R.—to which one might ascribe the fact that advertisements for Canadian firms and products clearly began to displace those of San Francisco in Victoria directories by about 1890.

And thus, in a sense, passed the San Francisco of the North, gradually to be replaced with today's centre of tourism and retirement enterprises, and of that truly big modern growth-industry, provincial government. Yet the businessmen who had seen Victoria rise from a fort or a gold rush tent town to a flourishing port city in well under thirty years, had no cause to minimize the comfortable affluence they had acquired, and done much to give to their adopted home.

What had the business community done for Victoria? In the first place—without at all forgetting other factors, the role of politicians and bureaucrats, of the labour force, or simply, the citizenry of consumers—they had essentially shaped its economic functions, furnished the bulk of jobs and services that made it an operative centre of urban population. In the second place they had considerably influenced its political, social and cultural life, businessmen having widely entered into provincial and municipal politics, benevolent and religious societies, educational movements, literary, musical organizations and the like. To deal with this would be to write another chapter. All that can be said here is that the record of early Victoria's business community in participating in primarily non-economic activities in their society seems as good as, or better than, the record of similar groups in comparable Canadian cities at similar stages of development. And this, again, is not to see this very human collectivity of fallible, self-interested individuals as peerless visionaries and altruists. It may have been more a result of Victoria's relative isolation, insularity and small size, whereby the entrepreneurial element readily came to know, and feel committed to a fairly compact local society that did not soon become heterogeneous and amorphous through continued rapid growth.

In the third place, the business community marked Victoria's character in the broadest sense: in its identity, to use a not-unheard of term. The city's affiliations with California that still exist surely relate not just to sea and sunshine (unlike the humidity of Vancouver and the northwest American coast) but to the historic communications and exchange that its merchants sustained with San Francisco. Victoria's oft-noted "British" attributes, also, may well be derived less from an obsolete Bay Company officialdom or a small emigrant English gentry than from the strongly British element in the dominant wholesale trades, which easily maintained the outlook and behaviour of the old gentry elite as it rose in wealth and social position. And finally, even the faint continuing touch of cosmopolitanism in an otherwise provincial city—which seems to give it a more mature ambiance than many an older Canadian town—assuredly may come from the original non-British, non-American component of the business community that largely persisted through Victoria's first formative decades. There is, then, much more in the early development of Victoria than the affairs of provincial governments or the vicissitudes of public men.

Notes

[1] On the general significance of this theme, see D. T. Gallagher, "Bureau crats or Businessmen? Historians and the problem of leadership in Colonial British Columbia," *Syesis,* Vol. 3, (1970), pp. 173-186.

[2] W. K. Lamb, "Early Lumbering on Vancouver Island," I, *British Columbia Historical Quarterly,* (January, 1938), p.43.

[3] *Ibid.,* p. 46.

[4] *Gazette* (Victoria), December 25, 1858.

[5] Alfred Waddington, *The Fraser Mines Vindicated* (Victoria, 1858), p. 19.

[6] *British Colonist* (Victoria), June 12, 1860.

[7] *The British Columbian and Victoria Guide and Directory for 1863* (Victoria, 1863), p. 49.

[8] W. Ireland, "British Columbia's American Heritage," *Canadian Historical Association Annual Report for 1948,* p. 68.

[9] *Ibid.,* p. 69.

[10] M. Ormsby, *British Columbia: A History* (Toronto, 1958), p. 141.

[11] R. E. and M. F. Stewart, *Adolph Sutro* (Berkeley, 1962), *passim*.

[12] "The Oppenheimers of Vancouver," typescript, British Columbia Archives (hereafter BCA).

[13] British Columbia Archives, Vertical Files (hereafter, BCAVF).

[14] Edgar Fawcett, *Some Reminiscences of Old Victoria* (Toronto, 1912), p. 60; British Columbia Miscellany, Bancroft Library, Berkeley.

[15] W. K. Lamb, *op. cit.*, II, *British Columbia Historical Quarterly* (April 1938), p. 114.

[16] Fawcett, *op. cit.*, p. 64.

[17] BCAVF.

[18] *Prices Current* (San Francisco). See advertisements from 1853 onward; also E. Mallandaine, *First Victoria Directory* (Victoria 1860), p. 42. For Samuel Price, *Gazette*, January 25, 1858—J. N. Thain was the local representative.

[19] *Colonist*, February 2, 1865.

[20] Fawcett, *op. cit.*, p. 62; *British Columbian and Victoria Guide*, p. 137.

[21] On the Lowes, see J. M. S. Careless, "The Lowe Brothers, 1852-70; A Study in Business Relations on the North Pacific Coast," *B. C. Studies*, No. 2 (1968-9), pp. 1-18.

[22] *Ibid.*, p. 10.

[23] I. M. Richard, "Gilbert Norman Sproat," *British Colonial History Quarterly*, (January, 1937), pp. 22-3.

[24] BCAVF.

[25] British Columbia Miscellany, Bancroft.

[26] BCAVF

[27] *Ibid.*

[28] *Colonist*, November 20, 1866.

[29] W. K. Lamb, *loc. cit.*, II, p. 105.

[30] *Ibid.*, p. 114.

[31] *Ibid.*, p. 121.

[32] BCAVF.

[33] P. A. Phillips, "Confederation and the Economy of British Columbia," W. G. Shelton, ed., *British Columbia and Confederation* (Victoria, 1967), p. 51, BCAVF.

[34] Phillips, *loc. cit.*, p. 51.

[35] Ormsby, *op. cit.*, p. 215.

[36] J. Audain, *From Coal Mine to Castle* (New York, 1955), p. 36.

[37] *Ibid.*, p. 51.

[38] M. A. Cox, *Saga of a Seafarer* (New Westminster, 1966), p. 8.

[39] E. W. Wright, ed., *Marine History of the Pacific North West* by Lewis and Dryden (New York, 1961), p. 81.

[40] *Ibid.*

[41] Careless, *loc. cit.*, p. 10. Lowe Papers, BCA, T. Lowe to A. C. Anderson, July 2, 1859.

[42] Lewis and Dryden, *op. cit.*, p. 140.

[43] *Ibid.*, p. 82.

[44] BCAVF.

[45] Phillips, *loc. cit.*, p. 57.

[46] S. Higgins, "British Columbia and the Confederation Era," *British Columbia and Confederation*, p. 28.

[47] Ireland, *loc. cit.*, p. 71.

[48] BCAVF.

[49] *British Colonist*, July 20, 1871.

[50] *City of Victoria Directory for 1890* (Victoria, 1890), p. 122.

[51] *Annual Report of the Minister of Mines* (Victoria, 1900), chart, n.p.

[52] *Ibid.*

[53] Phillips, *op. cit.*, p. 55.

[54] K. Ralston, "Patterns of Trade and Investment on the Pacific Coast, 1867-1892: the Case of the British Columbia Salmon Canning Industry," *B.C. Studies*, No. 1 (1968-9), p. 42.

[55] BCAVF.

[56] J. M. Grant. "British Columbia in Early Times," *British Columbia Magazine* (June, 1911), p. 494.

[57] Ralston, *loc. cit.*, pp. 42-3.

[58] Richard, *loc. cit.*, pp. 22-9.

[59] BCA, *R. P. Rithet Letterbook*, I, Rithet to G. Sproat, December 11, 1868.

[60] BCAVF.

[61] *Rithet Letterbook*, Rithet to Mrs. Sutton, April 16, 1870.

[62] *British Colonist*, November 11, 1869.

[63] *Rithet Letterbook*, Rithet to R. P. D. Duff, May 9, 1871.

[64] *Ibid.*, Rithet to A. Welch, August 24, 1871.

[65] *Ibid.*, August 25, 1871.

[66] *Colonist*, July 26, 1889.

[67] BCAVF. See also *Victoria Illustrated* (Victoria, 1891) pp. 77-8.

[68] *Ibid.*

[69] BCAVF.

[70] *Colonist*, April 17, 1889.

[71] Lewis and Dryden, *op. cit.*, p. 303.

[72] Audain, *op. cit.*, p. 52.

[73] *Ibid.*, pp. 65, 73.

[74] *Colonist*, April 13, 1889.

[75] Audain, *op. cit.*, p. 79.

[76] *City of Victoria Directory for 1890*, p. 122.

[77] *Annual Reports of the British Columbia Board of Trade*, 1887-1900 (Victoria, 1900), tables, n.p.

[78] *Victoria Illustrated*, p. 50.

[79] L. Makovski, "Rise of the Merchant Princes," *British Columbia Magazine* (June, 1911), p. 57.

[80] BCAVF. Francis Garesche was drowned in 1874, but the firm continued in both names.

[81] See directory and newspaper advertisements of period for indications of operations of these firms. On all three, for example, see *San Francisco Directory for 1873*, M. G. Langley (San Francisco, 1873), and on Falkner, Bell specifically, W. T. Jackson, *The Enterprising Scot* (Edinburgh, 1968), pp. 222, 374, *passim*. Falkner, Bell also appear in the Lowe and

Rithet letters—and Jackson's work notes that the Scottish American Investment Company, for and with which they dealt, bought extensive California ranch property on the recommendation of John Clay (who had been George Brown's estate manager in Ontario), as well as involving Thomas Nelson, the leading Edinburgh publisher in its investments. Nelson was Brown's brother-in-law, who with Clay succeeded in restoring Brown's Bow Park estate to financial health after the latter's death. One can see many ramifications here worth tracing out!

16. Population Growth and Change in Seattle and Vancouver, 1880-1960
Norbert Macdonald

A. NORBERT MACDONALD, *associate professor of history at the University of British Columbia, is a specialist in the modern United States, who approaches the study of Vancouver from a comparative urban viewpoint.*

All modern cities have a good deal in common. Whether it be the diversity of their inhabitants, the need for better transportation systems, the problems of air and water pollution, the elimination of sub-standard housing, the need to combat the sense of alienation and anonymity felt by many residents or the desire to improve local schools and art galleries—all seem to be shared by any large and complex city, at least in the developed sections of the world. For many urban historians, however, the real appeal in studying cities is not in showing how all cities reflect minor variations from a standard model, but rather in seeing how each city has a unique development and existence, quite unlike that of any other city. Although at long range two cities may appear to be quite similar in their geographical setting, population makeup, industrial structure, and historical background, when examined at close range they show a host of distinctive characteristics which make them unique.

Seattle, Washington, and Vancouver, British Columbia, are a pertinent case in point. These cities share much in common. Both are seaports far removed from national centers of population; both got their start in the late nineteenth century as logging and lumbering communities; both developed very slowly in their early years; and both began growing rapidly during the great railroad boom of the 1880s when the Northern Pacific and the Canadian Pacific reached the West Coast. The two cities prospered with the gold rush to the Klondike and Alaska in the late 1890s, and from then until World War I experienced a period of dynamic growth which they have never since equalled. Between 1897 and 1914 Seattle's population increased from 55,000 to 275,000, while Van-

Source: *Pacific Historical Review*, *XXXIX*, 3 (1970), pp. 297-321.
Reprinted by permission of the author and publisher.

couver's rose six-fold from 20,000 to 125,000. During these years each city became firmly established as a transportation, trading, and financial center for its respective region, and each depended primarily on the lumber industry for its economic prosperity. Throughout the prosperous 1920s and the depressed 1930s the two cities continued to develop along parallel lines. Only with World War II and the rapid expansion of the aircraft industry in Seattle did the American city depart sharply from its Canadian counterpart.

Although Seattle and Vancouver had much in common, they were obviously in different nations which had different governments, immigration policies, tariff structures, banking facilities, and legal systems. These differences had a decided impact on local development. The railroad that sparked Vancouver's growth, for example, resulted from national policies determined in Ottawa, whereas Seattle's railroad connections and early growth were in large part the consequence of private initiative. Similarly, differences in the pattern of municipal politics, in the behavior of businessmen, in the division of authority between federal and regional governments, in the nature of educational institutions, in characteristic housing types, in the attitude of workers to employers, and in the character and values of the two cities are all evident to the interested observer.

Histories of individual American and Canadian cities are numerous. But very little work has been done in isolating and identifying significant characteristics, and in showing in what way, if any, urban development in Canada has differed from that in the United States. As a first step in such a study this paper will focus on the way in which the population of Seattle and Vancouver has grown and changed.[1] Its aims are limited to showing the similarities and differences in this growth, and to suggesting some of the consequences of the distinctive population patterns.[2]

Seattle's first permanent settlement occurred in 1851, when a small party of immigrants from the Midwest under the leadership of David Denny, John Low, and Lee Terry chose Alki Point, in what is now West Seattle, as a likely spot for a townsite. The first winter was a miserable one for the twelve adults and twelve children who made up the group, and within a year most of them had relocated on Elliott Bay about four miles away. It was around this latter settlement that the city ultimately developed.

Seattle's early growth was very slow, and in its dependence on logging and lumbering the town resembled a host of other small communities which appeared on Puget Sound in the 1850s.[3] Seattle did have certain advantages. There were substantial coal deposits nearby which were gradually developed and the coal sold in San Francisco. In addition the town's central location on Puget Sound made it a logical entrepot and service center for the "mosquito fleet" of sloops, steamers, barges, and schooners which covered Puget Sound. It was this combination of lumber, coal, and lively supply trade which enabled Seattle to draw ahead of all its competitors by the early 1870s. Once in the lead, Seattle never fell behind. The number of settlers, however, remained very small. The federal census of 1880 gave Seattle's population as 3,533, and it was only after the Northern Pacific Railroad reached Seattle in 1884 that population spurted ahead.

Vancouver's early years were equally unspectacular.[4] In 1859-1860 a detachment of Royal Engineers constructed a rough road from New Westminster on the Fraser River to Burrard Inlet, and in 1862 land claims were first staked out. Three young Englishmen who had joined in the Cariboo gold rush thought that the coal and clay of the Burrard Inlet area might make it possible to develop brick making and pottery, but little came of this initial venture.

The real focus of activity on Burrard Inlet centered around three lumber mills, all of which were established in the mid-1860s. Moody's Mill, owned by Sewell Moody, was established on the north side of the inlet in 1865. On the south side Jeremiah Rogers began logging operations at Jerry's Cove (now Jericho Beach). Two years later Captain Edward Stamp established his Hastings Mill about three miles east of First Narrows. It was near this latter mill that a community dubbed Gastown developed. This in turn evolved into Granville and was ultimately incorporated as the City of Vancouver in 1886. Although the area exported a substantial amount of lumber (forty-five vessels loaded in 1869 alone), population growth was very slow.[5] By 1882 the various pockets of settlement around Burrard Inlet had a white population of about 900, and of this number some 300 lived in Granville.

While Seattle developed into the leading settlement on Puget Sound before it received its transcontinental railroad, Vancouver was of minor importance prior to the completion of rail connections with eastern Canada. Early in 1886, Vancouver had only about 600 residents and was dwarfed by both Victoria and New Westminster, the other provincial communities of any size. Conditions changed dramatically with the arrival of the first Canadian Pacific Railway train in 1887. In that year the city had about 2,000 residents, and by the time of the federal census of 1891, the population had jumped to 13,709. For all practical purposes it was the completion of the Canadian Pacific Railway which created Vancouver. The growth of the two cities, and of Washington and British Columbia, is traced out in Fig. 1.

Fig. 1 and Table I show that both cities experienced a rapid rate of growth in their early years when the population was small and could double in three years or less. The growth rate of Seattle and Vancouver in the 1880s was not significantly different from that of Pittsburgh or Toronto in the early years of the century, or from that of Kansas City or Denver in the mid-nineteenth century. Yet these cities in the Northwest were some of the last of the major North American cities to be established. With the exception of an occasional city, such as Miami, Florida, Tulsa, Oklahoma, or Edmonton, Alberta, which were yet to spring up, most American and Canadian cities destined to achieve even moderate size had been founded by 1890, and the urban network of both nations was substantially complete.[6] The dramatic growth of the two cities lasted until 1915.[7] Expansion continued after that date, but at a much reduced rate. Since 1915 Vancouver's growth rate has averaged 2.5 per cent per year, and Seattle's about 1.6 per cent per year.

These population data and growth rates refer only to the city proper, or central city, and do not include those persons in the suburban fringe. As in most North American cities, much of the population growth of Seattle and Vancouver has been in residential and industrial suburbs. Although legally not a part of the city, these thickly settled ring areas are an integral component of the total urban community. When they are included, the population growth of metropolitan Vancouver since 1915 rises to about 3.7 percent per year and that of metropolitan Seattle to about three percent per year. Such comparisons of metropolitan growth, or of the rates of suburbanization of the two cities, should be taken as reasonable approximations only. Not only does the definition of "metropolitan district" differ from nation to nation, but also from census to census within each nation. Consequently, the choice of data for a specific year is rather arbitrary.[8] But even with these reservations there can be no doubt that over the years a steadily larger number of the inhabitants of Seattle and Vancouver have located in the suburban rings of these cities.

All urban communities achieve population growth through three main channels: the arrival of immigrants, natural increase of the community, and annexation of new sections, As new communities in thinly settled regions, both Seattle and Vancouver grew primarily through the influx of migrants, especially native-born migrants. The U.S. Census of 1890, the first detailed statist-

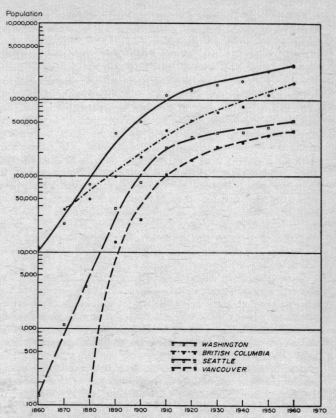

FIGURE 1. Population Growth of Washington, British Columbia, Seattle, and Vancouver, 1860–61 to 1960–61

Sources: *U. S. Census, Population, 1860 to 1960; Census of Canada, Population, 1881 to 1961; U.S. Census 1960,* Vol. I, Part 49, pp. 8, 10 (the population figure for Seattle in 1860 includes all of King County). *Census of Canada 1951,* I, Table 13. p. 2, gives British Columbia data from 1871 to 1951, and Table 17, p. 6, gives Vancouver data from 1891 to 1951; the Vancouver population for 1921 includes South Vancouver and Point Grey which did not officially join the city until 1929; the 1881 population figure for Vancouver is based on R. T. Williams, ed., *Bristish Columbia Directory, 1882–83* (Victoria, 1882), 236–238.

ical breakdown of Seattle's population, shows clearly the heavy dependence on migration. In that year out of a population of 42,837 persons, 39,335 (92 percent) were born outside the state of Washington, and 3,502 (8 percent) were Washington born.[9] Vancouver also relied on migrants for its early growth but many more came from the surrounding region than was true in Seattle's case. Out of a Vancouver population of 13,709 in 1891, some 8,552 (62 percent) were born outside the province and 5,157 (38 percent) were born in British Columbia.[10]

TABLE I

Population Growth of Washington, British Columbia, Seattle, and Vancouver, 1860-61 to 1960-61

	Washington	British Columbia	Seattle	Vancouver
1860-61	11,594		302	
1870-71	23,955	36,247	1,107	
1880-81	75,116	49,459	3,533	300
1890-91	357,232	98,173	42,837	13,709
1900-01	518,103	178,657	80,671	27,010
1910-11	1,141,990	392,480	237,194	100,401
1920-21	1,356,621	524,582	315,312	163,220
1930-31	1,563,396	694,263	365,583	246,593
1940-41	1,736,191	817,861	368,302	275,353
1950-51	2,378,963	1,165,210	467,591	344,833
1960-61	2,853,214	1,629,082	557,087	384,522

Sources: *U.S. Census, Population, 1860 to 1960; Census of Canada, Population, 1881 to 1961; U.S. Census of Population, 1960,* Vol. I, Part 49, pp. 8, 10 (the population figure for Seattle in 1860 includes all of King County). *Census of Canada 1951,* I, Table 13, p. 2, gives British Columbia data from 1871 to 1951, and Table 17, p. 6, gives Vancouver data from 1891 to 1951; the Vancouver population for 1921 includes south Vancouver and Point Grey which did not officially join the city until 1929; the 1881 population figure for Vancouver is based on R. T. Williams, ed., *British Columbia Directory, 1882-83* (Victoria, 1882), pp. 236-238.

The significantly greater number of British Columbians in Vancouver than Washingtonians in Seattle is accounted for by the fact that, with its terminal railroad facilities, Vancouver became the unchallenged center of the British Columbia mainland. No longer a local lumbering community, but a city with national and indeed international aspirations, it was the logical destination for

TABLE II

Central City Population and Ring Population in the Metropolitan Districts of Seattle and Vancouver 1900-01 to 1960-61

	Metropolitan District	Central City		Ring	
		No.	%	No.	%
Seattle					
1900	80,885	806,671	99.7	214	0.3
1910	255,622	237,194	92.6	18,428	7.4
1920	357,950	315,312	88.1	42,638	11.9
1930	420,663	365,583	85.9	55,080	13.1
1940	452,639	368,302	81.4	84,337	18.6
1950	621,509*	467,591	75.3	153,918	24.7
1960	864,109*	557,087	64.4	307,022	35.6
1950	844,572**	467,591	55.4	376,981	44.6
1960	1,107,213**	557,087	50.3	550,126	49.7
Vancouer					
1901	28,985	27,010	93.5	1,885	6.5
1911	123,902	100,401	81.1	23,501	18.9
1921	198,468	163,220	82.3	35,248	17.7
1931	304,854	246,593	80.9	58,261	19.1
1941	374,665	275,353	79.2	72,312	20.8
1951	481,442†	344,833	71.5	136,609	28.5
1961	621,773‡	384,522	61.8	237,251	38.2
1951	561,960§	344,833	61.4	217,127	38.6
1961	790,165§	384,522	48.5	405,643	51.5

*"Seattle Urbanized Area"

**"Seattle Metropolitan Statistical Area"

†"Vancouver Howe Sound Electoral Subdivision B"

‡"Vancouver Electoral Subdivision C"

§"Vancouver Census Metropolitan Area"

Sources: *U.S. Census 1910*, I, pp. 73-75; *U.S. Census 1920*, I, pp. 62-64; *U.S. Census 1940*, I, 1135; *U.S. Census 1950*, II, Part 47, p. 16; *U.S. Census 1960*, I, Part 49, p. 18; *Census of Canada 1911*, I, p. 39; *Census of Canada 1931*, II, p. 104; *Census of Canada 1941*, II, p. 143; *Census of Canada 1951*, I, Table 6, p. 85, Table 12, p. 2; *Census of Canada 1961*, I, Part I, Bull. 5, Table 7, p. 54, Bull. 6, Table 10, p. 3.

TABLE III

Birthplace of Seattle's Native-born Population, 1890-1930

	1890		1900		1910		1920		1930	
North East	6,871	23.6%	10,907	18.6%	23,743	14.0%	22,810	10.7%	20,697	7.2%
South	1,889	6.5	3,637	62	10,765	6.4	13,139	5.6	13,321	4.6
E. N. Central	6,842	23.4	12,341	21.0	41,432	24.4	47,452	20.2	45,257	15.8
W. N. Central	4,893	16.8	9,124	15.6	35,857	21.1	47,441	20.2	54,562	19.1
Mt. Pac. & Other	8,686	29.7	22,659	38.7	57,941	34.1	103,494	44.2	153,404	53.2
Total Native-born	29,181		58,668		169,738		234,336		287,241	
Total Population	42,837		80,671		237,194		315,312		365,583	

TABLE IV

Birthplace of Vancouver's Native-born Population, 1891-1961

	1891		1901		1911		1921	
Maritimes	860	10.0%	1,460	8.8%	5,698	12.8%	6,900	8.7%
Quebec	480	5.6	640	3.9	2,170	4.9	3,000	3.8
Ontario	2,420	28.3	3,950	24.0	16,663	37.8	21,200	26.6
Prairies	220	2.6	530	3.2	3,925	8.9	9,100	11.4
British Columbia & Other	4,572	53.6	9,968	60.2	15,522	35.4	39,720	49.6
Total Native-born	8,552		16,548		43,978		79,920	
Total Population	13,709		27,010		100,401		163,220	

	1931		1941		1951		1961	
Maritimes	8,033	6.3%	7,416	4.4%	8,903	3.8%	8,011	3.2%
Quebec	3,650	2.8	3,819	2.3	5,148	2.2	5,380	2.1
Ontario	23,809	18.6	22,920	13.7	25,153	10.8	21,723	8.7
Prairies	21,763	17.0	39,953	23.9	71,550	30.7	67,579	26.8
British Columbia & Other	71,141	55.3	92,986	55.6	121,837	52.3	148,994	59.1
Total Native-born	128,396		167,094		232,591		251,687	
Total Population	246,593		275,353		344,833		384,522	

TABLE V

Native-born Migrants in Cities of British Columbia and Washington

	% of British Columbia Population in Vancouver & Victoria	Canadian-born Migrants		
		British Columbia	Vancouver & Victoria	
		Number	Number	%
1901	27	40,023	9,890	25
1911	34	84,832	34,424	41
1921	39	107,003	47,132	44
1931	41	141,539	64,238	45
1941	39	197,467	83,795	42
1951	34	359,300	125,177	35
1961	27	445,111	117,960	27

	% of Washington Population in Seattle, Tacoma, Spokane	U.S.-born Migrants		
		Washington	Seattle, Tacoma, & Spokane	
		Number	Number	%
1890	28	205,140	47,151	23
1900	30	273,04	89,466	33
1910	37	623,055	240,869	39
1920	38	¾481,154	271,384	40
1930	38	741,778	284,326	38

Sources: This table is based on census material cited in Fig. 1 and Tables III and IV.

migrants from villages and towns throughout the province. Seattle had a larger regional population on which to draw, but many migrants in Washington preferred to locate and invest in Tacoma. That city, too, had mushroomed in the 1880s after it received railroad connections, and by 1890 its population of 36,006 was only 6,831 less than that of Seattle. The fact that many more persons boarded the Northern Pacific bound for Seattle than caught the Canadian Pacific Railway for Vancouver would also help account for the relatively small numbers of native Washingtonians in Seattle. As a rough rule of thumb, in the five-year period after the completion of the respective railroads, migrants arrived in Seattle at the rate of about 6,000 per year and in Vancouver at about 2,000 per year.

It is especially noteworthy that at any given time the bulk of these migrants came from comparable regions of the United States and Canada. In the 1880s, for example, most Americans arriving in Seattle were from New England, New York, Pennsylvania, Ohio, and Illinois. During the same decade Vancouver got most of its Canadians from the Maritimes and Ontario. Relatively few southerners went to Seattle in the 1880s, and relatively few Quebecers to Vancouver. These latter regions accounted for about one-third of the total population of their nations, but because of their distinctive culture and development they were considered to be outside the mainstream of national life. In the late nineteenth century a significant number of migrants left the South and Quebec, but not many of them went to the West Coast, preferring instead to migrate to nearby regions. The Canadian prairies were virtually unsettled in the 1870s and 1880s, and therefore very few prairie-born persons lived in Vancouver in 1891, whereas substantial numbers of Minnesotans, Iowans, Kansans, and Nebraskans lived in Seattle. Tables III and IV summarize this data for 1890 and for later years.

After the first surge of growth in the wake of transcontinental railroad connections, both cities subsided during the depressed years of the early 1890s. Not until the late 1890s and the gold rush to the Yukon and Alaska did a second major expansionary phase begin. During these exciting years, Vancouver replaced Victoria as British Columbia's largest city, and Seattle left Tacoma far behind in the population race.[11] Americans, Canadians, and a host of Europeans poured into Seattle and Vancouver in unprecedented numbers and continued to do so for almost twenty years.

By 1910 Seattle was approaching the quarter million mark, and Vancouver had reached about 100,000. Seattle still received substantial numbers of New Englanders, New Yorkers, and Pennsylvanians but the largest bloc of native-born migrants came from the heavily populated Midwest, especially Ohio, Indiana, Illinois, Michigan, and Wisconsin. Canada's thickly settled heartland of Ontario now provided most of Vancouver's new residents. With their United Empire Loyalist traditions, these immigrants from Ontario had a sharper sense of Canadian identity, were more outspoken about Canadian needs and accomplishments, and were more inclined than the contingent from the Maritimes to emphasize the blemishes and shortcomings of the United States.[12] With

TABLE VI—Birthplace of Seattle's Foreign-born Population (In Numbers and Percentages)

	1890	1900	1910	1920	1930	1940	1950	1960
England & Wales	1,871 13.6%	2,519 11.4%	6,267 9.3%	8,480 10.4%	8,106 10.3%	6,065 9.6%	5,158 8.6%	4,800 8.1%
Scotland	696 5.2	810 3.7	2,277 3.4	3,195 3.9	3,221 4.1	2,429 3.8	2,005 3.4	1,800 3.0
Ireland	1,133 8.3	1,576 7.2	3,177 4.6	3,455 4.3	2,855 3.6	2,014 3.2	1,628 2.7	1,740 2.9
Norway	1,353 9.9	1,642 7.5	7,193 10.4	9,119 11.2	9,745 12.4	8,436 13.3	7,827 13.3	7,286 12.2
Sweden	1,525 11.2	2,379 10.8	8,677 12.8	10,253 12.7	9,634 12.3	7,670 12.0	6,074 10.2	4,801 8.1
Denmark	457 3.3	641 2.9	1,879 2.8	2,228 2.8	1,987 2.5	1,514 2.4	1,261 2.1	947 1.6
Finland		424 1.9	1,299 1.9	2,256 2.8	1,950 2.5	1,740 2.7	1,458 2.5	1,021 1.7
France	197 1.4	258 1.2	646 1.0	717 0.9	550 0.7	421 0.7	416 0.7	430 0.7
Germany	2,195 16.1	2,735 12.4	6,176 9.2	4,827 6.0	4,608 5.8	3,581 5.6	3,141 5.3	4,887 8.2
Poland	49 0.4	78 0.4		881 1.1	975 1.2	858 1.4	899 1.5	763 1.3
Austria & Hungary	162 1.1	362 1.6	2,370 3.5	1,762 2.2	1,049 1.3	1,263 2.0	1,332 2.2	1,320 2.2
Russia	181 1.3	309 1.4	2,578 3.8	3,349 4.1	2,640 3.4	2,371 3.7	2,269 3.8	1,562 2.6
Italy	209 1.5	362 1.6	3,457 5.1	3,094 3.8	3,457 4.4	3,055 4.8	2,495 4.2	2,089 3.5
Greece	17 0.1	44 0.2	967 1.4	1,400 1.7	888 1.1	924 1.5	947 1.6	934 1.6
Canada	2,714 19.4	3,786 17.2	10,708 15.8	13,887 17.2	15,785 20.2	12,545 19.8	13,332 22.4	12,450 20.8
China	367 2.7	366 1.6	728 1.1	921 1.1	726 0.9	830 1.3	1,250 2.1	2,078 3.5
Japan	134 1.0	3,091 14.0	5,748 8.5	6,016 7.5	4,448 5.7	2,876 4.5	2,750 4.6	2,593 4.3
Other	396 2.9	621 2.9	3,300 4.9	5,136 6.4	5,714 7.3	4,878 7.7	5,199 8.7	8,219 13.8
Total Foreign-born	13,656	22,003	67,456	80,976	78,342	63,470	59,441	59,720
Total Population	42,837	80,671	237,194	315,312	365,583	368,302	467,591	557,087

Sources: U.S. Census 1890, I, Part 1, pp. 670–673; U.S. Census 1900, I, Part 1, pp. 485, 800–803; U.S. Census 1910, I, pp. 838, 858–859; U.S. Census 1920, II, pp. 697, 729–733; U.S. Census 1930, II, 234, 248–250; Census 1940, II, Part 7, pp. 304, 401, 403; U.S. Census 1950, II, Part 47, pp. 46, 54, 68, 100 (lists foreign-born white only). The number of foreign-born Japanese and Chinese are estimates, based on the total number of Japanese and Chinese. U.S. Census 1960, I, Part 49, pp. 147–148 (lists "mother tongue of foreign-born"). Estimates were made of the numbers from England and Wales, Scotland, Ireland, Canada, France, Austria, and Hungary on the basis of "country of origin of foreign stock."

their arrival, they added a significant and influential element to the city.

The growth rate of both Seattle and Vancouver dropped off in the 1920s, and by 1930 the origins of native born citizens in the two cities were strikingly similar. Persons born on or near the Pacific Coast now predominated, while migrants from the Great Plains and Prairies also made up an important bloc. It is pertinent to note that in 1930 persons born west of Ontario accounted for 72 percent of Vancouver's native born population, while in Seattle persons born west of the Mississippi and outside of the South also accounted for 72 percent of that city's native-born population. The similarity in the relative decline of the North East-Maritime, South-Quebec, and East North Central-Ontario regions in the population makeup of the two cities is also clearly evident.

Since 1930 eastern Canadians have accounted for a smaller and smaller proportion of Vancouver's population while persons born in the prairie provinces and in British Columbia itself have risen sharply. By 1961 Vancouver's native-born population was decidedly "British Columbian" and "western." Approximately eighty-six percent was born west of Ontario, with British Columbia itself accounting for fifty-nine percent. For these reasons it is not surprising to discover a general indifference to the issue of French Canadian rights or to the problems of farmers and coal miners in the Maritimes.[13] Even with national television coverage, Quebec and Nova Scotia seemed far away. By 1960 Seattle, too, had become a strongly "western" city. The U.S. census does not give detailed state-of-birth statistics for 1940, 1950, or 1960 but by the latter date approximately fifty-one percent of that city's native born population had been born in the state of Washington.[14]

Another interesting similarity between the native-born migration streams to Washington and to British Columbia is that in both cases the migrants showed a slight preference to settle in urban rather than in rural areas. Neither the Canadian nor the U.S. census provides sufficient data to establish this point conclusively, but the data that are available suggest that in both cases the westward movement to British Columbia and Washington tended to go in the direction of urban centers. In 1921, for example, Vancouver and Victoria possessed only 39 percent of British Columbia's population, but they accounted for 44 percent of the Canadian migrants to the province. Similarly, the three largest cities in Washington—Seattle, Tacoma, and Spokane— also received slightly more than their proportionate share of U.S.

TABLE VII—BIRTHPLACE OF VANCOUVER'S FOREIGN-BORN POPULATION (IN NUMBERS AND PERCENTAGES)

	1891	1901	1911	1921	1931	1941	1951	1961
England & Wales	1,551 30.2%	2,882 27.0%	18,414 32.7%	32,140 38.4%	46,151 39.0%	44,432 41.0%	44,287 39.4%	37,410 28.2
Scotland	580 11.2	910 8.5	9,650 17.1	14,900 17.8	21,613 18.3	20,080 18.6	19,265 17.2	16,551 12.4
Ireland	412 7.9	512 4.8	2,625 4.6	4,260 5.1	5,573 4.9	5,166 4.8	3,564 3.2	3,097 2.3
Norway	154 3.0	333 3.1	575 1.0	635 0.8	1,723 1.5	1,783 1.6	5,301 4.6	6,628 5.0
Sweden			952 1.7	920 1.1	2,136 1.8	1,802 1.7		
Denmark		46 0.4	180 0.3	276 0.3	715 0.6	720 0.7		
Finland			181 0.3	290 0.3	1,533 1.3	971 0.9		
France	23 0.4	48 0.5	266 0.5	379 0.5	441 0.4	416 0.4	1,386 1.2	8,618 6.5
Germany	108 2.1	180 1.7	733 1.3	264 0.3	893 0.8	956 0.9		
Poland	9			296 0.4	1,036 0.9	1,487 1.4		4,233 3.2
Austria & Hungary		23 0.2	500 0.9	237 0.3	664 0.6	1,022 0.9	1,834 1.6	
Russia	23 0.4	101 1.0	606 1.1	772 0.9	1,429 1.2	2,165 2.0		6,208 4.7
Italy	55 1.1	101 1.0	1,922 3.4	1,110 1.3	1,478 1.3	1,416 1.3		7,402 5.6
Greece		2 0.0	226 0.4	310 0.4	293 0.2			
United States	870 16.8	1,840 17.2	10,401 18.4	10,500 12.7	10,870 9.2	10,833 10.0	11,213 10.0	9,484 7.2
China	1,065 20.6	1,800 17.0	3,364 6.0	8,100 9.7	11,533 9.7	5,427 5.0	6,378 5.7	10,512 7.9
Japan		1,010 9.5	1,841 3.3	4,150 5.0	4,133 3.5	3,331 3.1		
Other	307 6.0	854 8.0	3,987 7.1	3,861 4.6	5,983 5.0	6,252 5.8	19,014 17.0	22,692 17.1
Total Foreign-born	5,157	10,642	56,423	83,300	118,197	108,259	112,242	132,835
Total Population	13,709	27,010	100,401	163,220	246,593	275,353	344,833	384,522

Sources: U. S. Census 1890, I, Part I, 580; U. S. Census 1900, I, Part I, 6-6-689, 710, 713; U. S. Census 1910, I, 730-734, 771-779; U. S. Census 1920, II, 626-630, 668-680; U. S. Census 1930, II, 153-157, 212-215. Census of Canada 1891, I, 332; Census of Canada 1901, I, 416-418 (Vancouver data have been calculated from Burrard District data); Census of Canada 1911, II, 426-428, 440-441; Census of Canada 1921, II, 315, 365-366 (Vancouver data have been modified to include South Va couver and Point Grey); Census of Canada 1931, II, 713, 739, 757-75 Census of Canada 1941, IV, 310-311, 418-422, 448-450, 528-530, 534-53 Census of Canada 1957, I, Table 45, pp. 1, 2, Table 48, pp. 9-10, Tal 49, p. 1; Census of Canada 1961, I, Part 2, Bull. 7, Table 49, pp. 1- Table 52, pp. 17-18.

migrants to the state, though the tendency was not as clear cut as in British Columbia.

A distinctive feature of native-born migration to Seattle that is not duplicated in Vancouver is the recent sharp increase in that city's Negro population. In 1900 about ninety percent of all American Negroes lived in the South. Like most northern and western cities at the time, Seattle's Negro population was very small, making up one-half of one percent of the city's population. By 1940 the 3,789 Negroes in the city had increased to only one percent of the city's population.[15] During World War II and the 1950s, Negro emigration from the South speeded up sharply, drawn by the economic opportunities in northern cities and by the hope, sometimes realized, of a better way of life. By 1960 Seattle's 27,000 Negroes made up 4.8 percent of the city's population.[16] As in the rest of the nation, Negro migration to Washington has been a strongly urban movement. Seattle, Tacoma, and Spokane together accounted for 32 percent of the state's population in 1960, and 72 percent of the state's Negroes.

Although not as significant as native-born migrants in shaping the population growth and composition of the two cities, foreign-born migrants have always played an important role in Seattle and Vancouver.[17] From the 1880s to the 1960s these newcomers from outside the United States and Canada have always had a much greater impact on Vancouver's growth and development than on Seattle's. The number of foreign-born in the cities is given in Tables VI and VII.

As can be seen from these tables, the most distinctive feature of this migration to Vancouver is that it has been predominantly from the British Isles. Until the opening of the twentieth century, British migrants made up a relatively small proportion of Vancouver's population. In 1901, for example, they accounted for sixteen percent of the city's population, but this changed dramatically in the following decade when migrants from Great Britain and the British Empire poured into Vancouver in unprecedented numbers.

During this exuberant period, Vancouver enjoyed some of its most prosperous years. It grew prodigiously and consolidated the basic system of streets, tramways, shopping districts, industrial centers, and residential suburbs. The great influx of English, Scots, Irish, and Welsh, along with the sprinkling of Australians, New Zealanders, and South Africans, gave a decided British cast to Vancouver's population profile. By 1911 there were 33,995 such migrants out of a total city population of 100,401.[18] In the years that followed, the patterns established so firmly during the early years of the century were maintained by continuing migration from the United Kingdom. As late as 1961, when the number of these migrants had declined somewhat, they still accounted for 15 percent of the city's total population and 45 percent of the foreign-born population.

This steady stream of migrants from the British Isles has had a profound effect on all aspects of Vancouver's life. Indeed, the influence is so pervasive, long standing, and taken for granted that there has been very little scholarly investigation of it. But the prevalence of British accents among Vancouver's clerks, mechanics, physicians, teachers, and businessmen and the more formal, precise nature of the exchanges is quickly apparent to the visitor. The abundance of Tudor and stucco houses, the popularity of flower gardens, the variety of British papers in newstands, the miles of public beaches, the number of public tennis courts, the layout of parks and playgrounds, and the absence of athletic scholarships at the University of British Columbia—all suggest the perseverance of this influence.

One area in which the role of the British migrant can be pin-pointed more precisely is in politics. Of the twenty-nine mayors who served Vancouver prior to 1960 at least seven were born in the British Isles.[19] The sustained growth of the Socialist party in British Columbia, and the close affiliation of organized labor with this party owes much to the leadership, ideas, and votes provided by generations of British migrants. In the 1890s the Vancouver Trades and Labour Council, representing a predominately Britsh group of skilled workers, urged the parent Trades and Labour Congress of Canada to establish an independent labor party.[20] During the 1930s British born leaders, many active in labor organizations in Vancouver, played a major role in establishing the socialist Co-operative Commonwealth Federation in British Columbia and in directing its activites in the provincial legislature.[21] Throughout much of the 1960s, when the rank and file of the New Democratic party (successor to the Co-operative Commonwealth Federation) were native Canadians, provincial leadership was provided by a Glasgow born Scot.[22] The general import of British migrants has undoubtedly declined since the early years of the century. But if any single feature has made Vancouver "different" from Seattle, it is this migration from Great Britain.

The first decade of the twentieth century was also a critical period in the evolution of Seattle's population. Vast numbers of migrants arrived in the United States during these years, and Seattle's early Scandinavian contingent was sharply reinforced with the arrival of 7,000 Swedes, 6,000 Norwegians, 1,200 Danes, and 900 Finns. By 1910 they accounted for eight percent of the city's population and helped provide the manpower for a host of logging, lumbering, and shingle operations. Only in the following decades did they move more into fishing and, to a lesser extent, into dairying. Scandinavian churches, banks, a variety of voluntary associations, and a general clustering in the Ballard district gave a distinctive coloration to the city. On the whole Scandinavians did not have a major impact on the political and social development of the city, but tended to assimilate quite rapidly in the new environment.[23] Substantial numbers of migrants also arrived from the British Isles. But in the American setting they were but one component of a diverse immigrant mix and did not achieve the size nor have the impact of their counterparts in Vancouver.

Both Vancouver and Seattle have always received large numbers of migrants from the neighboring nation. As was true throughout the United States and Canada, such persons were usually the most reluctant of all immigrant groups about acquiring citizenship, but otherwise they quickly became an integral part of the new community.[24] Canadians have consistently been the largest single bloc of foreign-born residents in Seattle, while next to Englishmen and Scotsmen, Americans have made up the largest foreign-born group in Vancouver. In 1910, for example, the 10,708 Canadian-born migrants in Seattle accounted for 4.5 per cent of that city's population, while 10,401 Americans were 10.4 per cent of Vancouver's population. This pattern has continued, though not at the level of importance of the early twentieth century. By 1960 there were 12,450 people of Canadian birth in Seattle (2.2% of Seattle's population) and 9,484 American born settlers in Vancouver (2.5% of Vancouver's population).

Another significant foreign-born bloc in both cities consisted of migrants from China and Japan. Vancouver's East Indian community was unique, but over the years Vancouverites and Seattlites showed little difference in their opinion and treatment of migrants from the Orient. Condescension, contempt, riots, and expulsion greeted them in both cities, and both nations considered the internment of Japanese residents necessary for national security in the early 1940s. Toleration, recognition, and assimilation are largely post-World War II developments.[25] Although the number of Chinese and Japanese has increased, their relative importance in both cities has declined. In 1900 they made up 4 percent of Seattle's population and 10 percent of Vancouver's. By

1960 the 4,700 foreign-born Chinese and Japanese in Seattle accounted for less than 1 percent of that city's population, while the 10,500 in Vancouver represented 2.7 percent of the population. As a general rule, Japanese outnumbered Chinese in Seattle by a ratio of four-to-one, whereas in Vancouver the Chinese predominated by a two-to-one margin.

Diverse European nationals have also contributed to the population of Seattle and Vancouver. Over the years these Europeans have been more significant for Seattle than for Vancouver. In 1910, for example, the number of French, Germans, Austro-Hungarians, Russians, Italians, and Greeks in Seattle amounted to 16,194 or 6.8 percent of the city's population. These groups numbered 4,253 in Vancouver, or 4.3 percent of the population. Similar patterns were evident in 1920, 1930, and 1940.

The period since World War II has seen some very significant changes in the mixture of foreign-born groups in the two cities. These changes are in large part a reflection of the differences in the immigration policies of the two nations. Seattle's foreign-born group has continued to decline from its numerical peak in 1920, just prior to the Immigration acts of 1921 and 1924 which effectively ended America's traditonal policy of unrestricted immigration. By 1960 Seattle's total foreign-born residents made up 10.7 percent of the city's total population and as in the past were mainly from Scandinavia, Canada, Great Britain, and Germany.

In Vancouver, the number of non-Canadian-born residents showed a sharp increase in the postwar period reaching 132,835 (35 percent of Vancouver's population) by 1960. About half came from the United Kingdom and the United States, yet it is significant that migrants from those nations showed both an absolute and a relative decline after 1940. The distinctly new feature in Vancouver's makeup was the great increase in persons of European origin. In 1960, for example, Vancouver had over 8,000 foreign-born Germans, 7,000 Italians, 6,000 Scandinavians, 6,000 Russians, 4,000 Poles as well as 18,000 persons of unspecified European origin. By 1960 approximately one Vancouverite in six was from a non-English speaking country.

Altogether this marked a sharp departure from Vancouver's traditional population makeup, and to a larger degree reversed the role of the two cities. Seattle, reflecting the more restrictive immigration policies of its federal government, had become by 1960 a much more homogenous community than it had been in the past. The immigration policies of the Canadian government, on the other hand, had indirectly softened the strongly British features of Vancouver's population profile and had made the city a much more diverse, cosmopolitan community than formerly. It might be added, however, that this emphasis on Seattle's homogeneity and Vancouver's diversity conveniently ignores the fact that the Canadian city had about 600 Negroes in 1960, while Seattle had some 27,000.[26] The Canadian government has never officially restricted Negro migration, but neither has it encouraged this migration.[27]

The stream of foreign migrants to Washington has nearly always shown a persistent urban tendency. Regardless of whether the migrants were Scots, Norwegians, Germans, Italians, or Chinese, or whether they arrived in the 1890s or the 1950s, all showed a preference to settle in a city, especially a large city,

TABLE VIII

Foreign-born Migrants in Cities of British Columbia and Washington

		Foreign-born Migrants		
	% of British Coumbia Population in Vancouver & Victoria	British Columbia	Vancouver & Victoria	
		Number	Number	%
1901	27	79,045	21,621	27
1911	34	223,158	75,117	34
1921	39	260,536	104,052	40
1931	41	319,529	137,406	43
1941	39	304,729	126,900	42
1951	34	339,197	130,703	38
1961	27	423,132	149,776	35

		Foreign-born Population		
	% of Washington Population in Seattle, Tacoma, & Spokane	Washington	Seattle, Tacoma, & Spokane	
		Number	Number	%
1890	22	90,005	25,964	29
1900	30	111,364	40,868	37
1910	37	256,241	111,774	44
1920	38	265,292	122,161	46
1930	38	255,258	115,327	45
1940	35	210,379	92,655	44
1950	33	198,000	85,000	43
1960	31	178,658	81,916	46

Sources: Table based on material cited in Tables I, III, IV, VI, and VII.

rather than in a small town or rural community. Whether it was the better job opportunities, the appeal of friends and relatives already living there, or the availability of houses, schools, churches, and taverns that drew these migrants to Washington's cities is unknown. But the evidence that foreign-born migrants preferred larger cities is unmistakable. In 1910, for example, only 37 percent of Washington's population was in Seattle, Tacoma, and Spokane; yet these three cities held one-half of the state's English, Welsh, and Scottish migrants and almost 45 percent of the state's Scandinavians, Canadians, Russians, Italians, and Chinese.

Across the boundary line in British Columbia some distinctive and significant differences are evident in immigration patterns. Migrants from the British Isles revealed much the same preference for cities as their cousins who located in Washington, but migrants from the continent tended to shun British Columbia's cities. With 34 percent of the province's population in 1911, Vancouver and Victoria held 40 percent of the province's migrants from Great Britain, but only 25 percent of those from the continent. This tendency prevailed until after World War II. Since then migrants from the continent have shown the same preference for British Columbia's cities as their counterparts had always shown for Washington's urban centers. With a quarter of the province's population in 1961, Vancouver held a third of the Germans, Poles, Russians, Italians, and almost two-thirds of the Chinese and Japanese.

Although Seattle and Vancouver account for only a small segment of their respective nations, they accurately reflect national trends. In the early twentieth century migrants from the continent tended to settle in Canada's rural areas and were not as heavily concentrated in cities as was the case in the United States.[28] Whether or not Canadians had any greater toleration for diversity than Americans, there can be little doubt that the relative isolation of these groups in rural Canada helps explain why they were able to retain their identity and resist amalgamation to a greater extent than in the United States.[29] Since 1945, however, the majority of migrants arriving in Canada have chosen to settle in major metropolitan centers. It is likely that in the future the conditions and pressures of urban life will lead to a much more rapid loss of ethnic identity in Canada than has been the case in the past.[30]

Throughout their early development there is no doubt that both Seattle and Vancouver grew primarily through immigration, whether from the region, the nation at large, or foreign lands. Natural increase was a minor factor in early population growth, but over the years it has become steadily more important. The lack of early statistics makes the task of assessing this component a difficult one, but fortunately detailed statistics are generally available for the years after 1910. Tables IX and X give birth and death statistics for the two cities.

The data show that in each decade between 1880 and 1910 natural increase accounted for less than ten percent of the population growth of the two cities, but since then has accounted for a steadily larger share of this growth. These tables should be taken as reasonable approximations only, for they tend to overstate the importance of natural increase. Some of the birth statistics for example are by "place of occurrence" rather than by "place of residence." Similarly, children born to migrants are classified as "natural increase" and not "migrants." In addition, the tables make no allowance for emigration of city-born children. But even with these qualifications there can be no doubt that the population growth of both Seattle and Vancouver has come to rely more and more on the natural increase of the inhabitants.[31]

Both cities have sharply increased their territorial limits over the years and this, too, has contributed to population growth.[32] During the nineteenth century Seattle's boundaries tended to stay well beyond the range of settlement with the result that annexa-

TABLE IX

Natural Increase in the Population Growth of Seattle

	Total Population Increase	Births	Deaths	Natural Increase	Natural Inc. % of Tot. Pop. Incr.
1880-1890	39,304	4,730	2,250	2,480	6
1890-1900	37,834	9,590	6,000	3,590	9
1900-1910	156,523	22,550	15,402	7,148	5
1910-1920	78,118	51,642	27,869	23,773	30
1920-1930	50,271	52,362	34,718	17,644	35
1930-1940	2,719	49,122	44,847	4,275	157
1940-1950	99,289	118,122	54,179	63,998	65
1950-1960	89,496	143,666	62,565	81,101	91

Source: See Table X.

tions had a negligible effect on population growth. Between 1905 and 1910, however, the annexation of a number of populated suburbs added some 48,000 persons to the city.[33] No further annexations of significance occurred until the 1940s when a number of small areas were added. Between 1952 and 1954, the city added some fifteen square miles of territory and about 62,000 persons when it annexed Northgate, Sandpoint, Lake City, and other areas in the North End.[34] This increased Seattle's incorporated area to some ninety-one square miles.

TABLE X

Natural Increase in the Population Growth of Vancouver

	Total Population Increase	Births	Deaths	Natral Increase	Natural Inc. % of Tot. Pop. Incr.
1881-1891	13,409	600	400	200	1
1891-1901	13,301	3,375	2,425	950	7
1901-1911	73,391	9,533	6,898	2,635	4
1911-1921	62,819	23,551	13,712	9,839	16
1921-1931	83,373	32,861	18,094	14,767	18
1931-1941	28,760	36,991	25,724	11,267	39
1941-1951	69,480	63,721	36,378	27,343	39
1951-1961	39,689	79,744	44,016	35,728	90

Sources: The mortality rate for 1900-1910, which can be found in the Bureau of the Census, *Mortality Statistics*, was applied to the 1880s and 1890s. The natural increase in population from 1910 to 1937 was based on data in *Reports of the Washington State Board of Health, 1911-1916*, and in *Births, Stillbirths, and Infant Mortality Statistics* of the Bureau of the Census. Death data were taken from *Mortality Statistics*. For the period after 1937, birth and death data have been taken from *Vital Statistics of the U.S.* Between 1930 and 1940 Seattle had a net loss of 1,556 migrants. The city's natural increase consequently exceeded the total population increase. Prior to 1913 statistics for Vancouver were published in *Report of Registrar of Births, Deaths, and Marriages of British Columbia*, and since then in *Vital Statistics of British Columbia, Provincial Board of Health, Annual Report*.

In Vancouver, too, the early boundaries remained well beyond the range of settlement. Not until 1911, when the annexation of Hastings Townsite and other smaller areas added 5,000 residents did boundary changes contribute to population growth. Of much greater importance was the annexation in 1929 of the municipalities of South Vancouver and Point Grey which had a combined population of 78,931.[35] This increased Vancouver's physical size from sixteen to forty-four square miles and with only very minor changes the city has since retained these boundaries.[36] It is likely that annexation of suburban areas, along with natural increase, will play a major role in the future population growth of both cities.[37]

A survey of population growth of Seattle and Vancouver since the 1880s reveals a striking similarity in the nature and timing of this growth. From earliest years to the mid-twentieth century each has felt the impact of a variety of forces that were largely beyond its own control. The railroad boom of the 1880s, the depression of the early 1890s, the gold rush to the Klondike and Alaska, the massive migration from Europe in the early twentieth century, and two world wars have largely ignored the existence of the 49° of North Latitude, and have caused the populations of Seattle and Vancouver to spurt and lag very much in step with each other.

Throughout much of their history these cities depended on the westward migration of native born Canadians and Americans for their growth. When Maritimers were pouring into Vancouver in the 1880s and 1890s, New Englanders were flocking to Seattle. The farmers from the Canadian prairies who headed for Vancouver in the 1930s, 1940s, and 1950s had their counterparts in the residents from Montana, Nebraska, and the Dakotas who preferred the mild winters of Seattle. Migrants from Britain and Europe also made major contributions to growth and, until the 1920s, they generally arrived in Seattle and Vancouver at similar intervals. But the 1950s found both cities relying on the natural increase of their citizens for a substantial part of their population growth.

Like all cities, however, Seattle and Vancouver each developed distinctive population characteristics. The strongly British image that Vancouver acquired in the early twentieth century has been substantially maintained by continuing migration from the United Kingdom. Seattle's European born element, especially its distinctive Scandinavian group, has slowly declined over the years. By 1960 diverse European groups were playing a much more important role in the life and growth of Vancouver than they had in the past. Seattle, on the other hand, had become a predominantly native born city possessing a significant Negro minority. During the 1950s both metropolitan areas grew about three-and-a-half percent per year, the central cities about one and a half percent per year. The inevitability of future growth surpassing that of Los

Angeles and New York remains an article of faith for many Vancouverites and Seattleites. The more realistic have their doubts.

Notes

[1] Other topics will be treated in a more detailed comparative study of Seattle and Vancouver on which I am working.

[2] A fundamental demographic characteristic that is not treated is the changing age and sex distribution of the two cities. Such information is of basic importance in explaining a host of urban characteristics and demands. The rapidity of population growth, the nature of the labor force, the kinds of homes, schools, and parks expected, the number of taverns and brothels, the interest in symphony orchestra and city beautification plans, or the demands for special municipal services—all reflect, in part, whether the population is predominantly male or female, young or old.

[3] For Seattle's early development, see Clarence R. Bagley, *History of Seattle from the Earliest Settlement to the Present Time* (Chicago, 1916) and Roberta F. Watt, *Four Wagons West: The Story of Seattle* (Seattle, 1931).

[4] See F. W. Howay and E. O. S. Scholefield, *British Columbia from the Earliest Times to the Present* (Vancouver, 1914); M. A. Ormsby, *British Columbia: A History* (Toronto, 1958); Helen R. Boutilier, "Vancouver's Earliest Days," *British Columbia Historical Quarterly*, v (1946), pp. 151-170; Alan Morley's *Vancouver: from Milltown to Metropolis* (Vancouver, 1961) is often lively and readable, but lacks documentation.

[5] F. W. Howay, "Early Shipping in Burrard Inlet, 1863-1870," *British Columbia Historical Quarterly*, I, (1937), p. 20.

[6] Charles N. Glaab and A. Theodore Brown, *A History of Urban America* (New York, 1967), pp. 107-132. Edmonton was incorporated in 1892, when it had a population of 700. See James G. MacGregor, *Edmonton: A History* (Edmonton, 1967).

[7] Vancouver reached its pre-World War I peak in 1912 with a population of 122,100. Wartime enlistments and dislocation led to a decline to 95,992 by 1916. Not until 1919 when the population reached 123,050 did Vancouver exceed its 1912 figure. *Annual Report, City of Vancouver, 1941*, p. 63, provides yearly population data from 1886 to 1940.

[8] If better data were available, more precise measurements of metropolitan growth and decentralization would be possible. For example, comparisons could be made of (1) growth rates of metropolitan centers and rings, (2) shares of metropolitan growth going to centers and rings, (3) shifts in the population contained in metropolitan rings. See Leo Schnore, *The Urban Scene* (New York, 1965), pp. 79-133.

[9] *U.S. Census 1890*, I, Part I, pp. 557, 580, 670-673.

[10] *Census of Canada 1891*, I, p. 332. (Vancouver data have been calculated from District of New Westminster data.)

[11] See Norbert MacDonald, "Seattle, Vancouver, and the Klondike," *Canadian Historical Review,* XLIX (1968), pp. 234-246.

[12] H. F. Angus, *Canada and Her Great Neighbor: Sociological Surveys of Opinions and Attitudes in Canada Concerning the United States* (Toronto, 1938), pp. 55-59, 108-110.

[13] British Columbia's exasperations and frictions with eastern Canada are not new phenomena (see Ormsby, *British Columbia, passim*), nor are they explained only on the basis of population makeup. British Columbia's distance from eastern Canada, its resource-based economy, its distinctive provincial political situation, and its very small French-Canadian element make for significantly different interests and goals than those found in Ontario and Quebec.

[14] *U.S. Census 1960,* I, Part 49, p. 130, shows that out of a total native-born population of 1,017,246 in the Seattle Standard Metropolitan Statistical Area, 520,769 were born within the state.

[15] *U.S. Census 1940,* II, Part 7, p. 401.

[16] *U.S. Census 1960,* I, Part 49, p. 46. The spatial distribution of a number of non-white racial groups in Seattle in 1920 and 1960 is available in Calvin F. Schmid, Charles E. Noble, and Arlene E. Mitchell, *Nonwhite Races, State of Washington* (Olympia, 1968), pp 57-69.

[17] In Canadian usage "foreign-born" refers only to persons born outside the British Commonwealth. The census of 1891 listed persons born in England, Wales, Scotland, and Ireland as "foreign-born," but this is the exception rather than the rule.

[18] This included 30,689 migrants from the United Kingdom, 2,125 from different British possessions, and 1,181 of unknown British origin.

[19] Biographical data were obtained primarily from Howay and Scholefield, *British Columbia,* the Vancouver *Sun,* and Vancouver *Province.*

[20] Harold A. Logan, *Trade Unions in Canada* (Toronto, 1948), pp. 60-61, 302-303; Thomas R. Loosmore, "The British Columbia Labor Movement and Political Action, 1879-1906" (M.A. thesis, University of British Columbia, 1954); and Paul A. Phillips, *No Power Greater: A Century of Labour in British Columbia* (Vancouver, 1967) show that the political orientation of much of the labor movement has continued.

[21] Among those active in the early years of the C.C.F. in British Columbia were Ernest Winch, born in Essex, England, emigrated to Canada in 1898, active in a wide variety of socialist and labor activities in Vancouver, served in B.C. legislature from 1933 until his death in 1957; Harold Winch, his son, also born in England, came to Canada in 1910, served in B.C. legislature 1933-1953, led provincial C.C.F. 1938-1953, elected to House of Commons 1953, active in the founding of the NDP; William A. Pritchard, born in England, president of Vancouver Trades and Labour Council in the early 1900s, active in the Winnipeg general strike of 1919, president of Associated C.C.F. Clubs of British Columbia in 1930s; Dr. Lyle Telford, Canadian-born C.C.F. member of B.C. legislature 1933-1935, mayor of Vancouver 1939-1940; Rev. Robert Connell, born Liverpool, England, Anglican clergyman in Victoria, first leader of C.C.F. in B.C. legislature. See Dorothy G. Steeves, *The Compassionate Rebel: Ernest E. Winch and His Times* (Vancouver, 1960), pp. 85-121. Biographical data

were also obtained from *The Canadian Who's Who, 1936-1937* (Toronto, 1936), and *The Canadian Directory of Parliament, 1867-1967* (Ottawa, 1968).

[22] Robert Strachan was born in Glasgow, Scotland, migrated to Canada in 1931, and served as provincial leader of C.C.F., NDP, from 1956 to 1969.

[23] Jorgen Dahlie, "A Social History of Scandinavian Immigration, Washington State, 1895-1910" (Ph.D. dissertation, Washington State University, 1967); Sverre Arestad, "The Norwegians in the Pacific Coast Fisheries," *Pacific Northwest Quarterly*, XXXIV (1943), pp. 3-17.

[24] See annual volumes of the *Statistical Abstract of the United States* and the *Canada Year Book* for a convenient summary of immigration and naturalization data.

[25] Jules A. Karlin, "The Anti-Chinese Outbreaks in Seattle, 1885-1886," *Pacific Northwest Quarterly*, XXXIX (1948), pp. 103-130; Shotaro F. Miyamoto, *Social Solidarity Among the Japanese in Seattle* (Seattle, 1939); H. F. Angus, *Canada and the Far East, 1940-1953* (Toronto, 1953).

[26] British Columbia had 1,012 persons of Negro descent in 1961. See *Census of Canada 1961*, Vol. I, Part II, Table 35, pp. 1, 2.

[27] See David C. Corbett, *Canada's Immigration Policy: A Critique* (Toronto, 1957) esp. pp. 52-55, 194-196.

[28] This generalization is based on a comparison of the number of continental migrants in the United States and Canada in 1910 and 1911 and on the percentage of these migrants living in the six largest cities in each nation. See also Donald G. G. Kerr, *A Historical Atlas of Canada* (Toronto, 1960), p. 66.

[29] See John Porter, *The Vertical Mosaic, An Analysis of Social Class and Power in Canada* (Toronto, 1965), esp. pp. 60-73.

[30] John A. Lee, "The Greendale Canadians: Cultural and Structural Assimilation in an Urban Environment," in Bernard R. Blishen *et al.*, *Canadian Society: Sociological Perspectives* (Toronto, 1968), pp. 636-647; Frank G. Vallee *et al.*, "Ethnic Assimilation and Differentiation in Canada," in *ibid.*, pp. 593-603; Frank E. Jones, "Some Social Consequences of Immigration for Canada," *ibid.*, pp. 629-635. Urban environments, especially at the neighborhood level, can also help sustain a variety of distinctive ethnic traits whether in social customs, religion, or speech. See, for example, Nathan Glazer and Daniel P. Moynihan, *Beyond the Melting Pot* (Cambridge, 1963), Oscar Handlin, *The Newcomers: Negroes and Puerto Ricans in a Changing Metropolis* (Cambridge, 1959), Sam B. Warner, Jr., *The Private City: Philadelphia in Three Periods of Its Growth* (Philadelphia, 1968).

[31] Leroy O. Stone, *Urban Development in Canada* (1961 Census Monograph, Dominion Bureau of Statistics, Ottawa, 1967), p. 179, concludes that between 1951 and 1961 net immigration accounted for 61.8 percent of the population growth of metropolitan Vancouver, and natural increase 38.2 percent.

[32] Seattle expanded from 10.89 square miles in 1869 to 91.57 square miles in 1960, while Vancouver went from 10.5 square miles in 1886 to some

44 square miles in 1960. See *Department of Engineering Report, 1960, City of Seattle,* and *Annual Report, City of Vancouver, 1960.* Additions to population by annexation have not been made a separate category since they are already included in the table of birthplace of native-born population (Table III). If detailed statistics on the annexed suburbs were available, it would show, for example, that some of the migrants who apparently arrived in Seattle between 1900 and 1910 actually arrived in the area before 1900.

[33] Calvin F. Schmid, *Social Trends in Seattle* (Seattle, 1944), pp. 56-59, 67-73; Russel W. Barthell, "Annexation and Consolidation of Local Government in the State of Washington" (M.A. thesis, University of Washington, 1931), pp. 89-109.

[34] *Annual Report, Department of Engineering, City of Seattle, 1950-1960; Seattle Times,* March 8 and Nov. 19, 1952, Sept. 10, 1953, Jan. 3, 1954.

Between 1950 and 1960 Seattle had a natural increase of 81,101 and also added some 62,000 by annexation. Since the total population growth was only 89,496, there was a substantial net migration out of the city. As a rough approximation natural increase accounted for about 60 percent and annexation 40 percent of the total population growth for the decade.

[35] For annexations to Vancouver, see *Annual Report, City of Vancouver, 1929,* p. 5.

[36] In 1960 Seattle had a population of 557,087 in 91 square miles, or approximately 6,100 persons per square mile. Vancouver with 384,522 people in 44 square miles had 8,700 residents per square mile.

[37] At the present time Vancouver's city council is investigating the feasibility of annexing the municipality of Burnaby with a population of over 100,000.

17. Regional Factors in Industrial Conflict: The Case of British Columbia
Stuart Jamieson

STUART M. JAMIESON, *professor of economics at the University of British Columbia, has written widely in the fields of industrial and labour relations. Here he offers an explanation of the growth of the traditionally militant British Columbia labour movement.*

There have been a number of ambitious studies on an international scale in recent years attempting to identify and compare "industry patterns" or "national patterns" of industrial conflict in different countries. Outstanding among these have been two analytical surveys, "The Inter-Industry Propensity to Strike," by Kerr and Siegel, and *Changing Patterns of Industrial Conflict*, by Ross and Hartman.[1] One of the findings in this latter study, incidentally, was that, among the fifteen countries surveyed, there has been a relatively high incidence of strikes in Canada—second only to the United States, in fact.

This paper is based on the premise that, in Canada, the individual *province*, or perhaps better, the *region*, is the most fruitful unit for studying such phenomena as industrial conflict. For regional differences in several respects are more pronounced in Canada then in most comparably industrialized countries, so that the portrayal of behaviour patterns in terms of national averages or configurations can lead to highly misleading conclusions.

British Columbia, next only to Quebec, perhaps, offers a particularly interesting area for research in this field, because it is a separate and distinct industrial complex, and has experienced patterns of industrial conflict that differ markedly in certain important respects from other major regions of the country.

It is not my intention, however, to emphasize the unique or special features of the labour scene in British Columbia. The field of industrial relations in general has suffered too much already, perhaps, from a plethora of detailed descriptive studies of matters of purely local scope and interest. What I am presenting here is a purely exploratory study, the purpose of which is to examine and discuss various types of situations that generate certain patterns of

Source: The Canadian Journal of Economics and Political Science,
XXVIII, 3 (1962), pp. 405-416. Reprinted by permission of the
author and publisher.

industrial conflict, in the hope that the approach may be useful for similar studies in other provinces or regions. The study will be confined to only one type of industrial conflict, namely, *strikes.*[2] It will attempt to portray, first, the main outlines of the special strike pattern in British Columbia, as compared to the rest of Canada; and, secondly, the main factors that account for this pattern.

There seems to be a fairly widespread impression that British Columbia is the most strike-prone province in Canada. The government of that province has fortified the impression by passing a series of new enactments in the Legislature that impose unusually severe restrictions on unions. Official statistics gleaned from both the federal and provincial Departments of Labour over the past decade seem to indicate that British Columbia *does* have an unusually high incidence of strikes. The non-agricultural paid labour force in that Province constituted about 10 per cent of the total for Canada from 1949 to 1959 inclusive. Workers in that province, however, accounted for almost 15 per cent of all strikes and lockouts, more than 15 per cent of all workers participating in strikes, and more than 21 per cent of all working days lost in strikes over the nation as a whole during this period.

A simple comparison on the basis of all paid employees, however, tends to be misleading. Strikes and lockouts, on this continent at least, are a highly institutionalized form of *overt* conflict between unionized workers and employers. They are rarely undertaken by unorganized or non-union workers.

A more meaningful comparison of the propensity to strike, therefore, would be to relate strikes and lockouts to union membership, in Canada and British Columbia respectively. This modifies the picture considerably. Almost one-half of all paid workers in British Columbia belonged to unions during 1949-59, as compared to less than one-third in Canada, or the United States, as a whole. Organized labour in British Columbia accounted for about 15 per cent of total union membership in Canada during this period. This percentage is roughly equal to British Columbia's average proportion of all strikes and of workers involved in strikes during this period. In general, then, unionized workers in British Columbia over the past decade have *not* gone on strike proportionately more frequently, nor in larger numbers, than their counterparts in the rest of Canada.

All this raises a whole new set of questions as to why workers in British Columbia are so highly organized as compared to other parts of Canada, and to the United States for that matter. Factors conducing to a high degree of organization into unions, of course, are likely to be important in explaining the pattern of industrial conflict in that province.

One important respect in which strikes in British Columbia *have* differed from the rest of Canada is that they have been much more prolonged (and strikes in Canada, on the average, have been more prolonged than in the United States since the Second World War).[3] Their average duration in B.C. during 1949-59 was 25.4 days, or almost 50 per cent longer than the Canadian average of 18.3 days during this period. Strikes and lockouts in British Columbia, therefore, while proportionately no larger or more frequent than in the rest of the country, on the average, have been longer and more difficult to settle.

Before pursuing this point further, however, it is necessary to state the obvious cliché that broad averages, over an extended period of time, tend to hide significant details. A further analysis of provincial labour statistics indicates that strikes in British Columbia have been heavily concentrated in certain years, and in certain industries. In 1952 and in 1959, for instance, that province, with only 15 per cent of all union members in Canada, accounted for almost 40 per cent of all workers involved in strikes, and 60 per cent of all man-days of employment lost in strikes. And, over the 1949-59 period, as may be seen from Table I below, only two industries, lumber and construction, with only 28 per cent of all union members in British Columbia, accounted for almost one-half of all strikes and no less than four-fifths of all losses of employment directly attributable to strikes, in that province.

This particular pattern of timing and location seems to indicate that strikes and lockouts in British Columbia tend to be concentrated in a few industries that are most vulnerable to cyclical fluctuations in output and employment, and that, in contrast to most other regions of this continent, they tend to concentrate in years immediately *following* periods of intense economic expansion.

Strikes occur for many different reasons and are expressed in a variety of forms. Any attempt to portray distinct patterns of industrial conflict and to explore their causes, therefore, requires some sort of classification. In the Canadian, and British Columbia, contexts, with their elaborate legislative provisions governing the prevention and settlement of industrial disputes, it would be legitimate, perhaps, to classify strikes into two broad categories: legally authorized, and other.

Legally authorized "interest" disputes and strikes arise in the course of negotiating new or revised agreements, and in most provinces, including British Columbia, the parties involved must go through complicated conciliation procedures required by law before reaching the overt stage of a walk-out or shut-down. The largest and most protracted strikes are almost invariably in this category.

Economic issues are at the forefront of such disputes. The overwhelming majority of them develop over organized labour's demands for higher wages or their dollar equivalent in "fringe" benefits, as against the employers' resistance to the increased costs that these would involve. Scholars in disciplines other than economics are prone to challenge the validity of a purely economic interpretation of "interest" disputes, however. The avowed economic issues, many sociologists, political scientists, and psychologists would contend, are merely symbolic of other deeper, more intangible goals (such as the struggle for greater power, status, recognition or prestige of the contending parties).

This is a matter of controversy too complex to pursue at this time. Suffice it to say that the position taken in this paper is that a fairly orthodox economic approach as regards causes tends to be the most fruitful in analysing "interest" disputes and strikes. In most cases they are undertaken only after fairly careful examination and articulation of the issues involved, and after fairly lengthy negotiation, and, in Canada, conciliation. And, in line with orthodox economic assumptions, to the degree that the pertinent facts are available for making realistic assessments, there is at least *some* effort by the parties involved at making rational calculations of their potential gains and losses.

The other main type of strike can be put in the "protest" or "wildcat" category: strikes undertaken without the prior authorization of the union officials, in violation of existing union agreements, or in contravention of disputes settlement procedure required by law. A cursory survey of those reported by Departments of Labour in Canada indicates that only a small fraction of them is rationally conceived and undertaken for specific economic goals. The vast majority are small, brief (of one or two days' duration), and motivated by non-economic sentiments, values, or objectives: support given to other workers on strike; threats to the survival of the group, as when non-union workers, or members of a rival union, are employed on work projects under a particular union's jurisdiction; protests against dismissals, demotions or other disciplinary actions by management; complaints about the quality of food, lodging, or transportation facilities; and a multiplicity of other issues.

Wildcat strikes seem to portray most clearly the types of collec-

STRIKES AND LOCKOUTS IN BRITISH COLUMBIA, 1949-1959*

Industrial categories in B.C.	Percentage total paid labour in B.C.	Percentage total union membership in B.C.	Strikes		Strike participants		Man days of employment lost		
			Number	Percentage of total in B.C.	Number	Percentage of total in B.C.	Number (000)	Percentage of total in B.C.	Average duration (days)
Logging and lumber	19	15	71	22.2	77,046	48.4	2,671	66.2	35
Construction	8	13	78	24.4	11,536	7.2	262	6.5	23
Sub-Total, two industries	27	28	149	46.6	88,582	55.6	2,933	72.7	33.1
All other industries	73	72.2	171	53.4	70,310	44.4	1,099	27.3	15.6
All industries	100	100	320	100	158,892	100	4,032	100	25.4

*Annual Reports for the years 1949 to 1959 inclusive, Department of Labour, Province of British Columbia.

tive action of major interest to sociologists and psychologists, and are least amenable to orthodox economic analysis. Annual Reports of the provincial Department of Labour from 1949 to 1959 inclusive indicate that, in both the lumber and construction industries in British Columbia, a large majority of strikes was in the unauthorized or wildcat category—specifically, forty-seven (compared with twenty-four "interest" strikes) in lumber, and forty-five (compared to thirty-three) in construction. Indeed, the prevalence of illegal "wildcat" strikes in these two industries has provided the main impetus and alleged justification for the punitive measures enacted by the British Columbia legislature in recent years. Wildcat strikes, however, as noted before, with few exceptions have been small and of brief duration. In virtually all industries, including lumber and construction, the less frequent "interest" disputes in the authorized category have accounted for the overwhelming proportion of strike participants and man-days of employment lost in strikes. The lumber and construction industries in British Columbia each experienced thirteen strikes of more than one month's duration during 1949-59. Of these, there were eight strikes in the lumber industry, and seven in the construction industry, that lasted for more than two months.

So much for the pattern. A large number and variety of factors could be offered as explanations for one or another of these aspects of industrial conflict in British Columbia. Some of these are more or less peculiar to the main industries involved, and some of them are peculiar to the special regional context in which these industries have carried on their operations.

There is, to begin with, the basic fact of *geography*. British Columbia in certain important respects is merely an extension of the larger Pacific Northwest and Mountain regions of the United States. Up to the Second World War, as a comprehensive survey by Clark Kerr in the late 1940's brings out,[4] these were the most highly unionized and most strike-prone regions in the United States. British Columbia over the past decade has been in a stage of development comparable to this section of the U.S.A. in the pre-war period, and manifests a similar pattern of industrial relations. This statement of course, still begs the main question as to what factors account for these special characteristics of labour in the Northwest Coast and Mountain regions.

One plausible explanation might be that British Columbia, because of its special location, topography and resources, has remained a frontier region up to the present day.[5] On the North American continent frontiers have been the main birthplace and nurturing ground of militant, and in the broad sense radical, labour movements and political parties (using the word "radical" in a descriptive rather than favourable or derogatory sense). The conditions that generate radical ideologies tend to create deep cleavages of interest and viewpoint between labour and management, and a high propensity to strike, for such ideologies provide a sanction and rationale for militant unionism and class conflict.

However, while radical ideologies may have been an important factor contributing to strikes in British Columbia in earlier decades, they appear to have had much less impact since the Second World War. There is little or no reliable evidence to indicate that unions under radical leadership have engaged in larger, longer, or more frequent strikes than those under conservative leadership in British Columbia. To take two examples: the mining and smelting industry of this province, under the jurisdiction of the Communist-led Mine, Mill and Smelter Workers' Union, has been relatively free of strikes of any consequence during the past decade, while among the most strike-prone have been certain organizations in the construction industry led by conservative "business" unionists.

A more pertinent factor that might help account for the high degree of organization and the intensity of industrial conflict in British Columbia, as in the Pacific Northwest and Mountain states in earlier decades, is that this Province specializes to a high degree in certain industries that have been found in other areas to be unusually strike-prone. (In this view, the prevalence of radical ideologies in frontier economies would appear to be a *result* rather than a *cause* of industrial conflict.) Clark Kerr and Abraham Siegel in their comprehensive survey covering dozens of industries in eleven countries,[6] found a remarkable degree of consistency in industrial relations patterns. In almost every country surveyed it was found that the industries with the highest incidence of strikes were, in order of frequency or impact: mining, maritime, longshoring, lumber, and textiles. The authors attributed the high incidence of strikes to such factors as: the large proportion of transient single workers employed in such industries (with the exception of textiles); the geographic and social isolation of the workers, like a "race apart," living in one-industry towns or special districts in cities where they have little contact with other occupational groups or classes; the limited opportunities for a stable family life; and other special hardships or limitations associated with work in such industries. These problems generate many frustrations and grievances, and more important, what Kerr and Siegel call the "totality of verbally shared grievances" tends to develop into a consensus of sentiment hostile to employers (particularly where these are absentee owners). To quote: "The strike for the isolated mass is a kind of colonial revolt against far removed authority, an outlet for accumulated tensions, and a substitute for occupational and social mobility."[7]

Several of these observations seem applicable to the British Columbia scene, and help account for the high incidence of conflict in the lumber industry of this province during the past decade—particularly the prevalence of wildcat strikes. A number of them also seem to apply, in British Columbia, to the construction industry.

Some of Kerr and Siegel's conclusions would have to be modified or rejected, however, in British Columbia's case. Mining and longshoring, for instance, have been virtually strike-free industries in British Columbia over the past decade. And their findings do not in themselves explain why loggers and sawmill workers, for instance, go on strike more frequently, and for longer periods of time, in British Columbia than in Ontario or Quebec.

Another factor of growing importance since the war, over Canada as a whole, and one that has a special impact upon industrial relations in British Columbia, has been the demonstration effect of United States wage and living standards. The higher wages and other benefits enjoyed by American labour have long been a source of unrest and dissatisfaction among many Canadian workers. In earlier decades these found their main outlet in large-scale emigration to the United States. Since the 1930's, and particularly since the Second World War, they have been channelled to a far greater degree into trade unionism and collective bargaining, supported periodically by strike action.[8]

Such pressures tend to be more intense in British Columbia than in other provinces for a number of reasons. There are, to begin with, the similarities in resource patterns and techniques, as well as in labour organization and in the ownership or control of major firms in the resource-based industries, as between British Columbia and the Pacific Northwestern region of the United States.

To a far greater degree than in other provinces also, workers employed in secondary and service industries as well as in the primary industries in British Columbia are strongly influenced by American wage and living standards, and thus have a stronger incentive to organize and strike for their objectives. This is most readily apparent, perhaps, in such industries as building construction. There is closer communication between Vancouver, B.C., and Seattle, Washington, than there is between any other comparable Canadian and American metropolitan centres, with the exception of Windsor and Detroit. But Vancouver and its surrounding urban municipalities, unlike Windsor in relation to Ontario, is the major metropolitan centre of British Columbia, and contains more than one-half the entire population of the province.

This leads up to another highly important causal factor influencing the pattern of industrial relations in British Columbia. Metropolitan Vancouver, as one of Canada's major seaports and the terminus for nearly all the Western region's major transportation and communication facilities, exerts a degree of centralized control over British Columbia's economic life probably greater than metropolitan centres in other provinces. This is most immediately apparent in such fields as credit and finance, wholesale trade and distribution, and special professional or technical services, as well as in corporate managements and trade unions. The trend towards larger-scale and more centralized organization has been particularly pronounced in the lumber and construction industries over the past decade, due primarily to the number of huge new industrial or resource-development projects whose operations have extended, directly or indirectly, over the whole province.

This trend, in turn, has encouraged the development of centralized industry-wide or multi-employer bargaining between unions and managements to a degree not usually found elsewhere in Canada. This is one of the most important factors that help explain the unusually large proportion of workers that are unionized, and the unusually long average duration of strikes in British Columbia. Broadening the scale of bargaining tends to reduce the number of "interest" strikes that develop over the negotiation of new agreements, but when they do occur they tend to be larger and more prolonged.

This trend towards large centralized organizations and industry-wide bargaining also helps to explain the high prevalence of wildcat strikes, particularly in the lumber and construction industries. Grievances and conflicts are frequent, for the type of reasons discussed at length by Kerr and Siegel. Many of the major construction and forest products development projects over the past decade have been carried out in remote areas in which working and living conditions are often unpleasant, and all sorts of difficulties, irritations, and misunderstandings arise. Often the Vancouver headquarters of both unions and employers are too distant to supervise or service their subordinates effectively, and to settle disputes quickly when they develop. Common grievances arising on the job tend then to develop into unauthorized or wildcat strikes, particularly on temporary projects in which workers are employed for only a few weeks at a time and which, therefore, cannot wait for protracted investigation and arbitration.

The final and most important factor accounting for the high incidence of industrial conflict in British Columbia, and particularly the heavy losses incurred in large and prolonged "interest" disputes, has been the rapid but uneven pattern of economic growth that this province experienced during the 1950's. This has arisen, of course, from the basically unstable nature of the British Columbia economy, specialized as it is in a few resource-based industries that produce largely for shifting and uncertain export markets.

Construction has played a central role both in the erratic course of the British Columbia boom and recession and in the comparatively turbulent state of industrial relations in that Province over the past decade. For a number of reasons, the construction industry on this continent, under certain conditions at least, seems to be inherently susceptible to recurrent long and bitter wage disputes between unions and employers. British Columbia appears to have been one of the more extreme examples of this pattern.

Because of their special vulnerability to seasonal and cyclical unemployment and high turnover of jobs, construction workers tend to put greater emphasis than do workers in most other industries on immediate gains in wages or equivalent fringe benefits, as against long-run security of jobs and incomes. Again, the organizational structure of the industry and the nature of its markets conduce to unusually rapid wage and price increases during boom periods. In each major region or metropolitan centre the industry comprises dozens of specialized unions whose leaders compete vigorously for prestige and leadership (as measured by wage increases or higher fringe benefits), and even larger numbers of specialized employers and trade associations competing for profitable contracts. The products of the construction industry are characterized by short-run price inelasticity and long-run income elasticity of demand. This combination tends to encourage excessive upward wage pressure by unions, and excessive optimism and overly generous concessions by employers, which result in periodic overexpansion and recurrent conflict. A series of large wage increases during a period of expansion tends to create "built-in expectations" which carry over into periods of decline or recession, when employers are forced to resist further union demands. The wage increases and other benefits won by the various building trades unions during periods of expansion, however, tend to vary widely, due to differences in elasticity of demand and supply in the various specialized labour and product markets within the industry, and differences in militancy and bargaining power among the various unions. Workers in the industry, at the same time, have a strong sense of status. This was reflected, up to the later 1940's, in a complicated but rigidly hierarchical structure of wage rates and fringe benefits based largely upon degrees of skill and training required. Unequal wage increases and other gains during periods of rapid expansion disrupted this established wage structure and generated widespread dissatisfaction and conflict. Unusually large gains won by a few unions occupying unusually strategic positions during a boom period set targets that other building trades unions were forced to seek by the "pressure of coercive comparison." When a time lag occurred in the exercise of the pressure, so that it met head-on with employer resistance during a down-turn, long-drawn-out strikes and lockouts ensued.

Maladjustments and conflicts arising from these conditions within the construction industry have tended to be made more extreme in British Columbia by the relatively greater magnitude of the construction boom, coupled with its greater instability in the province during the 1950's, as compared to the rest of the country. The annual volume and value of construction expanded far more in British Columbia than over Canada as a whole during the first half of the decade, specifically 137 per cent as compared to 92 per cent from 1951 through 1957.[9] Within this broad trend of expansion, the fluctuations in construction activity were far more extreme in British Columbia. During boom periods, construction expanded far more rapidly in this province (by more than 28 per cent in British Columbia as compared to less than 11 per cent in Canada in 1955 over 1954, and by more than 45 per cent as compared to less than 25 per cent in 1956 over 1955), and during recession years it has *contracted* far more severely (by 14.5 per cent for British Columbia as compared to less than 6 per cent for Canada as a whole in 1953 from the 1952 level, and by more than 25 per cent as compared to only 2.3 per cent for Canada during 1958 as compared to 1957).[10] A large part of this expansion and unevenness in growth can be accounted for by huge new industrial and resource development projects that have been carried out intermittently.

This "lumpiness" in investment tended to have further disturbing effects on industrial relations in construction in the province. Large firms handling multi-million dollar projects competed fever-

ishly for labour in boom periods, and offered wages and fringe
benefits higher than the smaller construction companies, or the
general public could afford over the long pull. In disputes with
major building trades unions in the middle of major projects, the
larger concerns were able and willing to make overly generous
concessions in order to win "peace at any price." The main
repercussions were felt in the subsequent periods of decline, after
completion of a series of major projects. Once a standard had
been set by a minority during the height of a boom, attempts by
other unions to win comparable wage increases came up against a
ceiling of stable or falling prices during the recession. Thus, as
noted earlier, the biggest and most prolonged "interest" disputes
in the history of the construction industry in British Columbia
occurred during 1952 and again in 1958-59. And practically all of
these were in the building section of the industry, and in major
metropolitan centres like Vancouver, not in large out-of-town
projects in the engineering category. Practically all wildcat strikes,
on the other hand, have occurred in the latter.

These main developments in the construction industry in British Columbia, the uneven rates of wage increases, and the dispari-
ties and conflicts they generated have had particularly strong
repercussions in the lumber industry, and appear to have been the
main immediate cause of the largest and most protracted shut-
downs in that field. The complicated interrelationships between
the two industries—particularly as regards labour and union
organizations—are provocative of maladjustment and conflict.
Certain broad similaries in conditions of employment, on the one
hand, lead workers in the two industries to look upon themselves
as comparable, and each group is within the other's "orbit of
coercive comparison," to use Arthur Ross's phrase. Both industries are largely in the capital goods category, and their workers
are particularly vulnerable to seasonal and cyclical fluctuations in
investment, output, and employment. There is a similar range and
variety of skills between the two main groups and a number of
occupations, particularly in mechanical work and maintenance,
are virtually identical in logging, sawmilling, and construction.
This factor has led, incidentally, to numerous jurisdictional disputes. And finally, on the Pacific Coast there has been intense
competition for leadership and prestige, and at times bitter
rivalry, between the International Woodworkers of America and
certain major building trades unions for several years.

The two industries differ markedly, on the other hand, as
regards such matters as the size and nature of their respective
markets, structures and techniques of production, and elasticity of

demand for labour. Equal or similar collective bargaining demands in the two industries, therefore, come up against different price and cost conditions and different employer attitudes and policies. Where the demand for construction goods tends to be price *inelastic* in the short run, in lumber it tends to be highly *elastic*. Where employers in the construction industry produce almost entirely for a local or regional market, and thus collectively have some control over the prices they can charge for their product, the lumber industry in British Columbia produces largely for export to the United States and overseas markets in close competition with other producing areas, and therefore has little or no control over the prices it can charge. Organization and collective bargaining in the construction industry in British Columbia, though operating on a larger scale than in most provinces, is still highly segmented and competitive, as noted earlier. Hitherto this has operated to the advantage of the unions in terms of bargaining power and wage or fringe-benefit gains, at least in the short run. In the lumber industry, by comparison, the union is industrial in structure, encompassing all types of workers, and it bargains collectively with all major employers acting as a unit, on a regional scale. And finally, where technological change has had a very limited impact on the construction industry, in terms of over-all displacement of labour, in logging and sawmilling it has been rapid and drastic in its employment effects. From 1949 to 1956 it made possible unusually large increases in output and profits for major firms in the industry without any appreciable increase in the size of the labour force. In general, then, the Woodworkers' union, while under pressure from its members to seek gains comparable to those won by the main unions in the construction industry, has been weaker in bargaining power, and has been faced with a group of larger and more unified employers who have had stronger incentives, and greater financial resources, to resist the union's demands. Wage increases for construction workers, consequently, were far larger than for lumber workers during the 1950's, and on those occasions where the latter made serious efforts to achieve parity with the former, protracted, industry-wide shut-downs resulted.

Because of these interrelationships and invidious comparisons, major disputes and strikes in the lumber industry have tended to follow closely on major disputes and settlements in construction. And, for reasons noted earlier, disputes in both industries have tended to concentrate in periods following major booms. The very size of the labour force employed in lumber production, and its exteme importance to the provincial economy, however, mean that, if need be, extraordinary measures will be taken to try to avoid industry-wide strikes. The eight-week strike of 1952 alone accounted for more man-days lost than in all other industries combined, from 1949 to 1956 inclusive. A threatened strike of 1957 was averted only by last-minute intervention of the premier of British Columbia, and another in 1958 was prevented only by the combination of depressed lumber markets and prices, and the long closure of the forests due to fire hazard, coupled with extensive third-party intervention. An even more protracted and costly strike than in 1952 finally developed in 1959 after lengthy mediation procedures.

The major wage disputes, strikes, and settlements in building construction and lumber have had their impact on other industries and occupational groups. The lumber industry particularly, because of its central importance to the provincial economy, and to the large size and prominence of the lumber workers' union, tends to be the main "pattern setter" for other unionized industries. And major disputes in these other industries, including the protracted and costly shut-down of the pulp and paper industry during 1957-58, have generally been linked, directly or indirectly, to those in lumber and construction.

One final factor possibly contributing to the peculiar pattern of industrial conflict in British Columbia, is perhaps the most controversial and most difficult to measure in its impact; namely, labour disputes legislation. This author, among others, has expressed the view elsewhere[11] that the compulsory conciliation procedures required in most Canadian legislation are important in helping explain the fact that, since the Second World War, the average duration of strikes in Canada is higher than in other countries, including the United States.

It would be difficult, however, to extend this argument to explain the longer average duration of strikes in British Columbia as compared to Canada as a whole. British Columbia's labour disputes legislation is based on broadly similar principles and procedures to those of the Dominion government and most other provinces. It does contain certain special provisions, particularly various penalties for illegal strikes and other irregularities, but it is difficult to derive any connection between these and the pattern of industrial conflict portrayed for that province.

One possible exception to this generalization, and a feature of British Columbia labour legislation that may be a contributing factor, is the provision that, in effect, requires a supervised secret ballot before strike or lockout action can be undertaken. This provision has been on the statute books, in amended form, since

1947. Critics allege that it tends to prolong strikes or lockouts when they do develop, because it gives them the aura of official government sanction.

But all this is by way of speculation. The notable fact that does stand out in the British Columbia labour scene has been the remarkable consistency of the cyclical pattern of industrial conflict, and particularly the similar sequence and incidence of strikes leading up to and including the peak periods of shut-down in 1952 and 1958-9. The consistency was evident in spite of numerous changes in legislation in 1954 designed to reduce the frequency and impact of industrial disputes. One is tempted to conclude that, in the unstable economic, social, and political context in which industrial relations are carried on in British Columbia, even the best designed and most far-sighted labour disputes legislation (or the most severe and punitive for that matter!) would have little or no effect upon the recurrent cycle of industrial conflict in that province.

Notes

1. Clark Kerr and Abraham Siegel, "The Inter-Industry Propensity to Strike: an International Comparison" in Arthur Kornhauser, Robert Dubin, and Arthur M. Ross, *Industrial Conflict* (New York, 1954); Arthur M. Ross and Paul Hartman, *Changing Patterns of Industrial Conflict* (New York, 1960).
2. The word "strike" is used in the generic sense in this context, to include what may be classed technically as "lockouts," as well as supplementary tactics such as picketing and boycotting.
3. Ross and Hartman, *Changing Patterns*, chap. v.
4. Clark Kerr, "Collective Bargaining on the Pacific Coast," *Monthly Labour Review*, April, 1947.
5. One index of this fact is that British Columbia is the only province in Canada, and the only regional political unit on the North American continent, in which, between 1941 and 1956, the population of the main metropolitan areas grew *less* rapidly than the population over the province as a whole.
6. "Inter-Industry Propensity to Strike."
7. *Ibid.*, 193.
8. Stuart Jamieson, *Industrial Relations in Canada* (Ithaca, 1957), chap. I.
9. Department of Trade and Commerce, Ottawa, *Private and Public Investment in Canada, Regional Estimates*, Series, 1952 to 1958.
10. *Ibid.*
11. *Industrial Relations in Canada*, chap. IV.

18. The Oriental "Menace" in British Columbia
Patricia E. Roy

PATRICIA E. ROY, *is an associate professor of history at the University of Victoria. Her article is part of a more extensive examination of the controversy over Asian immigration and the Asian immigrant, which has played so large a part in British Columbia public life since colonial days.*

The anti-Asiatic riots of 1907 and the *Komagata Maru* incident of 1914 are merely the two most vivid pre-war instances of those irrational fears and racial prejudices that British Columbians traditionally knew as the Oriental "menace." During World War I, the distraction of the war, the slackening of Oriental immigration, the departure of some Chinese, and British Columbia's dependence on the Japanese navy temporarily reduced agitation against the "menace."[1] Then, with the post-war resumption of large-scale Oriental immigration, the "menace" again became a lively issue. Throughout the 1920's politicians and publicists exploited and exaggerated it making the Oriental threat to British Columbia's future as a white province seem much greater than it actually was.

The idea of a "menace" flourished on fear. Anti-Asiatic agitators warned that "swarming millions" of Orientals would come to British Columbia if the federal government were not vigilant in passing and enforcing exclusion laws. The agitators, observing the "amazing" birth rate among the Japanese already in the province, predicted the submersion of the white race. At the same time, provincial government officials claimed that many Oriental births were not being registered. And those who were most fearful of the "menace" suspected that there was considerable illegal immigration.

The Chinese and Japanese population of the province seemed to be greater than the 38,539 indicated by the 1921 Census.[2] The distinguishing physical features of the Orientals and their concentration in particular areas, notably greater Vancouver, the lower Fraser Valley and Vancouver Island, made them unusually conspicuous. Restrictive legislation had confined them to a few

---

Source: Western Canadian Studies Conference, *The Twenties in Western Canada*, edited by S. M. Trofimenkoff (Ottawa, 1972), pp. 243-55. Reprinted by permission of the author and publisher.

industries, chiefly agriculture, the retail and service trades, certain aspects of lumbering, and fishing, where, after 1922, federal licensing regulations gradually reduced the number of Japanese fishermen. In these limited activities, the Orientals were usually so hard-working that their critics complained of "unfair" competition.

On first sight, the Oriental "menace" appears simply as a fear of economic competition. Indeed, it would be easy to select evidence to suggest that the question was largely an economic matter. Several of the most vocal anti-Oriental groups represented specific economic interests which faced direct Oriental competition. Accompanying almost every one of these objections to "unfair" competition, however, was a clear expression of fear for the future of a white British Columbia. Moreover, these ideas were shared by many white British Columbians who had no personal economic interest in the matter. The Oriental "menace," as explained by the politicians and publicists, was not just a threat to the pocketbooks of white British Columbians; it was a threat to the future of a superior white civilization.

A study of the reaction of the farmers of the province to the Oriental "menace" clearly shows how economic competition aroused traditional racial prejudices and made threatened individuals receptive to propaganda about dangers facing a white British Columbia. For many years white farmers had gladly employed cheap Oriental labour to clear land and to pick fruit and berries. During the latter stages of the war they even flirted with a plan to import indentured Chinese labourers. At the same time, Japanese and Chinese farmers were beginning to buy and lease their own land thus presenting white farmers with an Oriental "menace." A Victoria area farmer expressed the attitude of white farmers when he told readers of *B.C. Fruit and Farm Magazine* that "the proportion of Orientals to whites in B.C. is too great, but only in one sense, and that is owing to the fact that they are in business for themselves and are not, as they should be, working for white men."[3] The Orientals had ceased to be a subservient class. By aspiring to equality they threatened white dominance of British Columbia.

White farmers endorsed the popular idea of Oriental exclusion, that is, the banning of further Oriental immigration. And they were particularly anxious to have legislation to prevent Orientals from acquiring title to agricultural land and to limit the term of leases to them.[4] In their petitions to the provincial government, the farmers repeated the traditional argument that the lower Oriental standard of living undercut white men. They also claimed that the presence of Orientals depressed real estate values. With the help of statistics prepared by the provincial government, they showed that Orientals were increasing their control over certain aspects of agriculture.

The white farmers who were concerned about the existing situation were extremely fearful of the future. California propaganda about the Japanese stranglehold over some aspects of the state's agriculture haunted them. The editor of *Farm and Home*, a weekly newspaper, told his readers:

In California the Oriental situation is becoming more serious every day. Slowly the Japanese are taking charge of the agricultural industry. In certain districts where American farmers in other days lived and brought up splendid families, today the brown-skinned sons of Nippon control the land.

British Columbia is vitally interested in the Oriental question. The province, like California in so may respects is the favoured landing place of the Oriental.[5]

Such ideas fell on fertile ground. When the Advisory Board of the Farmers' Institutes met the Agricultural Committee of the Legislature, they referred to the seriousness of the California situation.[6] Throughout the decade other American examples were cited. In his first major address to the Legislature, J. W. Berry, the Conservative M.L.A. for Delta and a prominent dairy farmer, observed that the Japanese provided forty per cent of Seattle's milk supply.[7] At that time there were no Oriental dairymen in the Fraser Valley.

Similarly, the knowledge that Chinese and Japanese farmers had succeeded in coastal areas of British Columbia worried interior farmers. At Vanderhoof, for example, the annual meeting of the District Farmers' Institute in 1924 resolved that "while not affecting us here directly as *yet*, we still require to take a stand" on the Oriental question.[8] The best examples of apprehension are found in the Okanagan Valley. At Kelowna, more than 300 people attended a meeting called early in 1920 by the Great War Veterans' Association to "discuss the burning question of Oriental ownership of land."[9] At that time Orientals owned 112 acres in the Kelowna area. Six years later, when the Vernon Board of Trade informed the federal government of the inconvenience and detriment to white settlement which was likely to be caused by the sale of land to Orientals, it cited California precedents rather than local experience.[10] The very comprehensive *Report on Oriental Activities Within the Province* published by the Legislature in 1927, made no special reference to Oriental farmers or orchardists in the Okanagan.[11]

The farmers feared economic competition; they were also concerned about the future purity of the white race. Practically every resolution against Oriental land holding complained of the inassimilability of the Oriental. The Farmers' Institutes, for example, declared that the "Oriental race will not assimilate with the Caucasian race."[12] Assimilation, of course, was not desirable. At Fort Langley, where the Japanese were the chief "menace", the United Farmers unequivocally asserted that these people were "a serious menace to the social, economic and political life" of the community because they "do not assimilate with the white population—and it is not desirable that they should—and a homogeneous and largely self-contained settlement of non-assimilable aliens is an undesirable thing for Canada."[13] These ideas were consistently maintained. At their convention in 1925, the United Farmers of B.C. observed that "homogeneous and not a dual population is in the best interests of Canada, both for the strength of the nation in war and its institutions in peace."[14]

Such ideas were not confined to the agricultural interests of the province. The retail merchants of greater Vancouver and Victoria were also active in combatting the Oriental "menace" during the 1920s. For them, the "menace" was the post-war movement of Oriental merchants, particularly Chinese grocers, out of the Oriental sections of the cities and into white neighbourhoods. By keeping longer hours and more attractive stores, the Orientals drew away trade which the white merchants considered to be rightfully theirs. Notwithstanding their lack of merchandising initiative, the white merchants were effective campaigners against the Oriental "menace." Through their national organization, and in co-operation with Boards of Trade and other interested groups such as the Asiatic Exclusion League, the merchants sought to educate other parts of Canada about the seriousness of the "menace" on the coast. They lobbied parliamentary support for W. G. McQuarrie's resolution which, after declaring that the "rapid multiplication" of Orientals was "becoming a serious menace to living conditions, particularly on the Pacific Coast," called for the end of Oriental immigration.[15] Partly in response to this campaign, the federal government passed a Chinese Immigration Act in 1923 which effectively ended Chinese immigration.

The passage of this Act temporarily reduced the anti-Oriental agitation of the merchants but did not end Oriental competition in retail trade. A provincial Legislative Committee found that in 1925, 3,231 Orientals held business licenses in the province. Of these, almost two-thirds were in Vancouver and Victoria. The Committee reported that Chinese grocery stores were spread throughout the cities and had "replaced or driven out white storekeepers." Moreover, the Committee noticed that "Chinese residence in other quarters than their own followed this business penetration."[16] The idea that Chinese would live in white neighbourhoods was anathema to many white British Columbians.

The release of the Legislative Committee's *Report on Oriental Activities* coincided with new agitation. Through articles in the Vancouver *Star* and the Vancouver *Daily Province* and in his book *The Oriental Occupation of British Columbia*,[17] Tom MacInnes drew attention to the problem. In 1928 he got one hundred and forty-three Vancouver businessmen to sign a petition asking the provincial government to establish Trades Licenses Boards to check Oriental competition. He also secured the signature of sixty-seven of these businessmen on a petition calling for the partial repatriation of Orientals and the expropriation—"at fair market value"—of the property of those who were repatriated.[18] Among those signing the petitions were representatives of Vancouver's three large department stores who were not directly affected by Oriental competition.

The merchants, of course, feared competition in trade. They also shared the racial prejudices of white British Columbians. Writing to Prime Minister King in support of McQuarrie's Oriental exclusion resolution, the B. C. Board of the Retail Merchants of Canada declared:

> To us it is not merely a question of competitive merchandising, aggravated by a lower standard of living. It is in fact a struggle of far deeper significance in which home, family and citizenship considerations outweigh mercenary motives. . . . As Canadian citizens first and retail merchants afterwards, we ask that this issue be constructively dealt with at this Session . . . The situation of today is acute. The situation of tomorrow will be embittered. Can we with equanimity bequeath to the Canada of the future a race problem worse than the Negro heritage in the Southern States?[19]

And, in supporting MacInnes' repatriation petition, the Vancouver merchants demanded measures to "insure that British Columbia shall be a Province in which *Canadians of European origin*, and *incoming settlers of European origin* shall always be in a dominant majority for carrying on industrial, mercantile and agricultural pursuits."[20] For many merchants, the Oriental "menace" was a threat to the dominance of the white race as well as an economic concern.

Traditional trade unionists felt much the same way about the Oriental "menace". Despite socialist propaganda that the capitalists, not the Orientals, were the real enemies of the working classes and despite provincial legislation which was reducing the number of Orientals in the labour force, the trade unionists maintained their prejudices. Union leaders such as W. J. Bartlett and Percy Bengough played a prominent role in forming the Asiatic Exclusion League in 1921 "to keep the Province and the Dominion for the White Man, by stopping any further Oriental Immigration."[21] In 1928, the Vancouver and New Westminster Trades and Labour Council rejected a Canadian Labour Party resolution calling for the restoration of the franchise to Orientals in British Columbia.[22]

That racial prejudice was a major part of most complaints against the Oriental "menace" is clear. Resolutions endorsing Oriental exclusion inevitably referred to the inassimilability of the Oriental and the desirability of a "white British Columbia." Racial prejudices and fears for the future are evident in the statements of the politicians. A. M. Manson, the Attorney-General, frequently referred to the "ethnological problem"[23] despite the fact that intermarriage was rare.[24] These ideas were shared by Premier J. D. MacLean who told the Ottawa Rotary Club in November 1927 that British Columbians "had no complaint against the individual Oriental, who was, as a rule, honest, industrious and thrifty but it was a question of preserving the British white race."[25] A Conservative M.P., J. A. Clark (Burrard) who was familiar with Lothrop Stoddard's book, *The Rising Tide of Color*, told Parliament "the basic factor in the future of the white race is a racial type . . . if our race is to be mixed with that of an oriental country, we cannot have a racial type. We cannot assimilate the yellow races, nor as a matter of fact, any coloured race."[26] At the municipal level, a Vancouver school trustee, Major M. J. Crehan told a Commission investigating education in the province that "as a father I object to my little girl sitting next to a Chinese boy in school on general principal [sic]. I would keep Canada a white Canada as a heritage for my children."[27]

The active politicians were not alone in their racial views. A county court judge in Vancouver habitually denied Oriental applications for naturalization because, he said, "the question is whether or not this country of ours is to be filled up with Orientals from across the Pacific. . . . When I die I want to leave a country fit place for my children to live in. My duty is not to report any person [as eligible for citizenship] whom I don't believe would make the country better or keep it as good as it is." The judge wanted to preserve the province for the Anglo-

Saxon race and the Empire.[28] Christian clergymen also shared many of the current racial ideas. The Anglican bishop of New Westminster, for example, told his synod that "we should have a province that will be white; that will be British and that will be Christian."[29] Most Protestant spokesmen would probably have agreed with the Congregationalist and prominent social gospeller, Rev. A. E. Cooke, who declared that Orientals already in the country should be treated with kindness and courtesy but "the East for the Oriental, the West for the Occidental, with no attempt to keep house together, but for intermingling in international trade and brotherly friendship—that is the true solution of the Oriental problem."[30]

There was also a fear in some quarters that the Oriental, particularly the Chinese, was a corrupting influence. This was evident in provincial legislation which attempted to prohibit the employment of white women by Chinese.[31] The major concern of white spokesmen was the illegal drug trade. Early in 1922 the Vancouver *Daily World* attracted considerable attention by publishing a series of articles which argued that drugs were "the corruption of the little tawdry white girls who are taken round in curtained taxis to the Chinese labor camps and lodging houses—so that they might use the money to purchase more of the evil stuff."[32] After investigating the drug traffic, Judge Emily Murphy of Edmonton declared that it was "hardly credible that the average Chinese [drug] pedlar has any definite idea in his mind to bringing about the downfall of the white race, his swaying motive probably being that of greed, but in the hands of his superiors, he may become a powerful instrument to this very end."[33] The consequences of the drug trade were feared in the hinterland of the province as well as in the metropolitan areas where it was most prevalent.[34]

Throughout the 1920's, politicians actively discussed the Oriental "menace". Every politician who expected electoral success in British Columbia seemed to think it necessary to have an anti-Oriental statement in his record. The unanimity with which the provincial legislature passed anti-Oriental resolutions is one example. Federally, the general election of 1921 provides many good examples. It reveals how both major parties criticized each other's record on the Oriental question; it demonstrates how publicists aroused anti-Oriental sentiment and its shows how British Columbia Members of Parliament honoured one of their election promises.

During the campaign the Oriental "menace" was frequently mentioned particularly in coastal constituencies. Both Liberal and

Conservative candidates pledged to keep Canada "a white man's country." In fact, the matter was an issue only because candidates accused their opponents of being "soft" on the question. H. H. Stevens, the incumbent Conservative, warned a Vancouver audience that:

> the Liberal party, controlled from a portion of Canada where the Oriental question is not understood, openly and strongly advocated the extension of the franchise for the 50,000 Orientals in British Columbia. What a tremendous political instrument this would be on behalf of the Liberal party at an election.[35]

The Liberals countered such allegations with large advertisements in the Vancouver *Sun* and *Province* headed by the slogan "Liberal candidates are pledged to a white British Columbia" and featuring a cartoon showing an Oriental being warmly greeted as he entered the province through an arch decorated with the motto "Meighen Welcomes You."[36]

That the Oriental "menace" was widely discussed is not surprising. The anti-Oriental publicists who were active throughout the decade had been especially busy during the summer and fall of 1921. The Vancouver *Daily World* which regularly published anti-Asiatic editorials presented a series of sensational articles on "The Rising Tide of Asiatics in British Columbia." In them, J. S. Cowper described the penetration of Asiatics into industries in various parts of the province, suggested that some Japanese had entered the country illegally and complained of the apathy of eastern Canada to the problem. While the articles were appearing, Cowper was actively organizing branches of the Asiatic Exclusion League in several coastal centres. The League, however, had competition in seeking public support. In October 1921, another anti-Asiatic group, "The 'Danger' Publishing Company" began distributing *Danger: The Anti-Asiatic Weekly*. To quote its masthead, this journal was "devoted to an expose of the perils of the Oriental menace and to an effort to keep Canada and especially British Columbia a white country for white men." According to *Danger*, the Asiatic Exclusion League had noble motives but its small membership fee of 25¢ (soon raised to $1.00) led to dishonesty among canvassers and gave the League insufficient funds for publicity work.[37] The League survived for some years; *Danger* seems to have disappeared after the election.

Anti-Asiatic propagandists also used a novel as a means of impressing their message on the public. In August, 1921, the Vancouver *Sun*, which followed a moderate course in its editorial comments on the Orientals, published *The Writing on the Wall* by Mrs. H. Glynn-Ward, a Vancouver writer. The book was more of a diatribe than a story. It concluded with a nightmare scene revealing a glimpse of a future in which, among other things, the Mayor and all but two of Vancouver's aldermen were Chinese, as was the Attorney-General; white men were digging ditches for Chinese foremen and the Chinese who controlled the food supply were arranging the spread of typhoid and plague among the white population. The tale seemed to have a happy ending: troops from Alberta and the American army and navy were on their way to rescue the province from its Chinese masters! Alas, the Japanese navy with airplane support had already arrived to drive out the Chinese and take over Columbia for the Japanese.[38]

Such propaganda could have had little effect on the outcome of the election; all major candidates had included anti-Oriental planks in their platforms. The successful candidates honoured their campaign promises on the question. During the first session of the new Parliament, W. G. McQuarrie introduced a resolution favouring Oriental exclusion. The first reasons he cited for his proposal were the following:

1. They cannot be assimilated ... intermarriage between the white and the oriental has always produced unsatisfactory results. . . . The standards of living of the Japanese are certainly lower than ours. They live in a different way altogether, and in British Columbia they do not conform to our customs to any great extent.
2. If their peaceful penetration is allowed to continue it will eventually lead to racial conflict and international unpleasantness.

Only then did he raise the questions of economic competition, the illegal drug traffic and the dual nationality of the Japanese. He returned to the racial argument when he concluded, "it is desirable that we should have a white Canada and that we should not become a yellow or mongrel nation."[39] In the subsequent well-planned debate, every British Columbia Member of Parliament spoke in support of McQuarrie's resolution. The government accepted the idea but substituted a milder phrase, "effective restriction" for "exclusion" in the Chinese Immigration Act of 1923. Five years later, the federal government concluded negotiations with Japan for a reduction in the number of Japanese admitted under the Gentlemen's Agreement. In immigration matters at least, British Columbia had almost completely succeeded in combatting the "menace."

Nevertheless, the anti-Asiatic campaign persisted. After some internal re-organization, the Asiatic Exclusion League appeared in 1925 as the Oriental Exclusion Association which claimed to have forty-five affiliated organizations in Vancouver and approximately one hundred in Victoria. In 1929, another group, the White Canada Association—its very name suggesting concern for the "menace" to the white race—took over the leadership of the anti-Asiatic campaign. The White Canada Association had a wide base from which to draw support as its founders included representatives of the Union of B.C. Municipalities, individual municipal councils, several farm groups, Boards of Trade, the Retail Merchants Association and the Native Sons of B.C. Several of its founders were successful politicians: Reeve Thomas Reid of Surrey, a Liberal, defeated W. G. McQuarrie in the 1930 federal election; W. C. Woodward, the owner of a major department store had been a Liberal M.L.A. and F. J. Hume became mayor of New Westminster and later, of Vancouver. To be concerned about the Oriental "menace" was a part of a political career in British Columbia.

In the 1920's, the Oriental "menace" had a limited basis in fact. In absolute terms, the Oriental population of the province increased by slightly more than 10,000 or approximately 25 per cent during the decade. Because provincial legislation and policy limited the Chinese and the Japanese to a very few occupational fields, they were more conspicuous than they would have been had they been able to enter the labour market freely. While farmers and merchants promoted agitation against the Oriental "menace," their economic fears only stimulated traditional racial prejudices. They had tolerated the Orientals as long as they "kept their place." They spoke out against them as competitors for economic reasons and because direct competition implied racial equality. The racial argument was also one with which all white British Columbians could identify even though they might not be personally affected by the presence of Orientals in the province.

While the politicians and publicists did not create the Oriental "menace" out of nothing, they certainly exaggerated it. They observed the high Japanese birth rate but did not explain that this was likely to be a temporary phenomenon. They noted that the Oriental population of the province was increasing but they neglected to point out that the percentage of Orientals in the population of British Columbia was declining from 7.3 per cent in 1921 to 7.1 per cent a decade later. When the politicians and publicists could not find specific local evidence of the harmful effect of the "menace," they drew on California propaganda and, using examples from the south, warned of British Columbia's future. If they were in the interior of the province, they referred to the situation at the coast. Because much of the "menace" was based on apprehension, it seemed much greater than it actually was.

It is impossible to determine what the ordinary white British Columbian thought about the "menace." In elections he had little choice but to vote for an anti-Oriental candidate. It may be that he was not very concerned unless he was likely to be affected directly. White merchants complained that white housewives persisted in patronizing Chinese grocers. While McQuarrie's exclusion resolution was being debated in Ottawa, one provincial editor complained of general apathy about the question.[40] The very extent of the anti-Oriental publicity suggests that the fears of the "man in the street" had to be aroused. On the other hand, politicians would not have exploited the issue unless their campaign had evoked a sympathetic response. Given the extent of the anti-Oriental agitation, it is not surprising that white British Columbians believed that there was an Oriental "menace" which hurt the pocket books of some and threatened the racial purity of all.

Notes

[1] Public Archives of Canada (hereafter PAC), W. D. Scott, Superintendent of Immigration to the Niagara Falls Trades and Labour Council, August 21, 1917. Records of the Department of Immigration and Colonization, RG 76, Accn 70/47, File 729921.

[2] Canada, *Census*, 1921, vol. I, p. 357.

[3] *B. C. Fruit and Farm Magazine*, February 1919, p. 1165.

[4] E.g. *ibid.*, March 1917, p. 1185; March 1918, p. 20. For background on agricultural organizations in British Columbia see Margaret A. Ormsby, "The United Farmers of British Columbia—An Abortive Third-Party Movement", *British Columbia Historical Quarterly*, vol. XVII (January-April 1953), pp. 53-73.

[5] *Farm and Home*, July 15, 1920, p. 9.

[6] E.g. Vancouver *Daily Province*, February 28, 1921, p. 19; H. H. Stevens in Canada, House of Commons, *Debates*, April 26, 1921, p. 2595.

[7] Victoria *Daily Times*, February 27, 1929, p. 5.

[8] *The Agricultural Journal*, September 1924, p. 152. Italics mine.

[9] *The Kelowna Courier and Okanagan Orchardist*, January 22, 1920.

[10] Vernon *News*, March 18, 1926, p. 4. The letter may be found in the William Lyon MacKenzie King Papers, vol. 139, #118452, PAC.

[11] British Columbia, Legislative Assembly, *Report on Oriental Activities within the Province* (Victoria: King's Printer, 1927).

[12] Vancouver *Daily Province*, February 28, 1921, p. 19.

[13] *B.C. United Farmer*, July 1, 1921, p. 13.

[14] *Farm and Home*, March 5, 1925, p. 4.

[15] Canada, House of Commons, *Debates*, May 8, 1922, p. 1509; Vancouver *Daily Province*, November 30, 1922, p. 27. McQuarrie was the Conservative member for New Westminster.

[16] *Report on Oriental Activities*, p. 24.

[17] Tom MacInnes, *Oriental Occupation of British Columbia* (Vancouver: Sun Publishing, 1927).

[18] Provincial Archives of British Columbia (hereafter PABC), Vancouver Businessmen to J. D. MacLean, February 10, 1928, Attorney-General's Papers, 1918-17-2060, Microfilm. Vancouver Businessmen to J. D. MacLean, April 21, 1928, T. D. Pattullo Ppaers.

[19] PAC, George S. Hougham, Secretary, B.C. Board, Retail Merchants of Canada, to William Lyon Mackenzie King, April 28, 1922. Copy in RG 76, Accn 70/47, File 815661.

[20] PABC, Vancouver Businessmen to J. D. MacLean, April 21, 1928, T. D. Pattullo Papers. Italics in original.

[21] From a leaflet, "Asiatic Exclusion League of Canada", Vancouver, [1921]. (Copy in the Legislative Library of British Columbia.)

[22] Vancouver *Daily Province*, April 4, 1928, p. 7. The division of the labour movement within the province is described in Paul Phillips, *No Power Greater* (Vancouver: B.C. Federation of Labour, 1967), chapter 6 and Martin Robin, *Radical Politics and Canadian Labour* (Kingston: Queen's University, Industrial Relations Centre, 1968), *passim*.

[23] Victoria *Daily Colonist*, May 18, 1922, p. 5.

[24]. C. J. Woodsworth, *Canada and the Orient* (Toronto: Macmillan, 1941), p. 144.

[25] Ottawa *Citizen*, November 9, 1927.

[26] Canada, House of Commons, *Debates*, May 8, 1922, pp. 1522-1523. *The Rising Tide of Color Against White World Supremacy* was first published in New York in 1920 with an introduction by Madison Grant. For the role of Grant and Stoddart in inspiring American racism in the 1920's see John Higham, *Strangers in the Land* (New York: Atheneum, 1967 [first published, 1955]), pp. 270-277.

[27] Vancouver *Star*, August 6, 1924, p. 3.

[28] Vancouver *Daily Province*, June 5, 1922, p. 7.

[29]. Vancouver *Daily Province*, February 8, 1923, p. 17.

[30] Vancouver *Daily World*, July 30, 1921, p. 5.

[31] Ontario and Saskatchewan had laws with a similar intent.

[32] Vancouver *Daily World*, January 16, 1922. p. 4.

[33]. Emily Murphy, *The Black Candle* (Toronto: Thomas Allen, 1922), p. 188.

[34] E.g. *The Agricultural Journal*, February 1923, p. 287; Vernon *News*, February 9, 1922, p. 1. The latter reference was brought to my attention by Dr. Margaret A. Ormsby.

[35] Vancouver *Daily Province*, November 18, 1921, p. 4.

[36] Vancouver *Daily Province*, December 3, 1921, p. 7; Vancouver *Sun*, December 4, 1921, p. 19.

[37] *Danger: The Anti-Asiatic Weekly*, vol. 1, no. 3 (October 20, 1921), pp. 13-14. (Copy in Special Collections of the Library of the University of British Columbia.)

[38] H. Glynn-Ward [pseud. for Mrs. H. Howard], *The Writing on the Wall* (Vancouver: Sun Publishing, [1921]).

[39] Canada, House of Commons, *Debates*, May 8, 1922, p. 1516.

[40] *Farm and Home*, May 11, 1922, p. 8.

19. Joseph Trutch and Indian Land Policy
Robin Fisher

ROBIN FISHER, *who completed a doctoral dissertation at the University of British Columbia, now teaches at Simon Fraser University. He brings to the study of white-Indian relations in British Columbia the perspective of a student of white-Maori relations in his native New Zealand.*

. . . 1864 was a year of change in the administration of the colony of British Columbia; James Douglas retired from the governorship and Joseph Trutch was appointed Chief Commissioner of Lands and Works. In the area of Indian lands these changes in personnel were to be accompanied by a shift in policy, and the effects of these changes were to be profound.

As Chief Factor of the Hudson's Bay Company in Victoria and as Governor of Vancouver Island, Douglas negotiated a series of treaties by which the Indians of southern Vancouver Island surrendered their land "entirely and forever" in return for a few blankets and the reservation of certain lands for their use. Implicit in these treaties was the notion that the aboriginal race exercised some kind of ownership over the land that ought to be extinguished by the colonizing power, a view that was shared by Douglas and the Colonial Office.[1] By 1858, however, Douglas had relinquished his position as Chief Factor and could no longer dip into the stores of the Hudson's Bay Company for goods that would encourage the Indians to surrender their land. Dependent on other sources of finance, Douglas was unable to compensate the Indians for the alienation of their lands because the Vancouver Island House of Assembly and the Imperial Government each argued that the provision of funds for this purpose was the other's responsibility.[2] Although the shortage of funds placed limitations on the implementation of Indian policy, Douglas continued to defend Indian rights. He made it clear that reserves were to be laid out in accordance with the wishes of the Indians,[3] and once reserves were established insisted that they were not to be reduced, either by the encroachment of individual settlers or by the collective action of the House of Assembly.[4]

In retrospect at least, the Indians of the colony were satisfied

---

Source: Abridged by the author from *B. C. Studies, XII* (1971-72), pp. 3-33. Reprinted by permission of the author and publisher.

with the treatment they had received under Douglas.[5] In 1864 Douglas himself claimed that his reserve policy "has been productive of the happiest effects on the minds of the natives."[6] Seemingly his remark had some validity, and yet after his retirement many aspects of Douglas's policy were altered: and the man most responsible for the reversal was one whom Douglas had recommended for the position of Chief Commissioner of Lands and Works.[7]

Joseph Trutch had come to British Columbia in 1859 with eight years' experience behind him as a surveyor and farmer south of the 49th parallel. His interest in the gold colony in the early years was in building roads and bridges, surveying townships and establishing farms, and in amassing a personal fortune. To him the colony was an area of land requiring development. Consequently anything, or more importantly anyone, who stood in the way of that development had to be moved.

Moreover Trutch was very much a product of imperial England's confidence in the superiority of her own civilization. Other races came somewhat lower on the scale of human existence than the English, and the North American Indian was barely part of the scale at all. In a reference to the Indians of Oregon Territory Trutch used revealing terminology. "I think they are the ugliest & laziest creatures I ever saw, & we shod. as soon think of being afraid of our dogs as of them . . . "[8] The indigenous American tended towards the bestial rather than the human to Trutch; and his view was essentially unmodified by continued contact with the Indians. In 1872 he told the Prime Minister of Canada that most of the British Columbian Indians were "utter Savages living along the coast, frequently committing murder and robbery amongst themselves, one tribe upon another, and on white people who go amongst them for the purpose of trade."[9]

Trutch had stereotyped the Indians as lawless and violent, and was frequently preoccupied with the need to suppress them by a show of force. Douglas, on the other hand, had argued "that they should in all respects be treated as rational beings, capable of acting and thinking for themselves."[10] He had been firm in dealing with Indian "lawlessness," but also had an appreciation of the possible value of the Indians as allies and avoided offending them unnecessarily. Douglas had to cope with the potentially dangerous situation that followed the influx of miners in 1858, and in doing so he trod with great caution. His personal capacity for settling disputes was strikingly demonstrated at Hill's Bar in 1858. Strong words were said to each side, but he also took one of the Indian leaders involved in the affray into the government service. Douglas wrote that the man was "an Indian highly connected in their way, and of great influence, resolution and energy of character," and he proved to be "exceedingly useful in settling other Indian difficulties."[11] It was an action that Trutch would have been quite incapable of taking. Rather he enunciated the typical colonialist's misconception that the indigenous people had no mechanism for ending hostilities,[12] an attitude that would render him incapable of using Indians to settle disputes. Violence amongst the Indians themselves was bad enough, but violence directed against Europeans was the ultimate breakdown of the colonial situation. What was needed in such cases, thought Trutch, was a theatrical demonstration of European power. The dispatch of warships to coastal trouble spots, for example, would produce "a salutary impression" on the Indians.[13] Douglas wanted the law to operate "with the least possible effect on the character and temper of the Indians,"[14] while Trutch insisted that English law must be "enforced at whatever cost."[15]

Douglas most often referred to the "Native Indians," but Trutch seldom called them anything other than "savages," and was skeptical about their capacity for "improvement." After twenty years on the northwest coast, and even a visit to Metlakatla, he was to remark that "I have not yet met with a single Indian of pure blood whom I consider to have attained even the most glimmering perception of the Christian creed." The reason for this situation, according to Trutch, was that "the idiosyncrasy of the Indians of this country appears to incapacitate them from appreciating any abstract idea, nor do their languages contain any words by which such a conception could be expressed."[16] There is no evidence that Trutch was particularly fluent in any of the Indian languages, or that he had made any study of Indian religion, poetry or art. But then stereotypes are seldom based on concrete evidence; they are more often than not the product of ignorance.

It was these views regarding colonial development and the inferiority of the Indian that governed Trutch's attitude to the question of Indian land. His attitudes coalesced to produce something of an obsession with the idea that the Indians were standing in the way of the development of the colony by Europeans. The absolute superiority of English culture implied an obligation to colonize new areas. Therefore, to men like Trutch, the Indians had to be relieved of as much land as possible, so that it could be "properly" and "efficiently" used by Europeans. For Trutch British Columbia's future lay in agriculture. The colony's development had to be fostered by "large and liberal" land grants to settlers,[17] and Indian claims to land could not be allowed to hinder this development. In contrast to Douglas who wanted to protect the Indians from the progress of settlement, Trutch wanted to move them out of the way so that settlement could progress.

When Douglas recommended Trutch for the position of Chief Commissioner of Lands and Works it was because he thought he was an efficient surveyor and engineer, not because of any ability Trutch might have had to deal with Indian affairs. Perhaps Douglas thought that the governor would continue to dominate this area of the administration of the colony just as he had done. But, with the possible exception of Frederick Seymour, subsequent governors were neither as interested nor as competent to deal with the Indians. Unlike Chief Factor Douglas, Seymour took over the administration of British Columbia as a careerist governor, his most recent post having been Governor of British Honduras. He lacked no confidence in his own ability to deal with native races, however. Early in his governorship of British Columbia he gained local popularity and praise from 14 Downing Street for his dealing with the Indians responsible for the killings at Bute Inlet in 1864.

Efforts to suppress violence apart, however, Seymour's concern for the Indians of British Columbia was chiefly a matter of dispensing largesse rather than protecting their interests. Soon after his arrival Seymour became aware that the Indians felt that with the departure of Douglas from official life, they had lost a protector and a friend. The new governor determined to demonstrate to the Indians that he had "succeeded to all the powers of my predecessor and to his solicitude for their welfare."[18] His method of making this point clear was to extend an invitation to the Indians to come to Government House in New Westminster and celebrate the Queen's birthday. On the first of several of these occasions, in 1864, a luncheon was provided at the expense of the government; but the guests were informed that the rewards "to all good Indian Chiefs" would be greater next time.[19] Accordingly Seymour requested the colony's agents in London to forward "one hundred canes with silver gilt tops of an inexpensive kind, also one hundred small and cheap English flags suitable to canoes 20 to 30 feet long."[20]

These gatherings provided the Indian leaders with an opportunity to express their opinion on matters that concerned them more acutely than free luncheons and gilt canes. On at least three occasions the Indians present at the celebration petitioned Seymour to protect their reserves.[21] The first time the reply was clear. "You shall not be disturbed in your reserves," the Indians were told.[22] Three years later the reply was a little more equivocal, as the Indians were assured their reserves would not be reduced without Seymour's personal inspection.[23] The actual wording of the replies, is, however, somewhat immaterial. While Seymour was making reassuring gestures at Queen's birthday celebrations, Trutch was carrying out a reallocation of reserves that involved a considerable reduction in size, and there is no evidence that Seymour visited any of the reserves concerned. In relation to the Indians' land, Seymour's professed "solicitude for their welfare" was verbal rather than actual.

The restraining hand of Douglas had been removed, and Seymour was less concerned than his predecessor about Indian rights regarding land. Consequently Trutch was able to execute his policy of reducing reserves.

The first step in the process of whittling down the reserves was taken towards the end of 1865. In July of that year Phillip Nind, Gold Commissioner at Lytton, wrote to the Colonial Secretary regarding the reserves of the Indians of the Thompson River area. Nind claimed that "These Indians do nothing more with their land than cultivate a few small patches of potatoes here and there," although he noted that some groups were leasing grazing land to white settlers. The main point of his letter was that Indians were claiming "thousands of acres of good arable and pasture land admirably adapted for settlement."[24] This letter was apparently referred to Trutch for his comments. He made his views clear. He had already expressed the opinion that one of the most important ways in which the settler could prosper in British Columbia would be by farming to supply the mining population.[25] The thought of Indians standing in the way of this development was abhorrent to him.

I am satisfied from my own observation that the claims of Indians over tracts of land, on which they assume to exercise ownership, out of which they make no real use, operate very materially to prevent settlement and cultivation, in many instances besides that to which attention has been directed by Mr. Nird, and I should advise that these claims should be as soon as practicable enquired into and defined.[26]

Seymour felt that it was too late in the year for a general reduction of reserves but, forgetting his promise to the Indians, he agreed to the reallocation of the Thompson River reserves.[27] Walter Moberly, assistant surveyor-general of the colony was requested to inquire into the matter and on the basis of his report[28] Trutch informed the governor that the reserves were "entirely disproportionate to the numbers or the requirements of the Indian Tribes."[29] No accurate census had been taken of the Indians so Trutch could not know what their numbers were, and their land requirements were of course as Trutch, and not the Indians, assessed them. But these things were relatively unimportant for the land was valuable, and therefore, even though it had been reserved for them, the Indians had to make way for settlement. By October 1866 a notice was appearing in the *Government Gazette* indicating that the reserves of the Kamloops and Shuswap Indians had been redefined. The so-called "adjustment" meant that out of a forty mile stretch of the Thompson River the Indians were left with three reserves, each of between three and four square miles. The remainder of the land hitherto reserved for them was to be thrown open for pre-emption by settlers from 1 January 1867.[30]

The reallocations carried out in the Kamloops area provided a precedent that was applied by Trutch when he effected a second series of reductions involving the Indian reserves in the lower Fraser area. The move to reduce these reserves originated in the British Columbia Legislative Council, when John Robson moved in February 1867, that the governor be informed of the desirability of having the lower Fraser reserves "reduced to what is necessary for the actual use of the Natives."[31] Again it seems that Seymour referred the matter to Trutch for a report, and once again Trutch advocated reductions. His reasoning was similar to that adumbrated in the Kamloops case. The Indians were holding good land that they were not using in a productive way, therefore it ought to be made available to settlers. After all, wrote Trutch,

The Indians really have no right to the lands they claim, nor are they of any actual value or utility to them; and I cannot see why they should either retain these lands to the prejudice of the general interests of the Colony, or be allowed to make a market of them to Government *or to individuals*.[32]

Having denied the Indians any right to hold even land that had been reserved for them, and therefore to compensation for land that they were relieved of, Trutch initiated the policy of "adjustment." Again he had the approval of Seymour. It is difficult to discover the precise extent of these reductions, although there can be little doubt that they involved a considerable area. The report of one of the surveyors who marked out the reserves notes that the new boundaries would throw open 40,000 acres for settlement.[33]

The notion that Indian reserves were not to be violated by

Europeans was not the only policy that was transformed after the departure of Douglas. He had also favoured the idea of Indians leasing reserve land and benefiting from the income, but part of Trutch's rationale for reallocation was to prevent the Indians from receiving rent from the settlers. The reductions were therefore designed to leave them with no land to spare for leasing out to European farmers. Another option that was open to the Indians under Douglas was to pre-empt land,[34] but in 1866 this was virtually denied them. A Land Ordinance of that year prevented Indians from pre-empting land without the written permission of the governor,[35] and there was only a single subsequent case of an Indian pre-empting land under this condition.[36]

Of all the changes in official policy perhaps the most important, and certainly the one that can most clearly be attributed to Trutch, was the redefining of reserves. But Trutch was not only responsible for changing Douglas's policy, he also misrepresented the nature of that policy. Trutch made a series of inaccurate statements about earlier policy in an attempt to validate, or rather provide an excuse for, his own actions.

If there was any possibility at all after 1864 that the Fort Victoria treaties could provide a precedent for resuming the purchase of Indian lands in British Columbia the notion certainly did not enter Trutch's mind. On the contrary, he explicitly denied that the treaties signed by Douglas provided such a precedent. He claimed that the payments made under these treaties were "for the purpose of securing friendly relations between those Indians and the settlement of Victoria, then in its infancy, and certainly not in acknowledgement of any general title of the Indians to the land they occupy.[37] Such was not the view of those who had signed the treaties. Douglas clearly considered that he was purchasing Indian land,[38] and the Indians themselves, although they had yet to comprehend European notions of land ownership, knew that the paper they were signing involved more than a declaration of friendship.

It is comparatively easy to demonstrate that Trutch misinterpreted the nature of the treaties signed on Vancouver Island. In these cases we have as evidence a document that is still held to be legally binding in the courts of British Columbia. Throughout the rest of British Columbia no treaties were signed,[39] making it difficult for the historian to determine the exact nature of Douglas's policy, and much easier for men like Trutch to change the rules of the game. Nowhere in North America have Europeans ever lacked pretexts for taking land, and Trutch was certainly not short of one. In carrying out his policy of reduction his tactic was to claim that those responsible for marking out the original reserves had either exceeded or misunderstood their instructions.

William Cox marked out most of the interior reserves, while on the lower Fraser they were laid out by William McColl. Questions about the former's adherence to Douglas's instructions were first raised by Moberly when Trutch requested him to report on the interior reserves in 1865. It appeared to Moberly "quite out of the question that Governor Sir James Douglas could have given Mr. Cox instructions to make such extensive reservations."[40] The remark gave Trutch just the kind of pretext he needed. It seems that the Indians may have altered the boundaries of reserves by moving the stakes after Cox had laid them out, but that is not to say that he exceeded his instructions in the first place. In fact there are at least two specifically documented instances of Trutch reducing reserves in the interior that Douglas had been satisfied with. In 1861 Cox reported that he had laid out a reserve at the north end of Okanagan Lake. In accordance with his instructions the Indians had selected the location and pointed out where they wanted the boundary stakes to be placed. A marginal note in pencil, initialled by Douglas, gives no indication that he was dissatisfied with the report.[41] The following year Cox reported that he had laid out a reserve on the Bonaparte River, again adhering to the wishes of the Indians. Douglas's reply was that the reserves were satisfactory,[42] yet Trutch instructed Peter O'Reilly to reallocate the reserve in 1868.[43] These reductions in the interior involved an implicit denial of Douglas's policy.

In the case of the lower Fraser reserves Trutch went further. Here there was a definite falsification of the record. Trutch began his report on these reserves by stating that Douglas had never followed an established system regarding the reservation of Indian lands. He then claimed that those reserves that had been laid out were established on the basis of verbal instructions only: "there are no written records on this subject in the correspondence on record in this office."[44] The claim is, of course, quite untrue. There are numerous letters from Douglas containing instructions on marking out reserves in the files of the Lands and Works Department. It would have taken very little effort on Trutch's part to have found letters of instruction to both Cox[45] and McColl.[46] and with a little more work he might even have found the letter in which Douglas reprimanded his predecessor, Moody, for not laying out reserves in accordance with the wishes of the Indians.[47] Douglas's frequent repetition of this instruction makes it difficult to believe that Trutch was unaware of its existence: and the only other possible explanation for his remark is that he was attempting to distort the record.

Trutch was not alone in his effort to fabricate a pretext for reducing Indian reserves. W. A. G. Young, the Colonial Secretary, also had a hand in it. In his letter to Trutch conveying the governor's approval for the "defining" of reserves, Young also noted that "There is good reason to believe that Mr. McColl very greatly misunderstood the instructions conveyed to him." Young continued,

> The instructions given in Mr. Brew's letter of the 6th of April, 1864, are very simple, viz:—to mark out as reserves any ground which had been *cleared* and *tilled* for years by the Indians; and should the ground so circumstanced not be equal to ten acres for each *family*—each *adult male* being considered the head of a family—the reserve was to be enlarged to that extent.[48]

Yet when one compares Young's description of these instructions with Brew's actual letter, it is immediately apparent that he has neglected to include a crucial section. That "Mr. McColl will mark out with corner posts *whatsoever land the Indians claim as theirs*..."[49] is also part of the instruction. For some reason McColl claimed that the order to include all the land the Indians wanted had been given to him verbally by Douglas, thus making it easy for Young to claim that he had misinterpreted an unwritten instruction. Probably Douglas did give additional verbal directions, but the written ones are quite clear on the point that the Indians were to have whatever land they demanded. Young had access to numerous letters in which Douglas had over and over again repeated his instructions. One of the letters, conveying Douglas's orders to Moody, was even signed by Young;[50] as was another in which the governor expresses his satisfaction with Cox's allocation of the Bonaparte River reserve.[51] The probability of additional verbal orders is no excuse for Young to distort the written record, and certainly no excuse for Trutch to assert that there were no written directions on the subject.

Nevertheless, armed with a letter in which Young, representing Seymour, had "validated" his views, Trutch went on a tour of the lower Fraser area with the express purpose of repudiating the reserves defined by McColl. "I took occasion at each village, to inform the Indians that McColl had no authority for laying off the excessive amounts of land included by him in these reserves."[52] By saying that McColl had no authority to lay out their reserves, Trutch was misleading the Indians. He knew very well that McColl did have the authority to allocate reserves in accordance with the wishes of the Indians.

Having misled the Indians regarding past European policy, Trutch then proceeded to mislead the Europeans regarding present Indian attitudes. He informed the governor that there would be no difficulty in reducing the reserves "with the full concurrence of the Indians themselves."[53] The numerous complaints by Indians of the lower Fraser and other areas indicates that their real attitude was somewhat different from that which Trutch described.

When he began the reductions in the lower Fraser Trutch said that in carrying out the policy "firmness and discretion are equally essential to effect the desired result, to convince the Indians that the Government intend only to deal fairly with them and the whites."[54] The Indians, however, were a good deal more sophisticated than a man with Trutch's attitudes could appreciate. They were dissatisfied with the way in which their land was taken from them, and they knew very well that they were not being treated on anything like an equal basis with the Europeans. A good measure of Trutch's idea of fairness was his suggestion (incorporated in the 1865 Land Ordinance) that a European, in addition to a pre-emption of 160 acres, be allowed to purchase 480 acres,[55] while he was requiring that an Indian family exist on ten acres. This was the kind of inequality that even an "uncivilized savage" could appreciate. Undoubtedly Trutch was mindful of the comparative shortage of good agricultural land in British Columbia. Yet while this fact of geography may provide a reason for his ten-acre policy it does not provide a justification. Ten acres was not only insufficient for many Indian families to subsist on, it also failed to take into account the differences in the economic life of the various Indian groups.

Trutch's notion that Indian reserves be reallocated on the basis of ten acres per family involved another distortion of Douglas's policy. Douglas had included in his directions to those laying out reserves in British Columbia the provision that if the area demanded by the Indians did not equal ten acres per family then the reserve was to be enlarged to that extent.[56] Instead of using ten acres as a minimum as Douglas had intended, Trutch used it as a maximum figure. When instructing O'Reilly to reallocate the Bonaparte reserve, for example, Trutch wrote that "as a general rule it is considered that an allotment of about 10 acres of good land should be made to each family in the tribe."[57] Such was never the intention of Douglas. His opinion was clear enough in his instructions at the time, but he outlined it with even greater clarity some years later. "It was ... never intended that they should be restricted or limited to the possession of 10 acres of land, on the contrary, we were prepared, if such had been their wish to have made for their use much more extensive grants."[58] This letter in which Douglas recapitulates his policy indicates the extent to which Trutch brought radical changes to the colony's dealings with the Indians and their land.

Trutch's actions, moreover, involved a break with the usual British policy. In her haphazard way, Britain seems to have developed a policy whereby, if territory was occupied in a regular way, aboriginal possession was recognized, and therefore had to be extinguished before settlement could proceed. There was some kind of threshold over which Britain would recognize native rights to the land. The land ownership concepts of the Australian aborigine, for example, were not sufficiently clear for Britain to recognize, whereas those of the New Zealand Maori were. Given this threshold, then, were the concepts of territory and ownership of British Columbia's Indians sufficiently precise to be recognizable? It seems clear that they were. There were variations in different parts of the colony, but the Indians had precise concepts of territorial boundaries or ownership of specific areas. Douglas knew the Indians well enough to be aware of this aspect of their society and he tried to recognize it in his policy.[59] His attitude was sustained by the imperial government, and was clearly in accord with British policy throughout the rest of North America. Trutch, on the other hand, was not the least interested in Indian social usages. He denied that they had any rights to land at all.[60] Given the kind of man he was his lack of concern with aboriginal concepts of territory is not surprising. What is less explicable is his lack of concern for English law on native lands.

While Trutch's views on Indian land ran counter to those of Douglas and the imperial government, it seems that they were in accord with the opinions of most of British Columbia's population. To the extent that it is possible to assess the attitudes of the settlers, they coincided with Trutch's. Douglas had embodied many of the attitudes of the old fur trading frontier, whereas Trutch represented the attitudes of the new settlement frontier. An appreciable number of settlers in the colony adhered to the notions of "manifest destiny," and advocated ignoring Indian rights, or even their extermination.[61] Even the editor of The British Columbian, who claimed to be a constant defender of Indian rights, hastened to add that those rights did not include the right "to hold large tracts of valuable agricultural and pastoral land which they do not and cannot use."[62]

Editorials in *The British Colonist* were more forthright. Readers were told in 1863 that they could no more talk of Indian right to the land "than we can prate of the natural right of a he-panther or a she-bear to the soil."[63] To the editorialist both the problem and its solution were simple

> ...shall we allow a few red vagrants to prevent forever industrious settlers from settling on the unoccupied lands. Not at all. ...Locate reservations for them on which to earn their own living, and if they trespass on white settlers punish them severely. A few lessons would soon enable them to form a correct estimation of their own inferiority, and settle the Indian title too.[64]

These newspapers undoubtedly reflected the opinions of a good many of their subscribers.

One of the features of the colonial government's Indian policy in the years 1864-70 was that it closely reflected the aspirations of the settlers. In both colonies much of the pressure for removing the Indians from their land came from the governing bodies. On Vancouver Island the efforts of the Assembly resulted in the displacement of the Songhees from their reserve near Victoria. There was similar pressure on the mainland, where the Legislative Council also reflected settler opinion by urging the reduction of reserves. One member even felt that reserves of ten acres per family were unnecessarily large for the Indians.[65] Although government members advocated the interests of the colonists, it is perhaps Trutch's own official function that most clearly pinpoints the influence of settlers on government. That the Chief Commissioner of Lands and Works should also control Indian land policy goes a long way towards explaining why it developed in a unique way. Because the same person was responsible for allocating land to Europeans and to Indians he could not reflect the interests of both; and because that person was Trutch Indian rights were not considered important. British policy, and to a lesser extent Canadian policy, was formulated by men who were not so closely involved in the actual process of settlement.

As it developed under Trutch, British Columbia's Indian land policy was unique in two essential ways. First the non-recognition of aboriginal title, and second the comparatively small amounts of land finally allocated to the Indians. In a recent publication the history of dealings with the Indians over their land in Canada has been compared favourably with the repeated swindles in the United States. Indians in Canada, says Vine Deloria, did not "have their lands alloted and then stolen piece by piece from under them."[66] If the generalization is valid for the rest of Canada (and even that is dubious) it is definitely not true for British Columbia. Rather that is exactly what did happen under Trutch. It has been said that British Columbia's Indian land policy was "obscure and unsatisfactory" just prior to confederation.[67] To the Indians it was certainly unsatisfactory, but by no means obscure. They knew the colonists were taking all the land they could get. By 1870, however, British Columbia was in the midst of negotiations to unite with Canada, and Canada's thinking on the question of Indian land was not quite the same as Trutch's. The Indians were anticipating these changes in the white man's world in the hope that they would receive a better deal from Canada.

They were, however, to be disappointed, and an important reason for their disappointment was that Trutch was to be the first lieutenant-governor of the new province. Before 1871 Trutch had been largely concerned with making policy, and as lieutenant-governor he was determined to defend that policy against the encroachment of differing ideas held by the federal government on the question of Indian land.

Contemporary with Trutch's term as lieutenant-governor in British Columbia was the signing of the first four of the numbered treaties on the prairies. By making these treaties the Canadian government was enunciating an Indian policy that was quite different from British Columbia's in a number of ways. The treaties were an acceptation of the principle that the Indians had rights to the land that ought to be extinguished; the minimum of 160 acres per family was a much larger allocation of reserve land, and in addition there was provision for initial payments followed by annuities and other forms of assistance.

Now that Indian affairs were in the hands of the federal government it was possible that the policy on the prairies might be extended across the Rockies. One of the many reasons why this did not happen was the way in which Trutch defended, and misrepresented, British Columbia's policy as the most satisfactory one for all concerned.

His defence of what was largely his own policy began before he was appointed lieutenant-governor. Trutch revealed his basic beliefs about the Indian policy of the colony at a meeting of the Legislative Council in February 1869. He is reported to have maintained that

> our system of treatment of the Indians was more humane than in any other country. Our laws entitled them to all the rights and privileges of the white man; they have thriven under them and had vastly improved in every respect by contact with the

white man. The laws when applied to the Indian were always strained in his favour.[68]

Subsequent defences of policy involved an elaboration of this fundamental attitude.

In 1870 a letter written by William Sebright Green to the Aborigines Protection Society was forwarded to Anthony Musgrave, the new Governor of British Columbia. Because he was new to the situation, Musgrave, as Seymour had done, handed the letter to Trutch for a report. The burden of Green's criticism was that the Government of British Columbia had neither policy nor concern for the Indians. Part of Trutch's reply was that, on the contrary, the government had "striven to the extent of its power to protect and befriend the Native race." In fact, he continued, its declared policy had been that the Indians should, in all material respects, be on the same footing as Europeans. We have seen how his notion of equality worked in relation to land holdings. The Indians, as Trutch explained it, were given such lands "as were deemed proportionate to, and amply sufficient for, the requirements of each tribe."[69] The Europeans were treated equally because they were also allowed what was sufficient for their requirements. Perhaps Trutch really believed that ten acres per family did constitute equity for a savage?

The Terms of Union by which British Columbia joined Canada were an important delaying factor in federal involvement in the Indian affairs of the province. One cannot be absolutely certain, but it is highly likely that Trutch was responsible for the section that concerned Indians. During the debate on union in British Columbia there was some discussion of the Indian question, but the terms proposed contained no reference to Indians.[70] Presumably clause 13 of the final terms was added in Ottawa, and as Trutch was the only person closely involved with colonial Indian policy present at those discussions he can fairly be attributed with responsibility for the clause.[71]

The wording of clause 13 of the Terms of Union is very curious indeed. In transferring charge of the Indians to the dominion government it states that "a policy as liberal as that hitherto pursued by the British Columbia Government shall be continued by the Dominion Government after the Union."[72] A variety of words could be used to describe Trutch's policy prior to union, but "liberal" is not one of them. Subsequently, David Laird, the Canadian Minister of the Interior, thought that the framers of the clause "could hardly have been aware of the marked contrast between the Indian policies which had, up to that time, prevailed in Canada and British Columbia respectively."[73] Actually it is far more likely that Trutch was well aware of the discrepancy in policies but wanted to camouflage it.

Clause 13 was aptly numbered. It was unlucky for the Indians because it meant that some time was to elapse before the federal authorities realized just how illiberal the colony's treatment of them had been.

Trutch, meanwhile, continued to defend his views. In 1871 British Columbia's policy was again under fire, this time from Bishop George Hills of Columbia, who was particularly concerned about the paucity of government spending on Indians.[74] In reply Trutch first defended policy in general—it was described "as a well considered system, ably devised by experienced men and specially interested in favour of the Indians"[75]—and then went on to deal with the specific question of parsimony in the allocation of funds.

This point may have proved a little difficult for Trutch to refute, as the colonial estimates indicate that allocations for Indians were miserable; and often only a fraction of the amount included in the estimates appeared in the end-of-year statement of actual expenditure. This was at a time when the Indian population was declining rapidly through the impact of disease. Trutch conceded that "from the pecuniary inability of the Colony in the past no such appropriations have been made as could have been wished."[76] He did, however, neglect to mention the fate of money collected by leasing Indian reserve land, which Douglas had intended to be used for the benefit of the Indians.[77] Early in 1873 the newly appointed Superintendent of Indian Affairs was having difficulty in discovering what had happened to the sum of $1,984.82 that had been handed to Trutch in 1869 by the commissioners of the Songhee's reserve.[78] The reply was that, instead of being spent on Indian needs, the sum "formed part of the assets of the colony at the date of Confederation."[79] No action had been taken to distinguish the Indian's money from ordinary colonial revenue.

Trutch did, however, have other arguments to advance. While British Columbia had not spent directly on the Indians as much as she might have done, the Bishop of Columbia was forgetting that the Indians were partaking of "the advantages of civilization which we have brought to them." For example, the Indians could now use roads and trails without paying the tolls that were often imposed on white people. Europeans had also brought to the Indians implements "of husbandry and agriculture, the chase and fishing etc., which before they were without." Another of the benefits of civilization mentioned was one particularly close to his heart; namely "the blessings which result from the preservation of law and order throughout the colony, instead of those scenes of bloodshed and robbery which prevailed formerly among them, and amidst which their lives were passed in a state of constant dread and uncertainty of life and property."[80] With arguments such as these Trutch had little difficult in convincing himself that Indian policy in British Columbia had been "essentially benevolent towards the Indians."[81]

He concluded this letter by reminding the dominion government of the grave responsibility it had undertaken towards the Indian population of the province, and urged that such a responsibility should not be devolved on others for any reason. The meaning of the last remark became clear in 1872 when Ottawa appointed a Superintendent of Indian Affairs for the province. The appointee was I. W. Powell, a prominent member of the Victoria community and a friend of Sir John A. Macdonald. Trutch, however, had strong objections to the selection. In a letter to Macdonald he took exception to the fact that someone with no experience in Indian affairs should have been chosen for the position. Dr. Powell, according to Trutch, "might perform the duties of the office well enough if acting under the immediate direction and advice of someone of more experience here." Little imagination is required to guess who Trutch thought this experienced person might be, and it was certainly not left to Macdonald's imagination. "I may tell you," Trutch wrote to the prime minister, "that I am of opinion, and that very strongly, that for some time to come at least the general charge and direction of all Indian affairs in B.C. should be vested in the Lt. Governor."[82] If he had control of Indian policy he could be certain that things would remain as they were. Once the Powell appointment had been made, Trutch wanted to ensure that he retained absolute control, so that there would be no alteration of his policies.

To achieve this objective he was prepared to move from a verbal to an active defence of the status-quo. In 1874 the federal government tried to set up a three man board to deal with Indian affairs in British Columbia. Trutch was on this board, along with Powell and Lenihan, the two Indian Commissioners, but he was not interested in any board that he did not direct, and was prepared to hinder its work if he was not given a controlling position. Powell was preparing to visit Kamloops to discuss the land question with the Indians, and Trutch objected on the grounds that he was acting too independently. Trutch told the Minister of the Interior that he was prepared to act on the board only if he had authority to direct the management of Indian affairs in the province.[83] By now, however, the federal government was becoming aware of the situation in British Columbia. This awareness is reflected in Laird's reply. He told the lieutenant-governor, "I very much doubt . . . whether the Government would be prepared to delegate to any person in British Columbia the general control and management of Indian affairs in that Province."[84] Essentially Trutch wanted to abrogate the Terms of Union. Rather than control of Indian affairs being transferred to Canada he wanted them to remain in British Columbian, and preferably his own, hands. Ottawa, however, became determined to retain ultimate control, and yet was not prepared to go as far as a reversal of provincial policy.

In spite of Trutch's repeated misrepresentations of the situation in the years following union it became increasingly clear to Federal officials that British Columbia's Indian policy was far from satisfactory.

But as long as there was no major Indian outbreak and the government thought it could get away with it, Ottawa would not reverse British Columbia's policy.

Why, having conceded that provincial policy was unsatisfactory, did Canada take this line? One of the major reasons had been suggested to Macdonald by Trutch.

If you now commence to buy out Indian title to the lands of B.C. you would go back on all that has been done for 30 years past and would be equitably bound to compensate tribes who inhabited districts now settled and farmed by white people, equally with those in the more remote and uncultivated portions.[85]

To put it simply, it would cost too much to extinguish Indian title. Another reason for the Dominion's reticence about reversing provincial policy was that it had troubles enough with the "spoilt child of confederation" without instigating a furore over Indian land. The bitterness and frustration engendered by the railway dispute was sufficient for Ottawa to deal with.

Because of its initial unfamiliarity with the British Columbian situation, and then its unwillingness to take decisive action, the federal government was faced with a running battle over the acreage question during Trutch's lieutenant-governorship. In 1873 Ottawa suggested allotments of eighty acres per family, and British Columbia countered with an offer of ten. Powell managed to gain a shortlived agreement on twenty acres, but with the collapse of that accord no further bids were taken. The final stage of these negotiations was the acceptance in 1875 of a suggestion by William Duncan of the Church Missionary Society that no specific acreage be allocated, but rather that individual situations be examined by a commission and a decision reached on the basis of the local knowledge of the Indian agents.[86]

Powell was constantly faced with obstructionist tactics by the province, but his appointment did demonstrate one thing. His reports to Ottawa indicate that Trutch, the man of great experience in Indian affairs, was still not giving people accurate information about Indian attitudes on the land question. The general tenor of his reports as lieutenant-governor was that the Indians were satisfied with what had been done for them. In fact the Indians were no more satisfied in the early 1870's than they had been when Trutch "adjusted" their reserves; rather they were growing more and more dissatisfied. Yet, in his letter to Macdonald, Trutch pontificated that "our Indians are sufficiently satisfied."[87]

Indian complaints about treatment over land began when Trutch started whittling away the reserves, and during the years of his lieutenant-governorship they were feeling the situation more acutely. They were learning to understand the value of their land and at the same time "They know that they are rapidly being hemmed in upon their limited reserves, and that their domain is fast diminishing."[88] Indians were also beginning to realize what white ownership of the land meant. When Europeans owned land they fenced in the grass, and tended to bring trespassers before their courts. Areas cultivated by Indians, however, were not always similarly protected, either in the courts or from white encroachment. Indians who brought cases of their cultivated areas being trampled by Europeans' cattle before the courts failed to secure convictions,[89] whereas Indian defendants in similar cases were found guilty.[90] In other instances white settlers were granted pre-emption certificates for areas of land that included potato patches belonging to Indians.[91] No doubt the Indians concerned in such cases would have been intrigued with Trutch's claim that they were equal with Europeans before the law.[91]

The discontent produced by factors such as these can be directly attributed to Trutch's reduction policy. In a letter to Ottawa Powell wrote that the Indians were highly satisfied with things under Douglas,

But since that time his successors have, from time to time, at the request of the white settlers, who in some localities were envious of the fine tracts given to the Indians, cut them down or reserved other lands not so valuable as those originally laid aside for them. In this way they have become generally discontented. . . . [93]

Naturally Trutch would not have explained Indian discontent in terms of the inadequacies of his own policies, but he was undoubtedly aware that it existed. If he could not discern it for himself others were informing him of the situation. Powell wrote to him describing some of the injustices that had occurred and urging their settlement as a matter of paramount importance.[94] Settlers were also informing Trutch of instances of Indian dissatisfaction. He was told that the Chilcotin Indians, for example, were continuing their hostility to the intrusion of Europeans, maintaining that the land was theirs, and objecting to white men living on it.[95] This particular letter was forwarded by Trutch to the Secretary of State for the Provinces, although accompanied by some rather odd remarks. He said that the Chilcotins apparently thought that the Europeans were going to appropriate their land without any consideration rendered in compensation, and that they would be confined to certain limited reserves. Clearly the Chilcotin Indians had accurately assessed what had happened to the Indians and their lands in the rest of the province and did not want it to happen to them. Yet in his letter to Ottawa Trutch describes this concern as a "misapprehension."[96]

In spite of all expressions of discontent, Trutch was still blandly assuring Macdonald that the Indians were satisfied, and, in spite of all valid Indian grievances, advocating no change in policy.[97] Trutch sounds like the archetypal colonialist, protesting that "the natives are happy" while the revolution is battering down the walls. Also like the archetypal colonialist, this claim rests uneasily with his constant demands for sufficient military force to keep the Indians in subjection.[98] The revolt never came in British Columbia, but in the year after Trutch's retirement from the lieutenant-governorship the Indians of the interior were on the verge of rebellion. In these areas where Trutch first carried out his reduction programme, discontent had been steadily mounting. The Indians were becoming so wary of government officials that the bands of Nicola and Okanagan Lakes refused to accept presents from Powell "lest, by doing so, they should be thought to waive their claim for compensation for the injustice done them in relation to the Land Grants." Powell's opinion was that "If there has not been an Indian war, it is not because there has been no injustice to the Indians, but because the Indians have not been sufficiently united."[99] The voice of experience, however, spoke reassuringly from Victoria. An Indian outbreak in the interior is "highly improbable," opined Trutch.[100]

In fact the situation had reached boiling point. A desperate telegram was sent to Ottawa from the Reserve Commissioners claiming that an outbreak was imminent.[101] The freedom from Indian disturbances, particularly in comparison with the United States, was a major piece of evidence that Trutch had advanced to demonstrate the benevolence of Indian policy in British Columbia.[102] Now, not only did a revolt seem likely, but the Indians were talking of linking up with the resistance of Chief Joseph south of the border.[103] In the event the Indian Commissioners were able to cool the situation off, but there was no doubt in the minds of Canadian authorities that British Columbia's policy, as instituted by Trutch, was responsible for the very dangerous situation. It is obvious, said the Minister of the Interior, "that the discontent of the Indians is wholly due to the policy which has been pursued towards them by the local authorities." He even went so far as to say that in the event of an Indian war "the people of Canada generally would not sustain a policy towards the Indians of that Province which is, in my opinion, not only unwise and unjust, but also illegal."[104] In spite of Trutch's efforts to distort the situation the threat of an Indian outbreak had finally, although probably too late, awakened the federal government to a realization of just how unsatisfactory his policies were.

Another historian, writing about Trutch's lieutenant-governorship, has commented that he paid special attention to Indian affairs. John Saywell goes on to claim that Trutch laboured " to get the Federal Government to adopt an intelligent and consistent Indian policy."[105] This essay has tried to show that he was really attempting to convince the federal government to continue those policies he had originated before union. Neither the policies, nor his advocacy of them, was consistent or intelligent. Saywell provides no evidence that he has made any thorough examination of Indian affairs in British Columbia. He admits that Indian policy is important and yet apparently has canvassed no other opinions besides Trutch's on the matter; and as an adjudicator on his own policy Trutch is somewhat less than reliable.

Trutch's views and actions left British Columbia, not only with growing Indian discontent, but with a legacy of litigation that in the long run was to cost the province more than extinguishing Indian title and laying out reasonable reserves would have done. In most areas of Canada the Indian land question has been tied up in a neat European legal package called a treaty. In British Columbia by 1876, largely thanks to the influence of Trutch, it was still in the category of unfinished business.

Notes

[1] Carnarvon to Douglas, 11 April 1859, British Columbia, *Papers connected with the Indian Land Question, 1850-1875*, Victoria, 1875. (Hereafter cited as *B.C. Papers*).

[2] *The Daily British Colonist*, 18 June 1860. Newcastle to Douglas, 19 October 1861, *B.C. Papers*, p. 20.

[3] Moody to Cox, 6 March 1861, Good to Moody, 5 March 1861, Parsons to Turnball, 1 May 1861, Douglas to Moody, 27 April 1863, *B.C. Papers*, pp. 21, 22, and 27.

[4] Douglas to Lytton, 9 February 1859, *B.C. Papers*, p. 15. Douglas to Helmcken, 5 February 1859, Vancouver Island House of Assembly, *Correspondence Book, August 12, 1856 to July 6, 1859, Archives of British Columbia Memoir no. IV*, Victoria, 1918, p. 47.

[5] Lenihan to Superintendent General of Indian Affairs, 7 November 1875, *Report of the Deputy Superintendent of Indian Affairs for 1875*, [Ottawa, 1876], p. 54. (Hereafter cited as *Report on Indian Affairs*).

[6] Minutes of the Meeting of the Legislative Council, 21 January 1864, British Columbia, *Journal of the Legislative Council of British Columbia*, New Westminster, 1864, p. 2.

[7] Douglas to Newcastle, 14 September 1863, British Columbia, Governor's Despatches to the Colonial Office, 1858-1871, vol. III, (SC). (Hereafter cited as Governor's Despatches). Special Collections, University of British Columbia Library.

[8] Trutch to Charlotte Trutch, 23 June 1850, Trutch, Papers, Manuscripts and Typescripts, folder A1.b, SC.

[9] Trutch to Macdonald, 14 October 1872, Sir John A. Macdonald, Papers, vol. 278, Public Archives of Canada.

[10] Douglas to Lytton, 14 March 1859, Governor's Despatches, vol. I. Also in *B.C. Papers*, p. 17.

[11] Douglas to Stanley, 15 June 1858, Great Britain, *Paper 5 Relating to British Columbia, Part I*, Cmd. 2476, p. 16.

[12] British Columbia, *Report and Journal by the Honourable Chief Commissioner of Lands and Works, of the Proceedings in Connection with the Visit of His Excellency the Late Governor Seymour to the North West Coast, in His Majesty's Ship Sparrowhawk*, Victoria, 1869, p. 1.

[13] Trutch to the Secretary of State for the Provinces, 16 November 1871, British Columbia Lieutenant-Governor, Despatches to Ottawa, 14 August 1871 to 26 July 1876, Provincial Archives of British Columbia, (PABC).

[14] Douglas to Colonel Hawkins, 1 July 1861, Vancouver Island Governor, Correspondence Outward, 27 May 1859 to 9 January 1864, Private Official Letter Book, PABC.

[15] British Columbia, *Report and Journal*, p. 3.

[16] Trutch to Secretary of State for the Provinces, 26 September 1871, *B.C. Papers*, p. 101.

[17] Letter signed "British Columbian," *The Victoria Gazette*, 16 January 1860. A letter to his brother indicates that the one in the *Gazette* was written by Trutch under a *nom-de-plume*. Trutch to John Trutch, 20 January 1860, Trutch, Papers, folder A1.f.

[18] Seymour to Cardwell, 31 August 1864, Governor's Despatches, vol. IV.

[19] Enclosure in Seymour to Cardwell, 31 August 1864, Great Britain, Colonial Office Correspondence with British Columbia Governors, CO.60/19, University of British Columbia Library.

[20] Seymour to Cardwell, 23 September 1864, Governor's Despatches, vol. IV.

[21] Enclosures in Seymour to Cardwell, 31 August 1864 and 7 June 1865, Colonial Office Correspondence with British Columbia Governors, CO.60/19 and 21, also Seymour to Carnarvon, 19 February 1867, Governor's Despatches, vol. V.

[22] Enclosure in Seymour to Cardwell, 31 August 1864, Colonial Office Correspondence with British Columbia Governors, CO.60/19.

[23] Seymour to Carnarvon, 19 February 1867, Governor's Despatches, vol. V.

[24] Nind to Colonial Secretary, 17 July 1865, British Columbia Colonial Secretary, Correspondence Regarding Indian Reserves 1861-1865, 1868-1869, and 1874-1877, PABC. Also in *B.C. Papers*, p. 29.

[25] Letter by a British Columbian, *Victoria Gazette*, 16 January 1860.

[26] Trutch to Colonial Secretary, 20 September 1865, British Columbia Lands and Works Department, Correspondence Outward, 8 September 1865 to 11 July 1871, to Governor and Colonial Secretary, vol. 8a, PABC. Also in *B.C. Papers*, p. 30.

[27] Good to Trutch, 26 September 1865, British Columbia Colonial Secretary, Outward Correspondence to Lands and Works Department, PABC. Also in *B.C. Papers*, pp. 30-31.

[28] Moberly to Trutch, 22 December 1865, W. Moberly, Letters 1859-1868, Colonial Correspondence (CC), file 1145, PABC. Also in *B.C. Papers*, p. 33.

[29] Trutch to acting Colonial Secretary, 17 January 1866, Lands and Works Department, Correspondence Outward, Vol. 8a. Also in *B.C. Papers*, pp. 32-33.

[30] *British Columbia Government Gazette*, 6 October 1866. There is no indication of how far back from the river the original reserves went.

[31] Minutes of the meeting of the Legislative Council, 11 February 1867, British Columbia, *Journal of the Legislative Council*, p. 16.

[32] Trutch, Report on the Lower Fraser Indian Reserves, 28 August 1867, Trutch, Papers, (Hereafter cited as Report).

[33] Pearse to Trutch, 21 October 1868, *B.C. Papers*, p. 53.

[34] Young to Moody, 18 June and 2 July 1862, British Columbia Colonial Secretary, Outward Correspondence to Lands and Works Department.

[35] British Columbia, *Appendix to the Revised Statutes of British Columbia, 1871; Containing Certain Repealed Colonial Laws Useful for Reference, Imperial Statutes Affecting British Columbia Proclamations etc.*, Victoria, [1871], pp. 93-94.

[36] Report of the Government of British Columbia on the subject of Indian Reserves, 17 August 1875, *B.C. Papers*, appendix, p. 4.

[37] Trutch, Memorandum on a letter treating of conditions of the Indians in Vancouver Island, addressed to the Secretary of the Aboriginies Protection Society, by Mr. William Sebright Green, enclosure in Musgrave

to Granville, 29 January 1870, *B.C. Papers*, appendix, pp. 10-13. (Hereafter cited as Memorandum).

[38] Douglas to Newcastle, 25 March 1861, *B.C. Papers*, p. 19.

[39] With the exception of Treaty number 8, initially made by the Federal Government in 1899, and extended in 1900 to include the Beavers, and in 1910 to include the Slaves, both groups occupying the northeastern corner of the Province. Canada, *Indian Treaties and Surrenders*, Ottawa, 1912, vol. III, pp. 290-300. Wilson Duff, *The Indian History of British Columbia, vol. I, the Impact of the White Man*, Victoria, 1964, pp. 70-71.

[40] Moberly to Trutch, 22 December 1865, Moberly, Letters, CC, file 1145b. Also in *B.C. Papers*, p. 33.

[41] Cox to Colonial Secretary, 4 July 1861, William Cox, Letters 1860-1868, CC, file 376, PABC.

[42] Young to Cox, 14 November 1862, British Columbia Colonial Secretary, Outward Correspondence.

[43] Trutch to O'Reilly, 5 August 1868, Lands and Works Department, Correspondence Outward, vol. II.

[44] Trutch, Report, 28 August 1867.

[45] Good to Moody, 4 and 6 March 1861, British Columbia Colonial Secretary, Outward Correspondence to Lands and Works Department.

[46] Brew to McColl, 6 April 1864, William McColl, Letters 1860-1865, CC, file 1030, PABC.

[47] Douglas to Moody, 27 April 1863, British Columbia Colonial Secretary, Outward Correspondence to Lands and Works Department. Also in *B.C. Papers*, p. 27.

[48] Young to Trutch, 6 November 1867, British Columbia Colonial Secretary, Outward Correspondence to Lands and Works Department. Also in *B.C. Papers*, p. 45.

[49] Brew to McColl, 6 April 1864, McColl, Letters, CC, file 1030. Also in *B.C. Papers*, p. 43. Italics mine.

[50] Young to Moody, 11 May 1863, *B.C. Papers*, p. 28.

[51] Young to Cox, 14 November 1862, British Columbia Colonial Secretary, Outward Correspondence.

[52] Trutch to Young, 19 November 1867, *B.C. Papers*, p. 46.

[53] *Ibid.*

[54] Trutch, Report, 28 August 1867.

[55] Phyllis Mikklesen, "Land Settlement Policy on the Mainland of British Columbia, 1858-1874," M.A. Thesis, University of British Columbia, 1950, p. 100. British Columbia, *Appendix to the Revised Statutes*, p. 87.

[56] Brew to McColl, 6 April 1864, McColl, Letters, CC, file 1030. Also in *B.C. Papers*, p. 43.

[57] Trutch to O'Reilly, 5 August 1868, Lands and Works Department, Outward Correspondence, vol. II.

[58] Douglas to Powell, 14 October 1874, Sir James Douglas, Correspondence Outward, 1874, PABC.

[59] Douglas to Newcastle, 25 March 1861, *B.C. Papers*, p. 19.

[60] Trutch, Report, 28 August 1867.

[61] *The British Columbian*, 21 May 1864.

[62] *The British Columbian*, 2 December 1865.

[63] *The Daily British Colonist*, 21 March 1862.

[64] *The Daily British Colonist*, 8 March 1861.

[65] Resolution by the Honourable Mr. R. T. Smith, 3 May 1864, British Columbia, *Journal of the Legislative Council*, p. 41.

[66] Vine Deloria Jnr., *Custer Died for Your Sins, an Indian Manifesto*, New York, 1970, p. 55.

[67] G. E. Shankel, "The Development of Indian Policy in British Columbia," Ph.D. thesis, University of Washington, 1945, p. 89.

[68] *The Daily British Colonist*, 12 February 1869.

[69] Trutch, Memorandum, pp. 10-11.

[70] British Columbia Legislative Council, *Debate on the Subject of Confederation with Canada. Reprinted from the Government Gazette Extraordinary of March, 1870*, Victoria, [1870], pp. 157-159.

[71] Another student of the subject has come to the same conclusion on the basis of the similarity between clause 13 and Trutch's memorandum of 1870. Robert E. Cail, "Disposal of Crown Lands in British Columbia," M.A. Thesis, University of British Columbia, 1956, p. 327.

[72] Report on the Government of British Columbia on the subject of Indian Reserves, 17 August 1875, *B.C. Papers*, appendix, p. 1.

[73] Memo of Laird, 2 November 1874, *B.C. Papers*, p. 152.

[74] Bishop of Columbia to Secretary of State for the Colonies, 27 May 1971, *B.C. Papers*, pp. 97-98.

[75] Trutch to Secretary of State for the Provinces, 26 Sept. 1871, *B.C. Papers*, p. 99.

[76] Trutch to Secretary of State for the Provinces, 26 Sept. 1871, *B.C. Papers*, p. 100.

[77] Douglas to Helmcken, 5 February 1859, Vancouver Island House of Assembly, *Correspondence Book*, p. 47.

[78] Powell to Provincial Secretary, 4 February 1873, *B.C. Papers*, p. 112.

[79] Ash to Powell, 5 February 1873, *B.C. Papers*, p. 112.

[80] Trutch to Secretary of State for the Provinces, 26 September 1871, *B.C. Papers*, p. 100.

[81] Trutch to Secretary of State for the Provinces, 26 September 1871, *B.C. Papers*, p. 101.

[82] Trutch to Macdonald, 14 October 1872, Macdonald Papers, vol. 278.

[83] Trutch to Laird, 30 January 1874, Trutch, Correspondence with the Department of the Interior Regarding Board of Indian Commissioners for British Columbia, 1874, PABC.

[84] Laird to Trutch, 8 July 1874, Trutch, Correspondence Regarding Board of Indian Commissioners.

[85] Trutch to Macdonald, 14 October 1872, Macdonald Papers, vol. 278.

[86] Report of the Government of British Columbia on the Subject of Indian Reserves, 17 August 1875, *B.C. Papers*, appendix, p. 9.

[87] Trutch to Macdonald, 14 October 1872, Macdonald Papers, vol. 278.

[88] Lenihan to Superintendent General of Indian Affairs, 7 November 1875, *Report on Indian Affairs for 1875*, p. 53.

[89] *The British Columbian*, 9 July 1864.

[90] Powell to Attorney-General, 12 January 1874, *B.C. Papers*, p. 126.

[91] Powell to Trutch, 21 June 1873, *B.C. Papers*, p. 116.

92 Trutch, Memorandum, p. 10.
93 Powell to Superintendent General of Indian Affairs, 4 February 1875, *Report on Indian Affairs for 1874*, pp. 63-64.
94 Powell to Trutch, 21 June 1873, *B.C. Papers*, p. 116.
95 Riske and McIntyre to Trutch, 6 June 1872, Chilcotin, Correspondence etc. Relating to the District and the Natives, 1872, PABC.
96 Trutch to Secretary of State for the Provinces, 24 June 1872, British Columbia Lieutenant-Governor, Despatches to Ottawa, 14 August 1871 to 26 July 1876, PABC.
97 Trutch to Macdonald, 14 October 1872, Macdonald Papers, vol. 278.
98 Trutch to Macdonald, 16 July 1871, Macdonald Papers, vol. 278.
99 Memo of Laird, 2 November 1874, *B.C. Papers*, p. 153.
100 Ash to Powell, 30 January 1874, *B.C. Papers*, p. 127.
101 Telegram of Sproat and Anderson to the Minister of the Interior, 13 July 1877, Canada Indian Reserve Commission, Correspondence, Memorandums etc., 1877-1878, PABC.
102 Trutch to Secretary of State for the Provinces, 26 September 1871, *B.C. Papers*, p. 99.
103 Telegram of Sproat and Anderson to the Minister of the Interior, 13 July 1877, Canada Indian Reserve Commission, Correspondence. Speech of Mills, 1 April 1885, Canada, *Official Report of the Debates of the House of Commons of the Dominion of Canada, Ottawa, 1885*, vol. XVIII, p. 886. Cail, pp. 369-70.
104 Mills to Sproat, 3 August 1877, Canada Indian Reserve Commission, Correspondence.
105 John Tupper Saywell, "Sir Joseph Trutch: British Columbia's First Lieutenant-Governor," *The British Columbia Hisorical Quarterly*, vol. XIX, nos. 1 and 2, January-April 1955, pp. 85-86.

Select Bibliography on the History of British Columbia

British Columbians, as Margaret Ormsby has remarked, have always been literate: the volume of printed work by both inhabitants and visitors is immense. However, the handful of amateur and professional historians in the field have left many topics still untouched, wide-open to contributions by serious students. This bibliography is, therefore, a guide to further study. Works have been chosen for their representative character and their bibliographical materials, as well as their historiographical importance and interpretive skill. Manuscript materials, theses, local histories, travel literature, and fiction have been omitted as have all but a few articles and printed government documents.

Much primary and secondary material, in addition to reviews of books, has appeared in the *Annual report* of the British Columbia Historical Association, 1923-1929; the *Memoir* series of the Provincial Archives of British Columbia, 1914-1945; the *British Columbia historical quarterly*, 1937-1958; *B.C. historical news*, 1968- ; *BC studies*, 1968/69- ; *B.C. perspectives*, 1972- ; the Okanagan Historical Society *Report*, 1926- ; and the Vancouver Historical Society *Occasional paper* series, 1970- . Several historical articles have also appeared in British Columbia Natural Resources Conference, *Transactions*, 1948-1970.

Outside the province, articles on British Columbia have appeared chiefly in the Canadian Historical Association *Annual report* (now called *Historical papers*), 1922- ; the Canadian historical review, 1920- ; the *Canadian journal of economics and political science*, 1935-1967; the *Beaver*, 1920- ; the *Pacific Northwest quarterly* (formerly the *Washington historical quarterly*), 1906-; the *Oregon historical quarterly*, 1900-; the *Pacific historical review*, 1932-; and *Papers* of the Western Canadian Studies Conference, 1969-.

Multi-volume series which have volumes dealing with phases of British Columbia history include publications of the Champlain Society and the Hudson's Bay Record Society, both important for the fur trade, and of the Hakluyt Society for maritime exploration. The *Dictionary of Canadian biography*, now in progress, will become an increasingly important source for biographical information. About fifty biographies of British Columbians appear in volumes 9 and 10, covering those who died in the years 1861-1870 and 1871-1880.

Indispensable to the study of the history of British Columbia is the *Dictionary catalogue of the library of the Provincial Archives of British Columbia*, 8 vols. (Boston, 1971). This guide to the richest collection of printed materials in the field includes as well good coverage of the rest of the Canadian West and neighbouring American Pacific Coast. It is especially noteworthy for its "analytics" of articles appearing in the periodicals mentioned above, and other less important journals. *A bibliography of British Columbia*, now being prepared by the University of Victoria Social Science Research Centre, features books and pamphlets, but omits periodical articles and, with exceptions, government documents. Three volumes have already appeared: *Navigations, traffiques and discoveries, 1774-1848*, compiled by G. M. Strathern, (Victoria, 1970), and *Laying the foundations, 1849-1899*, compiled by B. J. Lowther, (Victoria, 1968). Each of these volumes includes writings about the years under review as well as imprints of the period. The twentieth century volume *Years of Growth, 1900-1950* (Victoria, 1975) was compiled by M. H. Edwards and J. C. R. Lont.

A guide to provincial government documents is provided by *Publications of the government of British Columbia 1871-1947*, (Victoria, 1950) and *Royal Commissions... in British Columbia, 1872-1942* (Victoria, 1945), both compiled by Marjorie Holmes. No similar guide to B.C. material in federal publications exists, although *Federal royal commissions in Canada, 1867-1966, a checklist*, compiled by G. F. Henderson, (Toronto, 1967) is useful.

Current books, pamphlets and government documents are listed in *Canadiana*; periodical articles in the *Canadian periodical index*. Handy guides to B.C. material also appear in each number of *B.C. studies*, the *Canadian Historical Review* and *La revue historique de l'Amerique francaise*. Provincial government publications are listed in *British Columbia government publications monthly checklist*, 1970- (limited distribution to Canadian libraries by the B.C. Legislative Library).

Much of the wealth of unpublished research in theses and dissertations is made available in *Theses on British Columbia history and related subjects in the University of British Columbia library*, (reference publication no. 35), UBC library, 1971. Graduate theses in progress are listed in the annual *Register of postgrauate dissertations in history and related subjects*, compiled by the Public Archives of Canada for the Canadian Historical Association. For Vancouver, scholarly work in progress in all disciplines is noted in the bulletin *Focus on Vancouver*, Vancouver Historical Society, P.O. Box 3071.

The standard history of British Columbia is Margaret Ormsby, *British Columbia; a history*, (Toronto, 1958; reprinted with corrections, 1971). Several older works are not completely superseded. In *British Columbia and the United States*, ed. H. F. Angus, (Toronto, 1942; reprinted 1970) the sections on exploration by F. W. Howay and on the colonial and confederation periods by W. N. Sage sum up each man's work. Volume 2 by Howay of E. O. S. Scholefield and F. W. Howay, *British Columbia from the earliest times to the present*, 4 vols., (Vancouver, 1914), is on a scale not yet duplicated. F. W. Howay, *British Columbia; the making of a province* (Toronto, 1928), is a one-volume survey. Part 2 by R. Edward Gosnell of Scholefield and Gosnell, *A history of British Columbia* (Vancouver, 1913), contains the shrewd comments of a participant in the politics of much of the period he surveys. Father A. G. Morice, *The history of the northern interior of British Columbia . . . 1660-1880* (Toronto, 1904; reprinted 1971), is still valuable.

Much of the history of particular localities is embodied in their place names. Two works on British Columbia place names are John Walbran, *British Columbia coast names, 1592-1906* (Ottawa, 1909; reprinted 1971), and G. P. V. and Helen Akrigg, *1001 British Columbia place names*, 3rd ed. (Vancouver, 1973).

Overviews of the European explorations that eventually reached what is now British Columbia are given by J. B. Brebner, *The explorers of North America, 1492-1806* (New York, 1933; reprinted 1955), and J. C. Beaglehole, *The exploration of the Pacific*, 3rd. ed. (London, 1966). Beaglehole's edition of *The journals of Captain James Cook on his voyages of discovery*, 4 vols. (Hakluyt Society, 1955-1967), will repay detailed study. A critical edition of Captain George Vancouver, *Voyage of discovery . . .*, is in preparation for the Hakluyt Society; meanwhile an introduction to his work is the biography by Bern Anderson, *Surveyor of the sea* (Toronto, 1960). For major overland explorers, we have W. Kaye Lamb's editions of *The journals and letters of Sir Alexander Mackenzie* (Toronto, 1970), and *The letters and journals of Simon Fraser, 1806-1808* (Toronto, 1960).

Richard Glover has edited the standard edition of *David Thompson's narrative, 1784-1812*, (Toronto, 1962). A shorter version by a Thompson enthusiast is *David Thompson, Travels in western North America, 1784-1812*, ed. V. G. Hopwood, (Toronto, 1971). Spanish contributions to the explorations of the area are outlined by Warren Cook, *Flood tide of empire: Spain and the Pacific Northwest, 1543-1819*, (New Haven, Conn., 1973). For Russian activities we must still rely in English on F.

A. Golder, *Russian expansion on the Pacific, 1641-1850*, (Cleveland, 1914; reprinted 1960).

Any assessment of the role of the fur trade in Canadian development must start with H. A. Innis, *The fur trade in Canada*, rev. ed. (Toronto, 1956). The best introductory account of fur trade activities on the Pacific slope is included in E. E. Rich, *The fur trade and the Northwest to 1857*, (Toronto, 1967). Rich covers the same ground in more detail in *The history of the Hudson's Bay Company, 1670-1870*, (Toronto, 1960). The H.B.C.'s role in the international politics of the Pacific coast is treated in John S. Galbraith, *The Hudson's Bay Company as an imperial factor, 1821-1869*, (Toronto, 1957). The North West Company's records did not survive in such profusion as those of the H.B.C., so histories of it must perforce be more impressionistic. Basic is W. S. Wallace's introduction to *Documents relating to the North West Company*, (Toronto, 1934), which is supplemented by his *The pedlars from Quebec and other papers on the Nor'Westers*, (Toronto, 1954). George Davidson, *The North West Company*, (Berkeley, 1918; reprinted 1967) has a useful emphasis on activities west of the Rockies. Marjorie Wilkins Campbell, *The North West Company*, (Toronto, 1957; reprinted with revisions 1973) is a popular history. Two authors deal specifically with fur trade activities on the Pacific slope between 1821 and 1846. W. Kaye Lamb's introduction to *The letters of John McLoughlin from Fort Vancouver to the governor and committee*, ed. E. E. Rich, 3 vols. (Toronto, 1941-1944), emphasizes company policy and administration, while the first part of John Hussey, *The History of Fort Vancouver and its physical structure*, (Tacoma, 1957), explains the workings of the trade. No good monograph has been produced on the maritime fur trade, but Howay's work on the subject is summed up in his contribution to *British Columbia and the United States*, (Toronto, 1942; reprinted 1970).

Willard E. Ireland, "The evolution of the boundaries of British Columbia", *British Columbia historical quarterly*, (October 1939), pp. 263-282, surveys the topic from Drake to 1866 with a look at the Alaska boundary dispute. Specific boundary disputes can be followed in Frederick Merk, *The Oregon question*, (Cambridge, Mass., 1967) and J. O. McCabe, *The San Juan water boundary question*, (Toronto, 1964). Norman Penlington, *The Alaska boundary dispute: a critical reappraisal*, (Toronto, 1972), is a short account with a bibliography. A work of a different kind, Barry Gough, *The Royal Navy and the Northwest coast of North America, 1810-1914*, (Vancouver, 1971), argues that British naval ascendency helped keep the "British" in British Columbia.

The dramatic aspects of the gold rushes which began in 1858 are a staple element of British Columbia historical writing; each of the general histories contains a narrative account. None of them, however, has the same trenchant analysis of the rushes themselves as that presented for the United States in Rodman Paul, *Mining frontiers of the Far West, 1840-1880* (New York, 1963). Paul's book is therefore a useful introduction, as is W. P. Morrell, *The gold rushes*, 2nd ed. (London, 1968), which sets the British Columbian rushes in the context of the world-wide "gold rush" phenomenon of the nineteenth century. Still the most extensive comparative work on British Columbia and the other rushes in western North America is W. J. Trimble, *The mining advance into the Inland Empire*, (Madison, Wisc., 1914; reprinted 1973).

The social effects of the gold rushes are treated by sociologist S. D. Clark in an essay and collection of documents in *The social development of Canada*, (Toronto, 1942). The essay is reprinted without the documents in S. D. Clark, *The developing Canadian community*, (Toronto, 1968). Isabel Bescoby, "Society in Cariboo during the gold rush", *Washington historical quarterly* (July 1933), pp. 193-207, is the substance of an M.A. thesis. The chapter by Cole Harris on "British Columbia" in R. Cole Harris and John Warkentin, *Canada before Confederation: a study in historical geography* (New York, 1974), not only provides an illuminating commentary on the period of the gold rushes and the preceding fur trade era, but also points to the nascent growth of those resource industries that were to shape the province's later economy.

The political history of colonial days can best be followed through the biography of James Douglas, chief factor of the Hudson's Bay Company in Victoria, and Governor of Vancouver Island (1851-1864) and of British Columbia (1858-1864). R. H. Coats and R. E. Gosnell, *Sir James Douglas* (Toronto, 1908), is superseded by W. N. Sage, *Sir James Douglas and British Columbia*, (Toronto, 1930). Of recent work, the best account of Douglas' life is by Margaret Ormsby in the *Dictionary of Canadian biography*, vol. 10 (Toronto, 1972). Dorothy Blakey Smith, *Sir James Douglas, father of British Columbia*, (Toronto, 1971), written for young people, excels in the portrayal of the human Douglas, while Derek Pethick, *James Douglas, servant of two empires*, (Vancouver, 1969), is a popular biography.

The circumstances of British Columbia's entry into the Canadian confederation have attracted much attention from historians. Besides the accounts in the general works, Howay, Sage and

Ireland have each written several articles on the subject, which can be traced through the *Dictionary catalogue of the Provincial Archives. British Columbia and Confederation*, ed. W. George Shelton, (Victoria, 1967), is a collection of essays of varying quality written to mark the 1967 centennial.

Considerable although spotty coverage has been given to the political history of British Columbia since 1871. Howay and Gosnell, in the works mentioned above, cover the period to 1914. A shorter treatment by Howay is "The settlement and progress of British Columbia, 1871-1914", *The Cambridge history of the British Empire*, vol. 6, *Canada and Newfoundland* (Cambridge, Eng., 1930). Two articles by Edith Dobie, "Some aspects of party history in British Columbia, 1871-1903", *Pacific historical review*, (1932), pp. 235-251, and "Party history in British Columbia, 1903-1933", *Pacific Northwest quarterly* (April 1936), pp. 153-166, give a survey to 1933. Margaret Ormsby, "T. Dufferin Pattullo and the little New Deal", *Canadian Historical Review* (December 1962), pp. 277-297, continues the story to 1939.

Valuable information on the transition to responsible government and the problems of nineteenth century provincial governments can be found in John T. Saywell, *The office of Lieutenant-Governor*, (Toronto, 1957). W. N. Sage, "Federal parties and provincial groups in British Columbia, 1871-1903", *B. C. historical quarterly* (April 1948), pp. 151-169, is a useful survey. Financial relations with the Federal government in Ottawa are dealt with in J. A. Maxwell, *Federal subsidies to provincial governments in Canada*, (Cambridge, Mass., 1937), which carries on into the twentieth century. The province's submission to the royal commission on dominion-provincial relations, *British Columbia in the Canadian Confederation* (Victoria, 1938), extensively documents British Columbia's grievances. The only nineteenth century premier to attract biographers has not been well served by them: Roland Wild, *Amor De Cosmos* (Toronto, 1958) is very slight, and George Woodcock, *Amor De Cosmos: journalist and politician* (Toronto, 1975), intended for juveniles, is superficial. Margaret Ross, "Amor de Cosmos; a British Columbia reformer", *Washington historical quarterly* (April 1932), pp. 110-130, is mostly about his colonial career. For the first half of the twentieth century there is only one published biography of a premier, James Morton, *Honest John Oliver*, (London, 1933). "Depression" problems of two premiers are dealt with by Ian Parker, "Simon Fraser Tolmie: the last Conservative premier of British Columbia", *BC studies* (Fall 1971), pp. 21-36, and by Margaret Ormsby in the article on Pattullo mentioned above. Russell Walker, *Politicians of a pioneering province,* (Vancouver, 1969), is the reminiscences of a newsman and political organizer in the 1920's and 1930's.

A two-volume political history of British Columbia by Martin Robin spans the whole period from 1871 to the present. Volume one, *The rush for spoils; the company province, 1871-1933,* (Toronto, 1972), however, covers the years to 1903 only in an introductory chapter. It is vigorously argued but marred by carelessness and inaccuracy. Volume two, *The pillars of profit: the company province, 1933-1972,* (Toronto, 1973), carries the narrative up to date. A short version of Robin's thesis on the "company" province is presented in his contribution to *Canadian provincial politics,* ed. Martin Robin (Scarborough, Ont., 1972). This latter essay should be read in conjunction with Alan C. Cairns, "The study of the provinces: a review article", *BC studies* (Summer 1972), pp. 73-82. Professor Robin's comment on the Cairns' article and Cairns' reply are in *BC studies* (Winter 1972-73), pp. 78-82.

The Cairns-Robin exchange reflects the current interest in recent B.C. political history, specifically in the CCF-NDP and Social Credit parties. Unpublished work by Thomas Sanford on the "politics of protest" provides the springboard for Edwin Black, "British Columbia: the politics of exploitation", *Exploiting our economic potential,* ed. R. Shearer (Toronto, 1968). Another interpretation is put forward by Martin Robin, "The social basis of party politics in British Columbia", *Queens quarterly* (Autumn 1965), pp. 675-690, reprinted in R. Blishen *et al, Canadian society,* 3rd ed. (Toronto, 1968). An analysis of the problem in a wider context than just that of British Columbia is Walter Young, *Democracy and discontent; progressivism, socialism and social credit in the Canadian west* (Toronto, 1969). The discussion on third party origins continued in *B.C. studies* (Winter 1971-72), with articles by Mark Sproule-Jones and Donald Blake, together with comments by Ed Black and Martin Robin. Succeeding issues of *B.C. studies* carry the Cairns-Robin exchange, a review by Norman Ruff of *The rush for spoils* and Robin's criticism of the review.

Other works on the CCF-NDP are Dorothy Steeves, *The compassionate rebel; Ernest Winch and his times* (Vancouver, 1960); chapters on J. S. Woodsworth's B.C. experiences by his daughter in Grace McInnis, *J. S. Woodsworth; a man to remember* (Toronto, 1953), and Daisy Webster's short sketches in *Growth of the* NDP *in B.C. 1900-1970; 81 political biographies (Vancou-*

*ver, 1970)*Walter Young, *The anatomy of a party; the national
ccf 1932-1961* (Toronto, 1969), has much to say about the role
in the party of British Columbia.

The British Columbia Social Credit party is not so well represented. Patrick Sherman, *Bennett* (Toronto, 1966), is a journalis-
tic biography of the province's longest-serving premier, while
Ronald Worley, *The wonderful world of W. A. C. Bennett*
(Toronto, 1971), is uncritical. What have since 1952 become the
"minor" provincial parties are represented only by MLA and former Liberal leader Patrick McGeer, *Politics in paradise* (Toronto,
1972).

British Columbia also has its own tradition of communist historiography, presented in three works: William Bennett, *Builders of
British Columbia* (Vancouver, 1937); Tom McEwen, *He wrote
for us* (Vancouver, 1951), a biography of Bill Bennett; and Harold Griffin, *British Columbia; the people's early story* (Vancouver, 1958).

A comprehensive economic history of British Columbia has yet
to be written. The standard text, W. T. Easterbrook and Hugh G.
J. Aitken, *Canadian economic history* (Toronto, 1956), has many
references to British Columbia. The historical volume (Book I) of
the *Report* of the Royal Commission on Dominion-Provincial
Relations (the Rowell-Sirois Commission), Ottawa, 1940, has
sections on the economic fortunes of British Columbia since
Confederation. It is abridged in *Rowell-Sirois report/Book* I, ed.
Donald Smiley (Toronto: The Carleton Library No. 5, 1963),
without, however, the material in the original on provincial and
municipal finances. W. A. Mackintosh, *The economic background of dominion-provincial relations* (Toronto, The Carleton
Library No. 13, 1964), reprinted from a study prepared for the
Powell-Sirois commission is also valuable. Morris Zaslow, *The
opening of the Canadian North, 1870-1914* (Toronto, 1971), has
chapters on the penetration of north-central British Columbia,
with a second volume to come on the years since 1914. The story
of the original London-chartered bank of British Columbia in
Victor Ross, *A history of the Canadian Bank of Commerce*, vol.
1 (Toronto, 1920), is in many senses a brief financial and economic history of B.C. and the U.S. Pacific Coast in the years
1862-1900. Robert E. Cail, *Land, Man and the Law; the disposal
of crown lands in British Columbia, 1871-1913* (Vancouver,
1974), is a mass of detail, from which can be pieced together a
picture of how land resources were used to fuel economic development.

A review of the present state of writing by economists on

British Columbia, doubly interesting for its attempt to outline a British Columbia point of view, is A. D. Scott, "Introduction: notes on a western viewpoint", *B.C. studies* (Spring 1972), pp. 3-15. An hypothesis about the process of growth of the province's resource industries is advanced by Ronald A. Shearer, "The economy of British Columbia", in R. A. Shearer, John H. Young and Gordon Munro, *Trade liberalization and a regional economy; studies of the impact of free trade on British Columbia* (Toronto, 1971), pp. 3-42.

Studies of specific B.C. industries are few, mostly pre-dating World War II, and histories of individual firms, even of corporate giants like Macmillan-Bloedel, are virtually non-existent. Harold Innis has chapters on mining in the Kootenays in *Settlement and the mining frontier* (Toronto, 1936). W. A. Carrothers produced a study on the forest industry as part of A. R. M. Lower, *The North American assault on the Canadian forest* (Toronto, 1938), and one on the fishing industry, *The British Columbia fisheries* (Toronto, 1941). A recent volume on B.C. Packers, Cecily Lyons, *Salmon: our heritage* (Vancouver, 1969), is a work of piety rather than scholarship. Agriculture is represented only by Margaret Ormsby "Agricultural development in British Columbia", *Agricultural history* (January 1945), pp. 11-20.

Works about British Columbia labour have told mostly about the growth of the trade unions of the province; little has been written about the conditions of life and work of members of the labour force. Paul Phillips, *No power greater* (Vancouver, 1967), is cast in this conventional mold. A concluding interpretative chapter can, however, be profitably contrasted with the analysis in Stuart Jamieson, "Regional factors in industrial conflict: the case of British Columbia", *Canadian journal of economics and political science* (August 1962), pp. 405-416. General histories of the Canadian trade union movement like H. A. Logan, *Trade unions in Canada* (Toronto, 1948), and Charles Lipton, *The trade union movement of Canada, 1827-1959* (Montreal, 1966), devote considerable space to events in B.C. Stuart Jamieson, *Times of trouble; labour unrest and industrial conflict in Canada, 1900-1966* (Ottawa, 1968), study No. 22 for the Woods task force on labour relations, details the more important and spectacular strikes in the province in the period.

The connection between the trade unions and radical political parties has interested several writers. The nineteenth century beginnings of this connection are traced in John T. Saywell, "Labour and socialism in British Columbia: a survey of historical development before 1903", *British Columbia historical quarterly*

(July-October 1951), pp. 129-150. Two works dealing with Canadian developments in general give attention to B.C. radicals: Martin Robin, *Radical politics and Canadian labour, 1880-1930* (Kingston, 1968), and Gad Horowitz, *Canadian labour in politics* (Toronto, 1968), the latter bringing the narrative up from 1930 to the 1950's. Irving Abella, *Nationalism, communism and Canadian labour; the CIO, the Communist Party and the Canadian Congress of Labour, 1935-1956* (Toronto, 1973), covers the same period as Horowitz from a different focus.

There are no full-scale histories of individual unions, but the forest industry is the subject of two works. Myrtle Bergren, *Tough timber* (Toronto, 1966), concentrates on the hardships of pioneer organizers of the logging camps, while the booklet, *The I.W.A. in British Columbia* (Vancouver, 1971), issued by the Western Canadian regional council of the union, is a short, but scrappy and disjointed outline of organization in the industry.

The early pages of George Hardy, *Those stormy years* (London, 1956), recall Hardy's activities as a union militant in Victoria before 1914. Another reminiscence is the vividly-told story of single unemployed struggles during the depression of the 1930's by Ronald Liversedge, *Recollections of the on-to-Ottawa trek*, ed. Victor Hoar (Toronto: The Carleton Library No. 66, 1973).

In the only work on the co-operative movement, A. V. Hill, *Tides of change* (Prince Rupert, 1967), traces the growth in the fishing industry of producers' co-operatives. George North and Harold Griffin, *A Ripple, A Wave* (Vancouver, 1974) is a brief history of unions in the same industry.

In an area like British Columbia, both mountainous and coast-fringed, transportation and access routes have always been of the utmost significance, yet no one has produced a history of transportation as such. Judgments about routes are, of course, implicit in all explorers' accounts, but the major writings on transportation devote their attention mainly to the building of railways. G. P. de T. Glazebrook, *History of transportation in Canada*, 2 vols. (Toronto, 1938; reprinted in The Carleton Library Nos. 11 and 12, 1964) gives a major part of his space to the national transcontinentals. The saga of the building of the Canadian Pacific Railway has continued to attract chroniclers, the latest and most spectacular production being Pierre Berton's two volumes, *The national dream* (Toronto, 1970) and *The last spike* (Toronto, 1971). Harold Innis, *A history of the Canadian Pacific Railway* (Toronto, 1923; reprinted 1971) is a detailed history of the Railway's early years of operation. J. L. McDougall, *Canadian Pacific, a brief history* (Montreal, 1968), is so short as to be almost perfunctory. The Canadian National railway and its predecessors have also been the subject of many volumes. G. R. Stevens, *Canadian National Railways* , 2 vols. (Toronto, 1960-1962), carries the story only until amalgamation. His *History of the Canadian National Railways* (New York, 1973), continues after 1922, while condensing the material in the earlier two-volume work. A. W. Currie, *The Grand Trunk Railway of Canada* (Toronto, 1957), and J. A. Lower, "The construction of the Grand Trunk Pacific Railway in British Columbia", *British Columbia historical quarterly* (July 1940), pp. 163-181, outline the construction in the province of a component line of the C.N.R. T. D. Regehr's forthcoming work on the Canadian Northern Railway will consider the third of the transcontinentals. The earlier history of what is now the provincially-owned British Columbia Railway is narrated in Bruce Ramsay, PGE; *railway to the North* (Vancouver, 1962). John Fahey, *Inland Empire; D. C. Corbin and Spokane* (Seattle, 1965), is the biography of a man important in the creation of the railway network in southeastern British Columbia. Essential in identifying the dozens of provincial rail projects, either still-born, or now merged or abandoned, is Canada, Department of Transport, *A statutory history of the steam and electric railways of Canada*, compiled by Robert Dorman (Ottawa, 1938).

A good deal of information about coastal ships and shipping in British Columbia is contained in *Lewis and Dryden's marine history of the Pacific Northwest*, ed. E. W. Wright (Portland, Ore., 1895; reprinted 1961, 1967), and the continuation volume *The H. W. McCurdy marine history of the Pacific Northwest*, ed. Gordon Newell (Seattle, 1966). Gerald Rushton, *Whistle up the inlet; the Union Steamship story* (Vancouver, 1974), traces the story of the Vancouver-based coastal fleet. The history of their rivals, the Victoria-centred CPR coastal steamship services, and its predecessors, is Norman R. Hacking and W. Kaye Lamb, *The Princess Story* (Vancouver, 1974). Lamb has already outlined the history of the Canadian Pacific service to the Orient in a series of articles in the *British Columbia historical quarterly* (July 1937), pp. 143-164, (January 1940), pp. 29-50. (April 1940), pp. 78-110, (January 1948), pp. 1-78. The other major trans-Pacific passenger and mail service, that to Australia and New Zealand, is the subject of James Hamilton, "The 'all-red' route, 1893-1953 . . . ", BCHQ (January-April 1956), pp. 1-126. The Canadian Pacific has published a summary account and fleet list of its coastal, lake, and ocean services in George Musk, *Canadian Pacific afloat, 1883-1968* (London, 1968). J. H. Hamilton, *Western shores* (Vancouver, 1932), contains anecdotes about the province's shipping industry.

The province's airlines have yet to attract their historian, but

Ronald Keith, *Bush pilot with a briefcase* (Toronto, 1972), tells how Grant McConachie's ventures finally emerged as C.P. Air.

A history of the diverse ethnic groups in British Columbia is *Strangers entertained*, ed. John M. Norris (Vancouver, 1971), a publication of the 1971 B.C. Centennial committee. The editor's introduction gives a general approach to the problems of immigration and ethnicity; the historical accounts originated with the groups themselves and vary in quality. The lack of a bibliography in *Strangers entertained* can be remedied from two sources: *Ethnic groups in British Columbia; a selected bibliography . . .*, compiled by Dorothy Blakey Smith (Victoria, 1957), for the 1958 B.C. Centennial committee, and *Canadian ethnic groups bibliography*, compiled by Andrew Gregorovich (Toronto, 1972), for the Ontario department of the provincial secretary and citizenship.

The Asian immigrant communities have been the focus of much of the interest in British Columbia ethnic groups. Two general works on Asian immigration and Canada's relations with the homelands of the migrants are Cheng Tien-Fang, *Oriental immigration in Canada* (Shanghai, 1931), and C. J. Woodsworth, *Canada and the Orient* (Toronto, 1941). A "state of the field" article for the Chinese by W. E. Wilmot, "Approaches to the study of the Chinese in British Columbia", *B.C. studies* (Spring 1970), pp. 38-53, includes an introductory bibliography. The forced relocation of the Japanese community in 1942 is the subject of Forrest La Violette, *The Canadian Japanese and world war* II (Toronto, 1948). An earlier work, C. H. Young, Helen Y. Reid and W. A. Carrothers, *The Japanese Canadians* (Toronto, 1938), analyses the situation before the uprooting. Jorgen Dahlie, "The Japanese in B.C.: a lost opportunity?", *B.C. studies* (Winter 1970-71), pp. 3-16, considers educational problems. Stanford Lyman, "Contrasts in the community organization of Chinese and Japanese in North America", *Canadian review of anthropology and sociology* (May 1968), pp. 51-67, is a valuable general article with extensive footnoting of literature on the subject.

Virtually the only historical treatment of the other major Asian community, the East Indians, outside of *Strangers entertained*, focuses on the refusal of admission to Canada of a shipload of East Indians: E. W. Morse, "Some aspects of the Komagata Maru affair, 1914", Canadian historical association *Report* (1936), pp. 100-109, and R. L. Reid, "The inside story of the 'Komagata Maru' ", *B.C. historical quarterly* (January 1941), pp. 1-23.

The standard work on another ethnic group that figures prominently in recent B.C. history is George Woodcock and Ivan Avakumovic, *The Doukhobors* (Toronto, 1968), which considers their history both before and during their stay in British Columbia. Irene Howard, *Vancouver's Svenskar* (Vancouver, 1970), is about the Swedish community. The history of Black migrants to B.C., particularly in gold rush days, is recorded in Robin Winks, *The Blacks in Canada* (Montreal and New Haven, Conn., 1971).

The native Indians cannot properly be considered just another ethnic group, but works on their history, as distinct from anthropological studies, are included here. A select bibliography of anthropology in British Columbia which includes a number of historical studies on Indians is published in *B.C. studies* (Autumn 1973). A B.C. provincial museum publication, Wilson Duff, *The Indian history of British Columbia, vol. 1: the impact of the white man* (Victoria, 1965), carries the discussion of changes in selected areas like population, material culture, and social organization up to the present. E. Palmer Patterson, *The Canadian Indian; a history since 1500* (Don Mills, Ont., 1972), promises more than it delivers, but the chapter on B.C. is informed by the author's special interest in Indian resurgence in this province. *Native rights in Canada*, 2nd ed., ed. Peter A. Cumming *et al* (Toronto, 1972), provides a convenient review of the Indian land question in B.C.

Educational history is represented by F. Henry Johnson, *A history of public education in British Columbia* (Vancouver, 1964), and his *John Jessop; gold seeker and educator* (Vancouver, 1971), a biography of the first superintendent of the provincial school system. For higher education there is Harry T. Logan, *Tuum est; a history of the University of British Columbia* (Vancouver, 1958), and a biography of UBC's first president by W. C. Gibson, *Wesbrook and his university* (Vancouver, 1973).

Writings on the religious history of British Columbia are confined to histories of individual denominations. The Roman Catholic faith is best represented; for the early period there is Father A. G. Morice, *History of the Catholic church in western Canada*, 2 vols. (Toronto, 1910). The histories of two missionary orders have also been written, that of the Oblates of Mary Immaculate in Kay Cronin, *Cross in the wilderness* (Vancouver, 1960), and of the Sisters of Saint Ann in Mary Margaret Down, *A century of service* (Victoria, 1966). A history of the most numerous protestant denomination, the United Church of Canada, has not yet appeared, but that of the second largest protestant group is the subject of Frank Peake, *The Anglican church in British Columbia* (Vancouver, 1959).

H. Keith Ralston
University of British Columbia
Aug., 1975

Other Titles of Related Interest